W9-CKK-496

Life is a Beach

Life is

A Vacationer's

McGraw-Hill Book Company

a Beach

Guide to the East Coast

Parke Puterbaugh and
Alan Bisbort

NEW YORK   ST. LOUIS   SAN FRANCISCO   BOGOTÁ   GUATEMALA   HAMBURG
LISBON   MADRID   MEXICO   MONTREAL   PANAMA   PARIS   SAN JUAN
SÃO PAULO   TOKYO   TORONTO

Copyright © 1986 by Parke Puterbaugh and Alan Bisbort

All rights reserved. Printed in the United States of America. Except as permitted under the Copyright Act of 1976, no part of this publication may be reproduced or distributed in any form or by any means or stored in a data base or retrieval system, without the prior written permission of the publisher.

1 2 3 4 5 6 7 8 9 SEM SEM 8 7 6

ISBN 0-07-050959-X

LIBRARY OF CONGRESS CATALOGING-IN-PUBLICATION DATA

Puterbaugh, Parke.
Life is a beach: a vacationer's guide to the East Coast.
1. Atlantic States—Description and travel—
1981–   —Guide-books.   I. Bisbort, Alan, 1953–
II. title.
F106.P98   1986   917.5'0443   85-23193
ISBN 0-07-050959-X

Book design by Kathryn Parise
Maps rendered by Paul Pugliese

Acknowledgments

When you travel for as long as we did, you will come to depend upon the kindness of strangers. The fact is, we got quite good at it. We would like to offer a sincere blanket thank-you to the many folks who did us a good turn in the course of our gypsy-like wanderings through fourteen states and two summers. But we'd specifically like to thank some of our friends who put us up—and put up with us—along the way, and did us favors. These good souls include Marge and Joe Dobarro, John Dunlap, Jane Karr, Errol Somay, Nicholas Schaffner, Abbie Miller, Brant Mewborn and Rhonda Granger. Hugs and kisses to Carol Hill for her generous assistance with the index and other help. Also, a word of thanks to our trusty '77 Toyota for not breaking down, and to Mike Smith for helping us find it.

We'd also like to salute our parents—Col. Harold and Penny Bisbort, and Helen Puterbaugh—for their help and support. Without the extended sanctuary, work space and board we received at the Puterbaugh household, we might never have finished this book. Finally, our appreciation to James Raimes, Jay Merritt, PJ Haduch and Ken Stuart, who helped get the book off to a running start, and to our editor, Lisa Frost, who was undaunted by the arrival of a mountain of paper on her desk and was a pleasure to work with.

Contents

Introduction

It was in the dead of a cold, storm-filled winter that we began developing our idea for a book on beaches. We both worked indoors—one of us buried in the catacombs of the Library of Congress, the other in an office overlooking Central Park. We liked our jobs, but we had the wanderlust. We wanted to travel. We wanted to write about America. We wanted someone else to pay for it.

Our beat would be the beaches. Beaches, we realized, are an all-American obsession. What red-blooded citizen doesn't put a beach vacation at the top of the list when it comes to plotting his or her two weeks in the sun? A little seaside R&R is not a luxury, it's an American birthright.

We grew up on the East Coast, so it was natural that we inaugurate our beach travels on turf familiar to us. Fortunately, these are the most popular beaches in the world. The statistics back us up. Seventy-five million people a year visit an East Coast beach. It is far and away the first choice when vacation preferences are polled. And yet it seemed that no one had written a general guide to the beaches of the East Coast. Having stumbled onto this idea, there was no turning back. We made a shopping list—suntan lotion, flip-flops, dark glasses—cut our jeans above the knee, bought a car, filled the tank and drove away. Starting point: north coastal Maine, by the Canadian border. Final resting place: Key West, Florida. We would follow that line on the map where the land

gives way to Atlantic Ocean blue, from top to bottom, come hell
or high water or even hurricanes (three of them, as it turned out).

Ours was no trivial pursuit. It was our aim to wriggle toes on
every reachable beach on the East Coast. To claim that we succeeded would be folly, inviting an avalanche of mail bellowing
that we missed a fjord in some forlorn corner of Maine or a step-
pingstone-sized key off the Florida coast. However, we did cover
an amazing amount of ground—er, sand—in the course of two
summer sojourns. From north to south, we scoured the beaches.
We swam on them, jogged on them, lay out in the sun and got
sunburned just like everyone else. We walked the beaches, study-
ing faces, listening. We tried the motels, the restaurants, the bars.
We ate a lot, drank our share and managed to remain merry through
it all. There was always a new beach down the road.

Now, we should perhaps explain a few things. We wrote this
book for, and as, vacationers. Our ideal beach vacationer is someone who enjoys the lure of the open road and the roar of the surf,
and who can appreciate the elemental solitude of a deserted shoreline as well as the animated press of a summer crowd. Hopefully,
he or she knows better than to trample on sea oats, makes an effort
to stop at red lights and doesn't leave empty burger wrappers lying
on the sand. But we learned that one can't be too idealistic on the
beach. That's the way the seashell crumbles.

We tried to approach each beach or coastal community without
preconceptions or prejudice, arriving with only a skeletal itinerary,
open to suggestion and eager to enjoy ourselves. We let impressions
roll over us like waves and wrote honestly about what we saw,
heard and felt. Throughout the project, we stuck to our original
plan—to report the good, the bad and the ugly—like barnacles to
a fishing pier. Inevitably, we realized, we'd wind up pinching a
few toes, but we're *not* just a couple of crabs. This odyssey of
ours, above everything else, was a labor of love.

We make no claims to being experts. We wrote about restaurants, but we aren't fussy gourmets or wine connoisseurs by any
stretch of the imagination. We wrote about night life,
but . . . actually, we *can* find our way around a bar pretty well,
so forget that. We describe the shoreline, but we are not qualified
to expound on coastal geomorphology. Nor are we marine biolo-

gists, though we might digress about shells or fish on occasion. Our grasp of history will not make the world forget Arnold Toynbee, but we diligently braked to read all historical markers.

In a sense, we regarded our minimal expertise in the relevant academic disciplines—not to mention our relative inexperience as travel writers—to be an advantage. Our qualifications, if you're wondering, are the same as yours, we hope. Childhoods spent frolicking in the sand and the surf. High school years spent ogling the opposite gender in their swimsuits. College years spent working at the beach all summer, and dreaming of it the other nine months. And now, in our alleged adulthood, we find ourselves trying to dodge nine-to-five jobs and returning to the one place that can rekindle the best times of our lives.

So we hope you read this in the spirit it was written. For the most part, we liked what we saw. We were pleasantly surprised—startled, even—on many occasions. Other times, we realized, to rephrase Thomas Wolfe, you can't go on vacation again—particularly when there's a big ugly condominium sitting where that favorite whitewashed cottage used to be and a sputtering moped is drowning out the surf. We were hard on development, especially when it was ecologically unwise and aesthetically unpardonable. The reality is that, in some places, there's not enough beach to meet demand, and so the buildup gets awfully thick and the oceanfront aggravatingly loud. This is a problem, and we will not be the first to point this out.

We've written about nearly 400 beaches here. Our idea was to achieve the inverse of the cliché: that is, to write a thousand words that are worth one picture. For each beach we've tried to create a postcard-perfect photograph in words that will give the reader a feeling for the place. Our general essays summarize each locale, from history to tourist traps, rustling sea breezes to overheard conversations, plus a gander at the beaches: who's on them, what they look like, what you can expect to do when you get there, rules and regulations . . . whatever. Further headings follow: Accommodations, Restaurants and Nightlife. While we did not sleep on every lumpy mattress or break bread at every fried-fish stall between Kennebunkport and Key West, we've tried to offer an overview of what you'll find on the beach with at least a few specific recommendations in every case. And, after dinner, we made tireless rounds of the seaside bars, taverns, nightclubs, discotheques—any place where people gather to have a good time. For this we deserve a Purple Heart . . . or a hole in the head. (We'd like to insert one disclaimer. Since survival is a season-to-season proposition for many establishments at the beach, we cannot swear that *every* place mentioned herein will still be there by the time this reaches your hands. A few will have been washed away by a high tide caused by hurricane, failure or foreclosure.)

You can read this book from cover to cover and follow our progress down the coast. Or you can randomly open it up and begin reading wherever your eye falls. For that matter, you can throw it against the wall. Our opinions might raise your eyebrow, or even your blood pressure. But hopefully you'll read of some far-off place you've never been—maybe never even heard of—and suddenly get the bug to go there. Use this book as a starting point. Follow it up by calling or writing for further information (we've supplied addresses and numbers with each entry). Maybe even book reservations at some of the places we've suggested, using the directory at the back of the book.

But for heaven's sake, don't just sit there. Take the plunge. Turn the page. Get wet. Surf's up!

Parke Puterbaugh
Alan Bisbort
December 1985

Maine Is for Lobsters

The state of Maine lays claim to more than 3,000 miles of twisting coastline along the Atlantic Ocean. This staggering figure—which takes into account every gnarled inch of its shore—is greater than the East Coast in its entirety, as the crow flies.

The reasons for this are buried deep in the geological record, hundreds of thousands of years ago when our coastlines were still being radically reshaped. After the granite ridges of north- and mid-coastal Maine were drowned by melting glaciers at the end of the last Ice Age, what was left peeping above water were the long, narrow ridge tops of these submerged highlands. Add to that the considerable volume of rock and debris gouged out, pushed along and deposited at land's end, and you have a geological goulash. As a result of all this, Maine's coast is not a neat, regular line like Florida's but a perpetual zigzag of fingerlets of land that reach far into island-studded bays. The distance from the tip of one peninsula to another might be only a few miles over water, but by car it can mean 50 or 60 miles of driving inland on the same road that brought you out, then negotiating the length of the adjacent reach of land.

On a map, the coast of Maine looks like a piece of cloth that was shredded roughly into unequal strips. Distances are deceptive, and the roads are hilly, winding, narrow and in frequent need of repair. If you plan to visit Maine, you should come fully warned about the drivers. They are among the world's worst. In these

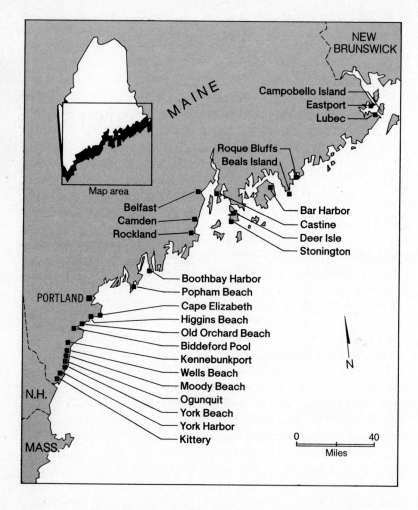

parts, the slogan "Buckle Up for Safety" is not simply a wise rule of the road, it's a commandment for staying alive. During our stay in Maine, we routinely witnessed maneuvers that made the Dukes of Hazzard look like driver-safety fanatics. All of these antics were perpetrated by vehicles sporting the cheery "Maine Vacationland" license plate.

Be forewarned: there is a hidden driveway around every bend.

Don't be surprised if some flyblown rattletrap with fins on its rusting frame comes snailing out onto the roadway, inviting a rear-ender. The purpose of all this is not to impute anything negative about the competence or intellect of Maine's "Down Easters"—as the native shore-dwellers like to refer to themselves—but merely to alert the reader to the matter of highway survival techniques and vacation safety in the isolated pine forests of "Vacation-land."

Still, as long as we're on the subject of IQ, it's worth mentioning that the delayed reaction time of the native Down Easter might give you some funny ideas about cognitive downward mobility. As one northern Maine restaurateur, a non-native, told us, fumbling for a tactful way to put it, "There's a gap. . . . Ummm . . . You'll find that you're talking to yourself a lot." Down Easters are not very forthcoming with speech or information. An innocent request for directions—e.g., "Say, where do you go to get the ferry to Isle Au Haut?"—will elicit a slow, curious cock of the head and a placid stare that will continue until you, unnerved, feel obliged to repeat the question. No sooner will you utter a few halting words, however, than you'll hear yourself interrupting the Down Easter, who has at last deigned to answer.

It all comes down to timing—they love to disarm unsuspecting outsiders by playing with the terms and conditions of conversation, which most of us observe as a way of expediting the everyday matter of living in an interactive society. Down Easters have no such sense of obligation. They are a breed apart. Not even the South has resisted assimilation into the mainstream of American life quite the way these salty, stubborn buzzards of backbay Maine have.

We heard the complaint of a Massachusetts-born woman who married a native of Boothbay Harbor, Maine. (They run a guest home there.) After twenty-three years, she still had not been accepted into their ranks as a local. She shrugged it off with a laugh, but the implication was clear: you either come from Maine or you don't come from Maine, and no amount of time spent here—most of a lifetime, even—will make you a Down Easter in the minds of those ornery cusses who were born here.

And so you'll ask a question and get a look as stony as the Maine shoreline. If a reply is given, take it with a grain of salt and solicit a second opinion, particularly if it's distances or directions you are seeking. The chances are about fifty-fifty that whatever figures or instructions you were quoted are almost useless. Three miles can mean 30 yards or 13 miles up the road. The state of Maine doesn't help matters. In its fever to rid its highways of the clutter of signs and billboards—a fever we wish were contagious—Maine has gotten positively stingy with directional signs and distance markers. You'll be following signs for a while and then come to an unmarked fork in the road. From that point on, you'll be following your hunches.

Yes, Maine is elaborately confusing. With its anything-goes geography, there are numberless nooks and crannies and coves and inlets in which to burrow anonymously. Thick forests of evergreens wander down to a rock-choked shoreline, which is often shrouded in mist. Perhaps this helps explain the sense of mystery and privacy, the guarded nature and suspicion of outsiders, that is branded upon the Down East character.

Certainly, they cling with exceptional tenacity to their habits and folkways, and the topographical and meteorological extremity of their state allows them to endure in their isolation. Don't try to figure out Maine. How can you expect to make sense of a state that has a stretch of highway simultaneously identified as Route 1 South, Route 3 West and Route 15 North? (This actually happens between East Orland and Bucksport.)

It's easy to get disoriented and lost along the Maine coast; indeed, this is why you should come here. To visit Maine is to drop back a century or so, to a time when shipbuilding, lobster fishing and other demanding maritime trades defined people's lives. North of Portland, which is to say for more than 80 percent of Maine's shoreline, the sea is treacherous. Tides rush in and out of inlets with monstrous speed and force. In some places, there is a 23-foot difference between high and low tide. At the Bay of Fundy, high tide arrives as a veritable wall of water. Often, a thick, blinding fog will roll up suddenly and unexpectedly. ("Don't like the weather?" goes a standard Maine joke. "Wait a minute.") And the shoals and shallows make for difficult navigation.

From Portland north, there is little ocean swimming and so few sand beaches that often the proper name is just that: Sand Beach. Of course, Old Orchard Beach, Kennebunkport, Ogunquit and the Yorks are beach resorts of a more conventional sort, but they occupy only the southernmost 30 miles or so of the Maine coast. Upcoast Maine, on the other hand, is a place for losing one's self in the measured cadence of an unhurried life. Once you acquire a taste for it, you'll begin to understand why Down Easters so steadfastly resist the intrusions of hyperactive East Coasters who hail from points south of the Kittery Bridge—and why a fancy car with New York license plates will more likely draw a scowl than a neighborly hello.

The Down Easter will be happy, however, to pocket your money. Tourism has become a state obsession of late, and U.S. 1—the primary north-south route along the coast—is lined with all sorts of fly-by-night shell shops, play parks and trinket stands. One ambitious shopkeeper, perhaps figuring he'll draw 'em in like flies if he offers something for everybody, advertises this mixed bag of tourist effluvia on the sign outside his store: "Folk Art, Gummy Bears, Carnations, Penny Candy, Antiques."

One more note. If you have a yen for lobster, Maine is your Shangri-la. Every decrepit lean-to from Eastport to Kittery is festooned with likenesses of the saltwater crustacean. Usually, they're depicted in something like a human standing position, as if dancing on their tails, with claws poised overhead like castinets. Not so jolly is the reality that they've been overfished for many decades and that their numbers are in precipitous decline. At one time so abundant that indentured servants would insert a clause in their work contracts mandating that they *not* be served lobster more than twice a week, this ocean favorite can hardly find a rock under which to hide in peace anymore.

Consider that it takes seven years for a lobster to reach a weight of 1 pound, which is the standard offering on restaurant dinner menus. Now ponder that the waters of the Atlantic were at one time filled with 20- and 30-pound lobsters. Though the presence of a 30-pound lobster in ocean waters might now cause a *Jaws*-like panic among the vacationing populace—try to picture the horrible things such a monster might do to an unattended child—well, hey, it was their ocean before it was ours. So think about it the next time you're wrestling with a boiled or steamed lobster and the slumgullion and brackish water start dribbling from its flame-red exoskeleton, and ask yourself: wouldn't the fried haddock have been just as good?

Lubec
Eastport
Campobello Island, New Brunswick

To get any farther east on the American map than Lubec, you would have to walk like a lemming into the rugged ocean surf at nearby Quoddy Head State Park. To go any more northeasterly than Eastport, you would have to take a long walk off the short wharf into its recently enlarged harbor. To get from one town to another—a distance, as the seagull flies, of less than 5 miles—you would either have to take a ferry that costs $6 and leaves from Campobello Island first or you would have to drive state roads that wind around these glacially formed chunks of Maine-land for almost 40 miles. This, indeed, is an out-of-the-way place. For the symbolism of the quest alone, a journey to northeasternmost Maine is well worth the fuel it takes to get here.

In addition to symbolism, there are some other, more tangible pleasures to be found by scouting around a bit—and whoever has taken the trouble to come this far will undoubtedly do so. As one congenial denizen of Eastport explained it: "You don't just pass through this area, because there is nowhere to go. . . . You have to *want* to be here." Although self-effacingly honest to us outsiders, he was not altogether accurate in his assessment. If you toss nearby Campobello Island (part of the Canadian province of New Brunswick) into your itinerary, a balanced sort of family vacation can be found, including camping, sight-seeing, beach hikes and boat trips. Even ocean swimming is not altogether unfeasible. It's been done, we've been told. (However, on a warm July day, according to a blackboard at the welcome center on Campobello Island, the ocean temperature was hovering at 50 degrees. *No thank you*.)

Crossing back and forth between Lubec and Campobello over the Franklin Delano Roosevelt Bridge can on occasion become a complicated transaction, what with U.S. Customs officials rooting around your luggage and asking all kinds of nosy questions. Be sure you know your answers beforehand when they descend upon you with the following frowning inquiries: (a) Where are you going? (b) Where did you come from? (c) Do you have any firearms? (d) Do you smoke? It's harder than you think *not* to feel like a criminal under interrogation. We were ordered out of our car while they searched every bag, knapsack and shaving kit they could lay their hands on. They were especially curious about the contents of a large box that contained nothing more than a zillion brochures about the East Coast beaches on our itinerary—perhaps they suspected us of trafficking pornography? At last, they located their contraband: a few cigarette butts in an ashtray. "I thought you guys told us you didn't smoke," one said with a triumphant grin.

On the crossing over to Campobello, the Canadian officials had asked us only if we planned to leave anything behind on the island. You do not, we discovered, need to include basic bodily deposits in your answer. Campobello Island is perhaps best known for the fact that Franklin D. Roosevelt maintained a summer residence here. (Imagine the uproar if a president were to keep a house outside the United States in these jingoistic times.) It is well worth a day trip at least. With a number of inexpensively priced motels and guest homes scattered about the island, one can even make a vacation of it.

The Lubec/Eastport area, which is where we based ourselves, has been suffering economic hardships in recent decades. Previously, the sardine industry sustained these towns. Now, however, sardines, a nonperishable product popular in a time before refrigerators, are neither in great demand nor in great supply. As with the lobster, these infant herring have been overfished, but, curiously enough, that apparently is not the full reason behind their decline in these parts. An Eastport waitress informed us that environmental laws, designed to protect the purity of the water, have driven the fish away. "The fish lived off the garbage," she explained.

It might say something about the general slowness of the area that it has taken so long to find alternate sources of income to replace the dinosaur-like canneries—and in Lubec's case, it is debatable whether any sort of even modest rebound is in the cards. But all in all, the impoverishment we'd been told to expect in this corner of Maine was not really in evidence—unless you find poverty in the small, neatly kept wooden homes and quiet summer cabins of Lubec, or the historic renovations of waterfront Eastport. Much of the latter community's stone and brick architecture dates back to the early 1800s, when Eastport was the busiest port in Maine.

Eastport has attempted to turn the clock back to those boom times by significantly enlarging its harbor to accommodate large oceangoing vessels. Every September, it trumpets its new status as a major-league port of entry with its Port Days celebration. Lubec, alas, endures on the strength of its few remaining canneries and as a quiet haven for tourists who prefer the road not, or seldom, taken. Those fascinated by extremities will want to visit *Quoddy Head State Park*, 4 miles east of Route 189 near Lubec. This is the easternmost point of land in the United States, and it can be a wild and forlorn place even in summer. The shore is rocky, the surf is terrifying at times and wind and fog make even picnicking a challenge. And if you chance to be strolling by the Quoddy Head Light when a fog rolls in, cover your ears: at close range, we were warned, a sudden blast from the foghorn can cause deafness.

Accommodations

The towns of Lubec and Eastport form one of the four true corners on the American map. If that map were made into an envelope (hey, you never know), the postage stamp would go here, on the top right-hand corner of Maine. Though it is certainly worth the effort to visit this unique spot, people don't exactly come here in droves. This is reflected in the choice of accommodations, or rather

the lack of them: without prior arrangements, you could be Returned to Sender, Address Unknown. We learned this the hard
way, our first night on the road.

Although we later discovered a handful of mom-and-pop (or
mère-et-père) motels over on Campobello Island, there was no room
at either inn in Lubec that mid-July weeknight. Grizzled and de-
lirious from having traveled nearly 700 miles from New York City
in a single stretch, we took the advice of a scarecrowish Lubec
innkeeper and headed back down the highway to Machias, a needless backtrack inland of 45 miles and an unfitting way to launch a
book about beaches. Nonetheless, we found a place that didn't
seem to care that our ravaged appearance suggested a pair of criminals on the lam, plunked down our $48 and dropped our suitcases
in a room that had all the sterile charm of a suburban guest bedroom—green Naugahyde chairs and all. As tired as we were, we
would have paid a hundred bills for it. Vacationer's Tip #1: Plan
well, make reservations and beware the bone-weariness of travel,
which will make even the Addams' Family's house seem like a
tourist's Valhalla.

For the record, the *Home Port Inn* in Lubec, a restored guest
home located within walking distance of town, is the choicest place
to drop anchor in these parts. The accommodations are limited to
a handful of rooms, however, so book early. The inn has a very
attractive dining room as well.

Hardier types might want to try one of the several fine campgrounds in the area. Up in these pine-scented woods, camping
somehow seems a more fitting way to visit. We made camp at
Cobscook Bay State Park, located smack dab in the middle of Moose-
horn National Wildlife Refuge about 10 miles from Lubec. A
hundred campsites are distributed around a beautiful bay. At high
tide, you'll find yourself a stone's throw from the water. At low
tide, there is no water—but you can go clamming in the tidal flats.
One caveat: beware the morning mosquitoes.

On Campobello Island, *Provincial Park Campground* offers eighty
sites situated near Herring Cove Beach, a mile-long beach on
the eastern side of the island, facing the Bay of Fundy. Herring
Cove has the distinction of being one of Canada's few true sand
beaches.

Restaurants

In Lubec, our inaugural meal consisted of fried fish on paper plates at the *Hillside Seafood Restaurant*. Maybe it was the magic of the moment, but food has seldom tasted better to us than it did on that particular afternoon. The place is no more than a barnlike roadhouse, resembling a Dairy Queen, but a more worthy recommendation would be hard to find than the one we heard spring from the lips of a crusty native regular: "I'm from around here, and the best food around here is here."

In Eastport, head straight for the *Cannery Wharf*, a complex of dining establishments and small shops dominated by the *Cannery Restaurant*. The latter has a varied selection of foods and styles of cooking, but you will more than likely want the waiter or waitress to throw a lobster bib around your neck. Lobster Duchess is the most civilized way to have at the creature, as the crustacean is baked, stuffed and relieved of its inedible innards. The Lobster Duchess at the Cannery Wharf was the best we would be served on the East Coast—and on our first night out, no less! Our host— a jolly man, and generous, too—joked that if we ate like this the entire trip, we'd look like him by journey's end. (He had a bit of a potbelly.) This cautionary observation, made in jest, alarmed more than amused us. We hadn't thought of that.

According to a native, there is not a single McDonald's around here for 120 miles. Just wait till the moguls figure out a way to mass-produce Lobster McNuggets.

Nightlife

Around midnight, look up at the sky. There's your nightlife: every star you ever wanted to meet. Meanwhile, back on planet Earth, aside from a few nocturnal beer-bar pool fanatics, most humans around here are in bed by nine o'clock. After dark, all the action is in the wildlife preserves.

Eastport Development Committee
78 High Street
Eastport, Maine 04631

Roque Bluffs

About 10 miles off of Route 1 just south of Machias, over a wind-ing, hilly road through country that looks more like the bluegrass of Kentucky than the coast of Maine, sits Roque Bluff State Park, a small public beach. The park offers its visitors a unique choice: saltwater swimming in the bay, and freshwater swimming in a pond just across the road. Both options were attractive, if chilly; and though the beach is pebbly, the small waves make a mellifluent singing sound as they rush over the stones and shells at the shore-line. We found it a peaceful, pleasant setting in which to spend an afternoon.

Beal's Island

Lest you be tempted to come here based on an innocent perusal of a map, as we were, be forewarned. Beal's Island is not a vacation resort but a fishing village in decline. To get there, we traversed a bridge that bore the singularly discouraging warning "Bridge Under Repair. Pass At Your Own Risk!" (We later discovered that this warning is posted at nearly every site where bridge- and road-work is being performed in Maine. Not a great confidence-builder.)

If that wasn't reason enough to make a U-turn, the slumlike conditions on the other side of the bridge were. Beal's Island looked like a seaside version of Appalachia: storm-tossed mobile homes set at crazy angles on small lots, surrounded by old tires and junked cars and patrolled by wild-eyed dogs. One look at this dismal setting, and the cesspool-like appearance of the bay at low tide, and we were only too glad to run the risk of crossing the bridge back over to the mainland.

Bar Harbor

Approaching Bar Harbor from the west, we began to fear the worst about this popular vacation resort from the 10-mile corridor of tacky tourist-trade establishments that leads into it: animal parks, lobster pounds, putt-putt courses, paddle-boat ponds and souvenir emporiums. Those fears were mostly put to rest, however, once we crossed the bridge over onto Mount Desert Island and rounded a curve into the town of Bar Harbor itself. For while Bar Harbor bustles with visitors during the summer months, the villagers take pains to maintain the aura of taste and manners that is its legacy from the days when millionaires summered here in opulent seclusion.

Bar Harbor was founded in 1796 by settlers who were so impressed with the natural splendor of the area that they named their new home Eden. Like that mythical garden of earthly delights, Bar Harbor has had its fall from grace, having taken a rather hearty bite from the poisoned apple of commercial tourism. Still, the pursuit of the lucrative tourist dollar—4 million people visit Bar Harbor annually—has been tempered by a staunch desire on the part of the townspeople to maintain something akin to an authentic village atmosphere. And thus the tourist quickly discovers he must accept Bar Harbor on its own uncorrupted terms, which is a pleasure.

The real attraction here is the island itself, which is mostly given over to *Acadia National Park* and is a study in geological contrasts. Mt. Desert Island is a mountainous island whose tallest peak—Cadillac Mountain, reaching an altitude of 1,532 feet—is the highest point on the Atlantic coastline north of Rio de Janeiro. There are, in all, eighteen peaks on Mt. Desert Island, which was severed from the mainland at the end of the last Ice Age when melting glaciers caused the ocean to rise. An ice sheet some 2 miles thick deposited huge boulders that had been carried great distances, and the abrasive action of the glacier rounded off the jagged granite peaks of the Acadian highland. The eastern egress of this glacial river carved out Somes Sound, the only true fjord in all of North America.

Within the space of a few miles, one will pass through cool evergreen forests, bare and steep-sloped granite cliffs at sea's edge and crystal-clear freshwater lakes. The one thing you will not find on Mt. Desert Island is much of an opportunity for ocean swimming. There is a public beach, prosaically called Sand Beach, off Park Loop Road in Acadia National Park. Bounded at one end by dense forest and by a wall of rock on the other, this small, crescent-shaped beach is a good place to sunbathe on a warm day. Only the hardier among the species, including the many French-Canadians one sees on New England beaches—who appear as oblivious to frigid waters as walruses—will want to brave the ocean. Those dead set on swimming should opt for Echo Lake Beach, a fresh-water lake off Route 102 on the western side of Mt. Desert Island (it, too, is part of the park). The mid-July water temperature at Echo Lake is 70 degrees—steamy compared with Sand Beach's shivering 55.

Acadia is worth a full day of sight-seeing at the very least. One should begin a tour of the park—the first national park established east of the Mississippi—at the visitors' center, located on Route 3 just outside Bar Harbor. A 15-minute orientation film will prep you for an afternoon of hiking, biking or auto touring. Our advice: buy the Acadia National Park *Motorist's Guide* (75 cents) and forgo the $8 cassette tour (why drag a chattering tape machine around when the beauty of Acadia is writ large before your very eyes?).

The one must-do item on your Acadian agenda is a drive to the top of Cadillac Mountain, with its striated, pinkish-tinted fields of granite and breathtaking views of the village below and the islands beyond. Go there at daybreak—which in the summer is around 4 A.M.—and you'll be the first to see the sun's rays strike the United States. A word of warning: Acadia is inundated with sight-seers in the summer months, so a midday drive along the 27-mile

Park Loop Road can become a bumper-to-bumper amateur Grand Prix up the mountain, overheating car engines and tempers. Those Winnebagos and their ample occupants do crawl along.

If the hordes begin to annoy, solitude can be found on the western side of the island, which hides a number of small fishing villages less touched by tourism. There are, in fact, some fifteen towns and villages scattered about the island. There are no blinking Holiday Inn signs to be found in Bernard, Bass Harbor, Seal Harbor, Southwest Harbor and Northeast Harbor—the largest communities, after Bar Harbor, on the island. You can watch boats bobbing idly in the bay and lose track of time.

All sorts of people are drawn to Bar Harbor. Old folks come in the autumn to linger over drinks and dinner in well-appointed dining rooms. Families flock by the thousands to splash around in heated motel pools, to browse the crafts shops and T-shirt dispensaries of Main Street and to undertake automotive circuits around Acadia. There are also a lot of college-age Yuppies, dressed for yachting.

A good many other under-forties, on the other hand, have found in Bar Harbor a mecca for new-age lifestyles: vegetarian gourmet restaurants, "world music" concerts by dulcimer players, fashions that tend toward peasant attire on the hirsute Rubenesque women and cutoffs and painter's hats on the guys, who look like members of the Grateful Dead. Bar Harbor and environs also draw a fair number of folkie entertainers—e.g., Jerry Jeff Walker, Tom Rush, anyone with the last name of Taylor—who still command a following here.

Bar Harbor is nothing if not colorful, given the panorama of people that pass down its streets. Second to nature-watching, people-watching is the most engaging pastime here. And certainly you will find yourself entertained in pleasant surroundings. The village green at the town center makes a good vantage point from which to watch the parade pass by. If you get restless, you can always take a trolley bus from town up to the top of *Cadillac Mountain*, or sign aboard an all-day cruise around the bay. Mt. Desert Island (pronounced dez-*zert*, as in blueberries and cream, a local specialty) offers plenty to do or nothing to do—it's your choice.

Accommodations

There are scores of motels and guest homes in Bar Harbor, all hoping to turn a profit in the brief, 90-day season. In an average summer, we were told, Bar Harbor's hostelries are booked up full an average of 30 days. But don't let a lack of reservations deter you from making a spontaneous trip to the island. There's room for everybody, it seems. Of all of them, *Atlantic Oakes By-the-Sea*, a moderately priced resort right on Frenchman's Bay, is the most enticing. The landscaping is environmentally oriented, with natural, wood-shingled buildings blending unobtrusively into spacious, forested grounds. There are six tennis courts and a large pool area, and frequently the proprietors throw an outdoor clambake. All in all, we found Atlantic Oakes to be an exhilarating place to unwind, with the bay in the foreground and the mountains as a backdrop.

In toward town, the *Cadillac Motel* sits on quiet, shaded grounds, just out of range of the Main Street hubbub. If you're hitting Bar Harbor on a busy weekend, you might first try the *National Park Motel*, which is much larger than most and often has vacancies. There is also a string of inns and guest homes on Holland Avenue and Mt. Desert Street, just blocks from the center of town.

Restaurants

Bar Harbor cuisine is definitely on the banal side. Buy anything with blueberries in them—pies, muffins, pancakes—because they're grown here. But be aware that even the best Bar Harbor has to offer in seafood is not going to be that much better than your average Howard Johnson's fried clam special. You'd be better advised to go and seek out a legitimate "Down East" outdoor clam and lobster bake.

The following restaurants, all of moderate-to-good quality, have something besides food to recommend them. The *Bar Harbor Motor Inn Restaurant* has the best view of Frenchman's Bay in town, which alone is worth the price of an entrée (don't ask which one). *Testa's*, which has a sister restaurant in Palm Beach, Florida ("Pines in the summer, palms in the winter" is their motto), serves reasonably priced Italian food and seafood in a warm, informal atmosphere. The *Mary Jane Restaurant* has generous portions of seafood and an outdoor patio from which to peruse the Bar Harbor bazaar.

For breakfast, scarf down a plate of blueberry pancakes ($1.69— wotta bargain) at *Jordan's Variety*. At lunch, they knock out a mean sub at *EPI's Pizza and Subs*, and the fifties-style jukeboxes on each table, complete with a service-call button for your waiter or waitress, add a nice antiquarian touch.

Nightlife

Bar Harbor after dark was neatly and succinctly summed up for us by an attractive bartender at an upstairs-downstairs club called *Geddy's*: "You have your one or two drinks and get mellow, then you go home and read your book." That assessment jibed with our own observations. While she chatted with us, Livingston Taylor could be heard plinking in the main part of the club overhead, singing about life on the Vineyard and other Sesame Street folk tunes that humored the Yuppie crowd.

We, meanwhile, entertained ourselves at our mug-covered table by defacing Liv Taylor posters with a Magic Marker, which amused our waitress and upset a drunken rich kid in a fishing hat, who unwisely attempted to engage us in repartee. And so it goes in Bar Harbor on a summer evening: lots of sidewalk strolling, but the nightlife never seems to rise above a polite simmer. Which was fine—we would see endless excess at the other end of the scale as we made our way south.

FOR FURTHER INFORMATION

Bar Harbor Chamber of Commerce
Box 158
Bar Harbor, Maine 04609
(207) 288-3393

Information Bureau
Southwest Harbor-Tremont Chamber of Commerce
Southwest Harbor, Maine 04679
(207) 244-3333

Stonington
Deer Isle

In the words of the wife of the service-station attendant who changed
our oil, *"This place is dead!"* Her son, who was lolling in a chair
with a catatonic, what-am-I-doing-here look on his face, couldn't
even muster that much enthusiasm on the subject. He just shook
his head slowly, as if he were watching his youth seep away like
a receding tide. Voicing the minority opinion was an old codger
with a rugged Maine set to his jaw and two bulging, asymmetrical
eyes. He declared that there was plenty to do—such as scavenging
for stones at low tide. Stonington, he vowed, has a greater variety
of stones "than anywhere else in the world." Beyond the idle
exaggeration of the boast—this was not the first time we'd heard
a Down Easter bestowing an improbable superlative on his neck
of the woods—it made us wonder just what would draw people
out here on one of Maine's farthest reaches of land. It couldn't just
be the stones, however magical and manifold they might be.

Other entertainment options presented to us in the course of
our stay included a tour of the local sardine cannery—"You watch
the ladies lop the heads and tails off the fish and pack 'em in cans"—
and a ride around the bay in a fishing boat. There are no bars
here on the isle, although you can bring your own beer to the
Fisherman's Friend or get drinks with your dinner up the road at
the *Clamdigger* in Deer Isle. There's freshwater swimming at the
Lily Pond in Deer Isle, but the only public saltwater sand beach
in the vicinity was disparaged even by the locals.

Picking up pebbles at low tide, watching sardines get decapi-
tated—really, what is a visitor to do in this place? Why come here?

Well, John Steinbeck made Deer Isle his first stop in *Travels with Charley* and briefly rhapsodized about the mystery and allure of the dark pine woods before heading out for points west. As for us, once we'd simmered down our city expectations we began to get hypnotized by the view out our bay window—a view that encompassed the numerous small, forested islands that dot Penobscot Bay.

Though Stonington is no Club Med, there are a few diversions worth mentioning. Foremost among them is a ride on the mail boat from Stonington to Isle Au Haut, which costs $4 each way. The island, part of which is included in Acadia National Park, is ripe for exploration. Commercial boat tours of the bay are available as well. Smaller pleasures include a visit to *Ames Pond*, just east of town, which is blanketed with pink water lilies, and a picture stop nearby at the Lilliputian neighborhood of homes, churches and stores, all of them built precisely to scale and none more than 2 feet high, that sits outside the dwelling of one Everett Knowlton, who spent forty years on his pastime. A patient man.

The communities of Stonington and Deer Isle have a rich, proud history. The area was settled in the seventeenth century by Frenchmen, as were many of the isles and islands along the Maine coast. By the mid-1800s, Deer Isle was second only to Gloucester, Massachusetts, as a fishing port. Later in the century, stonecutting became a major industry (it survives to this day). Deer Isle granite is what built the Brooklyn, Triborough, George Washington and Manhattan bridges in New York City, not to mention Rockefeller Center. During the so-called Gilded Age of the late 1800s and early 1900s, many a great yacht was docked in Stonington harbor, and the sons of Stonington crewed on many of America's cup-winning yachts.

Nowadays the economy is not so gilded, but the town is quite comfortable with its status as a self-described "working fishing village." It's impossible not to like a community that lists twice as many lobster dealers as lawyers in the Yellow Pages. And is it ever slow here. Walking down a Stonington side street, we overheard one resident thanking a neighbor for sending her a Christmas card. This conversation took place on July 24.

Accommodations

With a large wooden sundeck right on the bay, the *Captain's Quarters* is, to our thinking, *the* place to stay in Stonington. An enormous three-room suite, with complete kitchen facilities, a well-furnished living room and a picture window facing the bay, was going for $50 a night in season. Come armed with your thickest paperbacks, or a mantra. There is also a smattering of inns and guesthouses along the far side of Main Street. Among them, the *1872 Inn* had a whitewashed, colonial elegance that was especially appealing.

Restaurants

Look no further than the *Fisherman's Friend* for good, affordable seafood. This is where the locals come, and the locals are fishermen. The Mini Fisherman's Platter ($6.75) assuaged our maxi appetites; order the larger one only if you have a hunger on the order of Andre the Giant's. The *Bayview*, near the public wharf, is another good choice. It's family owned and operated, and ridiculously inexpensive.

Nightlife

When the sun goes down, so does the town. It's as simple as that.

FOR FURTHER INFORMATION

Deer Isle-Stonington Chamber of Commerce
Little Deer Isle, Maine 04650
(207) 348-6124

Castine

Castine has been called the most beautiful village in New England. It is hidden at the end of the Castine Peninsula, at some distance from the town of Bucksport on the mainland. As one star-struck visitor wrote a decade ago, "We thought the sea and sky fairer, the air clearer, the people truer, the prospect of water and islands more perfect than anywhere."

The town of Castine, unassuming as it may seem, has a lot of history behind it. It has flown under four flags (France, England, Holland, United States) and been known under three names (Pentagoet, Bagaduce, Castine). The British occupied Castine in the eighteenth century and built Fort George here to protect the town from invading American revolutionaries from the Commonwealth of Massachusetts. One of the most crushing naval defeats in U.S. history occurred at Castine, when the redcoats sank three dozen ships. The loss nearly bankrupted Massachusetts.

Perhaps this is why Castine remains New England's best-kept secret. In any case, Castine is an ideal place to get away from it all, to marvel at the beauty of the Maine woods and bays and to enjoy a town that has, miraculously, hardly changed a whit in the twentieth century. Castine has a few restaurants and a handful of lodging places—like the *Pentagoet Inn* and the *Castine Inn*—plus constant reminders of history in the form of forts, museums and historical markers. There are something like a hundred of the latter scattered in and around Castine.

Belfast

Located midway down Maine's coast just off Route 1, Belfast is a quiet bayside village of 7,000 described by its chamber of commerce as the "Greatway to Down East Maine," an ambiguous title at best. Therein lies an irony that seems emblematic of Maine in general. Maine is an economically depressed state (the third poorest in the country, behind Mississippi and West Virginia), full of hearty, hard-working people who cannot find work. Yet the state, trying to jazz up its image, bills itself to the world as "Vacationland." It is a sad state with a happy image, PR-wise. The real irony is that the vacation season in Maine is only as long as the summer, bounded by Memorial Day and Labor Day. The rest of the year, Maine is a deep freeze.

There are a number of mildly prepossessing coastal towns like Belfast that want to be part of the bigger Vacationland picture but have not quite figured out how to go about beating the drum. Belfast is the "Greatway to Down East Maine" simply because it is "the only way to Down East Maine." You must past through it. That doesn't mean there's any reason to stop here.

One Belfast bartender, a transplanted Mississippian, tried to explain the situation from the perspective of the reticent native Down Easters: "Nobody around here can find jobs, so they refer to Maine as Vacationland because they are on a permanent vacation."

Maine's dire poverty is most evident in its poorer northern counties, whose once-busy ports are now as useless as museum pieces. Belfast, especially, has seen better days, by the look of it. The unemployment rate is a staggering 20 percent. The town claims the only stoplight in the entirety of Waldo County. It tends to stick for moments at a time on yellow and red simultaneously. Yet Belfast's residents still stand by their humble township with exaggerated boasts of her "Greatway" virtues while stubbornly resisting the slightest whiff of change, particularly change wrought by money and outsiders, which is the only way an improvement in the big picture will ever be realized.

Belfast was a flourishing port in the days of the tall ships, and its grand past is very much in evidence in the old sea captains' homes along Primrose Hill or the completely restored wooden church, dating back to 1796, located on (of course) Church Street. Its tenuous present can be found in the center of town, near the wharf. There you will find a new seawall, a cafe that serves hot dogs and quiche, and a seafood restaurant whose daily special might just as easily be mako shark as fried clams. But beneath the level of these small concessions to progress, there is the much more revealing spectacle we witnessed on the main drag around midnight one evening, one that said more about Belfast than words or statistics. Outside a bar off the city square, an elderly man was performing a drunken improvisational dance, muttering and gesticulating threateningly to whoever it was inside the establishment who had just thrown him out. He was, we were told, the town drunk.

All of this begins to sink in only after a few days in the state. After a while, the stubborn reticence of the native Down Easter begins to seem more like self-spite. If you simply speed through Belfast, as most travelers do, you would see, tucked off in a side cove below the highway bridge, a quiet, solid-looking town with some notable old architecture in evidence and a couple of cherry-red tugboats tethered to the wharf. Scratch the surface and you find a town that is seething over the issue of change. The anchor of the past drags at the yacht of progress that wants to set sail for the harbor of revitalization.

When we visited, the telling issue in Belfast was—just coincidentally—a beach. The town's progressive wing wanted to create an artificial beach in Belfast City Park. Rock-strewn and peppered with small, sharp seashells, the public park extends south from the town center for a quarter of a mile along Penobscot Bay. It is not a bathing beach, but plans were heatedly afoot to make it one by dredging sand from the bay and depositing it on the shore. *Voilà!* A sand beach where none existed. They hoped that a new beach would entice visitors to the struggling community.

In editorials and conversations among the locals, there were worries voiced over the "wrong element" being drawn in—i.e., rowdy natives or the moneyed crowd that live on yachts and don't give a hoot about the communities where they dock them. It happened 18 miles down the bay in Camden, the locals insisted, and, by God, they weren't going to let it happen here. Never mind that Camden was prospering like nobody's business while Belfast was dying on the vine.

"You don't ruin natural resources," a crusty local shopkeeper told us in disgust. He did not elaborate upon his thesis, other than to give us the now-familiar Maine salute—a slow nod of the head. An on-site inspection of the park, however, revealed not a surfeit of natural resources but an area in dire need of maintenance and repair. A few picnic tables, a baseball diamond, some pockmarked tennis courts, one boarded-up set of toilets and an open rest room that a dead man would not wish to enter—it did not look like a Riviera in the making. The amount of money it would take to make it one is hopelessly beyond the town's means. But to import money and assistance from outside would destroy the very fabric of the town.

If they opt for development, they run the risk of becoming just another soulless haven for the summering jet set. If they resist the forces of change, the spoils of victory will be continued impoverishment. Belfast fascinated us. Outside of north coastal Maine, one does not very often encounter this sort of debate along the East Coast any longer. That is because there is hardly a shred of honest rusticity left anywhere on the East Coast.

Accommodations

A number of bed-and-breakfast inns are located in the Belfast area, and the quantity increases as you head north toward Searsport, a popular jumping-off point for antique hunters. One of the newest arrivals in Belfast, the *Penobscot Meadows Inn*, is definitely the nicest place to stay. In fact, it is so beyond the best that Belfast otherwise has to offer that it is downright anomalous. The Penobscot Meadows was opened in the summer of '84 by a trio of expatriate Washingtonians who are dedicated to the proposition that gourmet dining and gracious accommodations can be made to flourish even in Belfast. And so these pioneers-of-sorts converted a building that used to be a sailing school (and was "no better than a flophouse" when they started) into an inn and restaurant with an almost obsessively uncompromising sense of detail and style.

As for the weary motorist who doesn't want to deal with the ramifications of staying at a country inn (someone else lives there, so there is always an implicit obligation to act preternaturally well-behaved), try the *Yankee Clipper Motel* on Route 1.

Restaurants

Although you'd be hard-pressed to get a local yokel to admit it, the *Penobscot Meadows Restaurant* (attached to the aforementioned inn), is undeniably the best place to eat for many miles around. Upon asking directions there, we were told by a gas-station attendant in a rather outraged tone of voice that "you don't want to go there! They don't even have fried fish or potatoes!" He was right about one thing—no fried fish or potatoes—but wrong about the other. Yes, you *do* want to go here. In this land of lobster bibs and baked potatoes, they create astounding gourmet entrées like Fettuccine al Frutti di Mare and Lobster Sushi, and do so with an attentiveness that almost goes beyond the call of duty. Prices are moderate and reasonable, given the high quality of the food.

If you do crave the fried fish and potatoes, stay on Route 1 and you'll find, just north of the town's center, places with names like *Jed's*, where hungry crowds swarm like flies. In the heart of Belfast, down by the wharf, sits the *City Boat Landing Restaurant*, which specializes in fresh seafood and posts numerous daily specials.

Nightlife

The natives who are not abed by the time the dinner dishes are washed are probably about to commence drinking heavily. This, however, does not mean that they want to party hearty with a bunch of tourists. Mostly, an atmosphere of quiet, serious drinking pervades the local bars, as if the ship might never be coming in. Overall, the bars of Belfast did not appear particularly prone to sudden violence, but we took no chances and drank quietly, agreeing, with forced gaiety, with everything told us. The *Belfast Café*, on the city square, is a soulful little place that's a bit out of the ordinary, with original artwork and saxophones hanging on the wall. There we enjoyed a few mugs of Narragansett, our favorite New England brew.

FOR FURTHER INFORMATION

Belfast Area Chamber of Commerce
P.O. Box 58
Belfast, Maine 04915
(207) 338-2896

Camden

> *All I could see from where I stood*
> *Was three long mountains and a wood*
> *I turned and looked another way*
> *and saw three islands in a bay*

So wrote poet Edna St. Vincent Millay of her native Camden in her poem "Renascence," which she penned and recited in 1912 in what is now the Whitehall Inn, a guesthouse. There is a tradition of arts and letters in Camden that makes it a kind of oasis of culture in the barrens of mid-coast Maine. Millay found her voice here; one figures she would have lost it had she come from, say, Belfast, or at least written poetry of a very different stripe: "All I could see from where I stood/Was three drunk rednecks and a hood."

On Camden's streets, one would have no such problem. There are more bookstores and arts and crafts shops here than you can shake a scrimshaw at. Camden even has its own Shakespeare company! Not bad in a state where culture generally means scalloped potatoes.

Its sparkling blue harbor nestled up against Mts. Battie and

Megunticook, Camden recalls in its rugged natural beauty the northern coast of California. *Camden Hill State Park*, just north of town, encompasses both 1,600 feet of shoreline (no beach swimming, though) and *Mt. Battie's* 1,520-foot summit, which is accessible by car and worth the trouble. A tour of Camden's old homes, by car or on foot, is also recommended. A brochure outlining a route, prepared by the Camden-Rockport Historical Society, can be had at the local chamber of commerce, down on the waterfront near the public parking lot.

Camden is a former center of shipbuilding that currently caters to the yachting crowd. All of those two-masted schooners bobbing in the harbor spell prosperity for the community, and Camden seems to handle it well. The beach scene here is nothing much, however, and not the reason to come here. There's a small shoreline municipal park, Laite Memorial Beach, on Bayview Street. Up the road, there's an actual wide sand beach in the town of Lincolnville. One would have to have an arctic tolerance to want to frolic in these waters, however. More likely you'll wind up signing aboard a windjammer cruise around Penobscot Bay or taking a state-operated ferry to one or more of the larger inhabited islands—Vinalhaven, North Haven and Islesboro—out in the bay.

Accommodations

A quiet option is the turn-of-the century *Whitehall Inn* on High Street, which as we've said is where the young Edna St. Vincent Millay first read her poetry. The *High Tide Inn*, a mile north of Camden on Route 1, epitomizes all that's best about Maine's rambling old country inns. Located at the foot of Mt. Megunticook, the High Tide boasts 250 feet of private beach and many more rooms of all descriptions than the term "inn" usually connotes.

Over on Vinalhaven Island, the *Fox Island Inn* offers an inexpensive getaway. You can take your car over on the Maine State Ferry out of Lincolnville, but the owners suggest an adventurous alternative: leave your car on the mainland, ride the ferry and make the short hike to the inn from the ferry landing in Vinalhaven.

Restaurants

Jaunty yachtsmen and their mates repair to the *Waterfront Restaurant* for victuals and *après-sail* socializing. If someone in your party has had it with seafood, *Peter Ott's Tavern and Steak House* has a wide and varied menu and is informal and comfortable. Go to a place called *Swan's Way* (a Proust reference up here in wild moose country!) for coffee and one of their specialty desserts.

Nightlife

Little that we could detect. All the action, we surmised, was happening out on boats, if it was happening at all.

FOR FURTHER INFORMATION

Rockport-Camden-Lincolnville Chamber of Commerce
P.O. Box 919
Camden, Maine 04843
(207) 236-4404

Rockland

Route 1 through Rockland is a maze of gas stations and fast-food stands, a corridor of hellish motorway flanked by the golden arches on one side and Burger King's giant plastic Whopper on the other. Away from the highway, Rockland is home to a huge lobster boat fleet and is very much a working town. There are halfhearted attempts to make it seem as if there is something worthwhile to do here, like look at old houses, but this is just wishful thinking. Here's an image to sum it all up: outside of one of those ubiquitous roadside lobster pounds, a giant, man-sized wooden lobster was nailed atop a pole. From its tail dangled a beach ball onto which had been drawn a smiley face. This one separates the vacation winners and losers once and for all. Would you want to travel with someone to whom this enticement proved irresistible?

FOR FURTHER INFORMATION

Rockland Chamber of Commerce
Harbor Park
Rockland, Maine 04841
(207) 596-0376

Boothbay Harbor

There is, in the lore of this coastal area, an apocryphal story that
has circulated over the years. It involves a certain Luther Maddocks, a nineteenth-century entrepreneur of some local distinction.
Maddocks floated a whale he had harpooned from Boothbay Harbor to Portland on a wooden raft so a convention of businessmen
unfamiliar with the isolated coastal area might have a look at the
strange creature and, in the bargain, take notice of his own fledgling
developmental game plan. He underestimated their reaction. They
not only wanted to have a gander at the decaying narwhal, they
were willing to pay 10 cents a head to do it. The story, as the
merchants might tell it, would end here, perhaps closing with an
upbeat ". . . and the race was on."

But the story continues. When Maddocks was through, he tossed
the carcass into the ocean, where it floated ashore much farther
south, at Old Orchard Beach. There, another enterprising fellow
covered it with a tent, hawked it as a sea serpent and charged
admission to look at the by-now completely disfigured whale.

Though the tourist brochures proudly showcase this tale, it is
not the sort of flattering orientation that this quiet town deserves.
A single visit here will assure you that this is not a place with a
whale skeleton in its closet.

To get to Boothbay Harbor, turn off U.S. 1 to Route 27 and
head south toward the water. Be forewarned, however: this junction is not well marked, but for the record, it is 1 mile north of
Wiscasset. Once you've navigated it properly, you'll quickly find
yourself surrounded by acres of scrub pine and spruce and beautiful rolling terrain. Before you reach town, you might want to

stop at the *Information Bureau* on Route 27, 2 miles inland. Not only do they have lists of accommodations and restaurants on hand, they have information on availability and will phone in a reservation. And contrary to the Pavlovian conditioning that vacation expectations instill, the bureau will not suggest only the most expensive places.

Great pride is taken in the town by its permanent population, which numbers about 2,200. The houses are large but not gaudy, well-kept by any standards, even though the Maine winters take their toll on the paint. Flower boxes and gardens are not uncommon, and a stroll through the town is a pleasurable experience. In this relaxed atmosphere, the most popular diversion, shopping, can be done with a minimum of aggravation. The quality stores and gift shops outnumber the rinky-dink ones by a good three to one. Like Camden, there are lots of art galleries and record and book shops in Boothbay Harbor. We even found a thrift shop where, for 5 cents apiece, we bought oversized antique postcards with a typically sylvan Maine setting—a lighthouse set on a hillside—on the front. The card did double duty as a record, blaring a sassy version of John Philip Sousa's "Liberty Bell March" if you dared drop a needle on it. This was a major score.

But there's more to do in Boothbay Harbor. A free trolley offers rides around town for those who get tired of walking the hilly side streets, and every Thursday, in season, they have a free band concert on the green. Turning from the land to the sea, several daily cruises leave the *Fisherman's Wharf* to explore the surrounding islands and shoreline. Choose your cruise: the several offered have either a historical, scenic or natural (e.g., "see the seals on the rocks") theme. The tours start at $7 and go up from there; the more expensive ones stay out longer and include a lobster dinner. You can also, for $18 round trip, ride a boat out to *Monhegan Island*, where overnight accommodations are available.

As for beaches, a local innkeeper told us to look at *Barrett's Park*, an in-town plaza where the "young folks" go. An inspection, however, found the square roped off for repaving and no conceivable water sport possible on the rocks below. There is a big photo opportunity at the *Rowboat Memorial*, in which you can sit and pretend to be a Maine fisherman. We were also told about Ocean

Point, 7 miles east of Boothbay Harbor on Route 96. For our diligent efforts in seeking out this spot, we were rewarded with the sight of old folks playing shuffleboard and 100 feet of sand with more rowboats on it than people. Cape Newagan, 7 miles from Boothbay Harbor on Southport Island, does have an impressive private beach—but for the guests of the *Newagan Inn* only.

Accommodations

Prices for rooms in Boothbay Harbor are moderate to steep, but the range and availability are staggering. There is an irony to the price structure—the places that are homier and more indicative of Boothbay Harbor's quiet-village authenticity are the cheapest. Fine rooms in residential houses such as the *Harborage*, the *Hilltop House* and the *Welch House* (the latter two with beautiful views of the water) go for as little as $25 a night. In most such places, this means a shared bath, a reality that doesn't sit well with some travelers. If you're among them, you can opt for the *Fisherman's Wharf* or the *Boothbay Harbor Inn* (across the footbridge) for a considerably higher price. One thing to note: many establishments are open year-round, and prices are significantly lower before June and after Labor Day.

Alternatively, there are many inns and cottages for rent in the surrounding towns of East Boothbay, Southport and Ocean Point. Farther inland, there are the family-oriented motor courts—more expensive, more out of the way and most avoidable, in our estimation, unless there is not a single room to be had in town.

Restaurants

Boothbay Harbor has its priorities. On a Thursday, there were three full pages of restaurant advertisements in the local newspaper, but no sports section. A casual glance around will provide the reason: lobster eating *is* the primary sport in Boothbay Harbor. The entire state has a fixation with this beleaguered shellfish (if for no other reason than to lend credence to their substantial lobster T-shirt and toy industry), but in Boothbay Harbor it has been elevated to the major leagues. Most restaurants here feature some sort of lobster dish along with the usual other sea diversions, but the predominant method of preparation is a most unceremonious steaming. For those craving this ritual at its most primitive, you can walk via footbridge to the eastern side of the harbor and try out the *Lobstermen's Co-Op*, where you can drink beer, enjoy the view and perform major surgery upon your freshly steamed lobster. Or, you can stay right in town and do battle at the *Lobster Loft*, which has the cheapest price downtown for a steamed lobster ($6.95). The atmosphere is strictly "no-frills" (cement deck, healthy fly population, paper plates, bagged potato chips and hamburger-joint pickle slices as accompaniment). But the dripping wet, hot lobster itself is your real Maine acid test, for it can turn your stomach just as easily as it can satiate it. The detritus of our steamed lobster dinner included a generous quantity of mop-water-like residue sloshing around a paper tub; squishy green, white and pink slime left on our plates; two pairs of lobster eyes looking back at us, and the spent skeleton, crackly and pink, with spindly crustacean appendages and feelers lying around. If you can survive this ordeal without feeling squeamish, then your reward should be a trip downstairs to the *Smiling Cow Gift Shop* after dinner for a lobster T-shirt.

Nightlife

The only rock 'n' roll band in town during our visit played downstairs from a lobster restaurant. The joint was called *Upstairs/Downstairs*, aptly enough. The beer was cheap, the music loud and the bartender as big and friendly as a walrus. The band was rough—tons of Stones-like cover versions—but these Maine boys know how to play rough, and even the cops who dropped in for a song or two tolerated a bear-pawing from a bearded backwoods fellow who looked as if he was born intoxicated. For a measly two-buck cover, we had our first taste of live rock 'n' roll at the beach.

There are other venues for live music as well—mostly lounge acts with one name ("Vinnie," "Roberta," or "Lefty") and such esoterica as a self-described easy-listening banjo player who looked, in his promotional photograph, like Jim Nabors. If more conventional middle-class entertainment is desired, the *Boothbay Dinner Theatre*, located right in town, was posting moderate prices ($4.50-$7) and material (Neil Simon).

FOR FURTHER INFORMATION

Boothbay Harbor Region Chamber of Commerce
P.O. Box 356
Route 27
Boothbay Harbor, Maine 04538
(207) 633-2353

Popham Beach

Twenty miles down Route 209 out of Bath, on a finger of land pointing due south, sits Popham Beach State Park. Our arrival here was cause for celebration; it was the first wide sand beach, with real ocean waves and no rocks, we'd encountered on our north-to-south pilgrimage. Not that we stripped down to swim suits and made for the water. On a hot, late-July day, the water was still only 53 degrees, and it rarely surpasses 60 in the course of a summer. But the sand was soft, the sound of the surf pounding on the shore was balm to our ears, and the picnic tables at the beachhead made a fine place to spread out an impromptu lunch of canned Maine sardines, Muenster cheese, a loaf of Italian bread and fresh fruit.

On the way out, we learned that there was also a beach at Reid State Park, on an adjacent isle facing Sheepscot Bay. But the sand is more gravelly there and the swimming not as good, we were told by an attractive park attendant with a pretty smile. We had no reason to doubt her.

Portland

This city, the largest in Maine, is an amazing hub of highways. Interstate 95 (in this state a toll road, called the Maine Turnpike) and U.S. 1 go their separate ways here, not to mention the other state highways that jut into the city like acupuncture needles. The net result of all this hubbub—gateway to the north for vacationers headed upstate, gateway to civilization for those returning—is a subculture of squalid budget motels and malls with six-screen cinemas. The former are generally booked solid on weekends, and the latter offer whatever films any other mall in America would offer, plus the sequels.

Twin-towered Sheratons and Howard Johnsons cater to the convention and expense-account crowd, but the most egregious violators of the unsuspecting vacationer's wallet are the mishmash of privately run motels that sit, like lazy rockfish, in waiting for their meal (mmmm, here comes a tasty morsel . . . a beleaguered motorist in a wrinkled Hawaiian shirt, and he's reaching for his traveler's checks!). These places charge $45 minimum per night for a room, while letters or lightbulbs were missing from their signs out by the road and faded and cracked paint jobs attest to the fact that maintenance is not a high priority. They are the sorts of places where you walk into the office and are immediately struck by an odd codlike smell peculiar to people who sit in stuffed, cracked chairs in dark rooms all day long. One guy, an oddball who could have easily found a part in *Porky's II*, did not even bother with the courtesy of an office—he had merely taped a hand-penned "Office" sign on the door of an abandoned room, and the tools of his trade lay in cardboard boxes on the carpet around his feet. Room service might have been a scene out of *Halloween II*.

Take our advice. Get thee straight to the coast and take your chances there. Chances are, if you shop around you will find something for the same price and often for less in a smaller ocean community. Plus, you will have the ocean spray to salve your wounded wallet. Use Portland strictly as a last resort.

Portland Chamber of Commerce
142 Free Street
Portland, Maine 04101
(207) 772-2811

Cape Elizabeth

Within easy reach of Portland are two of the prettiest state beaches you are likely to find anywhere. They are almost within walking distance and certainly within biking distance of each other, but the appeal of both is quite different. *Two Lights State Park* is like an East Coast Big Sur, with a half-mile stretch of flat, slatelike rock tapering down to the very edge of the surf. There is no swimming here; the waves would fillet you against the rocks in no time. Two Lights is a place of solitude and meditation, with the rocks serving as a natural amphitheater seat and the ocean performing amazing feats onstage. Waves crash violently, sending ocean spray flying 20 feet into the air. Ducks swim nonchalantly farther out while shore birds frolic behind and over your head. It costs $1 to get into the park, and there is nothing in any drugstore, at whatever price, that will soothe the soul more deeply. A picnic area and playground are provided.

Near the lighthouse at Two Lights State Park is a place called the *Lobster Shack* that is extremely popular, judging by the line out the screen door at 12:30 on an overcast Saturday. For $3.75, you can get a lobster roll (a hot dog bun stuffed with lobster meat). The price is right, the location—atop a cliff overlooking the park— one rung below Nirvana.

Just 2 miles down the road is *Crescent Beach State Park*, which is truly a sand beach, with healthy waves breaking and seagulls overhead. Its beach is a 1 ½-mile-long stretch of soft white sand. A lifeguard does duty on busy weekends, and there are ample parking and showering facilities. Water temperature, however, was 59 degrees in late July, so brace yourself.. The cost for entry into the park is $2, but the ticket is good for admission at Two Lights State Park as well.

Higgins Beach

Farther south, reachable via Route 77 from Crescent Beach, is the community of Higgins Beach. It is truly a community, with six or seven blocks of privately owned homes along a gorgeous stretch of surf flanked by grass-covered rises of land. Without the American flags and omnipresent signs that say "No Parking on This or Any Other Street," you'd swear you were in Ireland. The skeletal remnants of a shipwrecked schooner give the place a haunted quality, especially if you take a stroll toward evening, as the quiet populace is inclined to do. During the day, younger folks were surfing and kayaking among the steadily crashing waves, with surfcasting coming in a close third in popularity. (A color snapshot, posted at the local inn, showed a man proudly hoisting a 43-pound sea bass caught here.) Swimming is for heartier types, with water temperatures rarely topping 62 degrees.

The ideal way to take in Higgins Beach is to stay at its only inn, chew the fat with the friendly folks at the *Country Store*, eat a home-cooked meal and fall asleep with a gothic-romance paperback facedown on your chest. It is difficult, from such a vantage point, to imagine that the honky-tonk Old Orchard Beach is only 15 miles south. The aforementioned *Higgins Beach Inn* is an extremely pleasant place, with lots of plain but functional rooms, a dining room serving home-cooked meals and a grandfatherly sitting room. A double room with running water is $38—a steal, given the solitude and the legal parking spot.

Old Orchard Beach

The map may indicate Old Orchard Beach is in Maine, but it really belongs to Canada. In the summer, this town of 6,000 swells to 100,000, and fully 80 percent of those transients are French-Canadian. Old Orchard Beach is the beach town that geography denied Canada. As sure as snow falls on the Great White North in December, vacation-starved Canadians roll down that 300-mile corridor from Montreal to Old Orchard Beach when July and August roll around.

The scene in Old Orchard Beach at the height of the season is a brawl of unfathomable proportions. It's the closest thing to Coney Island north of...Coney Island. Imagine our surprise upon rolling into town after several weeks of filling our eyes and ears with the quaint, picturesque and charming coastal villages of northern Maine. Having overdosed on quaint, picturesque et al., and after having had various innkeepers in the land of quaintness disparagingly describe to us the tacky amusement-park mob scene of Old Orchard Beach as if it were something only a cannibal could enjoy, we could hardly wait to get there.

We were not disappointed. The first sight that greeted our eyes, as we entered from the south side of town on West Grand Avenue, was an enormous replica of a Norse sailing vessel, grossly misidentified as a "pirate ship," swinging pendulum-style out over the roadway, seemingly in the path of our car. It was filled with hollering fun-seekers, as were the nearby Tilt-A-Whirl, roller coaster, bumper cars, "Liquid Lightning," water slide and arcades of the Old Orchard Beach amusement park.

There are two vastly different philosophies as to what a proper beach vacation ought to be. One cherishes the pursuit of Thoreauvian solitude and contemplation in a picturesque setting, unspoiled by the gross trappings of civilization. The other favors an oceanfront where tourists are crowbarred into every existing square foot of beach, where music blares from transistor radios and the salt air smells of Coppertone, and where an army of under-thirties can stroll a boardwalk till their feet blister, checking one another out. The majority of Americans would surely belch a loud preference for the latter type of vacation.

Such a place is Old Orchard Beach. The bars and clubs rock raunchily till one or two in the morning. The grease in the deep-fat pits bubbles later than that, cooking up french fries, fried dough, fried fish and other same-tasting sea creatures for all the walleyed disco insomniacs. During the day, you can drag your pounding head down to the beach, spread out on your Moosehead Beer beach towel (all good Canadians have them) and let nature gradually revive your appetite for another evening of arcade thrills, fast food and hearty partying.

It's a pretty splendid beach, too. At low tide, the strand is 50 yards wide, and the beach extends for 7 miles, from Pine Point in Scarborough (to the north) to the Saco River in Camp Ellis. A 7-mile beach! No rocks to hurt your feet! No boulders choking the ocean! No offshore islands to obstruct the surf and your view! Incredible waves! We had turned a corner in our beachcombing. Actually, it was Maine that turned the corner, in the vicinity of Portland, and the rocky coastline of the north was now a fading memory.

The only drawback was the water temperature, which was still a bone-chilling sub-60. Plenty of people were cavorting in the sea, though. Entire French-Canadian families would charge full force down the beach and dive into the ocean, hooting and kicking ice water on one another. This innocent frolicking and the genuine affection that French-Canadian family members seemed to have for one another was in marked contrast to the cantankerous public infighting we routinely witnessed on many an all-American beach.

Old Orchard Beach, fun as it is, still is not Malibu when it comes to frolics with the opposite sex, but at night, a healthy amount of prowling goes on indoors, under cover of a cover charge and a cover band. Manifesting a preference that we exercised whenever given a choice, we opted for rock 'n' roll clubs over the recherché *Saturday Night Fever* discos. Yes, we were ready for a baptism of beer to the strains of tawdry Van Halen tunes on crowded dance floors.

Even though Old Orchard Beach has its very own Triple-A minor-league baseball team, the Maine Guides, the most popular sport in the town is barhopping. Everyone does it, and it doesn't take much training to become good at it. There are lots of places to choose from at which to hone your skill. At *Porky's* we paid a dollar cover and two bucks for a bottle of Bud and got, in return, a grind-'em-out cover band and a leviathan sound and light system. At *Trader John's*, there was no cover and no band, and a 16-ounce Bud draft in a glass schooner was going for 75 cents.

The drunks, we noticed—the ubiquitous one-sip-over-the-line pub crawlers with wounded-moose expressions on their faces— were getting more interesting the farther south we traveled. At one rambunctious tavern, a guy was facedown bagging Z's while his friend tried for 2 hours to knead and slap him back to reality. At another, a stocky-looking sort who may have studied the martial arts—he was wearing a red "rising sun" T-shirt and white head-band—was carrying around a single long-stemmed rose while wearing a Rambo-like badass smirk. In all fairness, we witnessed no brawls or untoward behavior (except for three drunk hoodlums overturning garbage cans into the street), and it was your basic rabble-rousing Saturday-night beach crowd. Maybe not good clean fun, but good fun, certainly.

Old Orchard Beach is a curious mixture of the sacred and the profane. Families march shoulder to shoulder with bikers. Devout geriatric Catholics mingle with young scamps bearing clattering boom boxes. Mom, Dad and apple pie meet brown-bagged beer and heavy metal at the arcade. At the *Marie Antoinette Restaurant*, mealtime prayers for every religion and creed were printed on the cheap placemats, and beer and wine to go was sold in the back. Vacationers in Bermuda shorts and casual wear spilled out of a Catholic church following a midafternoon Saturday mass.

On Atlantic Avenue, the main street leading into town, and on Grand Avenue, the road that parallels the beach, a curious "store wars" was in progress. Prices on T-shirts, swimsuits, sound equip-ment and junk were being slashed in sales that began at 9 p.m. At that hour, the whole town resembled a giant turbine come alive, a symphony of noise comprised of revving bike engines, of ecstatic screaming from the amusement park, of stun-level rock music blaring from the Aqua-Scooter pool, of merchants trying to draw customers into tacky curio shops. And the crowds cruised the length of Grand Avenue, and traffic jammed up at intersections that badly needed stoplights and/or cops. And the night droned on in all its midsummer delirium.

The police seem to enforce only one law in Old Orchard Beach, a popular law to enforce these days: driving while intoxicated. They were snaring them right and left at closing time. Have a sober driver in your party (good advice in any case) or, better yet, walk. Most motels and cottages are within walking distance of the town center. Also, drinking openly in the street is prohibited; it carries a stiff fine and is enforced. Otherwise, the OOB police force is a fairly benign presence. We witnessed a SWAT team of four local cops patiently and paternally usher a girl who was drunk past talking, much less offering resistance, from a bar, with a fifth gendarme guarding the door, as Barney Fife might have.

Old Orchard Beach is, plain and simple, the biggest party town on the New England coast, and the town fathers and authorities must recognize that this is the key to its continued prosperity and popularity. Consequently, a laissez-faire attitude prevails here that is enticing to the beach reveler and to families as well. As one innkeeper told us, "Old Orchard Beach hasn't changed one bit in thirty years." Why should it?

On your way in or out of Old Orchard Beach, you'll probably have to pass through the eyesore towns of Saco and Biddeford. Do just that: pass through. But when you hit Old Orchard Beach, get ready to have a big yahoo of a time. If you can't have fun here, you can't have fun period.

Accommodations

Old Orchard Beach does virtually all of its business in July and August. June is still too cool, and business drops off precipitously after Labor Day. In a good summer, every room in the area is full every night of the month, at $60 or more a pop. But 1984 and '85 were not good summers. The Canadian dollar was worth 30 percent less than the U.S. dollar, and the Montrealers were visiting OOB in reduced numbers. Consequently, we found motels on the beach where double rooms went for $40 and $45 a night. The less expensive accommodations can be found on East Grand Avenue, away from the center of town. A favorite of ours was the *Biarritz*, run by a character named Ronnie La Pointe. Bear in mind that this is the Biarritz, not the Ritz. A nonfunctioning mini-refrigerator served as a bedside end table, and another lamp was supported by a rickety TV tray. But the price was right and the beds reasonably comfortable. And Ronnie will give you free tickets to the local minor-league baseball game just for the asking. In contrast to the usual stone-faced weirdos who run motels, Ronnie was a veritable beat-generation saint. One of our lingering images of Old Orchard Beach was seeing Ronnie cruising down the main drag on his Harley, feet propped, headed to a party with a madman's grin on his face. Surely he is the Zen king of Old Orchard Beach.

The massive hotel resort complexes sit over on West Grand— the ones with pools and pubs and restaurants on the premises. Seventy dollars and up a night is the rule here, even in a depressed summer season. There are plenty of these to choose from, but the *Waves Motor Inn* is among the friendliest and best maintained. It's also on the ocean side of Grand, so you won't hear the trains rumbling through town as you would on the far side of the street, where they pass no more than 25 feet away from your bedroom window.

Outside of town are a lot of older cabins and fifties-style motor courts, which have been steadily falling into disrepair since Eisenhower left office. Yet they tenaciously remain open, doing infrequent business. Often, you'll see a row of detached cottages, each a tiny unit with a narrow sloping roof that resembles nothing so much as a doghouse with shingles falling off. They're all over Maine. Given their often decrepit appearance, it would be safe to venture that an evening spent inside one would be just a hair less barbaric than sleeping in a treehouse.

Restaurants

Old Orchard Beach is not a bastion of haute cuisine. Forget about cloth napkins in the lap, fine wines and gourmet seafood. You're probably going to eat standing up, and the only table manners required are taking pains to keep the pepperoni from falling off your pizza. (We both failed at this one inebriated night, and wound up with tomatoey blotches on our pants.) The Old Orchard Beach gastronomic aesthetic is summed up in the name of an inexpensive feeding spot located right on the town wharf. The words were emblazoned on both sides of its roof in big block letters so as to be visible for a great distance in either direction: *SPAGHETTI HUT*. One native delicacy that appears to be quite popular is most often referred to as "fried dough." Everyone seemed to be tugging on a piece of fried dough, which is always sprinkled with a generous quantity of confectioners' sugar. Perhaps this fried dough is a crude form of carbohydrate loading, in preparation for a marathon evening of Skee-Ball or video games. In any event, those were the sorts of places that people were carrying their fried dough into.

Every creature of the sea and then some was being fried to crackling in deep fat in the vicinity of the arcades. Oh, you can shell out and eat reasonably well at some of the antiseptic restaurants in the multistory hotels, but if you're here for the real Old Orchard Beach experience, get in the game and ante up for fried clams and fried dough.

Nightlife

Old Orchard Beach is a good cheap thrill from stem to stern. Cruising Grand and Atlantic Avenues on foot, ducking into every other doorfront for a beer—now that's living. With a bit of persistence, you might luck out and find a good band. We did: a terrific all-girl hard-rock band called Fire, who drew us back to *Whitehall's Disco* three nights running. There's always the arcade and amusement park, though it is highly advised that you avoid the fried dough before boarding the heart-stopping roller coaster. Out away from town on Route 5 is where the *Maine Guides* practice America's favorite pastime. The minor league Guides are in the Triple-A International League, which means they're just a heartbeat away from the majors. Five bucks will procure a box seat, and on an early summer evening, what could be better than a few hours of beer and ball? The ballpark food ain't bad, either: deli quality hot dogs and sandwiches and cold Miller draft (which you must buy one at a time, one per person). Our only concern was the infrequent line drives that zinged into the unprotected stands directly at fans' heads; fear receded in direct proportion to our intake of beer.

Chamber of Commerce
Box 600
First Street
Old Orchard Beach, Maine 04064
(207) 934-2091

Biddeford Pool

The town of Biddeford Pool sits on a point at the end of a curlicue of land between Old Orchard Beach and Kennebunkport on Route 208. It is a private community with a 2-mile stretch of beach, and it does not want its privacy violated. To park on the beach, you need a permit that will set you back $10 and must be bought at Biddeford City Hall. Lodging is practically nonexistent. We drove through an exclusive compound (for whom, we couldn't determine) named the *Marie-Joseph*, which dominates the shore view and the shore. We nervously drove up the long drive to the entrance, where we were welcomed by intensely religious statuary and warned away by a lot of unfriendly signs. It was plainly not designed for our low-rent ilk. Though the bay glittered enticingly on this cloudless summer day, the unstated message seemed to be *We don't want you here. Go away.* As a parting shot, we were accused by a Biddeford Pool biddy of trying to run her down in her own yard. We were relieved to get back on Route 9, pointed south toward Kennebunkport.

FOR FURTHER INFORMATION

Biddeford-Saco Chamber of Commerce
170 Main Street
Biddeford, Maine 04005
(207) 282-1513

Kennebunkport

If the distance, beyond mere miles, is great between isolated, flag-bedecked Higgins Beach and wildly careening Old Orchard Beach, then the distance 15 more miles down the coast to Kennebunkport is almost immeasurable. It starts with the quality of the roads, which change markedly. As if to reward you for getting through the textile-town bottleneck of Biddeford and Saco (where both a "free eyebrow wax with every haircut" and Funtown USA await you), Route 9 suddenly, almost eerily, becomes less tortuous, the craters and crevices freshly blacktopped. And then Kennebunkport itself sneaks up on you. There is nothing to tell you that you have arrived—none of the usual warning signs, no "country stores" with lobster pots piled as high as Cadillac Mountain, no neon-fringed motels with "Pine" somewhere in the name, not even a city-limit sign (that we saw, anyway).

But finally, you do begin to apprehend a truth that emerges when the whole mosaic is taken together—the splendid architecture, the huge swaths of private beachfront property, the relaxed seaside cushiness of the village, its tony shopping district, the aerobicized bathing beauties in designer swimsuits and last, but not least, the inordinate number of Massachusetts license plates. What you soon realize is that you have not so much hopped 15 miles down the coast as you have leaped a symbolic 150. That is to say, Kennebunkport has more in common with Cape Cod than with the Maine coast, where it sits like a princess among less fortunate relations.

Though the emphasis here is on wealth, it is of the traditional sort (read: inherited) that makes flaunting it unnecessary and gauche.

It is simply here, like the rocks jutting out of the water, as if the very town were born into it. Just as it is difficult to enter this upper echelon of society if you don't already belong, it is not altogether easy to enter the town of Kennebunkport . . . or storm its beachhead.

Be that as it may, life here in Kennebunkport kind of rolls along at its own insular, well-heeled pace. The biggest controversy we heard discussed during our visit involved the only beach-cart hot dog salesman in the town's history. Not a community to trifle with wienies, Kennebunkport was one board meeting away from giving the vendor his walking papers, presumably loading him on the next bus up to Old Orchard Beach.

Instead of the usual image cultivated by most Maine seaside communities (quiet, leave-us-alone pick-yer-assqueness), Kennebunkport has clung to a rich, rarefied heritage. Think of it as Palm Beach North, with pines replacing palms. Many century-old merchants' and sea captains' homes dot this port town, spreading to the larger inland town of Kennebunk, unbroken by any suggestion of the twentieth century.

Travelers, be warned: Kennebunkport is entered in stages. Traversing Route 9, you first pass the more moderately priced bed-and-breakfast inns and woodsy motels, then you snake your way through the town's "designer" business district, and finally, by navigating either Beach or Ocean Avenues, you pass through the more expensive and exclusive layer, with the posh hotels on hillsides overlooking the sea, the private boating club near a beautiful riverside marina and the usual assortment of sprawling Cape Codder homes. Like El Dorado, the summer home of George Bush serves as the last stage, greeting you from Walker's Point. That's it. There is nowhere else to go. Despite the glares and frantic chatter on walkie-talkies from a phalanx of Secret Servicemen, an illegal U-turn in George's driveway is almost mandatory. Especially if you want to find your way back to the beaches.

Near George's manse, in fact, you can park your car legally along Parson's Way and walk down to Arundel Beach. It is the only public beach that's readily accessible from a free legal parking spot. Unless you are suddenly visited by Johnny Weissmuller-like delusions of swimming from Arundel Beach across the mouth of the Kennebunk River to the adjacent beaches of Kennebunkport, this may be the extent of your beach quest in this vicinity. From seawall to shining seawall, there is more than water preventing you from enjoying yourself in the heart of Kennebunkport. The chief obstacle is that the parking places along the town's two main beaches, Gooch's Beach and Kennebunk Beach, go to the guests of the inns and the town's citizens only. The more moderate accommodations are generally booked far ahead of time, and the fancier places may be beyond many a beach-hunter's reach. A walk to these beaches from locations where there is feasible parking is almost too long a hike, and the one popular beach besides Arundel that does not mandate a parking sticker from an innkeeper or a citizen, Goose Rocks Beach, does require a parking sticker from the authorities, obtainable at town hall for $2. As if to taunt you, Goose Rocks Beach is located 2 miles north of town off an unmarked road.

Kennebunkport is, when you come right down to it, more of a shoppers' town than a beach town. The business district is a compactly tailored consumer's mecca, sure to cause wear and tear on credit cards. There are beautifully crafted "authentic olde" wooden signs above nearly every storefront, but the names of these shoppes will remind you that you are not in Kansas anymore. In fact, you're barely in Maine. Some of the retail enterprises we sighted included Petite Etoile, a clothing boutique for children; Zamboanga—a Shopping Adventure (the challenge: can you escape an impulsive plunge into personal financial ruin?), and something called, simply, Alano Ltd., that had no window display and apparently didn't need one. Whatever it is, it was beyond our means.

Accommodations

Despite its reputation for exclusivity, Kennebunkport does offer some affordable lodging. This is a town known for its inns—fourteen are recommended in *100 Country Inns in Maine* (Down

East Books), and there are plenty more to choose from. Of the many fine inns we saw in and around Kennebunkport, *The Breakwater* is especially pleasant and reasonable ($36 and up *in season*) and has a harborfront patio. The *Captain Fairfield House*, a bit off the beaten path, offers similarly digestible rates and continental breakfast to make it go down even easier. For the family, *The Beachwood*, located on Route 9 toward Goose Rocks Beach in a quiet resort setting, offers a pool, beach permits and rooms with kitchenettes that start at $42. The in-town hotels are beautiful to look at and must be nice to stay at. (Don't ask us; we mostly shoe-stringed it through Kennebunkport.)

Many people own summer homes here, and recently condominiums have made their regrettable presence known—in the rather curious specter of "Narragansett-by-the-Sea," a monstrous structure built at Oakes Neck, the point of land that divides Kennebunk Beach from Gooch's Beach. From any vantage point you choose (sitting, lying down, standing on your head), it looks like a huge yellow whale. Of course, it's done up in a modified Cape Cod style, in keeping with the feel of the town, but it really seems inappropriate given the intentions of this immaculately formalized community. In the shadow of such a barn, why is a mere hot dog salesman the local whipping boy?

Restaurants

The food is *très bon* in Kennebunkport. Many of the restaurants are in restored inns. *The Breakwater*, already mentioned for its inn, also possesses a riverfront dining room. It is a popular place, for the fine 'n' fancy atmosphere and for the view of the Kennebunk River, as well as for the food. Among other things, you can feast on a full lobster clambake. *Arundel Wharf*, another restaurant along the Kennebunk, is more moderately priced than The Breakwater and more informal overall. Downright friendly, in fact.

Nightlife

. . . And as the sun set on another day along the banks of the lovely Kennebunk River, all was peaceful and calm as the restaurateurs geared up for a big evening. Even the traffic cop was puffing contentedly on his pipe as he gave an out-of-towner directions. But down on Arundel Beach, the sounds of conflict were heard, as two dogs at the ends of their fully extended leashes had suddenly squared off in coughing and snarling combat. The Pekingese won on points, but the poodle yelped one last time over his shoulder as he was led away, as if to say tomorrow was another day. The show over, we returned to Old Orchard Beach for the evening to see an all-girl rock 'n' roll band we had become smitten with. The trip may have been ill-advised, given the hour, the distance and the nightmarish darkness of the road, but the band was excellent. This is not something a sane person would do, though, we should point out.

Live music is available in Kennebunkport at the *Wine Cellar Pub* (located in the *Port Gardens Inn*) during July and August only—if you consider easy-listening folk singers to be alive. Other than that, there is always a Red Sox game on the radio or the tube.

FOR FURTHER INFORMATION

Kennebunk/Kennebunkport Chamber of Commerce
43 Main Street
Kennebunk, Maine 04043
(207) 985-3608

Wells Beach

The town of Wells is located between Kennebunkport and Ogunquit on Route 1, and is somewhat overshadowed by both as a beach resort. Wells proper purports to be the "factory outlet capital of New England," and you can take that for what it's worth. (To wit, you might save a few dollars on a pair of Hush Puppies.)

More interesting is Wells' early history. The town was named for the English city of Wells by Sir Ferdinando Gorges (pronounced "Gorgeous"), an Englishman who never laid eyes on his vast holdings in the New World. Too bad for Gorgeous. Located near the mouth of the Webhannet River, Wells became a center for lumbering and shipbuilding and a popular stopover for stagecoaches traveling the King's Highway (now U.S. 1). Today, Wells still draws travelers in large numbers, though the town itself is rarely anyone's final destination. Wells Beach and its neighbor to the immediate south, Moody Beach, are leisurely beach communities of private homes and a few small restaurants and inns. The beach is deserted, and one can park right off the road: no meters or fees, nor expensive permits. Boasting an ocean view and a reputation for good seafood, the *Greygull Inn* would make an excellent choice for dinner, and the *Webhannet Motor Court*, with its cool, shaded green, looked like an ideal place to get away from it all.

FOR FURTHER INFORMATION

Wells Area Chamber of Commerce
Box 256
Wells, Maine 04090
(207) 646-2451

Ogunquit

Of all the Maine beaches, Ogunquit walks away with the most superlatives. It is the quietest, most attractive, least pretentious, most well-mannered and habitable seaside community in New England. Situated along a 3-mile-long sandbar between the Atlantic Ocean and the Ogunquit River, Ogunquit also ranks among the two or three best sand beaches north of Cape Cod. Whatever it is they've done here—and it looks to be nothing more than building a vacation community upon the principle of sensible people enjoying themselves in relaxed environs—Ogunquit gets our Golden Sand Bucket award.

The town is steeped in early American charm. Ogunquit fans out toward the beach from where Shore Road and Beach Street meet at U.S. 1. The streets are lined with restored Victorian inns, fine restaurants and large, whitewashed resorts sprawled across well-manicured grounds. All the yards, parks and walkways are lined with flowers, and there is none of the chronic commercial despoilation so prevalent along the Atlantic Coast.

The beach consists of 3 miles of fine white sand and is reached from several crossing points over the Ogunquit River. There is swimming in both the ocean and the sand-banked river, which runs in both directions, depending on the tide. At high tide, the river swells to such a depth that people safely dive off the bridge that spans it. At low tide, such a stunt would deliver a fatal crack on the noggin, so drained is the rock-strewn riverbed. The tides also perform a miraculous disappearing act down at the beach, reducing a 50-yard strand to a thin ribbon of sand. The advancing tide necessitates frequent relocation of umbrellas and beach paraphernalia, and many unwary stragglers have found their towels, tote bags and torsos swamped in an onrushing wave. When the tide is fully in, the remaining beach is thick with bodies, giving an illusion of density that is all out of proportion to the actual numbers.

It's a fun crowd, too, a 50/50 mix of French-speaking Canadians and New England-speaking Americans. Demographically, Ogunquit attracts families, young couples and senior citizens in roughly equal numbers, along with a smattering of gays. A familiar daytime sight is a row of beach towels occupied by lissome, bronzed teenagers in large number—a testament to Catholic fecundity—with their gargantuan *mamans* posted in lawn chairs at an extreme flank, keeping watch like marble lions at the portals of a public library.

At the southern end of Ogunquit Beach, the sandy flats yield to a rocky upgrade, on the far side of which lies Perkins Cove, an artists' enclave as well as a fishing village. You can get there by foot along the Marginal Way, a mile-long path that follows the shore. It's an inspirational hike through breathtaking scenery. The path and the land it traverses were willed to the public. As you ascend to rocky rises that overlook the sea, the scent of juniper fills the breeze and the bright red berries of the bayberry bush stand out in the elemental landscape. A new vista appears at every turn, many with a bench from which to take in the view. The best time to walk the Marginal Way is in early morning, with the sun rising over the ocean. You can even swim at a small guarded beach called Lobster Point, located a few steps off the trail down a flight of stairs. Truly one of the most special spots on the Atlantic Coast.

As one public servant, a trolley-car driver and lifelong native, put it: "The Marginal Way is the only thing you get in Ogunquit for nothing, so take advantage of it." Well, at a quarter a ride, the trolleys themselves are a rare deal and another plus for Ogunquit. They run all day long from Ogunquit Beach out to Perkins Cove and points along the triangle formed by Beach Street, Shore Road and U.S. 1, where most inns, motels and restaurants are located. These open-air trolleys are a great way to see the whole town, even if you have no particular place to go. They are, surprisingly, built right in Ogunquit, used here for a summer, and then shipped out west to cities in Arizona and New Mexico. A new fleet hits the Ogunquit streets at the start of every summer season.

Though the trolleys make a lot of walking unnecessary, the town is laid out in such a way that one could get around quite comfortably without having to climb in a car or trolley. Walking is a great way to pass time in Ogunquit. No point here or in adjacent Perkins Cove is more than a mile or so away, and the beach is always beckoningly close, with many footpaths and footbridges aimed in that direction. At twilight, a hike around town or on the beach makes for pleasant recreation.

In addition to swimming, strolling and eating well (for its size, Ogunquit has the finest restaurants along seacoast Maine), there is a fair amount of antique-hunting to be done in the area. There are at least twenty antiques stores along U.S. 1 from Kennebunkport to Kittery (with Ogunquit at the midpoint of this relatively brief stretch). There are also a number of boat trips and fishing expeditions offered out of Perkins Cove, including a breakfast cruise on a real lobster-fishing boat for a reasonable $5.50.

The name Ogunquit comes from an Indian word that translates as "pretty spot by the sea." It's an apt description, understated even, much like the town itself. A visit to Ogunquit will restore both an appreciation of nature's handiwork and of man's ability to maintain and enhance the natural environment.

Accommodations

There are lots of resort-type hotels and motels in Ogunquit, but the best bargains are the inns. We stayed at the *Captain Lorenz Perkins* lodging house, a sprawling eighteenth-century colonial home, for an inexpensive $35 a night. There are numerous such inns and guest homes in Ogunquit. Among the more attractive and reasonably priced ones are the *Hayes Guest House* and the *Grenadier Motor Inn*. U.S. 1 is lined with large, modern motels with groaning ice machines and teacup-shaped pools "for the kiddies." Rooms here cost around $55 and $65 minimum in season, and you don't get a fraction of the personal attention or homey decor of a bed-and-breakfast inn. If you are going to spend that kind of money, you might as well stay right on the beach at *The Neptune*. The Shore Road, which leads to Perkins Cove, features a number of older, resort-type complexes. Again, you're better off paying a few more dollars to stay in these landed environs. Will people ever learn?

Restaurants

Ogunquit is known for its restaurants, which are not inexpensive. But seeing there is little else to drop your money on around here— eating and walking it off being the vacationer's yin and yang in this sleepy community—you could probably countenance dropping $11 to $15 dollars an entrée, which is the going rate in the finer restaurants. A few suggestions: the *Old Village Inn*, which has a genuine country-inn atmosphere, well-prepared gourmet food and great daily specials; the *Blue Water Inn*, located right by the bridge on the Ogunquit River, with a canopied outdoor patio and good seafood; and *Barbara Dean's*, a classy restaurant that overlooks the Atlantic from the head of the Marginal Way and has been around since 1929. Over in Perkins Cove, there are a number of restaurants on and near the water. The most popular place here, and indeed maybe in all of southern Maine, is *Barnacle Billy's*. It is generally jammed, and its specialty, served with a minimum of ceremony, is lobster doled out cafeteria style. Alternatively, you can cross the road and eat at one of the sit-down waterfront dining rooms, such as *Johnny Oarweed* or *Pirate's Cove*. Last of all, for breakfast head to *Einstein's*. Whoever makes their omelettes is a genius.

Nightlife

After the dinner hour fades to black, Ogunquit is as quiet as a church mouse. An occasional peeping or rustling lets you know that there are people scuttling around, but our several attempts to chase down action came up empty. The two places where nightlife ostensibly occurs are out on Route 1, well away from the town. There was, as it turns out, no need to sequester them. One, *The Maine Event*, is a disco lounge that caters to an older singles crowd and schedules events like tan-line contests to pep things along. The other, *Goodnight Ogunquit*, is set back in the woods on a drive that will torture your car's front end. This one is aimed more at the college-age and younger set. Again, business was slow, and we could hear the sound of rock 'n' roll bouncing off the walls of a largely empty room. Perhaps things are livelier on the weekend, but our evening's entertainment in Ogunquit on a warm late-July night consisted mostly of making U-turns in near-empty gravel parking lots.

FOR FURTHER INFORMATION

Ogunquit Chamber of Commerce
Box 2289
Ogunquit, Maine 03907
(207) 646-2939

Information Bureau
(207) 646-5533

York Beach

Long before the time when only Japanese science-fiction movies
had such names, this area was called Gorgeanna. And that unlikely
mouthful followed a name change from the original Agamenticus.
Although it is one of Maine's oldest and most historic communities,
it was not known as York, or the Yorks, until recently. Under-
standably hesitant, after such early monikers, to choose a final
calling card, York is actually made up of four separate villages:
Cape Neddick, York Beach, York Harbor and York Village. Each
has its own town center and its own distinct identity. Highway
1A forms a U as it swings accessibly through all four places like
a common driveway. Cape Neddick, at the northernmost tip, is a
quiet countrified village a mile from the coast. As you round the
bend out of Cape Neddick, York Beach takes center stage. Like
an aging entertainer down to his last toupee who keeps getting gigs
because people are familiar with his schtick, York Beach is the
recreational focus of the Yorks. In its tattered, peeled-paint rusticity, York Beach is like Old Orchard Beach with age on it and
not nearly so rabid a following. Both places do have one audience
in common: the man who sweats for his wage and the family that
loves him. York Beach is, as they proclaim, "a family-oriented
beach of bustle and fun" that draws visitors mostly from the tri-
state region of Maine, New Hampshire and Massachusetts. Most
of them are workingmen from the myriad plants that exist in all

three states, within 50 miles of York, and they move, whether they know it or not, to a motto that we saw on a plaque in a gift shop: "Vacation to me is no problem/As it is to other men/My wife tells me where/And my boss tells me when."

The village of York Beach is centered on the very buttocks of Short Sands Beach like a gargantuan deposit of sea residue left after a record tide. There is a ramshackle *Fun-O-Rama* that offers old-style beach diversions, like 10-cent Skee-Ball (it's gone up to 25 cents in most other towns), Pokerino and Woolworth's-type sidewalk contraptions (rocking horses, speedboats, helicopters). But today's progeny seem more enamored of the video games that take up the other two-thirds of the aging structure. There is also a newer complex for the youngsters called *York's Wild Kingdom* that has twenty-five rides and a zoo with a mascot called Yorkie the Bear.

Flanking Short Sands Beach are two remnants of the village's more storied past, the *Union Bluff Hotel* and the *Island Home*. Both are ancient wooden resort hotels that date from a time even before 10-cent Skee-Ball. They are in cracked-glass disrepair at the moment but are still open. The local businesses (e.g., restaurants and gift shops) are not memorable, nor are they meant to be, geared as they are for the beach crowd. But there is plenty of municipal metered parking on the beach and no signs of turmoil beyond the revving of a few motorcycle engines.

And even that seemed harmless enough. As we were leaving, a fellow in a Harley-Davidson T-shirt, leather vest and blue jeans ensemble kick-started his monster bike while his current blond girl friend, in bikini top and cutoffs, climbed aboard. Above the din, a leather-clad friend of his shouted, "Hell yeah, started on the firssss kick, heah-wooo!" and hoisted a tall Bud (it was still well before noon) in salute. Unperturbed, two healthy, milk-fed kids shot baskets at a nearby rim with no net. Their radio was blasting, "What's love got to *do*, got to *do* with it . . ." and they were quite content to think only on that.

Long Sands Beach is on the other side of *Nubble Light*, a much-photographed lighthouse that sits on a "nubble" of land between the two beaches. It is reputed to be the most pictured spot in Maine, or so the locals claim. Long Sands is a less concentrated, long stretch of perfect beach, much loved by the tri-state crowds who don't want to be caught up in the clamor of the town. (There is, in actuality, a mobile-home park nearby that is as big as some towns.) Its name is no exaggeration: Long Sands is so long and popular a beach that a special area is cordoned off for surfing— quite possibly the northernmost surfing beach on the East Coast.

The Yorks also have their true historical side, as seen in the final two of its villages, York Harbor and York Village. The former is a marina-oriented community with more money and shade trees than its sandy neighbor, and the latter is the centerpiece for local history, with its many original homes, taverns, schools and churches arranged compactly around a village green that dates back to the 1600s. The *Old Gaol*, built in 1719, is perhaps the best known of the structures, being the oldest jailhouse in the United States. But York Harbor's many intact colonial-era structures are all well worth seeing and easily done on foot or by car. There is also a trolley system that services all four villages during the summer months for only 75 cents a ride—a bargain, considering the ground covered and the running historical narrative provided.

Accommodations

Generally, prices climb as you approach the beach, but York Beach is so comfortably inelegant and devoid of pretensions at this point that you won't get ripped off too badly. The chamber of commerce maintains an information booth out on U.S. 1 and will help you find available rooms in a specified price range. The *Wooden Goose Inn*, in sylvan Cape Neddick, is one of the nicer bed-and-breakfast places we saw in Maine, but is no more expensive than a room in a beach motel and spares you the noise and fluorescent-porpoise decor. A full breakfast is provided and a quiet beach is easily accessible.

Restaurants

A visit to the Yorks is incomplete without donning a lobster bib at *Bill Foster's Downeast Clambake* in York Harbor. Similar in spirit and intensity to the southern "pig pickin' " or the western tent-style barbecue, Bill's clambakes are held nightly inside a huge screened-in area where picnic tables are covered with red checkerboard cloths, slop buckets are liberally placed on the tables, and the food never stops coming. The spread includes lobster, clams, corn on the cob, whole onions, potatoes and hot dogs, all of it cooked over a huge outdoor pit in a layer-by-layer heap that's covered with seaweed. When the heat reaches the weed, it yields its seawater drop by drop through each strata of edible food, literally steaming it. Just the way the Indians did it. Beer can be bought by the glass or the pitcher—just the way the Indians might have liked to do it. There is chowder before all this, coffee and watermelon afterwards and cornball musical entertainment throughout the 3-hour package. Bill himself leads the singing of "Roll Out the Barrel," "Take Me Out to the Ballgame" and "God Bless America." (Lyrics are printed on the paper placemats and hopelessly goo-soaked by the time of the singalong—that is, if you're doing things right). Bill also delivers a brief biology talk on the life cycle of the lobster that explains, among other things, that the male lobster has sex only once every two years—a sobering thought to two journalists who'd already spent the better part of a month in Maine and were beginning to feel like crustaceans themselves.

The whole wacky clambake shebang is watched over by a staff more wholesome than an Olympic athlete's family. The price, $15.95, might at first seem a bit high, but the tip is included, there's enough food served to keep you full for a week, children's plates are available, and this multimedia entertainment spectacular includes the aforementioned singalongs and victuals, as well as Ping-Pong, shuffleboard, basketball and spontaneous yahooing. Make my lobster good and red, Bill, you maniac. . . .

Nightlife

We were too full of lobster, "Roll Out the Barrel" and the contents of the barrel to poke around the obviously limited entertainment options in the York area beyond the clambake circuit. Some of the aging hotels advertised entertainers who appeared to be even more beyond reclamation than the hotels themselves. One band, judging by their black-and-white glossy, looked like they'd been born beaten up, and their repertoire was a lamentable melting pot of country-&-western, Irish traditional and contemporary disco borrowings. York Beach appeared to be a journeyman's last stand, the bottom rung on the hotel-bar ladder, and we feared from the looks of it that we might meet the aforementioned Harley-Davidson crew in less amenable circumstances. So we stuck to accordion jigs with the oldsters at *Bill Foster's*, and saved up our energy for warpaths farther south.

FOR FURTHER INFORMATION

York Chamber of Commerce
P.O. Box 417
York, Maine 03909
(207) 363-4422

Kittery

Settled in 1623 and incorporated in 1647, Kittery is the oldest township in Maine. It's also the southernmost city in coastal Maine, 293 miles from Eastport at Maine's northern tip. Located at the point where the Piscataqua River empties into the Atlantic, Kittery is popularly referred to as "the Gateway to Maine." Just south of the Kittery Bridge lies Portsmouth, New Hampshire, and the lives of the two communities intermingle in the extensive naval facilities that line both banks of the mighty Piscataqua. The Portsmouth Naval Yard, in fact, is mainly located on the numerous islands along the Kittery side of the river.

Shipbuilding has been the town's principal industry almost since its inception. The naval presence dates back to 1800, and indeed Kittery was the site of the first U.S. naval shipyard. The first ship to sail under the colors of Old Glory, John Paul Jones' *Ranger*, was launched from Kittery in 1817, as was the nation's first submarine (the L-8, in 1917). The navy shipyard is off-limits to the public, but the *Kittery Historical and Naval Museum*, located at the intersection of U.S. 1 and State Route 236, tells the story of the community with exhibits and so forth. Kittery is also becoming a growing home to factory outlets such as Bass Shoes and Lenox China. Recreationally, there is a beach with facilities for picnicking and fishing at nearby Fort Foster Park, on Gerrish Island, reachable by Route 103. The drive through these woodsy peninsulas, over many bridges and circuitous meanderings, is an interesting one.

And with our crossing of the Kittery Bridge into Portsmouth, it's goodbye, Maine, and adieu.

FOR FURTHER INFORMATION

Maine Publicity Bureau
I-95 and U.S. 1
Kittery, Maine 03904
(207) 439-1319

New Hampshire:
To Beach or
Not to Beach?

The Granite State wasn't entirely gypped when it came time to parcel out the coastline. New Hampshire wound up with an 18-mile stretch of oceanfront property—not much, but that's 18 more miles than Vermont (the only New England state with no Atlantic shoreline) can lay claim to. (Okay, okay, Vermont fronts Lake Champlain. Big deal.) From the old-time maritime charm of the city of Portsmouth to the controversial nuclear-energy facility set in the salt marshes of southerly Seabrook, New Hampshire has put its brief coastline to varied use.

There are numerous state beaches along Route 1A, three of them clustered in the vicinity of Rye, located mid-coast. And then there's the granddaddy, a sick old codger, Hampton Beach, which is ablaze with arcades, noise and traffic. After a stroll down the main drag, we were tempted to presume that the enigmatic "Live Free or Die" state motto actually was intended to warn folks away from a debilitating vacation here. If Old Orchard Beach in Maine is New England's answer to Coney Island, then Hampton Beach is its South Bronx, with a blush of the seamy side of Atlantic City thrown in for good measure. From its gaudy, dress-code discos to the clattering arcades, which assault the senses with cheap odors, idle youth and the ceaseless sounds of misspent quarters, Hampton Beach is run down, and runs the spirit down. The contrast between the heart of this vacation ghetto and the manicured, sprawling

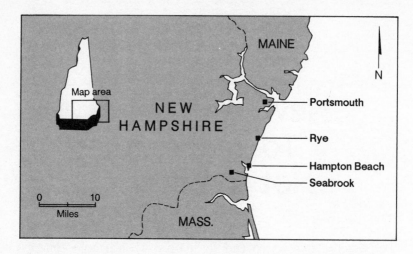

oceanfront estates of North Hampton just a few miles away makes one wonder whether the New Hampshire state legislature has ever had a coherent policy regarding coastal development. Fortunately, its coast is so brief that, passing through from Maine to Massachusetts, we didn't spend too much time worrying over it.

Portsmouth

Portsmouth is an active port town that, in combination with its kissing cousin, Kittery, Maine, is home to the United States Navy, as well as fleets of commercial vessels and the famous "tall ships." Shipbuilding has been Portsmouth's glory since the seventeenth century. Many a three-masted schooner has been midwifed in the Portsmouth shipyards from masts, spars and bowsprits of native oak and white pine. Those sorts of ships rarely patrol the seas under the Stars and Stripes anymore, but Portsmouth has kept an active hand in the military vessel trade: subs (not the meat-and-cheese variety) are made here, to go.

Since the turn of the decade, Portsmouth has been engaged in an ambitious program of renovation and preservation of its old homes and maritime tradition. The chamber of commerce publishes *A Walking Tour of Downtown Portsmouth's Waterfront*, a pamphlet that outlines a self-guided, 1 ½-hour trek that passes by the most historic and architecturally ornate of the town's colonial mansions.

The outlying Isle of Shoals, 10 miles into the Atlantic, can be visited via *Viking Cruise Ships*, which depart from Portsmouth's Market Street Wharf. Portsmouth itself has no beaches, but there are ocean beaches only moments away in either direction (York Beach, Maine, and Rye, New Hampshire).

FOR FURTHER INFORMATION

Greater Portsmouth Chamber of Commerce
500 Market Street
P.O. Box 239
Portsmouth, New Hampshire 03801
(603) 436-1118

Rye

Above the holocaust of Hampton Beach lies an undefiled stretch of seacoast under the jurisdiction of Rye township. Eight miles of New Hampshire's Atlantic Ocean doorstep fall to Rye. For what reason, one might wonder, should one small township deserve such a disproportionate amount of beachfront? For one thing, Rye hasn't allowed its beaches to be turned into a hooligan's amusement park. Much of the land is state-owned, with four state parks along Route 1A within Rye. The best swimming on the New Hampshire coast can be found at two of them: Jenness Beach and Wallis Sands. Both are wide sand beaches with rest-room facilities and metered parking.

The town of Rye itself is located a few miles inland. Founded in 1623, Rye—today a thriving town of 4,500—caters to a less hysterical type of vacationer. There are cottages for rent near the shore and motels and restaurants in Rye proper. We stumbled into a place called *Hector's Country Kitchen* and were greeted with more atmosphere and better food than we expected in this neck of the

woods. (Also more old people: several busloads arrived simultaneously as we did, creating an eerie, *2001*-style effect as we wandered among their endless numbers.) The owner, Hector Dionne,
proved an energetic host, giving us an unasked-for tour of the
kitchen and offering this pithy preview of Hampton Beach: "It's
a barnyard down there," he said, holding his nose. "You're much
better off up here." Given the peaceful setting of Rye and environs,
where woods, rocky cliffs and the blue Atlantic all come together,
we couldn't agree more.

Hampton Beach

Nothing in the darkest corner of your imagination or the farthest
cul-de-sac of your mind can prepare you fully for Hampton Beach,
New Hampshire. Certainly not the beautiful rolling yards and
gull-covered rocks to the north of here at Rye and New Castle,
not the slumbering inland community called Hampton and not
even its southern neighbor, the shrouded metal-and-concrete Seabrook Nuclear Plant. Hampton Beach is, quite simply and geographically, the armpit of New England.

The place yearly attracts hundreds of thousands of visitors, an
unusual number of them kids from 10 to 17 years of age. Yet inside
its Mordor-like walls, the childish spirit does not soar as it does
on many beaches; instead, it gets crushed out like one of the
plethora of cigarette butts in the sand. The faces you see on the
streets are not caught up in the magic of summer sights and sounds;
mostly they smirk and blow bubbles and suck on Goofy Pop and
Fry Doe (a local delicacy), occasionally breaking their monotonous
amblings along the paper-strewn sidewalks to yell at someone in
a passing heavy-metal-blaring automobile, something like, "Hey,
you owe me a quotah," or "Lenny, you SUCK!" Many of these
teen reprobates have run away from home. Our suspicions of this
were confirmed by a major article in the local newspaper that
coincided with our visit. The headline: "Hampton Beach Is a Popular Place for Runaways."

Hampton Beach is not even complex enough in its sociological undercurrents to be interesting. The best we could do was ferret out obvious contradictions and figure that those would tell the story. For instance, when you first enter the area, you are besieged with signs that read: "Alcohol Prohibited in Public, $100 Fine Strictly Enforced." But as you make your first sweep through the empty heart of this town on any given summer day, you will see that many of the souls who come here seem to be on all-too-familiar terms with the bottle: the older ones and even the middle-aged ones with their bloated flesh squeezed into tiny Jacques Cousteau swim trunks, the overhang belying a life of food and alcohol intake; the footloose revelers in their twenties and thirties dressed in ripped-up jeans and leather vests and jangling around like drunken mercenary soldiers in an occupied seaport; the teenagers who guzzle their beer on the sly at night near the beach, which is littered with their midnight confessions the next day; and then the youngest, dulled by the sugary grease in the air and the unspoken despair. They too will no doubt begin drinking some approaching summer and, if they visit Hampton Beach often enough to sour all their childish whims, they might just lose their virginity there, in a seamy rut on the beach.

One last image from our visit stuck out like a freeze frame from a bad dream: an elderly man in a goofy visor with a dolphin on it, overweight and dazed by the sun, entered the chamber of commerce's Sea Shell Office on Ocean Boulevard one blazing midafternoon in August. He fumbled, fighting palsy, for a wad of money in his pocket and finally placed it on the counter. He wanted to know how to play the New Hampshire Lottery Sweepstakes. They took his cash, gave him his tickets and then held his arm as he sloppily dragged a penny across the gray "Instant Winner" patch. He was not an instant winner. He said, "Oh . . ." and walked back out into the heat.

To be fair, Hampton Beach has a 5-mile beach. It's jammed all summer long and is graced by pretty, scantily clad girls taking carefully choreographed strolls, their every movement monitored by an army of wolfhounds. There is an amusement park, of sorts, with the usual creaking machines. They also have a trolley system that travels all the way up to the North Beach area. But that is only to be fair. To be honest, we advise you to stay away.

Accommodations

As it was in *King Rat*, Hampton Beach is a seller's market. In that classic tale of human enterprise, a group of American prisoners of war, weakened by a lack of protein in their diet, agreed to pay any price for a piece of meat. King Rat, sensing a good con, sold them meat—rat meat, to be sure—but at filet mignon prices. Not wanting to lose a captive audience, he of course told them it was something else, but even his most sun-crazed jungle-rotted customers knew the truth. They just could not admit it. And so they ate the rat meat and told themselves it was chicken or squirrel or rabbit.

In Hampton Beach, as in *King Rat*, you are sold rat meat at filet mignon prices. Double rooms that are glorified Penn Station lockers—just a place nearby to stash your bags—go for no lower than $60. And if you should, in disbelief, dally (i.e., shop around), you will find that something called a kitchenette, at $70 a pop, will be the only choice left by midafternoon. Actually, at this point, you have another, wiser option—to leave town—but should you accede to the demands of the market (e.g., a three-day minimum stay, not uncommon, even in midweek), then perhaps you have become a little sun-crazed yourself. But nonetheless, here is what you will find:

The marketplace for all this—a stretch of seedy, run-down real estate roughly twenty-five blocks long and two blocks wide, bounded by the aforementioned boulevards—looks at any hour like a late-breaking news bulletin from West Beirut and smells, after a good day's sun-baking, like a Lower East Side dumpster. Block after block of contradictory "Vacancy/No Vacancy" signs require the motorist to make frequent screeching halts to seek the truth, and the hairpin turn that is necessitated invariably scatters the teeming, nonstop rush-hour foot traffic. Approaching one of the rickety, paint-flecked structures that still has a vacancy is as unpleasant as it is depressing, like honoring an appointment to have several teeth pulled.

And we very nearly tried them all, starting at one o'clock in the afternoon and ending in frustration at four. The sorry lot of innkeepers we ran across might have given Charles Dickens serious pause: a young fellow who shouted to be heard over a countertop cassette player; an entire family, three generations of them, who never looked up from a soap opera while chanting "no rooms" in unison; a young woman, possibly 24 but with the ravaged spirit of an aged slattern, who was also seven or eight months pregnant, though she offered us a good deal ($45 for a room plus half price on breakfast). But then again, she was sorting out her dirty laundry on the front desk. And so on and so forth.

We finally settled on a place about 3 miles north of town in a no-man's-land with no distinguishing characteristics other than it was away from the horror show downtown. To describe the establishment and the room and our ordeal might appear to be flogging a dead horse, but in order to make a point, we will flog on. (Besides, the horse is very much alive.) The words "Coca-Cola" took up over half of the motel's sign. The charge, with tax, was $44.95, with no discount given for sharing the room with numerous flies, who were there before we walked in. Because there was a swimming pool on the premises, we figured that it was a relative bargain. We figured wrong—the water in the pool was colder than any ocean; the room had, in addition to a healthy fly population, a bad case of B.O., a smell not unlike that of downtown Hampton Beach; the television, a small black-and-white kit affixed ludicrously onto a huge, ceiling-mounted stand, had such bad reception that you'd guess you were somewhere in the Siberian steppes and not 75 miles from the eastern megalopolis; the shower had more caulking compound in it than the most hastily built low-rent suburban subdevelopment; the walls were so thin that even with the television on, every footfall, word and gesture of the family in the next room could be heard more clearly than the words of Fred Sanford on the tube; and the "family next door" was actually two families squeezed into a double room with a passel of whining, hyperglycemic children. That did it. We would have liked our $44.95 back, if for nothing else than to contribute to Planned Parenthood.

Though both of us were as exhausted as any two showgirls working the floor at the local lounge casino with the navy in town, when we laid our sun-crazed, jungle-rotted heads down on our double beds, sleep would not come. It wasn't just the dive-bomber flies entombed there with us in Room 32, nor was it the 2 A.M. disturbance next door—with a resounding thud, one of the children had fallen out of an overcrowded bed in Room 33 (with an accompanying hour's worth of sobbing and moaning and soothing). Nor was it the heat or the smell or the fact that just outside our back window an electric device was working overtime frying mosquitoes and moths. No, it was the feeling of violation that kept us awake.

As we were leaving the next morning, two flies were mating on the oleo-colored bedspread.

Restaurants

If, after a stroll down these streets toward day's end, you still have any kind of appetite, then Fry Doe is served. Bon appetit!

Nightlife

The predominant activities are as follows:

1. For teenagers—
   a. milling around discontentedly on putrid-smelling sidewalks in front of a paper-strewn "casino"
   b. shouting at one another from cruising cars
   c. smoking cigarettes in as many surly poses as possible
   d. drinking beer illegally and throwing up on the beach
   e. eating Fry Doe and french fries and throwing up on the beach
   f. taking street drugs in bad combinations and throwing up on the beach
   g. some combination of d, e and f.

2. For adults—
   a. listening to washed-up casino lounge talent
   b. dancing with orange-haired or toupeed divorcées under blinking, outmoded disco lights. That is, if you wear the proper attire (no jeans, no sneakers . . . at the beach!)

   c. listening to overweight folksingers doing improbable versions of "New York, New York" (our ears did not deceive us)

   d. drinking mirthlessly and staring at a television above a bartender's head.

3. For children—
   a. video games
   b. falling out of an overcrowded bed and banging your head on the floor
   c. sunburn and diaper rash
   d. crying.

FOR FURTHER INFORMATION

Hampton Beach Area Chamber of Commerce
Box 596
180 Ocean Boulevard
Hampton, New Hampshire 03842
(603) 926-8717

IMPORTANT LOCAL PHONE NUMBERS

Police—926-3333
Ambulance—926-3315

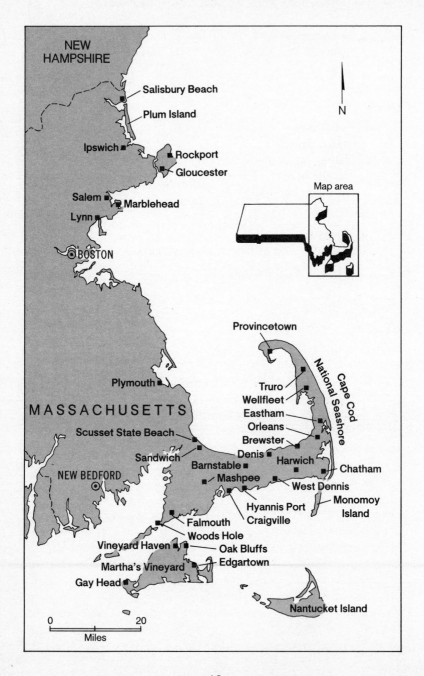

Massachusetts: Life, Liberty and the Deep Blue Sea

From Plymouth Rock to powdered Whigs to Paul Revere, Massachusetts' colonial history is pretty much the early history of our nation, and chances are if you didn't learn it in grade school, you're a Communist. Nowadays, the Bay State—which ranks a mere forty-fifth in land area—offers itself as a living, breathing refresher course in early American history, and a vacation here is almost bound to plop you knee-deep in it. Can you say "Miles Standish"? Can you say "Pass the turkey, Pilgrim"?

All joking aside, Massachusetts is the seat of democracy as we know it, with some of its most fundamental principles hammered out in town meetings, defended by gallant citizens in tricornered hats and theorized by great minds. The state of Massachusetts has given this nation an inordinate share of poets, politicians, presidents, priests, philosophers, and philanthropists.

For its authentic claims to history alone, Massachusetts is a rewarding vacation spot, and a tip of the sun visor goes to its many tireless local historical societies. But what you may not realize about Massachusetts is that the Puritans are gone and it's okay to have fun here. The state is surrounded by water. This means-- you guessed it—beaches. Everyone knows Cape Cod, the defiant arm of land that juts into the Atlantic Ocean, shaking its raised fist at the rest of the East Coast. Twelve million people a year visit Cape Cod. It is no secret that summer traffic on the Cape is horrendous. Many argue that it is worth the hassle; others who can

69

afford it simply gravitate to trendy enclaves like Kennebunkport, Maine. But there is something about the Cape that cannot be duplicated anywhere, with any amount of money.

Other principal resort areas include the North Shore (Salem, Marblehead, Newburyport and Cape Ann—an unheralded delight); the South Shore (from Boston to Plymouth) and the islands of Nantucket and Martha's Vineyard. Indeed, if it weren't for a couple of mild disclaimers, Massachusetts could pass for a vacationer's Promised Land. As it is, it comes close.

The disclaimers: you will need to get used to the roads. Very few directional signs (or any other kind, for that matter) are provided for the stranger, and you'll often find yourself playing highway roulette. You'll need to get used to the drivers, too, most of whom drive as if they are both blindfolded and angry. Accustom yourself as well to the rotary, or traffic circle. This motorist's merry-go-round is an exercise in barely controlled hysteria.

Salisbury Beach

Salisbury Beach is really a barnacle encrusted onto the hull of New Hampshire. Despite the presence of a state beach (which costs $3 to park at), this parched, decaying town is spiritually aligned with its neighbor across the bridge, Hampton Beach, offering such amusements as a minibike track, Go-Kart rides and temporary tattoos. On that note, you might want to make your visit here temporary as well—like two minutes.

Plum Island

Located a few miles east of the town of Newburyport, Plum Island is a six-mile barrier beach and national wildlife refuge. At the far southern end is a state park that's seasonally very popular.

Ipswich

Ipswich refers to itself as the Birthplace of American Independence because there was a rebellion here that predated the American Revolution by nearly a hundred years. But Ipswich is better known to the rest of the world as the home of the Ipswich clam (a tasty bivalve) and Crane's Beach (one of the East Coast's finest). Located at the mouth of Ipswich Bay, Crane's Beach runs for five wide, white miles, encompassing sturdy dunes and excellent bay swimming. It is named for Richard T. Crane, Jr., a wealthy benefactor whose Castle Hill mansion, built in 1927 and overlooking the beach, is an area attraction.

FOR FURTHER INFORMATION

Ipswich Chamber of Commerce
P.O. Box 456
Ipswich, Massachusetts 01938
(617) 356-3231

Gloucester

Perched between New Hampshire and Cape Cod, the little jut of land on Massachusetts' North Shore known as Cape Ann is a veritable valley of humility 'twixt two mountains of conceit. It is, shall we say, a road less traveled that takes you out to this small c cape and its several artist colonies and fishing towns, the best known of which is Gloucester.

"They that go down to the sea in ships" is the legend that is inscribed beneath the bronze statue of a fisherman at the wheel of a ship, a famous landmark near the Gloucester harbor. We that went down to the sea in a Toyota paused contemplatively for a few moments before this monument to bravery. Gloucester is a modest workingman's town over which hangs the smell of fish— the perfume of its primary source of revenue. Gloucester has been and is one of the great fishing ports of the world. It is also America's oldest seaport, having been continuously active in the maritime trades since its settlement in 1623. (Its discoverer was Champlain, who named it La Beauport; it was rechristened by the English fishermen who established a settlement here under the tutelage of a company of "merchant adventurers.") The waters off of Gloucester, around Cape Sable and the Grand Banks, have provided an ample harvest of cod, mackerel, halibut and herring since the earliest days of the fishing industry. Today, the Gloucester Fleet comprises more than 250 fishing boats, and the town has more cold storage capacity than anywhere in the world. That's a lot of fish sticks, Jack.

Fishing and fish processing are Gloucester's main industries, but tourism is a not-insubstantial industry in itself and is on the upswing. There is a big reason for that: the whale. Gloucester has, since 1979, been billing itself as the whale-watching capital of the world. The shallow waters of the Cape serve as feeding grounds for four different species of whale—the finback, the humpback, the minke and the right—and half a dozen different firms offer whale-watching cruises. So prevalent are these leviathans that a sighting is *guaranteed*.

There are, would you believe, 20 beaches along Cape Ann, some of them among the best New England has to offer. Locals and loyal vacationers alike insist that Good Harbor Beach, off of Bass Avenue in Gloucester, is the finest little swimming hole in creation. The topography of the beach was drastically altered—for the better, people say—by a cataclysmic storm in February 1978. The result is a gently sloping, wide sand beach that at high tide offers rejuvenating swimming in limpid pools of cool, green water. It was the first swim of the trip that did not engender Arctic discomfort. At low tide, you can walk out several hundred yards, exploring the rocks that frame the half-mile beach at either end without getting more than your ankles wet. Just beyond the north end of Good Harbor Beach lies Long Beach, which technically belongs to the neighboring community of Rockport. It too offers excellent ocean swimming in a peaceful setting.

Accommodations

There are more than two dozen inns and motels in the vicinity of Gloucester, among them *Bass Rocks Motor Inn*, a modern-looking motel with a spectacular ocean view. If you are arriving without a reservation, stop by the chamber of commerce, located downtown at the top of a hill just off Rogers Street. They will know where the vacancies are and point you in the right direction.

Restaurants

Your nose isn't playing tricks on you: that pungent incense that hangs over Gloucester is fish, brought in fresh every day, ton after ton. You can be assured that your seafood—the locally caught stuff, anyway—will be as fresh as any that can be had, for love or money, on the East Coast. For atmosphere, the *Gloucester House* and *Captains Courageous* are two harborfront restaurants with excellent views from their dining rooms and top-quality seafood. The *Down East Oyster House* will interest aficionados of local color. It's a favorite chowing, and chowdering, spot with the natives, whose boisterous, friendly laughter rings out over the booths and tables. Listen attentively—they talk loud, so you don't exactly have to eavesdrop—and you just might overhear a tale as tall as any ship out in the harbor.

Nightlife

We had our doubts. Walking through the narrow, zig-zag streets of its compact downtown district on what seemed a quiet weeknight, we figured to strike out in Gloucester after dark. After all, Gloucester is a working community first and a tourist haven second. What we didn't realize is that its bars and taverns are filled with working people looking to blow off steam at the end of the day. We chanced into a place called the *Rigger*, and it appeared that every stocky boatswain and wench in town was jammed in, dancing lewdly and loudly to ZZ Top and other tunes spun by an insane deejay who would cut in with his own suggestive lyric variations. To the unattached, he attempted to play matchmaker; to dancing couples, he stoked already libidinous fires. In a moment of drunken epiphany, a guy with a broken leg suddenly took to his feet, strumming his crutch like an electric guitar while a heavy-metal screech from a band called Ratt rattled the rafters. A policeman, stationed at the door all night, smiled upon the revelry.

FOR FURTHER INFORMATION

Cape Ann Chamber of Commerce
128 Main Street
Gloucester, Massachusetts 01930
(617) 283-1601

Rockport

Round the north side of the Cape from Gloucester sits the town of Rockport. In contrast to the industrial-strength bustle of Gloucester's working harbor, Rockport is a quieter place, a haven for artists and browsing tourists. Its narrow streets are crammed with crafts shops and galleries, ice-cream shoppes and vegetarian pizza stands. If you eventually come to suspect that there's an air of manufactured quaintness about Rockport, at least it's not being done indecently, and its streets make for pleasant strolling.

Rockport has a long and fascinating history. Originally known as Graniteville, the town at one time provided the United States with most of its granite. The beds of dark granite upon which Rockport sits provided an inexhaustible store, and attracted many skilled Finnish stonecutters during the granite boom of the 1800s. Granite has gradually been phased out of the construction industry in favor of cement and concrete, but Rockport endures on the strength of its lobster-fishing industry. It's also become a fashionable place for artists, who come and paint portraits of harbors and sunsets, and for tourists, who buy them. Rockport has the upscale bohemian feel of Provincetown on Cape Cod, without the gay community.

Rockport does have one drawback (or asset, depending on which way you teeter on the alcohol issue). The town has been completely dry of alcohol since 1856, when the ladies of Rockport made their way through the bars, smashing every bottle and vessel containing demon alcohol. You'll just have to settle for a cup of Pudge's Old-Fashioned Slush, a local concoction we couldn't work up the stomach to try, or go thirsty.

Manchester-by-the-Sea
Essex

There are other, smaller waterfront villages along Cape Ann, among them Manchester-by-the-Sea, with its 4 miles of shoreline, and Essex, a clamming town with the distinction of being the birthplace of the fried clam. This is not in itself reason enough to make a pilgrimage to Essex, even though you can eat your fill and then some at any of the fourteen restaurants in town that serve them. But Manchester-by-the-Sea does have a worthy calling card in Singing Beach, one of the very best on the North Shore. As you walk across the beach here, the sand will literally "sing" beneath your feet.

Salem

Established in 1626 by maverick colonialist Roger Conant, Salem was "the first Towne in America" and an early capital of the Massachusetts Bay Colony. Conant, as Salem's founder, can perhaps be excused for the hubris of the following statement, which is inscribed on the base of his statue in the Salem Commons: "I was a means, through grace assisting me, to stop the flight of those few that then were here with me and that by my utter denial to go away with them, who would have gone either for England, or mostly for Virginia." Translated, he would not let the poor buggers out of his sight, come hell or high water, Indians or numbing New England winters. Today, he would forthwith be asked to seek asylum for such audacity, but back then, you must remember, they were given to wearing upside-down pepper shakers on their heads and had to deal with an often hostile wilderness and an always unsmiling God.

After a day of walking through this endlessly fascinating town—the only real way to see it, built as it was before the automobile created suburbs and parking problems—such seemingly bizarre pieces of its history begin to take on coherence. Eventually, if you walk long enough through Salem's narrow streets, a full portrait of a historical moment begins to emerge. More than history, however, there is a feeling preserved here—from the ancient *House of the Seven Gables* to the sounds of "Let Me Call You Sweetheart" rolling out of the pipe organ at the Polish Rectory on Bingo night; from the restored Pickering Wharf, a waterfront mall-and-restaurant area to the statue of the Very Reverend Theobald Mathew, an apostle of temperance whose fingers have been chipped away by vandals or divine intervention. In other words, Salem is not just a few plaques nailed to a wall and some guy in a powdered wig hollering historical "facts" through a bullhorn.

Salem can, among other things, boast that it was the site of the first armed resistance against the King of England, resulting in a British tactical maneuver thereafter laughingly known as Leslie's Retreat. Salem was also the site of America's first naval sea battle, and after independence, it became a powerful seaport. It was also Nathaniel Hawthorne's birthplace and the source of his literary inspiration.

Despite all this, Salem is most widely remembered for the witch hysteria of 1692. The witchcraft mania actually broke out in Salem Village (now Danvers) when the Reverend Samuel Parris' Carib Indian slave, Tituba, began telling "forbidden stories" to the children of the parish, who lapsed into *Exorcist*-like fits said to be divinely inspired. Being a young and very religious community filled with the offspring of persecuted Christians, they accepted this behavior as evidence of the Devil's presence in their midst. They did the only sensible thing that a vigilant community could do: they held trials, based on the testimony of the children who were speaking in tongues, and nineteen women were hanged while one man was pressed to death (hold the starch). Like the latter-day witchhunt of the fifties, it lasted a few years before fizzling out with a lot of finger-pointing, false arrests and confusion. These days few people have even heard of Tituba.

Be that as it may, Salem makes no effort to hide this strange slice of American pie. In fact, it has proudly been known as "the Witch City" for generations now, with the usual commercial exploitation verging on the tasteless. And thus, even a run-down gas station can be called "Witch City Auto Body Co." This is all a rather sad attempt to court the tourism that has supplanted the waning maritime industry since the tall ships became obsolete for anything but July 4th celebrations. In recent years, a *Witch Museum* and a *Witch Dungeon* have opened their doors, the former recounting the witch hysteria of 1692, the latter the witch trials and tortures. (Bring the mother-in-law to this one.) Still, it is all held in some perspective by the locals. One elderly Salemite, when asked if there were witches in his hometown, replied: "You'd better watch out, son, because there's witches in every hometown."

Though beach- and water-related activities are not major draws to Salem, they can provide supplemental recreation. A history-oriented cruise of the harbor and surrounding coastline leaves several times a day from the *Salem Maritime National Historic Site*, and a sunset tour leaves at 7:30 P.M. in season from the *Salem Willows Park*. There is also a whale-watch excursion that leaves from the wharf. A whale sighting is promised on every trip.

As for beaches, on the yon side of the historic Salem-Beverly bridge, the town of Beverly has a half-mile stretch of rocky beach with a dock set far enough off from shore so that kids can dive off it safely. In town, Salem has its ancient Salem Willows Park, a public amusement area 1 mile out from the town center on Derby Street. They ban motorcycles here, and for that reason alone the town fathers should be sainted. There are neatly kept recreational facilities—tennis and basketball courts, a picnic area and two small beaches. But the centerpiece is *Kiddie Land*, where the cutest tots this side of a Jell-O Pudding Pop commercial ride miniature caterpillar roller coasters and merry-go-rounds, eat E. W. Hobbs' "world-renowned" popcorn and play games at the smallish arcade. Well, not just the kiddies play the arcade games. We confess to scoring an all-time high of 320 on a Skee-Ball alley here, not to mention mopping up on an adjoining pinball bowling game.

Together, we made off with a huge haul of loot, towering over the heads of our envious preteen competition. Along with the prizes, we were the recipients of dirty looks from the matrons behind the counter. Our goofy take included fake cigars, crazy sunglasses, combs shaped like six-guns, pirate eye patches and assorted noisemakers that we knew would, in time, be put to good use somewhere on our continuing journey down the East Coast.

Accommodations

Salem, to be honest, is not blessed with a huge number of accommodation options. It is not exactly a seaside resort, and tourists who come here to soak up its bewitching history are mostly day-trippers. But if you want to do justice to the city's vast historical holdings and enjoy this quiet green town at a more leisurely pace, there is a haven that's well worth seeking out: the *Hawthorne Inn*. Double rooms fall in the $60 range, and are worth the money for the location alone, next to the Salem Common and catty-corner from the Witch Museum. But the inn itself is a marvel of preservation, and there are other plusses as well: the view of Salem from lace-curtained windows, the antique Early American decor, the high-quality shops that adjoin the inn, and its commodious tavern (not necessarily in that order).

Restaurants

Pickering Wharf is where you will undoubtedly be steered if you don't feel inclined to wander far afield. A glorified shopping mall along the waterfront, it houses yogurt parlors, carry-out food joints and serviceable sit-down seafood restaurants. Its location is the real treat—*Chase House* looks out over a watery parking lot full of small craft of all description. For the best seafood, the natives swear by *Folsom's Chowder House*, a family-run establishment that's been around since 1934, and the *Beef and Oyster House*, set smack in the middle of the restored *Essex Street Mall*. The latter is a multileveled facility that includes sidewalk seating and a relaxed atmosphere, as evidenced by the sight of a patron wandering from an inner dining room to scrape the remains of his meal into a gaggle of happy pigeons on the brick walkway outside. For breakfast, the best bet is *As You Like It*, also in the Essex Street Mall, which offers large omelettes, homemade pastries and soothing Elizabethan recordings for a fair price ($2.95 and up). For inbetweenies, there is *Café La Espresso*, catering to the beatnik crowd, located near the Hawthorne Inn. Gastronomic curiosity seekers might want to check out a place called *In a Pig's Eye*, on Derby Street, which is a self-described "eating saloon" with everything named after some part of the pig's anatomy (even the drinks).

Nightlife

Kick off your evening with a trip to the *Hawthorne Inn's Tavern-On-the-Green*. It looks out over the common and is decorated with tasteful oriental bric-a-brac. Draft beer is $1.30, and the people don't all wear funny nautical hats. If you're already with someone you like, you might just want to encamp here for the evening, because Salem's nightlife options are not altogether staggering (although we were by the time we finished checking them out).

On the night we visited *Jonathan's*, the local rock 'n' roll venue, they were charging a five-buck cover (and requiring "proper attire") to watch a deejay spin nightmarishly loud disco favorites. After close consultation and a lengthy stroll past myriad outdoor dinner patios ("Do you wear soft lenses or hard lenses?" we overheard from the direction of one Cinzano umbrella), we determined that most robust goodtimers gravitated down to the *Chase House* on Pickering Wharf. Around the witching hour, in fact, most of Salem's youthful, devil-may-care crowd can be found down here. A good chunk of them are of the Yuppie nautical ilk—pretty girls in floral-print dresses bobbing their heads to the idle chatter of guys in Docksiders with properly groomed mustaches. Everyone was casually sucking on drinks of every imaginable color in the Kool-Aid rainbow. "You haven't had a green one yet," we chided a tableful of girls.

A piano sat in the corner of the patio, begging to be banged on, and we obliged. Though neither of us plays the instrument, we wrote and performed a spontaneous composition, titled "At the Wharf" (set to the tune of "At the Hop"), which went largely unnoticed by the chattering multitude. (Except for one killjoy who was overheard to say, "If they play one more note, I'm going to break their fingers.") At midnight, a strange rite takes place at the Chase House: everyone on the outdoor patio is made to move inside. At first thought to be related to the superstitions of the town, it is in fact a retreat made in deference to the condo owners next door.

There are other places to drink quietly and sanely, but as with most historical towns that eschew brouhaha, Salem's nightlife centers around the dinner ritual. Oh yes, for our kinky readers, there is a liquor store on Derby Street named The Bunghole—as God is our witness.

FOR FURTHER INFORMATION

Salem Chamber of Commerce
Old Town Hall
32 Derby Square
Salem, Massachusetts 01970
(617) 744-0004

Marblehead

Originally part of Salem back in the seventeenth century, Marblehead (then known as Marble Harbor) is a wealthy bayside village that's popular with the yachting set and has been a yachtsman's enclave (artist's and craftsman's, too) pretty much through the entirety of the twentieth century. Marblehead's prime asset is a fine, deep harbor that's practically landlocked; the town itself sits on a rocky promontory overlooking Massachusetts Bay. Sixteen miles south lies Boston. The popular beach in Marblehead is Devereux Beach. It turned out to be harder to track than a snow leopard. Take Route 114 East out of Salem, and then . . . ask for directions. Several sets of directions never got us there, though we did see a lot of nice summer houses and drove through cool woods. Devereux is purported to be worth the effort it takes to get there. *Bonne chance.*

FOR FURTHER INFORMATION

Marblehead Chamber of Commerce
62 Pleasant Street
Marblehead, Massachusetts 01945
(617) 631-2868

Lynn

Lynn is a commuter town of 80,000 perched a few miles above Boston. The principal industry is shoemaking (like Marblehead, which was renowned for the manufacture of children's shoes), and there is really little for the vacationer to do here but get lost in its perplexing maze of streets. In that regard, it is kind of a warm-up for the massive catastrophe of driving in Boston—an ordeal that is worth driving 50 miles out of the way to avoid. (And avoid it we did. Thankfully, Boston did not fall conceptually within the scope of our particular expedition—i.e., it has no ocean beaches.)

The anomalous fact of the matter is that Lynn does have 3 miles of wide, sandy beaches as attractive and archetypally recreational as any in Massachusetts. One surmises that lots of Bostonians break for here on the weekend, toting beach blankets and iced-down coolers. Sure beats steaming in Bean Town. There is a restored inn dating from 1835, *Cap'n Jack's Waterfront Inn*, right on the beach. While you'd be ill-advised to book a vacation in Lynn, it might make a convenient overnight stop to points north, particularly if you allow enough daylight to enjoy its fabulous King's Beach.

FOR FURTHER INFORMATION

Lynn Chamber of Commerce
170 Union Street
Lynn, Massachusetts 01901
(617) 592-2900

Plymouth

The town of Plymouth is a living textbook of early American history. The pages come to life as Pilgrims walk around the town just as if it was 1620 and not the Us Decade. The first question that we, being enterprising students of history, were inclined to ask the wandering Pilgrims of Plymouth was, "Aren't you hot in those clothes?" The second was, "Is this a summer job, or . . . do you really think you're a Pilgrim?" Judging from the ex-acidhead look of some of these folk, particularly the long-haired men, there was a glimmer of doubt in our minds on that latter point.

The early Pilgrims' settlement of Plymouth was no laughing matter. The year was 1620; the ship, the *Mayflower*; their leader, Captain Miles Standish. And what a time they had: half of them died in the first year, succumbing to malnourishment, disease and the elements. When spring came, they plowed over the graves of their deceased fellow travelers and sowed grain, so that the Indians would not perceive the magnitude of their reduced numbers. Yet fortified with new arrivals, the colony took hold, and other colonies—Duxbury, Scituate—were founded in the vicinity. America was off and running on its manifest destiny.

It's interesting to note that Plymouth was the Pilgrims' *second* attempt at colonization. Before charting a course for the New World, the Pilgrims—religious separatists from the Anglican Church—settled comfortably in Holland for twelve years. Wary of becoming assimilated into Dutch culture (was it the wooden shoes?), the Pilgrims embarked for what is now Massachusetts in a British wine-carrying ship, the *Mayflower*. After disembarking at Plymouth Rock and setting up housekeeping, the colonists did not live as ascetically and severely as is popularly believed. By one historical account, "The Pilgrims preferred wine, ale, beer and cider to water."

They would have been very much at home in modern-day Plymouth, which seemingly has a package store, bar or spirit-dispensing restaurant on every corner. They'd also find plenty of the previously mentioned Pilgrim lookalikes to mingle with, and would feel right at home, if mildly querulous, with these imposters' daily routines: hoeing a garden out of season at the *Plimoth Plantation* or signing the Mayflower Compact ten times a day aboard the one-third-scale replica of the *Mayflower* (called the *Mayflower II*) docked down at the State Pier. Should you choose to visit these attractions, an adult combination ticket will set you back $7.

Another big attraction in Plymouth is the Rock. Plymouth Rock has the number "1620" inscribed on it and is interred in a cage, of sorts, out of the reach of eggheaded tourists who have been known to try to chip off a souvenir. You can look in, and people toss pennies at it for good luck, but you can't touch America's favorite pet rock. Plymouth Rock, legend has it, is the first solid ground the Pilgrims of the *Mayflower* touched in the New World. Technically, there is legitimate debate over that, and the weight of evidence seems to indicate that the *Mayflower* first dropped anchor on the tip of Cape Cod, at what is now Provincetown. To redress this historical inaccuracy, Provincetown has erected its own Pilgrim's Memorial, a tower intentionally built high enough so that it can be seen from Plymouth on a clear day. The implication is clear: *they stopped here first, and pooh on your big rock.*

All of the above-mentioned sights, and many other buildings of historical import, can be quickly toured via trolley. The Plymouth Trolley makes a 3-mile circuit around town, hitting about fifteen of the main tourist stops for a mere 50 cents. So pick up a map of the town from the chamber of commerce (at 44 Samoset Street), and hop the trolley for some soulful sight-seeing.

Options along the waterfront include bay and harbor cruises. *Princess Cruise Lines* operates a popular day-long cruise from Plymouth to Provincetown that includes a 4 ½-hour layover in colorful P-town. There is also a 35-minute harbor tour that leaves every half hour from an adjacent berth on the State Pier. But we've saved the best for last. Plymouth is the home of Ocean Spray, the cranberry sauce company, which offers tours out of its mammoth, completely modernized *Cranberry World Visitors Center*. Heck, you can lose the better part of an afternoon ogling the scale-model cranberry farm or trudging about a moist, loamy bog. To think that Ocean Spray is now cultivating the world's largest commercial cranberry crop where once humble Pilgrims dropped their seeds into the ground!

Incidentally, the superabundance of history can overshadow the fact that there are some exceptional beaches in the Plymouth area. Nelson Beach is a public beach with free parking; it's located just north of the center of town, off of Water Street. The longest, and most popular, is Plymouth Beach, about 3 miles south of town via Route 3A . There's also a small public beach at Stephen's Field, south of the town business district, adjacent to the yacht club. Few folks come to Plymouth for the swimming—they'll curl out onto Cape Cod for that—but the beaches provide a good sideshow to the main event of the town and its history.

Accommodations

Lodgings are pricy, in season. The *Governor Carver* and *Governor Bradford Motor Inns*, centered downtown amid all the various Pilgrim memorials and museums, have the market cornered on location, though you'll pay $60 or $70 a night to stay here. There are numerous inns in town and along Route 3A. Do book ahead, though. Arriving late on our first night in town sans reservations, we were consigned to what appeared to be the last available motel room in Plymouth. It was expensive, by our standards, and while it was not quite the debacle we had in Hampton Beach, it was nothing to shout about and certainly not worth $50 a night. The imprint of ruined springs on our spines from such places haunts us still.

Restaurants

There are 550 restaurants in Plymouth County. Grading them would make a book in itself. You can (and we did) simplify matters by making straight for the waterfront, where, along Water Street and Park Avenue, some of the best of them are clustered. *McGrath's*, located right at harborside, is among the most popular, with a large dining room and seafood with a gourmet Italian touch, e.g., seafood Alfredo. A local favorite is *Bert's On the Beach*, south of Plymouth on Route 3A, near the neighboring town of Manoment.

Nightlife

In a word, tame. Prepare to grimace to "soft rock" cover bands in dimly lit, nearly empty cocktail lounges, most of them appended to restaurants to catch the dinner-rush spillover. Best bets: the upstairs lounge at *1620* and the *Park Avenue Pub*, both in downtown Plymouth. If you luck out, you might catch a Top Forty cover band that won't have you reaching for the extra-strength pain reliever. But Plymouth after dark is generally as dull as a Puritan sabbath. As it turned out, we wound up importing our nightlife from Los Angeles: the summer Olympics, on a flickering motel-room TV set.

FOR FURTHER INFORMATION

Plymouth Area Chamber of Commerce
44 Samoset Street
Plymouth, Massachusetts 02360
(617) 746-3377

Waterfront Information Center
Park Avenue
Plymouth, Massachusetts 02360
(617) 746-4779

Cape Cod Bay

The public beaches along the northern edge of Cape Cod exist on maps, but finding them is like stalking small game. Some of them we had no luck sighting at all. Of course, once you get out to Provincetown, all is forgiven. But the beaches of the Cape Cod Bay are elusive, their still waters warm and brackish, often plopped down in marshy wetlands. They seem to exist mainly for the sunning pleasure of the locals, with roads and facilities ill-equipped for a steady influx of outsiders. Still, they do exist, and we trekked over bumpy and unmarked roads in what became a challenge to our map-reading and navigational skills. Read on.

FOR FURTHER INFORMATION

Cape Cod Chamber of Commerce
Routes 6 and 132
Hyannis, Massachusetts 02601
(617) 362-3225

Scusset Beach

Scusset Beach State Reservation is a state-run stretch of sand located, as you are heading toward Cape Cod on Route 3, just before you reach the Cape Cod Canal. In fact, it claims one of the spokes off the rotary that precedes the bridge. Allow a complete circuit of the thing to identify the proper turnoff. Several more circuits ought to get you in a safe enough position to attempt making the turn. (The rotary, or traffic circle, fortunately exists in abundance only in Massachusetts. It is the highway-engineering equivalent of the Pinto with the gas tank in the rear. On summer weekends, driving the rotaries along Route 3 out to Cape Cod is a nightmare out of a grade-B drive-in drag-strip flick.) Once you've aimed your car in the direction of Scusset Beach, follow the looming smoke-stacks of the local electric plant. The entrance gate is about a mile down the road. A day pass costs $3, and the beach is open from 8 A.M. to 8 P.M..

Sandwich
East Sandwich

Once you have crossed the bridge over the Cape Cod Canal and are heading east on Route 6, you will need to take a very sudden exit onto Route 6A, an offshoot of the main highway that runs through the historic villages of lower Cape Cod and much closer to the shore. If you keep your eyes peeled and your nose clean, you will find several public beaches within minutes of your turnoff.

Almost immediately, you are in the historic town of Sandwich. Settled in 1637, it claims to be the oldest town on the Cape, and the list of attractions are suitably antique to verify such a claim: the *Dexter Mill*, a still-functioning gristmill that dates back to 1654; the *Hoxie House*, which dates back to the late 1600s; the *Sandwich Glass Museum*, containing a large collection of American glassware (much of it made in the Sandwiches between 1825 and 1888); and *Heritage Plantation*, an offbeat museum of American history.

As for the beaches, Town Neck Beach is adjacent to the Plank Walk near Sandwich Harbor. Getting to it requires a labyrinthine series of turns—keep the car moving, that is the key. Farther down Route 6A, after you have entered the town of East Sandwich, turn left on Beach Road, drive 1 ½ miles and take another left on North Shore Drive, where the road will end, for all intents and purposes, in a sandy parking lot. The stone walls at either end of this 300-yard-long beach serve notice that beyond them, the shore is private and off-limits. But East Sandwich Beach is a pocket of rocky sand "for the people."

FOR FURTHER INFORMATION

Greater Bourne-Sandwich Chamber of Commerce
Bourne, Massachusetts 02532
(617) 888-6202

Barnstable

The turnoff for Sandy Neck Beach, the next public beach down the bay's shoreline, is just inside the Barnstable town limits. Signs to this swath of beachfront allegedly exist, but just in case you miss them (and we did), look for any public road or machete-cut path or deer crossing—anything heading north off of Route 6A after you leave East Sandwich. This being Cape Cod, the worst you will encounter, should you get lost, is an old man with loafers and a hoe staring up from his petunias.

Yarmouth

This is the next old township you encounter as you head east on Route 6A. Yarmouth is chockful of inns in all shapes and sizes, including one aptly named *The Gingerbread*. A left turn on Centre Street takes you past one of New England's ancient sprawling cemeteries with thin slate headstones that bend forward or back like messages from disturbed otherworldly occupants. Soon, you'll reach the free parking area for Gray's Beach, which is not so much a beach as a marsh. There are swimming spots protected by the marsh that are popular with the kids—though these are too low at low tide to be good for anything but a mud bath. But the real treat is the long wooden walkway that takes you into the heart of a living salt marsh, where every little pool of water can be heard percolating with tiny organisms. It is these vital life beds that feed the fish that feed us. At low tide, you can practically squish your way through the ooze and muck of Gray's Beach all the way over to the town of Dennis.

FOR FURTHER INFORMATION

Yarmouth Chamber of Commerce
1 Springer Lane
West Yarmouth, Massachusetts 02673
(617) 775-4133

Dennis
East Dennis

Speaking of Dennis, if you proceed eastward on Route 6A, you will find it (or him). Should you wish to forgo the old homes and stately inns and the *Capetown Playhouse* located in town (the third oldest continuous summer theater in the nation) in search of a beach, turn left on Beach Street, follow it to Taunton Avenue and then look for the signs to Chapin Public Beach. This one is fairly popular, despite the fact that it costs $4 to park here and caters to the dune buggy crowd. For the record, there is a public beach, of sorts, in East Dennis. Turn left off of Route 6A on Sea Street, make another left on Point of Rocks Road and you'll find yourself on a tiny public beach requiring a community parking sticker. Oh well.

FOR FURTHER INFORMATION

Dennis Chamber of Commerce
P.O. Box 275
Dennis, Massachusetts 02638
(617) 398-3568
Alternatively, you can visit the Information Booth at the intersection of Routes 28 and 134 in South Dennis, or call (617) 398-3573.

Rock Harbor

We found Skaket Beach outside of the township of Rock Harbor, just around the bend of Cape Cod's foot. There is ample free parking, to be sure, but swimming was conducted by dogs and children in a glorified ditch, and after a hardy half-hour hike across sandy muck in the direction of the bay, we still had not reached our destination. A puzzle, this one.

Provincetown

The herbs and fruits are of many sorts and kinds.
   —JOHN SMITH ON NEW ENGLAND, 1616

Though these words were written over three centuries ago, John Smith could easily have been peering into a crystal ball at modern-day Provincetown. Following Smith's early explorations, the first shipload of settlers from England touched land here (aboard the *Mayflower*) in 1620. Three hundred and sixty-six years later, the pioneer spirit lives on in Provincetown. The frontiers being explored these days have nothing to do with wilderness and Indians, however. Today, Provincetown is on the cutting edge of alternative lifestyles in the eighties, a liberated free zone at land's end.

At any given moment, you'll find more varieties of colorful creatures ambling along the sidewalks of P-town than anywhere this side of the Bronx Zoo. And here, contrarily, the straighter you are, the more eccentric you appear. At the center of town, in front of the town hall, a statue has been dedicated to the American tourist, mocking his obesity and her big-bosomed hauteur.

Still, everyone—even garden-variety tourists—finds what they're looking for in Provincetown. There are harbor cruises and whale-watching expeditions at the wharf. The 260-foot-tall *Pilgrim Monument*, from whose summit you can see the Boston skyline on a clear day, is an aerobic workout for those up to it. There are lobsters to be wrestled with, and those wacky lobster bibs to be laced about the neck by smiling waitresses. And, finally, at the tip of the cape, there are wild, unspoiled stretches of national seashore with cliff-like dunes. Here you will find the finest ocean beaches in New England, bar none.

Then there is the other side of Provincetown, the full-tilt Bohemia that people make for when they want to come out of the closet and bring the closet with them. Writers and artists come here in search of inspiration, solitude and/or camaraderie among their own kind. College students flock here in the summer to work as busboys and chambermaids, and to party like there's no tomorrow.

Provincetown, 70 miles from the mainland, is the crooked finger at the tip of the bent elbow of land called Cape Cod. The finger spirals inward, so that Provincetown practically surrounds itself. Out here, protected from scrutiny, social mores have taken a bold turn. At land's end, you can be—as the army recruiting jingle goes—all that you can be, and a lot of things you *can't* be most anywhere else. Gay culture seems to flourish with a particular abandon here, embracing a wide cross-section of gay lifestyles, male and female.

The action in this bizarre bazaar centers around Commercial Street, the more traveled of the two parallel streets that traverse Provincetown longitudinally. Commercial and Bradford Streets extend for about 3 miles along the bay. The town is laid out like a giant ladder, with approximately forty rungs connecting the two main streets. Because of the peculiar contour of the Cape out here, Provincetown runs east to west. You enter town on Route 6A from the east end, which is largely private residences, plus a few inns and guesthouses. Proceeding west into town, you start to hit a stretch of P-town's better restaurants—intimate hideaways on the far side, and casual, open-air restaurants on the bay side—and a few art galleries. The pace picks up a bit: you hit a cluster of boutiques that sell women's clothes to members of both sexes, leather-goods stores and astrology shops that specialize in occult jewelry and mystical knickknacks. You'll know you've hit the center of town when the words "Saltwater Taffy" begin appearing on every other storefront.

The promenade begins in earnest after dark, when the most interesting and variegated crowd of people on the East Coast can be found wandering up and down Commercial Street like a drugged wolf pack. Everyone has their eyes open, and the procession is as strange and wonderful a cast of misfits as one will find in any science-fiction flick. Just park yourself on one of the benches outside town hall on a muggy summer night and watch the parade go by.

The town itself is such an entertaining diversion that one is tempted to overlook the scenic appeal of the nearby beaches. P-town's main public beaches are Race Point and Herring Cove. The latter is a pebble-strewn, calm-water beach that's narrow but runs for a great distance. Race Point, only a couple of miles away, faces the ocean head on and is pounded by a steady surf. The water

here is colder and deeper than at Herring Cove, the beach wide
and sandy, more hospitable to the feet. Sunset-watching at Race
Point is a popular ritual. Here, as in Key West, the setting sun
becomes a broad red disc as it nears the horizon, until it suddenly
drops out of sight over the water. This dazzling display always
draws appreciative applause.

Parking at either beach during the daylight hours costs a paltry
$1, and your receipt will get you into any of the other National
Park beaches on the Cape that same day. There are also some nude
beaches hereabouts, but these are known more by word of mouth
than by outright designation. (There are other books devoted to
nude beaches, to which the interested reader/gawker is referred;
we kept our suits on.) Finally, the bay itself, mere feet from Commercial Street, is a popular and convenient swimming hole. The
tidal exchange is extreme, however, and the best swimming is
done at or near high tide. Also, since a large and active fishing
fleet, not to mention many pleasure vessels, are docked down at
the town wharf, don't be surprised if some strange debris floats
by on the lazy waters of the bay. We found ourselves face to face
with a disembodied tuna head one unforgettable afternoon.

Bicycling is a cheap, quick way to get around P-town—in fact,
it's actually more sensible than driving. Commercial Street is a
narrow one-way thoroughfare that is jammed with pedestrians and
cyclists by midday and at night, with cars creeping along more
slowly than even the most red-faced tourist who's hoofing it. You're
better off just parking the car and forgetting about it while in
Provincetown. *Arnold's Bicycle Rentals*, downtown, rents funky but
serviceable bikes by the hour ($1) or the day ($3). There are paved
bicycle trails all through the dunes and salt marshes outside of
town, and you can follow them out to Race Point or back toward
Boston.

Provincetown has for many decades been a haven for artists and
writers. Artists claim the light is exceptional, and writers have the
best of both worlds: you can be a desolation angel if you wish, or
you can have your wicked kicks in kindred company—i.e., you
can have your naked lunch and eat it, too. The presence of so
many creative talents elevates the town to something more than
just a fashionable, moneyed resort à la Kennebunkport. Turned

inward on itself by geography, Provincetown is a self-contained, self-indulgent community: regal in its bearing and desirous of beauty and order but driven by instincts that come from a primal, decadent place. It has personality, perversity, aliveness, zeal and daring.

Accommodations

Holiday Inns on the highway, real inns in town. There are many old captains' houses dating from the 1800s and earlier right on the fringes of the town's center, along Commercial and Bradford Streets. A personal favorite for many years has been the *White Horse Inn*. The rooms are simply but tastefully appointed, and the house feels comfortable and lived in. The abundance of original art on the walls is a tipoff to the aesthetic sense of the inn's owner, Frank Schaeffer, who's a walking authority on Provincetown—from tourist info to town gossip—and a generous supporter of its artistic community. Runs a good inn, too.

Some of the other first-rate inns in town are *The White Dory* and *The Ship's Bell*. Both have private beaches on the bay across the street and are located in the quiet East End. Another prime choice, sort of a cross between a hotel and an inn, is the *Hargood House*, which has spacious rooms and efficiencies, plus sundecks that catch the best of the bay breezes. If you require the amenities of a heated pool, color tube, private bathroom, etc., you might stay at the *Surfside Inn*, which, unlike the luxury chain motels stranded out on the highway, has its own beach on the bay and is situated just a stone's throw from the downtown area, again in the East End.

Restaurants

There are a plethora of good restaurants in Provincetown and very few bad ones. Deciding where to go is a difficult task, and indeed one could spend a week eating at two- or three-star restaurants and not repeat oneself. As their names suggest, *The Everbreeze* and *The Landmark Inn Restaurant* have been around awhile (the latter is located in a home built in 1840) and are dependable, especially for lobster and seafood. *Ciro & Sal's*, too, has been around forever (or so it seems). The emphasis here is Italian, and the small dining room is cozy and intimate. *Café at the Mews* is a sure bet for gourmet seafood. As an added plus, it overlooks the waterfront.

The native Provincetonians are Portuguese in ancestry, and good Portuguese cuisine can be had in P-town. *The Moors* specializes in Portuguese-prepared seafood. If you're sick of the sea, order linguine—a Portuguese specialty. The *Pilgrim House* and *Poor Richard's Buttery* boast large outdoor patios for dining. Both offer excellent vantage points from which to peruse the ceaseless Commercial Street procession, and are good for breakfast, brunch or dinner. For good, cheap fare in a homey atmosphere, the *Mayflower Café* gets a hearty thumbs-up. A swordfish-steak dinner cost us only $7.

We donned bibs and did battle with lobsters at the *Lobster Pot*. In contrast to the mannered decor of Provincetown's more elegant eateries, this place dispenses with the protocol and gets right down to the nut of it: food. Lobster, especially. There are lines going out the door in the summer and it's a mite noisy, but the food is good—probably the best mass-produced lobster on the Cape. It's worth a visit, as are many other restaurants that space prevents us from mentioning. Perhaps we can absolve ourselves of these sins of omission by suggesting that gourmet Provincetown is perhaps best experienced by personal investigation. Stroll the streets, read the menus and set the lion's share of your vacation budget aside for wining and dining.

Nightlife

Well, you walk from one end of downtown to another, then back again, back and forth, over and over, until you get the uncanny feeling that you've checked out the same people (and have likewise been checked out by them) a few times too many. So then you angle out onto one of the town wharfs, sigh contentedly at the sight of the moon and the harbor lights on the water and at last drowsily return to wherever you're staying to be lulled to sleep by the distant sound of a foghorn.

If you are a restless goonie, you may actually be a tad disappointed by P-town nightlife, which is not as cosmopolitan as the town's reputation. Unless, of course, you're plugged into some sort of private-party circuit, in which case you'll never lack for things to do. If you live here, visit often and/or have friends who do, chances are you'll fall in with a fast crowd, if that's where your tastes lie. If not, you can still bar hop and have a pretty good time. Lots of places are gay only, if not by strict door policy, then by clientele. Others operate on more of an open-door philosophy. P-town's rowdiest clubs that cater to a general crowd are the *Governor Bradford* (downtown, on Commercial Street) and *Captain John's* (out a short distance, on Shank Painter Road). If you're lucky, you just might catch a good band and/or deejay. Of course, a night out at the beach is often only as good as the Top Forty at that moment in time, since cover bands and deejayed turntables are often the only entertainment sources. But a good ballgame on TV will do in a pinch.

Tuesday is two-for-one night all over town, ensuring crowded bars, and the weekends always pack 'em in. Two-for-one night at Captain John's is an especially hot ticket: the place is packed with summering collegians and the atmosphere is swampy and wanton, complete with disco blare. A calmer time among an older crowd can be had at *Pucci's*, an attractive bar and bistro with a deck on the bay, over in the East End. A few of its tall drinks at sundown will have you feeling positively rosy. There are other popular bars of long standing, like the *Fo'csle*, which cater primarily to fishermen and are raucously rambunctious in the grand tradition. Sea shanties can sometimes be heard spilling out of the doors like bilge water. In keeping with its reputation as a place where the gate swings both ways, Provincetown has a number of drag shows, which draw mixed crowds of gays and straights, all of whom hoot uproariously to the antics of the Phyllis Diller/Bette Davis-impersonating she-men. (The euphemism is "illusionist.") Your initiation into the quaint folkways of P-town isn't complete until you've sat through one of these.

Provincetown Chamber of Commerce
307 Commercial Street (at MacMillan Wharf)
P.O. Box 1017
Provincetown, Massachusetts 02657
(617) 487-3424

Cape Cod National Seashore

The 30-mile length of Cape Cod from Provincetown to Chatham
is variously known as the Lower Cape, the Outer Cape, the "fore-
arm" (in anatomical lingo, it runs from the "elbow" of Chatham
to the "fist" of P-town). It doesn't matter what you call it—this is
quintessential Cape Cod country. The Lower Cape is as beautiful
as portions of Maine, and otherwise has no rivals on the East Coast.
The scenery is striking—woodlands and ponds line both sides of
Route 6, and rugged cliffs drop down to the cold, blue waters of
the Atlantic.

You have entered the Cape Cod National Seashore. Established
in 1961 by an act of Congress and signed into law by President
Kennedy, it became our second permanently established National
Seashore. The following quote, from the August 1962 issue of
National Geographic, captures the urgency that was brought to bear
on this most wise purchase: "The National Park Service says that
this is the only extensive area on the Atlantic Seaboard (excepting
the Cape Hatteras National Seashore) which is not already so built
up that its pristine values have been submerged." This is a sobering
statement, particularly when one considers the exponentially greater
damage that has been meted upon the Atlantic Seaboard since
1962.

Concern over the fate of Cape Cod predates the early sixties. In
fact, much of the Cape was in sorry shape by the thirties. The
virgin pine and oak forests were long gone, and meadows and

farmlands had been overgrazed. By the fifties, the new prosperity that followed World War II sent middle-class America on the road. They had no trouble finding Cape Cod, and the sudden tourist inundation alerted conservationists that something must be done quickly, or the beautiful ocean beaches of the Lower Cape—those on the east side, facing the Atlantic, collectively known as the Great Beach—would soon become just another all-American eyesore. After years of studies and surveys, preservation came not a moment too soon with the establishment of the Cape Cod National Seashore.

Cape Cod National Seashore runs for 42 miles, encompassing approximately 27,000 acres—roughly 9 percent of the Cape's total land area. There is a string of accessible beaches and four "developed areas" within the confines of the National Seashore. At these developed areas—Nauset, Marconi Station, Pilgrim Heights and Province Lands—one will find interpretive exhibits, picnic areas, nature and bike trails, guarded beaches and rest-room facilities.

Despite the Herculean legal efforts that have been made to set aside this land for future generations, its permanence is still in question. According to a sign at the breathtaking overlook by the *Cape Cod Lighthouse* (near the town of Truro), the seaside cliffs are sliding away at the rate of 3 feet per year. This famous lighthouse, also known as the *Highland Light*, has been moved twice. At this rate, perhaps it should simply be moved for safekeeping onto the fairway of the nearby Highland Golf Course.

Yet while the ocean gobbles up the cliffs, the government keeps up its land-acquisition strategy. Much of the Lower Cape was already private land when the government stepped in, and it agreed from the start to honor all existing land and ownership rights. As land becomes available, and as budgetary provisions allow, Cape Cod National Seashore continues to grow by increments.

The National Seashore lands surround and adjoin the towns of Provincetown, Truro, Wellfleet, Eastham, Orleans and Chatham (moving from north to south). Though they all have the wild beauty of the National Seashore in common, each village has a distinct character of its own.

FOR FURTHER INFORMATION

Cape Cod National Seashore
South Wellfleet, Massachusetts 02663
(617) 349-3785.

Truro

Truro is a small town (the villages of Truro and North Truro have
a combined population of 1,200) whose "center" is the intersection
of Pamet Road and Route 6. There are plenty of beaches within
arm's reach of Truro, however: Ballston, Longnook, Highland and
Head of the Meadow. The last of these is easily one of the nicest
ocean beaches on the Cape, just the sort of place for a picnic or
cookout at sundown. Next to it is Highland Beach, which looks
up at the aforementioned *Cape Cod Lighthouse*. Near the lighthouse,
the Truro Historical Society maintains the *Highland House Museum*.
Farther down the Cape, between Truro and Provincetown, the
Pilgrim Heights Area of the National Seashore takes up a healthy
bite of the Cape. A nature trail leads around Pilgrim Lake, down
to a freshwater spring where the Pilgrims of the *Mayflower* toasted
their arrival in the New World.

FOR FURTHER INFORMATION

Truro Chamber of Commerce
Route 6 at Head of the Meadow Road
P.O. Box 26
North Truro, Massachusetts 02652
(617) 487-1288.

Wellfleet

While Provincetown bustles about gaily all summer long, Wellfleet
moseys at a more unhurried pace. Both towns have a Commercial

Street, and both attract artists and art galleries. There are over a dozen reputable galleries clustered in Wellfleet, while the artists are scattered all over the moors. This village of 2,000 is more sedentary than P-town, and less oriented to transients. There are a few motels out on Route 6 to catch the P-town overflow, but at the town center you'll find not much more than a handful of inns. There are a reasonable number of restaurants, though, and you'll not want to miss a chance to eat at the *Wellfleet Oyster House* if you find yourself at this end of the Cape.

The village of Wellfleet is on the bay side of the Cape. There are several beach-access points off Route 6, however, and the smaller communities of South Wellfleet and Wellfleet by the Sea face the Atlantic. The Marconi Station Area of the Cape Cod National Seashore is near Wellfleet. Named for Guglielmo Marconi, who transmitted the first wireless transatlantic message from this beach in 1903, the Marconi Area includes a guarded beach, nature trails and National Seashore headquarters. Just north of here are three other beaches: Lecount Hollow, Cook's Beach and Newcomb Hollow. Ocean View Drive connects the first two of these, and offers a rare chance to drive along the ocean for a distance. Other Wellfleet-area attractions include the *Wellfleet Historical Museum*; a 700-acre *Audubon Wildlife Sanctuary*; and a place called *Great Island*, a 7-mile peninsula on the bay side of Wellfleet. You can hike but not drive out here. Your reward will be the unparalleled solitude of Chequessett Beach.

FOR FURTHER INFORMATION

Wellfleet Tourist Information Center
Route 6 at Davis Corner
P.O. Box 571
Wellfleet, Massachusetts 02667
(617) 349-2510

Eastham

The *Salt Pond Visitors' Center* of the Cape Cod National Seashore is located right off Route 6 in Eastham, one of the four original Cape townships. Here, you can equip yourself with maps and brochures and walk around the Salt Pond—in essence a controlled nursery for shellfish, which are then used to seed the salt marshes. Eastham (pop. 1,100) is abuzz with early colonial history. Like every crossroads on the Cape, it has its own historical society. Unlike any historical society we've ever heard of, however, you enter this one through the jawbone of a whale. The eastern edge of Eastham has two superior ocean beaches: Coast Guard Beach and Nauset Light Beach. A steep wooden staircase descends to the latter, with the lighthouse presiding above it all on a high bluff. There is parking at Nauset Light, while Coast Guard is reached via shuttle bus from the Salt Pond Visitors' Center, and there are lifeguards at both, in season. Over on the bay side, tiny First Encounter Beach commemorates the spot where the first European arrivals from the New World had their initial encounter with the native Indians—a meeting that was, by one account, "anything but cordial."

FOR FURTHER INFORMATION

Eastham Tourist Information Center
Route 6 at Fort Hill Road
Eastham, Massachusetts 02642
(617) 255-3444

Orleans

Located midway between the Cape Cod Canal and Provincetown, Orleans was originally part of Eastham, from which it split in 1797. Named for the French Duke of Orleans, who graced the Cape with a visit, Orleans is worthy of more than a few historical footnotes, not all of them stemming from the days of the Pilgrims, either. During the War of 1812, British troops tried to extort $1,000 from the townspeople; they refused, and the British frigate *Newcastle* was deliberately run aground by a crafty Yankee captain. It is not difficult to run aground off the coast of Orleans—3,000 ships have done it, including the first recorded shipwreck, in 1626. Even today, Orleans' harbor is navigable only around high tide. Orleans has the distinction of being the only place in America to be fired on in World War I. A German sub, which had been attacking American coal barges, apparently unleashed a barrage of shells, one of which landed onshore.

Today, Orleans is out of the line of fire, though it bustles as the center of commerce for the Outer Cape. New growth is creeping in this direction, and the Orleans-Chatham area threatens to get as out of hand as the towns of the Middle Cape. While waiting for some money in the lobby of an Orleans bank, we flipped through a slick magazine called *Cape Cod Life*. To our dismay, our eyes fell upon the following quote, uttered by the president of an outfit known as American Heritage Realty: "Pound for pound, Orleans outsells Chatham." He was not referring to fish.

But enough of this. One can still find solace on Nauset Beach, on the long spit of land between the ocean and the town of Orleans. It'll cost you $3 or $4 to park here (unlike the National Seashore beaches, which charge only $1), but it's an archetypal Cape Cod beach with breakers big enough to draw a cult following of surfing aficionados. There are restaurants and accommodations along Routes 6, 6A and 28, but the only motel you'll find right on the beach is the *Nauset Knoll Motor Lodge*. It's at the end of Beach Road and, like most establishments on the Cape, is operated seasonally, from about April to November.

FOR FURTHER INFORMATION

Orleans Tourist Information Center
Route 6A and Eldredge Parkway
Orleans, Massachusetts 02653
(617) 255-1386

Chatham

Chatham is one of the smallest townships on the Cape, but it is circumscribed by an amazing 65 miles of waterfront. Chatham is situated at the elbow of Cape Cod, where it bends north to the fist of Provincetown and west toward the biceps of the Middle and Upper Cape. The town of Chatham is on a nub of land that is three-quarters surrounded by water.

Chatham has the look of old money about it. There is the musky smell of antique prosperity here. The village of Chatham was the railhead for the Chatham Railroad Company, which hauled Cape Cod freight (shoes, salt, fish) to inland markets. The original train station, built in 1887, is now a museum. The museum of the Chatham Historical Society is located in the *Atwood House*, which holds an extensive collecton of glassware, manuscripts and antiques. Finally, there are splendid examples of Victorian, Cape Cod and "bow roof" architecture to be found all over town.

Beach-wise, everyone makes for the Chatham Light, at the end of Shore Road. It's a small cove beach, protected from the Atlantic by the Nauset Beach spit. From the bluff above the beach, shutterbugs will find an unmatched view of the Atlantic. People also gravitate to the *Chatham Fish Pier*, both to watch the fishing fleet and to buy the day's catch as it's off-loaded. Though Chatham is becoming more "fashionable" to the yachting set every year, as gentrification moves out the Cape from Hyannis, one can find ample vestiges of its charmed past, and it's still possible to get lost on country roads in the rolling, wooded highlands.

FOR FURTHER INFORMATION

Chatham Tourist Information Center
Main Street
Chatham, Massachusetts 02633
(617) 945-0342

Monomoy Island

Monomoy Island is a 9-mile sandbar south of Chatham. Some 300 species of birds nest and rest here, and it has been set aside as a National Wilderness Area. You can't get here by car, but boats make the trip from Chatham. Monomoy Beach is up at the northern end of the island.

Harwich

There is not one Harwich but seven, arranged in bicycle-spoke fashion around the hub of Harwich proper. The Harwiches boast five protected harbors. Indeed, the fledgling fishing industry got its start here. Every spring, an annual pilgrimage of herring makes its way up the Herring River to spawn. Inland, cranberry bogs abound in classic New England terrain.

Most of the tourism is centered in Harwich Port and West Harwich. The Harwiches' sole public beach, Red River Beach, faces Nantucket Sound; its waters are calmer and balmier than those of the Outer Cape.

FOR FURTHER INFORMATION

Harwich Tourist Information Center
Route 28
Harwich Port, Massachusetts 02645
(617) 432-1600

West Dennis

Dear old Dennis again. We have already mentioned his cross-Cape kinfolk, East Dennis and Dennis proper. This westerly one has one of the best beaches on the middle Cape, with the unconfusing name West Dennis Beach. Located off Lower County Road, this beach will take on all comers—there is parking for 1,500, at $3 per day for nonresidents.

Hyannis
Hyannis Port

You can take a boat over to Martha's Vineyard or Nantucket from here, there is a huge harbor at which to dock your yacht, you can get a good meal at any number of fine and fancy restaurants, and these are the main reasons you'll want or need to sail close to these tourist middens. Everyone equates Hyannis with the Kennedys, and indeed, there is little reason not to. Their compound is set somewhere behind the walls and hedges of Hyannis Port, and there's a JFK Memorial and an adjoining Veterans Park Beach. But tour buses choke the streets of this overcrowded town, and factory outlets and malls overrun it. This is historic Cape Cod? This is, as the quote on the brochure suggests, "where the blue begins, and the frets of life cease"? Humbug.

FOR FURTHER INFORMATION

Hyannis Board of Trade
319 Barnstable Road
P.O. Box 547
Hyannis, Massachusetts 02601
(617) 775-2201

Craigville

It is impossible not to be confused by the way towns are organized on Cape Cod. The game seems to be that there are "towns," which have wide boundaries and also incorporate "villages." Technically, for example, Hyannis is a village in the town of Barnstable. But what is Craigville? Craigville is said to be part of the village of

Centerville, but it's actually closer to West Hyannis. So does Craig-ville enjoy any autonomy at all, or is it merely a subdivision of a village that falls within the sphere of Hyannis, all of which belongs to Barnstable township? No need to get tongue-tied over all this—just find your way down to Craigville Beach, the largest beach on the south Cape. The water is as calm as a birdbath, the view over the bay is unobstructed and there is plenty of sand to spread out on. Parking is $3 per day.

Mashpee

"Industrial Lots Are Available" bragged the sign on Route 28, just inside the historic town of Mashpee. There used to be Indians around here somewhere, the Massipees by name. Their ranks were thinned by European diseases, and they were run off the lands they had farmed from antiquity. Today, the descendants of the Massipee tribe continue to sue for land rights, demanding their return. Fat chance of that; among other things, a 2,000-acre resort complex is harvesting a new crop—tourist wampum—and the whole vulgar sprawl along Route 28 from Falmouth to Mashpee to Hyannis is mocked by the cretinous grins of giant seahorses, cowboys, Pilgrims, lobsters and—ugh—Indians. There is, sur-prisingly, a nice, unspoiled beach off the beaten path of Route 28. Take the Great Neck Road from the Mashpee Rotary. Your pot of gold at the end of the road is South Cape Beach. Again, parking costs $3 a day.

Falmouth
Woods Hole

The town of Falmouth is the second largest on Cape Cod. Bar-tholomew Gosnold arrived here on March 23, 1602; it is the first place Englishmen landed in the New World. (Seems like we've heard that one before, or 10,000 variations upon it.) In any event, the British explorer named it after the port of Falmouth, from which he had set sail. The area was settled later in the century by Quakers, who farmed the land. With the rise of whaling in the 1800s, Falmouth became many a stalwart sea captain's home base; a number of their houses survive. As whaling declined, a flood of proper Bostonians streamed in this direction, finding the woods and bays of Falmouth to make a commodious summering place. The imprint of their wealth is etched upon the town, which is a pretty one to walk or bike around. There are bike paths and a village green, old homes and the museums of the Falmouth Historical Society.

If you walk, bike or drive from Falmouth to nearby Woods Hole, you'll find quite a different village—one that makes its living not from recycled history but from the most progressive scientific inquiry. Woods Hole is the home of the Woods Hole Oceanographic Institute, the Marine Biological Laboratory and the Northeast Fisheries Center. You'll also find the *Island Queen*—the popular ferry that makes a dozen round trips a day (in season) between Woods Hole and Martha's Vineyard, 6 miles away. To cap it all, there are beaches: Old Silver Beach, which faces Buzzards Bay from North Falmouth, and Surf Drive Beach, where Mill Road deadends into Surf Drive in downtown Falmouth. Parking is $5 at Old Silver, $4 at Surf Drive.

FOR FURTHER INFORMATION

Falmouth Chamber of Commerce
Academy Lane
Falmouth, Massachusetts 02540
(617) 548-8500

New Bedford

With a population pushing 100,000, New Bedford is a prosperous New England city and the gateway to Cape Cod. Fishing and textiles are the major industries—the largest fishing fleet on the

East Coast is headquartered here—but tourism figures into the town's life as well. The main attractions are the cobblestoned streets and restored sea captains' houses of the town's *Historic Waterfront District*. At one time, New Bedford was the whaling capital of the country. The story is told at the enormous *Whaling Museum*, a seven-building complex on Johnny Cake Hill. Indeed, you can't get away from reminders of whaling days. A pedestrian mall is named Melville Mall, in honor of the author who commenced his whaling epic *Moby Dick* in New Bedford. As barbaric as whale hunting seems in hindsight, some peculiarly romantic notions survive regarding the rugged masculinity of those who lived to harpoon these huge, beautiful creatures. However indirectly, whaling continues to fuel the economy of New Bedford, even though it no longer lights the lamps.

There is a municipal bathing beach in New Bedford, at the foot of *Hazelwood Park*, and one can swim in Buzzards Bay at the small beach out at Fort Phoenix Beach State Reservation, east of New Bedford in the neighboring town of Fairhaven.

FOR FURTHER INFORMATION

Bristol County Tourist Information Office
70 North Second Street
New Bedford, Massachusetts 02744
(617) 997-1250

Nantucket Island

Nantucket! Take out your map and look at it. See what a real corner of the world it occupies; how it stands there, away off shore, more lonely than the Eddystone Lighthouse. Look at it—a mere hillock, an elbow of sand; all beach without a background.

When Herman Melville wrote this passage in *Moby Dick*, he had not yet visited Nantucket. Perhaps the island he described is the one that any man of the sea might have imagined upon staring at a map in 1850. In any case, it still holds true today that the island can seem more lonely than the Eddystone Lighthouse, though not entirely for the reasons that Herman, in his imaginative zeal, conjectured. Read on.

> *The Nantucketer, he alone resides and riots on the sea . . . to and fro ploughing it as his own special plantation.*

In Melville's famous novel—disparaged upon its publication, a required-reading classic today—the narrator ("call me Ishmael") first came to Nantucket Island along with his savage buddy, Queequeg, to book passage on a whaling ship. Being tender of feet, the unlikely pair did not book reservations ahead of time. They were not punished for this oversight—one of the few advantages of being young and impulsive in 1850—and after a brisk stroll through the main harbor town, they managed to secure room and board of a sort. The "board" prompted Ishmael to query, "Queequeg, do you think we can make supper for us both on one clam?" As for the room, the only stipulation their innkeeper made was that Queequeg not take his whale harpoon to bed with him. Should Herman or even Ishmael arrive in Nantucket today with no prearranged plans for room and board, however, they might want to carry their big buddy's harpoon along to defend themselves. Nowadays, historic Nantucket is really two islands in one: the whaling port of Melville's musings, where scrub trees grow out of sandy soil and the Atlantic beats relentlessly on the eastern shore; and then, the latter-day resort where, instead of harpooning whales, they harpoon tourists.

> *For the sea is his; he owns it, as Emperors own empires; other seamen having but a right of way through it.*

As you enter sleepy Nantucket Harbor aboard the ferry from the mainland (either Hyannis or Woods Hole), you can almost hear the town gear up for the next boatload of traveler's checks. The gift shops tidy up their whale memorabilia, the ice-cream parlors stack up new piles of sugar cones, the chef tests the temperature of the deep-fat fryer by tossing in a sacrificial clam. You feel, in short, as any newcomer does in an unfamiliar or exotic spot, that you are "just off the boat," marked instantly as an off-islander. This is the Scarlet Letter you will carry around with you for the duration of your stay.

For instance, the brain trust of Nantucket likes to discourage people from bringing their cars. They don't prohibit it outright, but they make it prohibitively costly. Not only is ferrying your car over from Hyannis expensive ($47.50 one way), but spaces aboard the boat are as rare as whale's teeth. This supply-demand imbalance prompts the handwritten pleas you read on all the island bulletin boards, e.g., "Wanted, one car reservation for Aug. 29." So, not wishing to rock the boat and/or with no alternative, you pay to leave your car in a Hyannis parking lot (run by the same Steamship Authority that operates the ferries, and costing $4.50 a day) and come to Nantucket fully expecting a reasonable island mass-transportation system.

Not necessarily. You are greeted by a town stuffed with private cars and gas fumes and very little viable alternative transportation. To be sure, there is a bus system, but it runs sporadically and doesn't go to every corner of the island. There are mopeds, available for a whopping $30 per day, and ten-speed bicycles that rent for $15 daily, but try riding the cobblestones for a few hours, and then attempt to do anything that requires standing. (For the same money, a rental car might be a better bet—particularly if you're traveling with someone.) Before you can even digest all this, however, contemplate that you and your mate have already spent $41 just to get here ($32 round-trip ferry fare for two, plus $9.00 to park your car on the mainland for two days). Soon enough, the message becomes clear: the Nantucket they want you to see is not the island, but the town that's spread out before the ferry landing: cobblestoned, restored, dripping with designer quaintness and jet-set money, overphotographed, overrun . . . yet more lonely than the Eddystone Lighthouse. Most visitors are trapped here like fish in a barrel, whether they know it or not.

Not that there aren't things worth seeing in Nantucket. The *Whaling Museum* is a fitting memorial to Nantucket's Golden Age, when the oil taken from the big critters lit up the homes of the world. The streets of Nantucket, as it recedes from the waterfront, beg to be explored on foot. For instance, a hike up the hilly cobblestoned streets to the *South Church* (built in 1809, it houses the town clock) is a good way to get the blood circulating. Even today, nautical charts still cite it as a navigation guide for ships approaching America, and the community continues to use it as a meeting place. As you approach the church, you cannot help but notice the surrounding buildings, so magisterial in their centuries-old grandeur. Should you be capable of closing your mind to the clothes boutiques and balloon shops for one glorious moment, you can imagine yourself bumping into Queequeg with his harpoon, on his way down to the harbor.

> . . . [T]hat they wear quicksand shoes . . . that they are so shut up, belted about, every way inclosed, surrounded and made an utter island by the ocean.

All this brings up a curious phenomenon that we noticed not only in Nantucket, but on islands and coastal enclaves along the whole Atlantic Coast: the "burn the bridges" mentality. Often a group of early and regular visitors claim to "discover" a place, and then, when the multitudes begin to storm the ramparts for a looksee, this band of originals (who, in their minds, have by now created a distinct "way of life") will adopt an attitude of aloofness and even outright hostility toward "outsiders." They, in fact, come to think of themselves in all seriousness as the real, true natives of a place. These people—usurpers themselves—will actually refer to themselves as natives, though the only thing that separates them from the tourists whose infestations they despise is that they, at least in the case of a summering place like Nantucket, have been around since May and not since last Monday.

We heard disdainful and condescending comments from the likes of college kids, who were working on the island as summer help, yet who seemed to believe they were as native as the Indians. Meanwhile, the unflappable tourists, with whom we began to feel a *soupçon* of sympathy, are creating the economic base that supports this snooty young party society.

No, Nantucket is not "inclosed" anymore, nor surrounded and

made an utter island. Rare indeed is the true Nantucketer. Although the well-ensconced New York/Palm Beach set would love to see the day when it was possible, they alone cannot support 54 guesthouses, 19 hotels, 17 variety stores, 16 clothing shops, 15 antique stores, 12 gift shops, 6 basket shops, 5 jewelers, 5 caterers and 1 perfumer.

One Nantucket hotel owner, whose rambling inn is located in the hard-to-reach community of Wauwinet, put it this way: "Without the tourists, this island would be like the Falklands. . . . Maybe the college kids could learn to raise a few sheep."

But these extravaganzas only show that Nantucket is no Illinois.

Luckily, however, this is a bigger island than you might think, an "elbow of sand" that is 15 miles long and 8 miles wide. There are four or five other communities tucked into hidden corners of the island, away from the port of entry. There are also hills, valleys, ponds, moors, cranberry bogs and exceptional beaches— 88 miles of the latter. The most crowded public beach is Jetties Beach, because of its accessibility to the town of Nantucket, the lifeguard and facilities provided and the safer waters of Nantucket Sound. Less populous and equally tame is Dionis, on the north shore.

For the surf-lover, there are spectacular ocean beaches on the south side of the island. These include Nobadeer (most popular with teenagers), Surfside and Cisco. Much of the coastline outside the town of Nantucket is utterly isolated and begs to be wandered for the sensation Melville described—"all beach without a background"—the dunes, the ocean, the sky, and only you and an occasional gull to witness it.

Accommodations

The vast majority of accommodations on the island are located in the town of Nantucket. An extraordinary number of them are bed-and-breakfast inns in old whaling-captains' homes and so forth. It should come as no surprise, however, that they are not giving away rooms here—$50 for a room is about the rock-bottom lowest price we found anywhere, and most places are dramatically higher than that. The room tariff often comes freighted with stipulations, too, such as four- or five-day minimum stays, in season. All reservations should be booked well in advance, for July and August particularly. For guidance and reservations, *Nantucket Accommodations*, at (617) 228-9559, is well worth a call. The chamber of commerce operates an information bureau on Federal Street that can help orient you about the island. Camping, incidentally, is allowed nowhere on Nantucket.

Should you want to see the island in all its unspoiled isolation, far from the maddening crowd and all that, there are alternatives. The *Wauwinet House* is one, and it's as isolated an establishment as one will find 'twixt Maine and Key West. A self-described "country inn by the sea, away from the bustle of town, overlooking the beaches and the bay," it is located on the eastern shore of Nantucket in the "community" of Wauwinet—a community so small as to be fictional, like Lake Wobegon. The inn is 9 miles away from town on a strip of land, with Nantucket Harbor on one side and the Atlantic Ocean on the other. It is so far out that the owner advises careful cogitation before planning a vacation here. Without a car, it is a $10 cab ride into town (and $10 back), and once you are here, you are not going to be wandering far, unless you suddenly sprout a beak and a pair of wings. But there is sailing and tennis, and enough solitude on the beach to placate Thoreau, if this is what you are seeking. Once a stunning, celebrated resort complex that catered to the sailboat crowd, the hotel—which has been in continuous operation since 1896—does show its age. It is not an exclusive luxury hotel now, but a reasonably comfortable one whose rooms, though a bit dingy, have lots of character. The real key, however, is the setting: empty stretches of shore, nature at its most unblemished, and elemental silence.

Restaurants

For welcome relief from the classic stylings of gourmet Nantucket, the locals troop to several less-hurrahed restaurants, most notably the *Atlantic Café* (or, more succinctly, "AC") and the *Brotherhood*, the latter a pleasant bit of funkiness (good sandwiches and drinks) in a sailor's-bar setting. Of the more well-heeled spots, *The Second Story* has quickly earned a following, and *Obadiah's* is the first choice for seafood. Obadiah's is located in the home of a merchant-ship owner, Captain Nickerson by name, built in 1847. The prices are fairly reasonable, too. Another restaurant in an old-inn setting is the *Jared Coffin House*. They have a fairly simple soup-and-sandwiches lunch menu, and more specialized fare at dinnertime. (They also rent rooms; theirs is one of the finest and fairest of the inns on Nantucket.)

Try the quahog chowder, by all means, wherever you go. (*Quahog* is the anglicization of the Indian word for "clam"; they really do seem bigger out here on Nantucket. Howard Johnson, eat your heart out.) And then there is the other side of Nantucket dining—places with names like *The Chanticleer* and *The Opera House*. At the latter, omelettes were being hawked for seven bucks a throw. Chances are, if you are able to meet such prices without flinching, you wouldn't be reading this book in the first place. So take our advice—brave the crowds at *The Downyflake* for breakfast, and save your seven bills for something more cost-effective than a plate of eggs.

Nightlife

On this historic island, you will occasionally hear references to something called a Nantucket sleigh ride, a phenomenon from whaling days: after being harpooned, a sperm whale would attempt to get away from the pain in his ass by making a deep dive. In the process, he invariably would drag the boat, like a reluctant water skier, behind him. This "sleigh ride" ended when the whale was exhausted or the boat capsized.

Presently, after a full day's "sleigh ride" of touring Nantucket, the exhausted visitor can come up for air in one of several places. Live rock 'n' roll can be harpooned at the *Chicken Box*, on Dave Street. It's as good a spot as any to see the islanders, mostly the well-groomed college-kid population that works summers here, let their hair down and get wild. In addition to that element, the Chicken Box attracts "anything from teenyboppers to island dirt-balls," according to our cab driver, a college boy who bragged of having taken acid the night before and then nearly rear-ended us into a station wagon a heartbeat later.

As for mingling with the golden goddesses from Vassar or the bronze Adonises from Yachtland USA, you can hang your shingle at the *Rose and Crown* (conveniently located across the street from the police station) or *The Muse* (where those who aren't at the Rose and Crown go, and vice versa). Finally, if you hang around the docks after-hours or meet the right people at the bars, you might bluff your way onto a yacht or sailboat party—in which case, scrounge up a pair of Docksiders and a rugby shirt and leap aboard, mate. If you laugh enough in all the right places, who knows: you might get a Nantucket sleigh ride you never bargained for.

FOR FURTHER INFORMATION

Nantucket Chamber of Commerce
25 Federal Street
Nantucket Island, Massachusetts 02554
(617) 228-0925

Martha's Vineyard

It costs just 25 cents for the ferry from Manhattan to Staten Island, which is said to be one of the last bargains left in the civilized world—but when you get across the water, you are on Staten Island. It costs $3.75 for the ferry to Martha's Vineyard—but when you get across the waters of Nantucket Sound, you are in heaven. That is not just a bargain. That is a godsend.

And, like heaven, Martha's Vineyard seems larger than life, or its modest dimensions, because of all the stories, the myths and the geological diversity that exists here. Martha's bodily statistics varied with each source we checked; having neglected to bring surveying equipment ourselves, we settled for round numbers.

Roughly, the island is 20 miles long and 10 miles wide, and, like a compact fantasy world, she possesses a little bit of everything within her borders: rolling hills, glimmering ponds, fields of hay and horses, deep forests and multicolored cliffs. The people who come here are a varied lot, too, from the beer-guzzling fishermen Down Island to the rare-vintage Burgundy sniffers Up Island. Contrary to popular myth, Martha's Vineyard is not all James Taylor lookalikes and/or Yuppie overachievers battering their Gold Cards.

Before there was an American Express, or even an America, there were Brits roaming around Martha's Vineyard and adjoining islands. As early as 1602, they came. Under the provenance of one Captain Bartholomew Gosnald, the first English settlement in New England was established, in fact, on what is now Cuttyhunk Island—the next hunk of rock down from Martha's in the chain of sixteen islands known as the Elizabeth Islands. Martha's Vineyard was originally christened *Martin's Vineyard*, after one of the members of Gosnald's crew. Luckless Martin lost out to history on that one, as the name and gender of the Vineyard were changed to Martha by Thomas Mayhew, a member of the Court of Massachusetts who made the deal of the century. For an alleged $200, Mayhew purchased both Nantucket and Martha's Vineyard, plus the smaller surrounding islands. The legality of the sale was challenged, however, and the citizens of Martha's Vineyard disputed both Mayhew's and Massachusetts' claim over their sovereignty in any aspect. Yet eventually Mayhew was accorded the title "governor for life" of Martha's Vineyard. The "Martha" in question, incidentally, was either his daughter or wife—the facts of the case are hazy.

Returning to the heaven metaphor, Martha's Vineyard is not necessarily for everyone. Some hell can be raised here, but it is not the kind that leaves unaccountable bruises on the body and mind or even, for that matter, the wallet. Most people who come to the island come often, quietly renting houses or cottages summer after summer for a week or more at a time. The wealthier residents who are more or less full-timers—the island is virtually uninhabitable during the winter, when cold temperatures and gale-force tempests pummel the place—tend to live Up Island. The term

"Up Island," in native parlance, signifies the hilly western end, away from the tourist centers of Edgartown, Oak Bluffs and Vineyard Haven. The island, which is mostly flat, rises at its northwestern extremity, near the townships of Chilmark and Gay Head, to heights of 200 and 300 feet. And then the cliffs abruptly drop down to the sea—an impressive and picturesque sight.

Generally the Up Islander can be identified on sight as that very natural-looking person who is frequently heard to intone the island's sanctified nickname—"the Vineyard"—much the same way that a New Yorker will, when homesick or flustered in some backwater social situation, refer misty-eyed to Manhattan as "the City." But even for the folks who do not belong to this clique, there are ways to get to know Martha's Vineyard without feeling (as on Nantucket) as if you should crawl on your belly like a reptile at the ferry landing to beg forgiveness from the locals for your tourist garb and manners. First of all, the island is set only 7 miles off the coast of Cape Cod, and on clear days you do not lose sight of this fact. The sense of isolation is not so intense as on Nantucket, and the ferry ride is not so expensive.

Ferries leave from Hyannis, Falmouth, Woods Hole and New Bedford on the Massachusetts mainland, and cost $3.75 one-way per passenger and $30 each way per car. Only the Woods Hole ferries provide car passage, and you should phone way in advance (like one lifetime) for reservations. The Steamship Authority's number is (617) 540-2022. Should you park your car on the mainland you will discover upon landing in Vineyard Haven that the island has a viable shuttle-bus system that runs to the two Down Island population centers of Edgartown ($1.25) and Oak Bluffs (75 cents). Most hotels and inns are located in these three towns, and the buses make a car fairly unnecessary, unless you are counting on doing some Up Island exploring or want to hang out at Carly Simon's nightclub. The latter is located mid-island near the airport, more accessible to Lear jets from Nova Scotia than Okies from Muskogee on bicycles.

Bus tours are the best way to see how the other side lives. Regular jaunts that circumnavigate the island for upwards of 2½ hours cost but $5.50 and are led by Vineyard natives who have lifetime love affairs with the place. These trips are a quick-and-dirty way to get a handle on the land and its inhabitants. The list of residents who own the palatial Down Island harborfront homes and those who maintain the expensive wooded properties in and around the Up Island communities begins to smack of a Hollywood Who's Who tour. Jackie O., William Styron, Patricia Neal, Ruth Gordon, James, Carly and John Belushi (yes, his grave was pointed out) are but a handful of the names dropped relentlessly by the tour guide.

By the time you get to Gay Head, however, you are in Indian country. That is to say, this land was once a reservation for the Wampanoag tribe, and the remaining Indians here—about 125 families, most of whom have intermarried with white islanders— decided to incorporate as a town. Even more boldly, they now wish to sue for the worth of the whole island (which, given the net assets of all the celebrity landowners, is probably more than the national budget). However, our avuncular tour guide was quick to reassure everyone on the bus that the Indians would peacefully settle for the 500 acres they have been offered in compromise. Once clear of the Gay Head area, he then launched into a string of mildly derogatory Indian jokes that would have turned Bob Hope green, including one with the memorable punch line, "He drowned in his own tea pee."

Bicyclists are in their glory on Martha's Vineyard. Bike paths connect the Big Three towns Down Island (Edgartown, Oak Bluffs, Vineyard Haven), and an amazing 125 miles of bike trails wind their way through the State Forest. A bicycle can be brought over on the ferry for an extra $2.50, or can be rented from any number of places on the island. Finally, for those disinclined to pedal, there is the moped. Several outlets rent them for around $20 a day. Many people ride them, and everyone who lives here hates them. 'Nuff said.

Then there are the beaches. The northern and eastern sides of the island—which front Vineyard Sound and Nantucket Sound, respectively—offer protected, calm-water swimming. Oak Bluffs Town Beach runs a short distance from jetty to jetty. While rocky and strewn with debris, it's an okay place to unroll your beach towel for a few hours of sun. If you're going to make a day of it, head on down to the State Beach, which runs for several miles between Oak Bluffs and Edgartown. *Jaws* was filmed here, and they'll never let you forget it. The beach is narrow but long, and people park along the side of the road. There is a small harbor beach, Lighthouse Beach, at Starbuck's Neck in Edgartown. And over on Chappaquiddick, there's East Beach at Cape Pogue.

The south side of the island gets the full force of the Atlantic, and so, needless to say, the best beaches run along the island's nearly straight, 20-mile south edge. Unfortunately, much of this stretch is either privately owned or accessible only to residents of specific townships. Lucy Vincent Beach, for instance, has a much-vaunted reputation as a nude beach, but it is technically off-limits to all but Chilmark residents. Skinny dippers flock here, however, and they can't all live in Chilmark, so you can draw your own conclusions. The beaches at West Tisbury, Lambert's Cove, Squibnocket, Gay Head and Lobsterville are similarly semiprivate. But just south of Edgartown, on the Katama Road, lies Katama Beach (a.k.a. South Beach)—3 miles of ocean-fronting barrier beach that is ample compensation for having been denied access elsewhere.

Moving clockwise around the island, up along the north shore, there are three public beaches. Menemsha Public Beach is located just around the Gay Head cliffs at the western end of the island. It is quite scenic—maybe the loveliest public beach on the island— as it fronts the cool, clear waters of Vineyard Sound. And back near the top of the island, in the vicinity of Vineyard Haven, are a pair of harbor beaches—at Lake Tashmoo and Owen Park—that are open to all.

As for the towns on the island, all the action seems to be in Edgartown and Oak Bluffs. Vineyard Haven has the best harbor on the island and is where some of the tourist boats arrive, but most everyone heads over to the eastern shore. Edgartown remains one of New England's most elegant communities. It is one of the great yachting centers of the world, and row upon row of well-preserved captains' houses make it an architecturalist's delight. It also has an aura of permanence from its more or less year-round population that one doesn't feel in rowdier Oak Bluffs. In Edgartown, for instance, a battle was brewing as residents were attempting to ban tour buses from their streets. Since the buses do nothing more than pass through town in what is an almost un-avoidable route, given the circuitous nature of the tour, this seemed an extreme reaction—a typical hoarding of privacy in the New England tradition.

Oak Bluffs, which is where we headquartered ourselves while on Martha's Vineyard, came to life as the Siamese Twin of Edgartown back in the 1800s and has since developed along very different lines. Originally founded by Methodists in 1835 as a site for camp meetings, Oak Bluffs was a temporary tent community that grew into something more permanent. Year by year, the canvas walls of the tents gave way to sturdier cottages of wood, and the austere spirit of Methodism yielded to a more freewheeling lifestyle. In the end, the Methodists could not contain the fundamental human need to enjoy, not deny, the pleasure-giving and uplifting things in the material world that God created—particularly in a place as paradisiacal as Martha's Vineyard.

In 1880, Oak Bluffs became autonomous from Edgartown. Unlike Edgartown and Vineyard Haven, Oak Bluffs had no centuries-old tradition of whaling and other maritime trades. As the emphasis swung from spiritual to secular, Oak Bluffs became the playground of Martha's Vineyard. Today, rest and relaxation are the big drawing cards. Oak Bluffs is, in the summer, the largest town on the Vineyard, with a population that swells to 20,000.

Architecturally, parts of Oak Bluffs look like something out of *Hansel and Gretel*. The first revivalist visitors to throw up sturdier housing constructed cottages built to look like gingerbread houses out of a child-fable fantasy. These "gingerbread cottages" survive in all their multicolored glory, set as close together as bowling pins and painted and trimmed in various candy-colored schemes, like dollhouses. They are impeccably maintained, and to this day look good enough to eat (especially if you're sick of seafood). Particularly impressive are the cottages that rim the outdoor tabernacle on the Grand Circle.

By way of summing up this varied and versatile island, there is much to be seen (beaches, forests, towns, cliffs, ponds and harbors), as well as many places to be seen at (nightclubs, gourmet restaurants, nude beaches). The best part of all is that you can choose your own road, spend as much or as little as you want and, regardless of the kind of vacation or visit you design, one thing will be certain: once you get here, you will find it hard to leave.

Accommodations

As it is in Nantucket, many people flock to Martha's Vineyard during the summer for longer than a weekend or even a week. Some live here in summer homes, while a younger population works the entire season at the inns and restaurants. The permanent population of 9,000 grows to 50,000 after Memorial Day. There is a heavy bias toward long-term seasonal rentals, but there are ample options for visits of shorter duration as well—e.g., inns and rental homes and cottages. So that you don't get stuck like Gilligan on the island, utilize one of the central reservation services—either Martha's Vineyard Reservations at (617) 693-4111, or Island Reservation Service at (617) 693-5300, will set you up with a confirmed reservation. And write ahead for a copy of the local chamber of commerce's visitor's guide, titled *The Island of Martha's Vineyard*. For ferry fares, schedules and reservations, contact the Steamship Authority at (617) 540-2022, or write the Steamship Authority, Woods Hole, Cape Cod, Massachusetts 02543.

If you are planning to rent a house, try for something Up Island and bring (or rent) a car. The isolation is worth it, but you will have to get there first, and eventually you will want (or need) to make forays Down Island. If you wish to stay Down Island, you can do no better than an inn or hotel in Edgartown or Oak Bluffs. *Point Way Inn*, for instance, is one of many affordable inns in historic Edgartown—a renovated 1830 captain's house with working fireplaces and a free continental breakfast.

The *Wesley House*, in Oak Bluffs, deserves special mention. This ancient hotel, painted yellow, dominates the Oak Bluffs harborfront. Built in 1879 to house the spillover from the nearby Methodist camp-meeting grounds, the Wesley House is basically unchanged from those days, save for an in-lobby color television set. Filled with stuffed couches and old magazines, the lobby is as comfortable as Grandma's drawing room, and from the front porch, which is lined with rocking chairs, one may stare out over the harbor in idle reverie. The Wesley House is run by a disarmingly ebullient man, Paul Chase, who is a Martha's Vineyard perennial and something of a head cheerleader for the island. Sporting a crew cut and a bola string tie, and displaying the warm grace and hospitable manner of a country preacher, Mr. Chase is a fifth-generation owner of the Wesley House and a man who loves his roots on the island. There are buckets of water in the hallways for "fire security," the floors creak and sag a bit, and many windows go screenless, but seldom will you find such overall comfort in the most important sense, as in peace of mind and relaxed contentment. If you need to get up early, for instance, Mr. Chase will pull a shoe box out from under the counter and let you choose an alarm clock from it. This is the sort of touch that defines the homespun informality of the Wesley House.

Restaurants

There is a variety of dining opportunities available on Martha's Vineyard, from fine French cuisine to firemen's fish fries. For instance, there are many Up Island restaurants of distinction: the *Beach Plum Inn* in Menemsha specializes in nouvelle cuisine, *Lambert's Cove Country Inn* in West Tisbury is set snugly in a vine-covered farmhouse, and *La Grange* in Chilmark emphasizes dining in the French *provençal* style. All also feature large dinner crowds, so make reservations. There are Down Island restaurants of equal rank, most notably *Chez Pierre* in Edgartown. Moving down from those upscale heights, there are numerous places of merit that don't stand on ceremony to that degree—e.g., the *Ocean Club* and the *Black Dog Tavern*, both in Vineyard Haven, and both quite popular. Expect to queue up for a little while if you come at the height of the dinner hour. Oak Bluffs offers casual dining somewhere on a scale midway between Vineyard Haven and Edgartown. For seafood, try the *Ocean View Restaurant* or *David's Island House*. And we can't get away without mentioning a local institution, the *Edgartown Delicatessen*—an inexpensive, locally popular hangout.

A few more bits of information that might help you plan your dinner itinerary: the buses stop running at 11 P.M., and you can order alcohol only in Oak Bluffs and Edgartown restaurants.

Nightlife

Carly Simon's *Hot Tin Roof* nightclub is the place to go; there's virtually no competition. Located at Martha's Vineyard Airport, off the Edgartown-West Tisbury Road, the place is acrawl with beautiful people. Depending on the night you go, there can be deejays, live rock bands, comedy acts and jazz, reggae and pop music. Saturday is the designated dancing night. Don't expect to see the Ramones perform here, but the *Hot Tin Roof* is as *chaud* as this little island gets.

Meanwhile, back in Oak Bluffs, there are bars along Circuit Street to be ducked into. Sometimes the crowds can be pretty lowlife; at one dive, we were whacked across the calves with a metal crutch while picking tunes at the jukebox. Our assailant was a legless biker trying, in his subtle way, to get our attention. His request—"Play 'Outlaw Man' by the Eagles"—came out more like an order, and we didn't disobey. Other times, the bars are more civilized. One particularly commended bar/restaurant is *David's Island House*. But in general, the password on Martha's Vineyard is "mellow." When down in Edgartown, angle on over to the *Square Rigger*, a good watering hole.

Somehow fittingly, Arlo Guthrie was playing when we were in town, at the outdoor tabernacle in Oak Bluffs where the Methodists formerly held their camp meetings. The spirit of Guthrie's music, with its roots in the counterculture sixties, burns on in the alternative-lifestyle preferences of the many Vineyard inhabitants (read: hippies) who turned out to catch the concert on this warm summer night. The message hit home when a puff of wind carried the singalong chorus of Guthrie's signature tune, "Alice's Restaurant" (the hippie Magna Carta), into our hotel-room window. Some things never change.

Martha's Vineyard is, all in all, not a wild place. Except for Edgartown and Oak Bluffs, the island is, in fact, dry of alcohol. So settle back on a porch rocker with a bottle of Vine—a native bottled drink made of carbonated well water and a splash of natural grape flavoring—and watch the sun go down. If you must—well, okay, walk into town and get that ice-cream cone you've been craving ever since you shoveled down that plate of fried oysters. But pick carefully! There are over twenty-five flavors to choose from—and forget about sundaes. . . .

FOR FURTHER INFORMATION

Martha's Vineyard Chamber of Commerce
Beach Road
Vineyard Haven, Massachusetts 02568
(617) 693-0085

Rhode Island:
Less Is More

In statehood, as in many areas of life, bigger is not necessarily better. Just ask the citizens of Rhode Island. Theirs is the smallest state in the union. You could fit 475 Rhode Islands inside one Alaska, and indeed there are many counties in America that can best Rhode Island's 1,214 square miles. But you won't find too many states with so admirable a historical record and such great geographical and industrial diversity.

Rhode Island was the thirteenth of the thirteen original colonies. It was founded by religious dissident Roger Williams, who sought to escape the austere severity of the Puritans. Williams was a free thinker who chartered Rhode Island as a place where one could believe, speak and act without censure. In sequence, the towns of Providence, Portsmouth, Newport and Warwick were founded between 1636 and 1642. In accordance with its feisty beginnings, the state of Rhode Island renounced its allegiance to the Crown two months *before* the Declaration of Independence was signed.

Rhode Island's nickname is "the Ocean State." Here again, size and appearance are deceptive. Though only 37 miles wide, Rhode Island has 500 miles of shoreline indenting the Narragansett Bay and fronting Rhode Island and Block Island Sounds. For a tiny state, you've got a remarkable breadth of vacation opportunities. There's wealthy Newport, upon whose headlands the biggest names in America built Brobdingnagian mansions. Today, prestigious

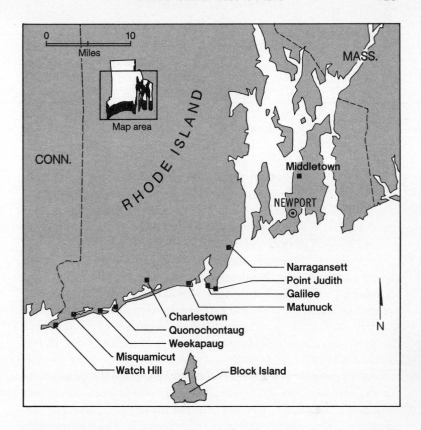

tennis tournaments, yacht races and jazz festivals draw folks to Newport. Along the South Shore, from Narragansett to Watch Hill, is a string of regular barrier-island beaches. And 9 miles out to sea, there's Block Island, a beautiful island that, on the map, looks like a stepping-stone between the end of Long Island and Martha's Vineyard.

A storybook island, great beaches, a moneyed resort—and the Rhode Island Red hen, a breed of chicken developed by Rhode Island farmers. What more could anyone ask of a state?

Newport

We had just crossed the giant suspension bridge that ushers traffic into Newport, Rhode Island, when we noticed our first license plate. It was from Palm Beach, Florida, and it was attached to the formidable, barge-sized automobile we found ourselves tailgating after disengaging our humble compact from the jaws of the bridge and Route 138. Gulp. The next thing we spied was a stray dog— a pedigreed fox terrier, to be precise, strutting nonchalantly down the sidewalk by Farewell Street. Big gulp. Our third sight, after parking on a cobblestoned side street, was a nun purchasing $16 worth of placemat-sized postcards from a gift shop. As if overcome by a sudden wave of guilt or the need to explain, she turned to us and said, "I'm only going to be here one day."

Welcome to Newport, home of yachts and mansions, tennis lawns and Kool jazz. Summer home of corporate presidents and chairmen of the board and snobby blue-blooded DAR socialites. Winter home of . . . a skeleton staff of domestics. You know, those cavernous mansions are such a headache to heat in the winter, and besides, there's polo to be played down in sunny Palm Beach. Tally ho!

Yes, Newport comes with its own prepackaged image of exclusivity. The town boosters go to great lengths to promote its affluent past and ritzy/trendy present ("See the mansions on Bellevue Avenue. . . . Drive along private Ocean Drive"), while losing sight of the equally engaging side of Newport that does not trade upon snob appeal. For while it is true that the pastel-lipped crowd can be seen here in the summer, Newport is *not* Palm Beach. Above and beyond the lure of wealth, Newport is a well-rounded, full-blown American town—no more, no less and no different, in many ways.

And so our initial impressions were mitigated by a flood of other images, gathered over the course of a three-day visit—images of tired, tattooed men dragging home after a day of pulling at the fish nets; a man walking down Broadway at night with a bag of groceries in one hand and a baseball bat in the other; a mob of chattering kids spilling out of an old brick fortress of a high school at the last bell; the legend "Remember Duane Allman" spray-painted on the cement wall behind First Beach; the quiet suburban neighborhood known as Purgatory Chasm, barely a mile from the "stately mansions" . . . and so on.

It is certainly understandable why Newport would choose to emphasize its glamorous past. When the U.S. Navy began pulling out of the area in 1973, tourism had to be dragged into port to replace the lost revenue. Despite its glittery heritage, the town fell on hard times for a while. Even the jazz festivals, yacht races and tennis tourneys couldn't do the job alone. The town had to cultivate tourism, but it presented a tricky proposition—how to entice people by flaunting vast wealth without making them feel too poor to come here.

Which leads to the fourth thing we saw (in fact, *ate*) in Newport that first day: a hearty breakfast at a fancy restaurant on one of the poshest blocks in town that cost us each a thoroughly reasonable $2.50. In other words, Newport is affordable.

The road we were on is known as Thames Street, pronounced phonetically (not "Temz") by the locals, perhaps a deliberate and lingering snub of the British. Invariably, you will be directed to Thames Street by the guidebooks and brochures, which you will have dutifully picked up at the eager-to-please chamber of commerce information center, centrally located on a street with the fancified name of America's Cup Avenue.

If you read the literature closely, you'll learn that Newport has had two vastly different pasts. Newport was founded in 1639 by dissidents who broke away from the original colony of Providence, which itself was founded by dissidents who'd fled ascetic Puritanism. The original inhabitants of Newport were double dissidents, so to speak. Soon enough, Newport became a booming seaport, one of the busiest in the colonies. Some of the churches, mills and homes from that era are among the oldest buildings still standing in America. Recommended for a visit are the *Touro Synagogue* (the oldest synagogue in America), *Trinity Church* (built in 1726, and in continuous use since), the *Quaker Meeting House* and the *Old Stone Mill*, a mysterious tower of stone believed by some scholars (and a few dimwits) to have been built by Vikings.

The scam that brought Newport to its preeminence as a seaport was known as the Triangle Trade, an infamous and lucrative setup whereby African slaves were traded for West Indian sugar and molasses to be used in the manufacture of Newport rum. The rummy port of Newport thus attracted all manner of mankind and mayhem, a legacy that has not entirely disappeared to this day. The city's symbol is the pineapple, as unlikely as that might seem in New England. (Pineapples were another prime item of trade that arrived from the West Indies.) The seaport, alas, went out of business when the British occupied the harbor in 1776. Their blockade lasted for four years. The wharves were destroyed, the wood was burned in fireplaces, and the sailor boys scattered to the four winds.

Newport's second past began years later, in the late 1800s, when some of the most powerful men in America began summering here, building seasonal homes in exaggerated imitation of their European forebears. The French courts of the various and sundry Louises seem to have been the prevailing models of choice. This period has become known as the Era of the 400. Today, you can tour these architectural fossils from Newport's second heyday. There are more such tours than you could possibly care to take, in fact, especially if you eschew the crammed bus/loudspeaker/roped corridor style of touring. These mansion tours, in particular, smack of a Six Flags Production, perhaps "Lifestyles of the Rich, Famous and Deceased."

Well, there's always the vaunted *Cliff Walk*, a self-guided trail that runs along the outer perimeter of most of the Bellevue Avenue mansions, between the cyclone fences and the sea down below. You can see the Breakers, the Château-Sur-Mer, Rosecliff, et al., from a legal distance. You can also see the fortress mentality in the barbed wire and signs that say things like: "Warning! This Area Patrolled by Trained Attack Dogs."

The 3-mile Cliff Walk was designated a National Historical Landmark in 1976 and has since been restored by the Cliff Walk Committee (Claus Von Bulow, chairman). Parts of the path, however, are in such disrepair and other parts so nonexistent that walking it can be more of an adventure than hiking the Appalachian Trail. We made it, out of breath but safe, though toward the end—around Sheep Point and Land's End—we had our doubts. These two spots were virtually impassable, and for older people who have been misled by the guidebooks into thinking it's a pleasant little stroll in the country, the Cliff Walk is just plain dangerous. Oops. Over the edge and onto the rocks—splat. Enough of this, however, because it is a safe and scenic trail for the first mile or so, but walking the entire length of it is for the hale and hearty only.

Many of the beaches in the Newport area are private—e.g., Hazard's Beach, Bailey's Beach—and are not visible as you pass by them on Ocean Drive. Gooseberry Beach is an exception; it is open to the public for a parking fee of $4 on weekdays and $6 on weekends. The longest and widest stretch of sand—variously known as Newport Beach, First Beach and Easton's Beach, take your pick—is open to the public. It's located just beyond the head of the Cliff Walk on Route 138, between Newport and Middletown. Get there early on a hot summer day, because First Beach is one of the more popular places around Newport. Farther into Middletown, off Purgatory Road, lies Sachuest or Second Beach. (Once again, the choice is yours.) It has the only sand dunes in the area. Parking is limited and facilities are nil, making it and the other harbor beach around the corner—yup, Third Beach—more popular with the natives.

Accommodations

By driving around Newport and its outlying areas, you will soon realize that the budget motels are not a bargain and that the prevailing motif out there is Early Drive-In Theater (with *Friday the Thirteenth, Parts 7 Through 11*, playing). There is one exception—the *Seaview Motel* in Middletown, which boasts a panoramic view of the ocean and 40 nicely maintained rooms.

By retracing your steps to the chamber of commerce information center, you will soon learn that the best places to stay are the guesthouses and the bed-and-breakfast inns. The chamber keeps a running list of them, complete with up-to-the-minute availability and prices. Just by strolling in off the street, we obtained suitable lodgings for $30 in a retired navy couple's home. There are inns and guest homes all over Newport; ours was a 5-minute hop away in Middletown, a name that adequately describes the community. We were given our own key to their modest suburban split-level house, and we came and went as we pleased. Mostly went.

Because of the influx of visitors to Newport during various special events, it's often impossible to find a room here. You will want to book early or come midweek, even after Labor Day. Without previous arrangements, you might be left with no alternative but a triple-figure room in one of the corporate lodges. Or, you can always brave the barbed wire and trained attack dogs and camp out, like a piece of litter, on the far end of a castle lawn. Just don't call us from jail.

Restaurants

Everything you read is not true. Everything you are told is not true. Life is unfair. You can count on that. We were so misled, for instance, while trying to select a restaurant in Newport that a bad comedy shtick could be built around our visit to one place in particular: "Hey, the food was so bad we saw the roaches giving each other the Heimlich Maneuver. . . ."

Normally, we don't single out restaurants by name for damnation (we only do that to bad bars). But one restaurant we went to, on advice from more than one source, was so awful that it simply must be mentioned, if only to prove that reputations can be way out of whack with reality when it comes to almost every aspect of traveling.

So here goes.

Welcome aboard the *S.S. Newport*, ladies and gentlemen, the *only* floating restaurant in town, docked at Waite's Wharf, off Lower Thames Street. Lower Thames, we'd heard, was where you go for the best seafood at the lowest prices. The S.S. Newport was unanimously singled out for praise. Okay, ahoy, mateys, and off we went to board the S.S. Newport.

First of all, Waite's Wharf is a parking lot on one side and an industrial work area on the other, surrounded by rusted oil tanks straight out of Bayonne and wooden pallets straight out of the Big Red Furniture Barn. There was no menu posted at the gangplank entranceway. That's okay; we'd heard great things. After being seated, we saw that the menu was top heavy with tourist-trap fried food, not nearly as inviting as the Calabash-style seafood platters that dominate the Carolinas (down there, you *knows* what you's gettin'). The draft beer was warm, the waitress was forgetful (e.g., she forgot to return our credit card), and . . . we could go on and on nitpicking, but the bottom line is the food, right?

Well, the chow aboard the S.S. Newport would turn the scurviest seaman's stomach. Starving sailors would toss it overboard and then mutiny. The oyster stew was not stew but a lukewarm dish of milk with grease spots floating in it, and a few sickly oysters submerged in the solution. You'd get better fried shrimp at a five-and-dime lunch counter, and the cocktail sauce was served in cheap plastic thimbles too small to jam a shrimp in. The vegetables of the day were, in some fancy mimicry of a "nice" restaurant, doled out in measly portions from plastic bowls. The baked potato was so overcooked it was yellow. And so on.

These are basic things, the bare minimum one deserves for plunking down, oh, $10 or $15 for a meal. Don't repeat our mistake. Having said this, we will summon our remaining resources and recommend *Salas'*, also on Thames Street. They serve all kinds of fresh, steamed and spiced seafood. The price is right and the food is good. And you are on dry land the whole time.

Nightlife

Newport's various social strata have not quite achieved a happy equilibrium. The rich kids hang out at a cluster of bars and discos down near the upscale Bannister's Wharf, and the poorer folk hit the beer joints strung out, like a snaggled set of teeth, along Broadway, barely four blocks away.

At a crowded see-and-be-seen bistro called *Black Pearl Pub*, on Bannister's Wharf, we overheard a couple of jauntily togged preppies scoping out the scene: "Well, what do you think?" "Let's go back to the boat, Kev."

We did not stay at a no-name bar on Broadway long enough to overhear anything except the sound of our own guzzling. You might say that any messages we needed to hear were relayed to us by telepathy, in the stares and glowers from a bull-like guy at the far end of the bar who had a huge bandage on his face.

A happy medium was found not in Newport but in adjacent Middletown, at the *Starboard Tack*. There was nothing pretentious or dangerous about the place—just a decent jukebox, a big-screen TV and a few pool tables in the rear. A pack of pretty, smiling Rhode Island redheads were toting the cue sticks the night we were there, while the guys were in the front room, ogling a baseball game on the big screen.

When there's no festival in town, live music in Newport is dominated by jazz and/or lightweight lounge music. The *Blue Pelican* on West Broadway will occasionally book a rock act, but more often than not, it—like most every club in Newport—favors jazz and folk and blues and soft rock, showcasing it in a very homey setting.

For a real authentic rock 'n' roll scene, you'd have to drive an hour or more to Providence. There's always something going on up there at *Lupo's Heartbreak Hotel*, *The Living Room*, *The Cage*, *The Last Call* and so on. Whatever happened to rock 'n' roll at the *beach*?

FOR FURTHER INFORMATION

Newport Chamber of Commerce
10 America's Cup Avenue
P.O. Box 237
Newport, Rhode Island 02840
(401) 847-1600

Narragansett

"Narragansett Has No Peer" reads the slogan on one chamber of commerce handout. "World's Finest Beaches" brags the cover of another. Somebody up there has got a ripe sense of humor, or else is laboring under a tragic delusion. Ah, we get it—it's a pun!

"Narragansett has no *pier*" is how you're supposed to read it. But wait: there is a state pier right down from the main beach. In fact, the whole area is called Narragansett Pier—meaning the long, gentle cove on the east side of the Narragansett Bay, which seems to be the heart and center of the town of Narragansett.

And it *is* nice. The beach goes on for quite a distance, the water is calm and refreshing, and there's lots of sunbathing action on the wide, sandy flat. The road, "Scenic 1A," and a cement wall follow the contours of the beach. They curve in, then curve out in a perfect little mile-long semicircle. Right around the middle, there's an impressive edifice: two towers linked by an overhead arch, under which traffic passes. There's always a fresh breeze blowing off the bay. Nice. Real nice. But *peerless?* To a Narragansett Indian, maybe. . . .

The name Narragansett is taken from a great Indian tribe that was routed and dispersed by King Philip's War in the 1670s. Though the area has been settled continuously since 1675, the town of Narragansett was not incorporated until 1901; previously, it was part of South Kingston. Like Newport, albeit on a smaller scale, Narragansett enjoyed a gilded age when wealthy who's-whos began building summer mansions on the shores of Rhode Island and Cape Cod. Those drawn to Narragansett were a less ostentatious breed then those who built show-off palaces in Newport. In Narragansett, you really are out of the mainstream.

Less traveled though it was, Narragansett still had its grand hotels and estates, not to mention an impressive casino that was the scene of many a gala. The Narragansett Pier Casino, built by Stanford White, was a mammoth social, recreational and dining complex. The crowning touch was the *Towers*. Built in 1882, the Towers are all that remain of the casino complex, which burned to the ground on September 4, 1900. Nowadays, the Narragansett Chamber of Commerce houses its Tourist Information Center in the Towers. Narragansett is not as exclusive as it once was, yet is a pretty residential community of 12,000. Many of its inhabitants make their living at commercial fishing.

Recreationally, the Narragansett area offers a choice of five beaches: Narragansett Beach, a town beach; and four state beaches, at Scarborough, Galilee, Wheeler and East Matunuck. Interestingly, there is purportedly good surfing at Narragansett Beach, and the fact that the Northeast Surfing Championship is held here annually would seem to confirm it. Scarborough is about 3 miles south of Narragansett Beach, and also gets the full force of the ocean surf; the others are all on the other side of Point Judith, where the coast runs along more of an east-west axis.

The village of Galilee is worth a look in its own right. If ever the words "picturesque fishing village" rang true, it is here. Galilee is home to a sizable local fishing fleet, is the putative "tuna capital of the world" and is the site of numerous big-time fishing tournaments. For basic beach recreation, however, any of the five area beaches will do. Parking runs about $2 or $3 at all of them, there are pavilions and facilities and the sound gleams like diamonds. Maybe they aren't the finest beaches in the world—really, now— but you'll be glad you sought them out and will leave happy as a clam.

Accommodations

The guest home and the bed-and-breakfast inn thrive in this corner of New England. Seemingly every couple with a spare bedroom will open their doors to overnight boarders. We quickly counted twenty-five such lodging houses. Among the most impressive of these is *The Phoenix*, another Stanford White creation with an 1889 birthdate. For a modest $30 to $50, you can stay in a large bedroom overlooking a private green, and the price includes a real breakfast—anything from eggs Benedict to lobster quiche. As a bonus, the beach is within walking distance.

Restaurants

We walked the length of the wall, north to south, from one end of Narragansett Beach to the other. We passed lots of bodies, basking in the still-warm early September sun. It was a long walk, but hardly an unpleasant one. At the end of the wall, we ran smack into the *Café at the End of the Wall*, which is something like a gourmet clam shack, if you can imagine that. For $1.95, we feasted on clam fritters and clam chowder, which fortified us for the hike back. Sometimes life is so easy.

Nightlife

For all we know, the lobsters and the crabs get together on the beach after the last jeepload of teenagers has pulled away and play strip poker all night long.

FOR FURTHER INFORMATION

Narragansett Chamber of Commerce
P.O. Box 742
Narragansett by the Sea, Rhode Island 02882
(401) 783-7121

South Kingston

The town of South Kingston was settled in 1723 as Pettusquamscutt. A decisive battle in which the Narragansett Indians were nearly exterminated was fought here. An obelisk marks the spot of the Great Swamp Fight. At the intersection of Route 138 and U.S. 1 rises a 100-foot-tall wooden observation tower, from whose summit one is rewarded with a panoramic view of the Rhode Island coastline. There are old, restored houses and the largest freshwater pond in the state hereabouts, but the real attraction is a string of three beaches—Green Hill, Moonstone and Matunuck. The one with all the *u*'s in it was singled out for special praise by a Rhode Island surfing nut who seemed to know his stuff.

FOR FURTHER INFORMATION

South Kingston Chamber of Commerce
Main Street
Wakefield, Rhode Island 02880
(401) 783-2801

Charlestown

Charlestown is Indian country. The Narragansett tribe barely escaped total annihilation at the hands of their New World usurpers, and every year in Charlestown their descendants hold an August "pow-wow" complete with "peace pipe ceremonies." There are Indian burial grounds and an old Indian church, and a new Indian cultural center is on the way.

The Rhode Island countryside is heavily wooded in these parts. *Burlingame State Park*, a 2,100-acre park, offers 755 campsites. Swimming options include a freshwater lake, Watchaug Pond, and easy access to East Beach, a mile away on the ocean. Be forewarned that from Memorial Day to Labor Day, people begin queuing up for a campsite at six in the morning.

The town of Charlestown claims nearly 10 miles of barrier-island beaches. At the flanks on its oceanfront are the villages of Quonochontaug and Charlestown Beach. The middle section of this stretch is a protected conservation area, but Quonochontaug, Charlestown Beach and East Beach are public. Parking is limited to a few small gravel lots, however. Quonochontaug is especially known for good fishing. To get there, you follow the signs directing you off U.S. 1. After driving past miles of cornfields that give way to marsh grass, you're at the beach. There's a colony of modest summer houses, but beyond that we saw nothing here but a man in a football jersey giving us funny looks.

FOR FURTHER INFORMATION

Charlestown Tourist Information Center
U.S. 1 at Route 216
Charlestown, Rhode Island 02813

Misquamicut
Weekapaug

Misquamicut needs a press agent, a PR person, someone to spread the word. Little gets written about Misquamicut; indeed, it was one of the last beaches that came to our attention. Here it is, the finest, most even, longest and widest beach in Rhode Island, and hardly a word is breathed about it out-of-state. Part of the problem might be that Misquamicut is filed under Westerly. In the confusing New England municipal schemata of villages and towns, Misquamicut is a village incorporated into the town of Westerly. But Westerly is inland, up the Pawcatuck River on the Connecticut border. This is confusing. Westerly is not a beach town. Any fool can see that from the map. But Misquamicut frequently gets included under the umbrella of Westerly.

Another problem might simply be the name. Who can pronounce it? Who even wants to try? It's pronounced like it looks, more or less, and it sounds wrong even when you get it right.

A final reason for its relative obscurity may be that in New England, where every twig and stone has historical significance, Misquamicut seems to be nothing more or less than a good place to swim. A few spur roads lead here off of Scenic 1A, there's a huddle of motels and restaurants on the beach and for a few blocks back, and—bingo!—that's all there is to Misquamicut. Nothing to study but starfish.

Perhaps the Rhode Islanders have simply closed ranks and decided not to bellow about their sandy paradise. Misquamicut does draw healthy crowds all summer long. In every picture we've ever seen, there are crowds. The crowds had largely left by the time we got here, but on a warm fall afternoon, a stroll up in the direction of Weekapaug—Misquamicut's kissing cousin to the east— was as satisfying as any we'd taken in two summers. The water was even warm enough to be swimmable, though strewn with round stones, seaweed and starfish.

All of which brings up an issue that's hotly debated in Rhode Island. To wit, who owns the beach? The beach at Misquamicut is one of the four main public beaches in Rhode Island, the others being Matunuck (in South Kingston), Scarborough (in Narragansett) and First Beach (in Newport). There are 470 miles of twisting and turning coastline in Rhode Island, of which 74 miles can be classified as sandy beach—the kind that people like to frolic on. Of those 74 miles of beach, 52 are private. Which leaves 22 miles of beaches for Rhode Island's 950,000 citizens. That works out to nine-tenths of an inch of beach per person. Remember that Rhode Island is nicknamed the Ocean State. No wonder they're up in arms.

In any case, you wouldn't know that people are getting red in the face over anything but too much sun here in Misquamicut, where there's plenty of beach to go around. But up at Weekapaug, just up the road, the beaches are for "residents and guests only." Beach buttons are required, and they promise "strict enforcement." Thank heavens you can always go right back to the little town with the big beach and the funny name.

Accommodations

Most of the motels here will meet your basic needs while stopping short of swaddling you in luxury. In other words, you'll get a room, and you can count on a pillow, clean linen, cable TV and a shower stall. The motel owners surmise, rightly, that you did not come here to count the flowers on the wall. You will pay an average price ($45 or $50 a night) for an average room.

There seem to be some strange regulations in force here. We stayed at the *Sandpiper Motel*. On a card stapled to the inside of our motel-room door was printed a list of rules. At the top, it said, "Thank you so much for staying at our motel." A few lines down, it said, "No visitors allowed in rooms. Violation will result in loss of room with no refund."

An upscale exception to all this is the *Pleasant View House*, an oceanfront complex that has the look of a large inn and the appointments of a modern luxury motel. The Pleasant View House is on the beach; most rooms have oceanfront or poolside balconies, and there is a lounge and gourmet restaurant on the premises as well. There are patios at poolside and by the ocean, and lawn chairs to be pulled out in the sun. All in all, this is *the* place to stay during your Misquamicut vacation.

Restaurants

The clambake is a Rhode Island tradition. This seems a good place to talk about clambakes, which, it is claimed, were invented in Rhode Island. (The idea was purloined from the Indians, in fact.) As long as we talk about clambakes, we won't have to talk about the restaurants of Misquamicut. We tried several that were average, as in disappointing. Bland food, priced too high, even with the free salad bar come-ons. No, we wished we could have gone to a clambake instead: all those layers of food—clams, mussels, lobsters, fish, corn, potatoes, sausage, onions—steaming on a bed of hot rocks and hissing seaweed. If that doesn't whet your appetite, read on: "When the bake is ready to be served," reads one account, "the traditional ringing of the bell takes place, as all the guests gather round to watch the unveiling. Billowing clouds of steam rise up as the canvas is removed, and the air is filled with a great surge of delicious aromas." Ding-ding-ding.

Nightlife

In the catacombs of the *Pleasant View House* is a watering hole with a to-the-point name: the *Down the Hatch* lounge. You can watch colorful fish swim around an aquarium, play the jukebox and eavesdrop on older couples, as we did, while you keep pouring 'em down the hatch. Beyond the haven of the Pleasant View, one can always shimmy over to the *Captain's Galley*, which has both a raw bar and a tropical drink bar. We spent a slow Sunday night watching a trio of surfers from Connecticut get inebriated on elaborate concoctions with names like Hollywood Mudslide. There are other outdoor/indoor bars and even a disco in Misquamicut. (The disco is the place with the hot-pink neon in the window.)

FOR FURTHER INFORMATION

Greater Westerly Area Chamber of Commerce
159 Main Street
Westerly, Rhode Island 02891
(401) 596-7761

Watch Hill

Out where the land runs out, by a lighthouse and an old carousel,
sits the town of Watch Hill. This is the oldest beach resort on the
South Shore—a lighthouse keeper built a beach hotel here in 1840—
and the most moneyed one as well. 'Twas a time when Watch
Hill could challenge Newport and Narragansett for fashionability.
It is still very rich; enormous Victorian houses rise behind hedges
trimmed as neatly as Sergeant Carter's crew cut. The *Watch Hill
Lighthouse*, a formidable granite tower, dates back to the mid-1800s,
and its light shines still. The *Watch Hill Carousel*, finished in 1867,
is reputed to be one of the oldest in America. But the real attraction
in Watch Hill is the waterfront. There's a lot of yacht traffic here,
and Napatree Beach extends out for half a mile on a narrow point
of land. With its picture windows and hillside perch, the *Inn at
Watch Hill* offers sublime accommodations from which to watch
it all.

FOR FURTHER INFORMATION

Greater Westerly Chamber of Commerce
159 Main Street
Westerly, Rhode Island 02891
(401) 596-7761

Block Island

The first thing we saw on arriving in Block Island was a moped accident. It was a simple matter of physics: the road made a 90-degree turn and the driver didn't. The sputtering two-wheeler rudely came to a halt against a curb, and its inept operator wound up eating sidewalk. Aside from a few scrapes and scratches, the driver—a sour-looking woman with a brazen manner—was all right. It was her dignity that was bruised, since she'd executed this nimble maneuver in full view of two hotel porches and several restaurants, and she inexplicably began ranting at her beleaguered male companion, who had been following her at a safe distance on his own motor scooter.

The only reason we're mentioning this up front is that Block Island has had a celebrated, nationally reported feud with mopeds. So vehement have the islanders been on the subject that they've even threatened secession from Rhode Island, which was not recognizing the legality of its anti-moped legislation. (Among the comical sidelines to the debate was an offer from the state of Colorado to "adopt" Block Island.) Should Block Island succeed in its crusade, it will be one of the noblest acts of rebellion since tea was tossed into Boston Harbor. No sanctuary as peaceful as Block Island should be sullied with the noise and bloodied bones for which these contraptions are responsible.

Having got this sermon out of our system, we shall turn to the subject at hand. Without ceremony or hyperbole, let it simply be said that whenever we're asked to list our favorite beaches (and we've been asked this question daily for years), Block Island is one of the first names out of our mouths. To our thinking, it is Eden North. (Kiawah Island, in South Carolina, gets the garden of earthly delights award on the yon side of the Mason-Dixon line.)

Geographically, Block Island is a pork chop-shaped piece of real estate off the Rhode Island coast, south of Newport and east of Montauk Point (the tip of Long Island). It is 6 miles long and 3 miles wide, at its extremist dimensions, and encompasses 11 square miles, making it not a tenth the size of Martha's Vineyard. But what it lacks in size, it makes up for in natural beauty. Block Island is an exceedingly pleasant place to come, whether for a day, a week or an entire summer.

The island is the best of all possible worlds. It's more affordable than Nantucket, less populous than Martha's Vineyard, and there's that sense of apartness from the mainland, where you can always sense the wheels of civilization grinding away just over your shoulder. The pace of life is slow and deliberate, the lack of tourist diversions a blessing when you've got a wide veranda and an empty chair from which to gaze out over the blue waters of Old Harbor. If you get restless, there is a whole island beyond the main town center that begs to be explored (preferably on a nonmotorized two-wheeler, or on foot). Hundreds of freshwater ponds are scattered about, and there are bay and ocean beaches. There are bluffs that tower 200 feet above the shoreline, and there's an inland hollow that is actually *below* sea level.

In all likelihood your vacation will commence in the village, located midway along the eastern shore of the island at what is known as Old Harbor. It is here that most of the ferries and boats from the mainland drop anchor, and here that you'll probably be staying. Ferries make daily trips from Providence and Newport, on the Rhode Island mainland, and from New London and Point Judith, on the Connecticut coast. There are arrivals and departures to all four points every day, and one-way passenger fare averages around $5. (For a full schedule and fare information, write Box 482, New London, Connecticut 06320.)

Additionally, there are passengers-only ferries over from Montauk Point, on Long Island. These dock on Block Island at New Harbor, located at the head of the Great Salt Pond on the island's western side. New Harbor, a well-protected deep-water harbor with extensive marina facilities, is the only hub of activity on Block Island besides Old Harbor. The two harbors, though on opposite sides of the island, are actually pretty close to each other, since the island narrows at its midsection, like an aerobics instructor.

If you are debating whether to bring your car, it's not necessary (and if you're coming from Long Island, not possible). The town—technically known as New Shoreham, although Block Island will suffice to cover both town and island—is easy to explore on foot and fronts the best ocean beaches. Crescent Beach is the island's main swimming beach. About 1 ¼ miles long, it begins at the Surf Hotel at the center of town (Water and Dodge Streets) and runs north. There is a stretch in the middle known as State Beach, with a bathhouse, parking lot and lifeguards. It's all a few easy paces from town.

The beaches on the bay require a bit more cunning and determination to find, as only one paved route, Cooneymus Road, cuts across to the western side. But the isolation is worth the effort. Up island from Crescent Beach is "the Maze," an area filled with hiking trails. Eleven miles of paths wind through pine forests, emerging at cliffs that drop precariously down to the Atlantic. On the south side of the island, trails lead out to the still-functioning *Southeast Light* and Mohegan Bluffs—the highest shore overlook on Block Island.

Inland, there's an interesting spot known as Rodman's Hollow. It's a glacially gouged-out ravine whose floor is beneath sea level. From the road, an informational marker congenially invites walkers down. The hike in is something akin to cutting your way through the bush country of Africa, however. Most visitors stare quizzically from the road, wondering how hiking is possible on a trail that is practically vertical. Being intrepid travelers, we slid in, limbo-ing under a canopy of gnarled bushes and shrubs. Was it worth it? Yes, but Rodman's Hollow is more for Outward Bound enthusiasts than your average foot soldier.

Block Island is a pastoral paradise of lakes, wildflowers, rolling hills and stone walls. First settled by Europeans in 1661 and a popular vacation retreat since the last century, the island has been kept remarkably free of disfiguring development. Even now, none of the hotels, restaurants or other commercial establishments are obtrusively "modern." The stately Victorian look of the town has been maintained through conscientious preservation and restoration. There are no blinking neon signs, whirring air conditioners, honking horns—and not a single stoplight on the island. You can thank your lucky stars, and a provident citizenry, that such a place still exists in the present day, mere miles over water from major centers of clanging tourism and commerce.

By the way, the day we left town a new ordinance governing mopeds went into effect. It required that moped renters either have a motorcyclist's license or undergo a brief safety course before driving away. We saw the safety course being administered at one of the moped rental lots. Two parallel rows of inverted plastic beer cups had been set up on a barren gravel lot, and a long-haired employee was showing a middle-aged man how to maneuver his moped between them in a straight line. Would he also learn, we had to wonder, thinking back to the luckless accident victim, how to make a right turn?

Accommodations

The multimillion-dollar renovation of the *National Hotel*, erected in 1888, is among the most impressive such efforts we witnessed in our coastal travels. The National is a real beauty: its outside is constructed of white clapboard, with green shutters and a gabled, black mansard roof. Inside, a Victorian cabbage rose carpet with a dark blue background runs throughout the hotel's three stories. The rooms have been appointed with refinished original furnishings and delicate lace curtains. And there are some contemporary touches: modern bath fixtures and cable TV, for instance. All in all, they've succeeded in re-creating the grandeur of a bygone era. Located where Dodge and Water Streets meet, the National is not inexpensive ($95 to $105 per night for a double room), but the extraordinary quality and attention to detail justify the price tag.

Compared to the elegant National, the *Surf Hotel*, located across the street is funky but chic. It too is a landmark (dating from 1876) filled with antique lamps and furniture. The Surf Hotel is a bargain ($42 per night for a double with shared bath) but fills up months ahead of time. As we listened in the lobby one morning, a dripping-wet matron, easily in her seventies, was blocking out her reservations for the next summer with the desk clerk.

Situated west of town, on a terraced hill that slopes down to the ocean, the *Spring House* is a marvelous colonial leviathan that is Block Island's oldest inn, dating from 1852. The rooms are

graded "special," "choice" and "other," and range t.
per day for a double, with both private and shared bat.
The grounds alone are so inviting you may never walk i.

The *Highview Hotel*, also perched high on a hill, is one c
Island's most visible landmarks. Another oldie but goodie (i
the Highview offers spartan but serviceable rooms, a fine on-premises restaurant and a wonderful view of Old Harbor. Rooms range
from $42 to $55 per night (most share a bath), and are—take note—
half that in the off-season.

This listing could go on and on: there are forty such lodging
establishments on Block Island. When planning a stay, be aware
that many places on Block Island, as elsewhere, mandate a minimum stay of two or three days, especially over weekends in season.
Write the Block Island Chamber of Commerce for a directory, and
you'll wind up with a mailbox full of brochures.

Restaurants

Most of the restaurants on Block Island are family oriented and
relatively affordable. *McAlloon's Saloon* at the National Hotel has
both an indoor dining room and tables that line the front and side
porches outdoors. It's the best place in town to catch a late-afternoon breeze and watch the action along Water Street, the main
drag. The menu starts cheap—hamburgers and salads—and works
its way up to pricy seafood entrées. The *Harborside Inn*, located at
the ferry landing on Water Street, is another must-visit spot. It's
both an inn and a restaurant, set in a sprawling Victorian manse.
There are a couple of Block Island specialties to be tried, namely
Block Island swordfish and Block Island chowder. The former is
not some new species of swordfish—the "Block Island" label only
attests to the freshness of what is caught in very local waters. Block
Island chowder is more of a novelty—yet a third way to prepare
clam chowder. In this variation, big chunks of potato and clam
pieces float around in a clear, briny broth made from salt pork.
It's not half bad, but can't be regarded as serious competition to
the standard Manhattan and New England clam chowder recipes.

Nightlife

If the ocean breezes do not suffice as after-dinner entertainment, there are a pair of clubs on Block Island where you can kick out the jams till long after the ferries stop running. They are, by name, *Captain Nick's* and the *Yellow Kittens*. Both are located within spitting distance of Crescent Beach and walking distance from any place you'd conceivably be staying. Each has live bands, dancing, deejays and well-stocked bars. Mostly, they attract a college-age crowd, and the atmosphere is one of frivolous fun. As luck would have it, we caught up with our favorite all-female hard-rock cover band in the world, Fire (see OLD ORCHARD BEACH), who were playing a week-long stint at the Yellow Kittens. But we bounced back and forth between both places and had a ball. Make mine a sea breeze, bartender: cranberry juice, grapefruit juice and vodka. And let me hear Bruce Springsteen's "Dancing in the Dark" one more time—definitely the song that defined our summer sojourns.

FOR FURTHER INFORMATION

Block Island Chamber of Commerce
Drawer D
Block Island, Rhode Island 02807
(401) 466-2982

Connecticut: Declare Your Independence

Connecticut calls itself the Constitution State and seems inordinately attached to its American heritage, placing the word "historic" next to anything that hasn't moved, or been moved, in the last hundred years. Though the I-95 corridor from New Haven to Manhattan is all urban blight—and one of the most hellish stretches of pavement on the East Coast—the state is surprisingly rural, with three-fourths of its land given over to farms and woods. Down along the coastline, the roads wind through green country. Expect to make lots of hairpin turns and get hopelessly lost on shore loop roads. Then suddenly you'll round a corner and find yourself in a well-groomed, picture-postcard village by the sea.

On some other mission, we might have spent more time in Connecticut, but owing to a geographical technicality, we gave it only a cursory once-over. We came looking for beaches—sand, waves, ocean water—and the Connecticut shore winds up getting stiff-armed out of the picture by Long Island. Like an overprotective parent, Long Island cradles the 90-mile Connecticut shore from direct assault by the Atlantic.

Many travelers will recognize the names of coastal Connecticut villages such as Mystic, Stonington, New London and Old Saybrook. Mostly, they are geared to the boat crowd or to those eternally fascinated by anything remotely resembling the "historic." A sign we saw in the window of a shop in the overpriced

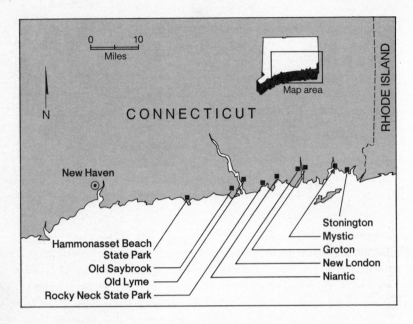

former whaling town of Mystic said it all: "Gift Shop—Scrimshaw, Harpoons, Tee Shirts, Rose Bracelets, Salt Water Taffy."

To be fair, there are some state park beaches on the Long Island Sound. But all things considered, if you're after a viable beach vacation, you are hereby advised to declare your independence from the Constitution State.

Stonington

This is a small maritime village, dating from the 1700s, which looks over the waters of the Little Narragansett Bay to Watch Hill, Rhode Island. Stonington manages to avoid the tourist claustrophobia of nearby Mystic. The *Old Lighthouse Museum*, full of artifacts from land and sea, is worth a peek, as is the village, which is the home port of Connecticut's only commercial fishing fleet. Stonington may well be the only town on the Connecticut coast where real ocean waves roll into shore.

Mystic

Mystic is the sort of place that will try to con you into surrendering cash simply by uttering the magic word "historic." The town's past is real enough, but its present is mostly tourist razzle-dazzle. On the plus side, Mystic's glory days as a shipbuilding town are authentically re-created at *Mystic Seaport*, the nation's largest maritime museum, encompassing 17 acres and 200 boats. The century that is documented spans 1814 to 1914, and the many restored vessels include the 1841 whaleship *Charles W. Morgan* and the 1882 square-rigger *Joseph Conrad*, not to mention many smaller craft used in the maritime trades.

But Mystic knows it has a captive audience, and the throngs flock to such dubious attractions as *Olde Mistick Village*, an "eighteenth-century-*like* colonial shopping center with more than 60 shops and restaurants *including banks and a theater* [emphases added]." On a further note of inauthenticity, it is located adjacent to cacophonous Interstate 95. We have heard too that some of Mystic's high-priced motels require full prepayment from their guests. Sorry, no.

FOR FURTHER INFORMATION

Mystic Chamber of Commerce
2 Roosevelt Avenue
Mystic, Connecticut 06355
(203) 536-8559

For information regarding the greater Connecticut shoreline:

Mystic & Shoreline Visitors' Information Center
Olde Mistick Village
Mystic, Connecticut 06355
(203) 536-1641

Groton

One of the largest cities on the southeast Connecticut shoreline, Groton touts itself as the "submarine capital of the world." Heavens, when this gets out, they'll have to beat the tourists off with a stick.

New London

Another in a series of former eighteenth-century whaling towns, New London has the added novelty of Ocean Beach Park. This unexpected bonanza offers a mile-long beach and boardwalk along Long Island Sound. There are also bathhouses, an Olympic swimming pool and an amusement arcade. Parking is only $2 a day. Fun for the whole family.

Nowadays, New London has a more modern look, as befits a town that is the center of commerce for southeastern Connecticut. But reminders of the seagoing life are everywhere—from the *Bank Street Waterfront Historic District* to the *Tale of the Whale Museum*. Ferries to Block Island and to Orient Point, on the tip of the north fork of Long Island, can be taken from New London.

FOR FURTHER INFORMATION

New London Chamber of Commerce
1 Whale Oil Row
New London, Connecticut 06320
(203) 443-8332

Rocky Neck State Park

Near the village of South Lyme, between Old Saybrook and Niantic, one will find Rocky Neck State Park, which has a mile-long beach and a boardwalk, plus facilities for fishing, camping and picnicking.

Hammonasset Beach State Park

A 932-acre oceanfront park near the town of Madison. Again, you can do everything but launch a boat here.

New York:
The Empire State
Strikes Back

New York. These two seemingly harmless words conjure more images than can be feasibly recorded with the naked eye, ear, nose, throat or typewriter. Everyone has his or her own private stockpile of rants and raves, and no other state in the union, not even California, will elicit such a cross-section of opinion. No wonder. New York is really two states in one, and few people know both of them well. There is "upstate," and there is "the city." The city occupies 314 of New York's 49,576 square miles. Seven million people are crammed into those 314 square miles, while the 10 million other New Yorkers are spread out over the remaining 49,262 square miles. In other words, the population density in the city is 110 times greater than upstate. We are talking about two different worlds here.

Topographically, the state embraces the extremes as well, from the Finger Lakes to the Great Lakes, the Catskills to Coney Island, dense evergreen forests to teeming urban jungles. At the bottom right-hand corner sits the greatest metropolis in the world—a city so full of vice they named it twice. Extending out from New York City is the largest island on the East Coast. Long Island itself partakes of extremes. The first 30 or so miles is all urban rotgut, from which the unflattering stereotypes are drawn. But then the concrete maze clears away, and you pass miles of farmland and small villages. At the far end of the South Shore, you are 125

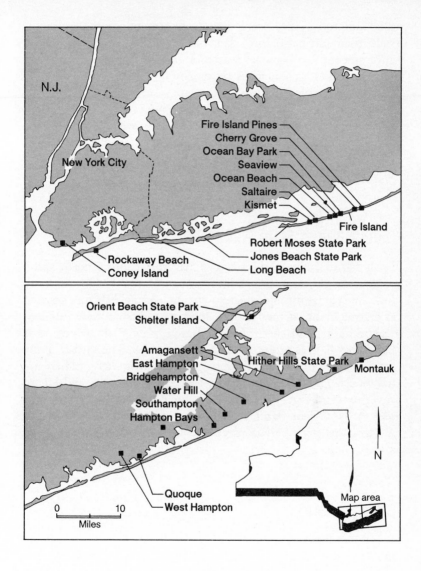

miles away from New York, standing on desolate dunes and looking out over an uncrowded beach.

The beaches of Long Island are some of the finest in the world
and include such familiar names as Jones Beach, Fire Island and

the Hamptons. Jones Beach is protected from development by the state (it's a state park); Fire Island has been preserved by the federal government (it's a National Seashore); and the Hamptons are spared a Jersey Shore denouement by money (i.e., the rich folk and an organization called Nature Conservancy keep a tight rein on development). You simply cannot believe how remote and untrammeled these beaches are. If you can make it over the bridges and out the tunnels of Manhattan onto the parkways of Long Island, you will discover a world that you would never guess could exist so close by.

Orient Beach State Park

Long Island splits at the town of Riverhead into a north and a south fork. The south fork leads out to Montauk. On the north fork, one passes through small towns and cornfields before arriving at Orient Point, at the tip. The ferry to and from New London, Connecticut, lands here. Orient Beach State Park, which faces Gardiners Bay, is protected on nearly all sides. The surface of the bay is like a mirror, and they say you can swim here. (There are bathhouses, and you can picnic, too.) There is sand, and lots of coves to wander in and around, but the beach is chockful of rocks and shells. Orient Beach is so far out in the middle of nowhere, though, that it's a perfect place to come for serene meditation on a warm day.

Shelter Island

If the two forks of Long Island resemble a pair of open jaws on the map, then Shelter Island is the morsel of food the creature is about to swallow. You cannot get here except by private boat or expensive ferries—from Greenport on the north fork and North Haven on the south. It's an idyllic little world within a world, if you can afford it. Mostly, you'll find lots of tucked-away summer homes and high-priced resorts.

FOR FURTHER INFORMATION

Shelter Island Chamber of Commerce
17 Grand Avenue
Shelter Island, New York 11964
(516) 749-0399

Montauk

The Hamptons are far from Manhattan in terms of distance, but not in terms of manners. Montauk is only 10 miles beyond East Hampton, but it's a million miles away in temperament. For one thing, it's at land's end on the south fork of Long Island, at the tip of a finger of land that protrudes from the broader arm of Long Island. Formerly inhabited by the Montaukett Indians, Montauk has traditionally been known as a fishing village and a blue-collar resort.

The most varied land forms on Long Island can be found in and around Montauk—everything from wide sandy beaches to rocky, wind-whipped points of land, from freshwater ponds and forests of tall pine to rolling hills carpeted with wild grape and honeysuckle. Montauk's isolation is its most appealing quality, and its sleepy-village rusticity is genuine. Any early riser can walk into a place like the *Village Restaurant* and find the local fishermen guzzling coffee and talking shop before setting off. This is not the four-star travel guide "quaintness" of a re-created village like Mystic; this is real people making a real living.

Lately, though, Montauk has become another bauble to be sold to the highest bidder. The gentrification everyone feared would creep east from the Hamptons has begun. Montauk has informally become known as "the Hamptons' cheaper brother." Co-ops and condos and other forms of developmental vulgarity are advancing on Montauk like a red tide, and the unholy partnership of those who deal for profit and those who buy for tax shelters is conspiring to wreck the life of this village.

Montauk is a beautiful place, and there is no mystery why people would find it desirable. Miles of undefiled beaches run along the Atlantic, protected by high dunes and always uncrowded. New York City is just an ugly memory by the time you reach Montauk, and it's not yet within the sphere of the Hamptons, so the money parade trickles out as well. Still, the specter of development is worrisome. Montauk residents are attempting to throw a wrench in the works by withholding building permits, but this is just a case-by-case stopgap, not a comprehensive answer. The saddest thing is that escalating real estate values are driving lifelong natives and their children away from the town they were born in. As one told a *New York Times* reporter in 1984, "We're attracting tennis players and golf players, and leaving our kids no place to live." Dick Cavett, a celebrity who cherishes his privacy out here, laments, "I wish I could reverse the trend." (Maybe he could start by moving away himself.)

Even though the type of person who is drawn to Montauk is changing, nothing irrevocable has been done to ruin its natural beauty—except, maybe, for the seven-story condominium built on the traffic circle at the center of town. Two state parks help keep the oceanfront unobstructed. At *Montauk Point State Park*, the island comes to an end on grass-covered bluffs that drop down to the rocky shore. *The Montauk Light*, erected in 1796 by order of George Washington, sits at the head of one such promontory. West of the village of Montauk, where the old and new Montauk Highways fork, is *Hither Hills State Park*. There are lots of campsites behind the dunes, and a broad ocean beach.

Though the rich sporting dilettantes would like to own it, Montauk properly belongs to serious fishermen. For both surfcasting and deep-sea game fishing, these are some of the most fertile waters on the East Coast. The celebrated "cod ledge" is right off the banks of Montauk. Cod and flounder are year-round residents of these waters, while ocean and sound are visited seasonally by migratory schools of bluefish, striped bass and sea trout. But it's the big fish that excite the diehard fishermen. In the summer months, the Gulf Stream brings up the southern game fish—marlin, swordfish, tuna— and from June to October the fishing frenzy reaches its zenith.

Incidentally, one night we dined on swordfish steak cut from a 300-pound monster that had been caught off the continental shelf not 24 hours earlier. Even if the idea of catching fish doesn't hook you, Montauk is a wonderful place to nab some rest and relaxation. Between the casual ebb-and-flow of village life and the elemental sublimity of its beaches, harbors and highlands, Montauk is a prime cut of paradise twelve months a year.

Accommodations

There is a glob of both plain and fancy motels down by the beach, where the Montauk Highway comes into town. These are generally cheaper than comparable accommodations down the road in the Hamptons, besides being right on the beach. Among the more inviting of these are the *Stingray Motor Lodge*, the *Royal Atlantic Motel* and the *Beach House Ocean Resort*. The Montauk style is more relaxed than the Hamptons. At one place, we were invited to name our own price if we didn't like the one we were quoted.

If price is no object, however, you will want to stay at *Gurney's Inn*. As it does with food, Gurney's sets the standard for accommodations on this end of Long Island. It also puts a premium price upon them (around $200 a night). But if you can afford it, you will not live better than at Gurney's, which, as they tell you, is right "on the brink o' the beach." Secluded from town on the Old Montauk Highway, Gurney's has been in the resort business on this very spot for more than sixty years.

If you're on a shoestring budget, or simply looking to soak up the outdoors, camp at *Hither Hills*. Unfortunately, many people want to camp here, so reserve a site early—like eight weeks ahead—if you can.

Restaurants

Montauk offers food to fit all budgets. Folks who favor a Cinzano-umbrella motif and on-the-waterfront dining love *Gosman's*, a complex with a clam bar, seafood restaurant and retail fish market. Gosman's is by Montauk Harbor, on the sound side of the island. They make a promise that says it all: "The fish we serve you tonight was caught on our boats this morning." When we passed through, a lobster dinner—including steamers, corn and chowder—was going for $11.95. Not bad at all.

The dining room at *Gurney's Inn* offers an extensive menu of seafood, beef and Italian dishes. For appetizers, try raw oysters (among the biggest we've seen) or the Clams Alla Monte (from an eighty-year-old family recipe). For dinner, you're on your own. Whether you choose steak au poivre or seafood au gratin, it's all excellent. And don't pass up the dessert menu. Dinner here is a rich experience.

For lunch, head down the highway to the *Lobster Roll*. It is so renowned as a lunching spot that it's known among cognoscenti simply as "Lunch." Across and up the road is an informal outdoor restaurant and snack bar called the *Clam Bar*. Watch for its lunch specials. For $3 we were served fried fish sandwiches, locally grown corn and cantaloupe that tasted as sweet as ice cream. Finally, there are straight seafood houses such as *Salivar's Restaurant and Marine Bar*, out on the docks. The fishermen themselves eat here. And you won't pay an arm and a fin, either.

Nightlife

There's nothing here to compare with the Hamptons, as far as nightlife. The two are as different as a seagull and a sand crab. There is a beach club called *Waves* and a place called *The Place*, but the latter proved to be a poor imitation of the moneyed splendor of the Hamptons hotspots. There's no action, or not much, in Montauk. Nor does there need to be; out here, the crashing surf is music far sweeter than any you'll hear at Danceteria.

If you're seeking racier thrills, you can always point your car west and traverse the darkened dune country toward the Hamptons. What you will find in Montauk are small bars beloved by locals. A couple of such places, like the *Shagwong Tavern*, are conjoined to the several decent restaurants on the main drag in "downtown" Montauk. Two types of people drink here, among the nautical bric-a-brac and comfy booths: those waiting to be seated for dinner, and those who'll not leave their stools unless they fall off. Several characters were so befuddled with drink by eight o'clock that they couldn't decide whether to shake hands or duke it out. There were flubbed attempts at both courses of action. Finally, they just gave up and bought another round.

FOR FURTHER INFORMATION

Montauk Chamber of Commerce
Box CC
Montauk, Long Island, New York 11954
(516) 668-2428

"The Hamptons":
Amagansett
East Hampton
Bridgehampton
Water Mill
Southampton
Hampton Bays
Quogue
Westhampton

Moving from east to west, this 40-mile lineup of villages is loosely and collectively known as the Hamptons. The name has a suitably patrician ring to it—the Hahmmmptons, dahling—that somehow befits this magical Gatsby land on the far South Fork of Long Island. In fact, as the farmland out here gets sold off acre by acre, these villages are beginning to have more in common than they have differences. And so, like it or lump it, the Hamptons it is: a world where money grows while people play tennis.

You begin to suspect as much as soon as you are halfway out on Long Island, when the Levittown tract homes give way to Canaan-like acreage. This improvement in the landscape is especially evident if you're traveling the Sunrise Highway (Route 27) and not the Long Island Expressway, which it parallels. For one thing, the Sunrise Highway does not require the Road Warrior tactics of the LIE. (Have you ever had a flatbed truck tailgate you at 75 mph—in the right lane? Or followed a ramshackle pickup that things began falling out of? Or been in bumper-to-bumper traffic going 80 mph? No? Well, by all means visit the LIE!) Once you are past the town of Patchogue, the process is almost complete—in every direction you begin to see rolling, verdant farmland, not unlike the Pennsylvania Dutch country. A first visit out here usually elicits this response: "I can't believe all this is so close to New York!"

Well, by the time you reach the Hamptons, you are not that close to New York. You are, in fact, 100 or so miles away. Allowing for traffic, this much-traveled route can take upward of 3 hours, and many more on summer weekends. So, quite literally, the Hamptons are a world away from Manhattan. This is a land of high hedges and higher tax brackets, old oak trees and older money, private clubs and summer mansions, manicured lawns and pedigreed pets, indoor pools and grass tennis courts, dashingly handsome men and women who always look *mahvelous*. (Why are there no ugly rich people?) They travel in Lear jets, jitneys and helicopters, always hurrying off to urgent appointments and ready to indulge any old Elvis-style whim. Their BMWs and Mercedes putter about the town like oversized golf carts. In short, if the people who live out here are not America's landed gentry, at least they *think* they are, and that's about as close to the old British model as this country's ever going to get.

It should come as no surprise that this entire area was settled by the English. The town of Southampton, established in 1640, is the oldest English settlement in New York State. Everybody knows, of course, from watching "Masterpiece Theatre," Sir Laurence Olivier and Benny Hill that Britain is a land of country gentlemen and royal ladies. The British upper crust have always coveted lawns large enough for polo, croquet, cricket, fox hunts and steeplechases, and they grow their hedges tall enough to ensure privacy. The country life of a squire is a grand British tradition. Nowadays, however, that world is more nostalgia than reality—

castles and estates having become whistle stops on travel-bureau bus tours.

Ah, not so in the Hamptons. These folks may have inherited the manners and desires of the British lords and ladies, and even some of the town names, but they have grown the hedges even higher, and in the grand American tradition, have continued to make more money. The wealth is well hidden from sight. And so you end up driving the shaded back streets, ogling and gawking at the manicured beauty of it all, catching glimpses of grandeur through an occasional break in the hedges.

The Hamptons are genuinely pleasing to the eye. There are windmills and ponds, stone stables and woods, old cemeteries and great mansions. And then they have the beaches—a treasure trove of sand and dunes that are hauntingly windswept and wild, and curiously deserted. (We learned that private native conservancies own a lot of the oceanfront.) The best way to see the beaches is to get off the Sunrise Highway at Exit 63 and head south to Westhampton Beach. If you keep winding your way through the maze of back roads, you will eventually come to a drawbridge that will cross over Moriches Bay onto a thin strip of barrier island that would be the easterly continuation of Fire Island had an inlet not been cut. Turn right on Dune Road and drive out to where the island ends at Country Park. Then turn around and travel east for the road's entire length. Perhaps the quietude of places like Quogue and Tiana Beach seems all the more profound after 3 hours on the expressways, but this is an enjoyable, rejuvenating drive along a beach that has an ethereal calm. We even watched two foxes (the animals) chase each other crazily into the underbrush. Foxes on Long Island? Wha?

Although there are intermittent homes on this and every stretch of sand in the Hamptons, there are giant gaps and spaces between them, and the tall dunes remain unmolested. These Hampton beach homes are worth mentioning. Built by what must be some of the hippest Dutch futurists on the architectural scene, they look like Martian Tinkertoys. Their severe modernism is in stark contrast to the desolate beachscape. For the record, most of the town beaches have signs that say things like, "Bathing beach restricted to resident taxpayers only." The rest are private.

Beyond the trend-setting homes and the quiet landscapes, those who live in the Hamptons like to think they have a sense of community out here. And they do have a sense of community—it's just hard to see it from the other side of the hedge. We, for example, overheard this conversation in a Westhampton coffee shop one morning: "Don't work too hard, George. Are you going to play golf today?" "No, I got a big land deal just about in the bag. . . . I gotta stay at home by the phone."

Accommodations

In the figurative ocean known as the Hamptons, a grouper is not a fish. It is a creature, just barely human, who works at a mid-level job in the professional trades (publishing, banking, law, writing memos, sitting at desks in tall buildings) and, to blow off steam, comes here in the summer from Manhattan. The grouper—or so this fish tale goes in the minds of the more moneyed and permanent Hamptonians—begins spawning and frolicking in the nearby waters with thousands of others of its kind, choking the streets of the quaint little villages with car exhaust, jogging madly on the fringes of private lawns, hogging the *New York Times* and the wines and cheeses at the local delicatessens and, in general, befouling the shoreline worse than a hundred grounded oil tankers.

A grouper, in reality, is someone who wants a little seaside rest and relaxation from the summer hell of Manhattan and does not make enough money to buy a house and does not see the Jersey Shore as his or her last resort. The beaches of the Hamptons are beautiful and uncluttered. The motel lodgings are sparse, full of rules and regulations, overpriced and often too far from the water to be worth pursuing. Therefore, a group of like-minded adults of roughly similar economic standing pool their money and rent a house for the summer in one of the Hamptons. Then (this is the tricky part) they attempt to figure out who gets the house on which weekends, how many guests they can bring, where they will all sleep, what everyone owes and when. (Perhaps one in their number is an accountant.) You now have an official school of groupers.

As snooty as the more entrenched citizens can be, they manage to tolerate this invading army, summer after summer. Perhaps this has to do with the fact that everybody out here is involved, in some way, shape or form, with the perpetual recycling of real estate. An unofficial count from the brochures and Yellow Pages yields the names of 45 separate real estate agencies. Our heads spun at the prospect of 45 firm handshakes, 45 proffered cigars and, after our "no thanks," 45 dirty looks, so we headed to Montauk and the Hither Hills campgrounds.

Far be it from us to crack this grouper network, but of the villages that make up the Hamptons, Amagansett and Bridge-hampton seemed the quietest, Southampton and Westhampton the busiest, East Hampton the most exclusive. Gear your vacation expectations accordingly, and realize that you'll probably be spending all summer in traffic. But then, you already know all this. . . .

Restaurants

To borrow a line from a local publication, the cuisine of the Hamptons features "everything from curry to cous-cous." That should tell you what they do not have out here—no burger joints, fast food, pizza deliveries. They will remind you of these things if you get out of line. For instance, here is a personal rebuke, taken from a local gossip column: "Chappy M. is happy to be back in Metropolis after summering in Bridgehampton 'cause now he 'can have his pizzas delivered'! If that's all this 'chap' looks for in the Hamptons, I can suggest a pizzeria that delivers . . . in Des Moines!" Ouch.

What the Hamptons do have is as diverse a selection of cuisine as you are likely to find at any seashore, based as it is upon the Manhattan expectations of the clientele. This translates into genuine haute cuisine—no phony French accents and canned mushroom soup here. We are talking chefs, assistant chefs, wine stewards, maître d's, jackets required, not to mention valet parking and effete snobbish vintners (one of the latter breed subtitles his local wine column "Life After Liebfraumilch"). It goes without saying that the restaurants of highest distinction are fully deserving of their reputation. A "bad" gourmet restaurant in the Hamptons would lose its lease in a week as word got around . . . that sort of thing really, like *really*, ticks them off. A few of the top-rated ones are the *Casa Albona*, the *House on Toilsome* and *Club Burgundy*. And then there is the celeb-dotted gourmet delicatessen known as the *Barefoot Contessa*.

Surprisingly, a goodly number of restaurants eschew such an image. Some even go out of their way to bend against the prevailing winds of snobbery. There is the *Great Hampton Chicken and Rib Co.*, on Route 27 in Southampton. The name alone suggests a gloriously sloppy dinner. Then you can imagine the scene at *PB's Tequila Flats* in East Quogue, which boasts of "the best Tex-Mex on the East End." But the most amusing place has the frumpish-sounding name the *Old Stove Pub*. Located between Bridgehampton and East Hampton, their motto is: "When you're fed up with the chic, come to the Greek."

Nightlife

It is not impossible for an outsider to crack the inner social circle of the Hamptons, just as it is not impossible for a plumber from Bayonne to swim the Hudson River with a meatball balanced on his head. There are probably ways to become one of the beautiful people of the South Fork without having been born into it. For starters, you could get a date with Brooke Shields and take her to the annual Shinnecock Indian Powwow in Southampton. You could be a writer with a hot new "property," preferably a scandalous, name-dropping best seller. You could pretend to know George Plimpton.

Of course, the odds of any of this happening are long. The mannered folk of the Hamptons cling pretty tightly to their illusion of community, and as hard as it may be to believe, money will not necessarily gain you entry into their private world. As a constant reminder of its impenetrability, you will read accounts such as this one in the local papers: "Tanya Brooks, who is from Palm Beach and New York, gave a delightful cocktail party at Tides End, the home of Grenville Walker. . . . The party was limited to 200, which really made it into a large, almost private party."

One repeated visitor to the area, an investment banker by trade, was able to break down this slow melting process into its component parts. He asserts that it takes six years for them to say hello to you, and then six more years for them to remember your name.

If you scan the entertainment guides and newspapers, you will find more names dropped per square inch than there are bluefish off Montauk Point. If those named are not at one of their seemingly endless "large, almost private" parties or twisting and shouting to the oldies (read: *Big Chill*) music at one of their members-only beach clubs, then you might find them mingling with the groupers and gropers at one of several trendy nightspots in the area. (Remember: in the summer, this is the transplanted cream of the Manhattan scene.)

There are two clubs that merit special mention. They don't need to keep up with trends, because in the grand tradition of Studio 54, they set them. First, there is the *Danceteria*, located on Montauk Highway in Water Mill. It's a state-of-the-art dance club owned and operated by the same folks who run the original Danceteria "back home" in Manhattan. The cover charge on the weekends is $15 or $20; anyone who's ever lived in Manhattan is used to this. Often, the club will be used for a semiprivate party ("semi," because the ads imply that peons like you, yes you, are invited, too . . . just be sure to bring $20). Take this party, please, which we regretfully missed: "Nick Oshyo Scirgio and Mitch Paul warmly invite you to a party celebrating the making of their First Million." Or this one we decided to forgo: "Anthony Addison, Phil Siegel and Meghan Boody invite you to a Whip Cream and Handcuffs Party." We didn't know what to wear.

The other Titan of the club scene is a place called *LeMans* (a.k.a. "the Hamptons' Racy Night Club"), located where Routes 27 and 27A converge in Southampton. Resembling a small airplane hangar, LeMans is a summer dance club (it closes after September) with a car-racing obsession. On the next to last weekend of the season, they give away his and her Alfa Romeos. On other nights throughout the summer, they have drawings for cash, handing out up to $1,000 as if it were a bowl of Beer Nuts. The unasked, unanswered question is, how do they do it?

Some of the better places for live rock 'n' roll are the *Canoe Place Inn* (in Hampton Bays) and *Wilson's Garage* (at Westhampton Beach), offering local groups with names like Alive 'n Kickin' and Astriligy. For national acts, *Bay Street* in Sag Harbor (an artist and writer's colony on the north shore of the South Fork) seemed the place to go. James Brown played there the week before we arrived. Good Gawd, y'all.

FOR FURTHER INFORMATION

East Hampton Chamber of Commerce
74 Park Place
East Hampton, New York 11937
(516) 324-0362

Southampton Chamber of Commerce
76 Main Street
Southampton, New York 11986
(516) 283-0402

Westhampton Chamber of Commerce
Riverhead Road
Westhampton Beach, New York 11978
(516) 288-3337

Fire Island

Contrary to what has been said, written, joked about and retold into legend, you do not have to be gay to visit Fire Island. In fact, most of the towns along this 30-mile-long barrier island off the south shore of Long Island are decidedly not gay, in more ways than one. Excepting the exclusively homosexual community of Cherry Grove and the more singles-oriented township of Ocean Bay Park, Fire Island is essentially a family-oriented residential summering outpost. Somewhat oddly, the string of towns along the western half—the most concentrated and populous area of the island—have branded upon all who visit or live in them a bewil-deringly Byzantine set of rules and regulations. Each community has its own variations, posted along the walkways as you enter. These span the societal spectrum, from the brilliant ("no cars are allowed anywhere on the island") to the commonsensical ("no person shall take part in riotous assemblages"), from the near-unconstitutional ("no idle congregating or loitering on public walks") to the Ayatollah-inspired ludicrous ("women must be covered from shoulder to thigh in the business district"—this bit of lunacy was Ocean Beach's, if memory serves). In short, the residents bring their PTA/Boy Scout leader view of reality over with them from the mainland and impose it with the iron hand of a Latin American dictatorship. This is in marked contrast to the social philandering going on in the gay, easterly townships, which are as footloose as the straight communities are philistine. How do they coexist on the same narrow strip of island, year after year? You figure it out . . . we can't. Maybe, without cars, the two populations find it easy to ignore one another.

Before delving further into the issue, we should say that Fire Island possesses a stunning natural beauty and beaches as inviting and swimmable as any on the Atlantic Coast. Fire Island is part of the East Coast's first great barrier-island chain (as you move from north to south); as such, it is constantly shifting—eroding from the east end, primarily—and moving in tune to the whims of the ocean and the storms that blow through. These can do devastating things to private property on both the ocean (through the direct force of waves) and the bay (through overwash) sides of the island. It is a narrow strip of sand, and its ecological balance is precarious. People still talk of the great hurricane of '38, and storms in '84 and '85 served as reminders that nothing is permanent on the beach—even the beach.

Still, it is the sort of place that makes you want to sink roots, even in sandy soil. The lack of cars is a glorious boon to the quality of life; the air is clean (off in the distance, one can see the dome of pollution that envelopes Manhattan); the ferries that run back and forth to the Long Island mainland are swift and efficient; and the beaches are unspoiled and gorgeous. It is only the people who set the municipal agendas who sound a sour note.

Consider this case in point, which is both comical and perverse: the Great Pizza Controversy of 1984. Not since the Cookie Monster was arrested seven years earlier for eating a promotional chocolate-chip cookie on the street has the Fire Island community of Ocean Beach been shaken so deeply. Two teen-age boys were caught redhanded eating slabs of pizza outside the Ocean Beach pizzeria where they had purchased them. They were sitting on the steps of the establishment because there were no more seats available inside. By local ordinance, it is strictly forbidden to eat food on the sidewalks of Ocean Beach; they were arrested, and their moms appealed the $25 fines. The incident escalated into a minor civil war. A court date was set. The community was rocked right down to its cookie sheets.

Ocean Beach is the most stringent community on the island. It posts more signs forbidding you to do things than you'll find on the site of a nuclear-reactor facility. In addition to numerous signs along the walkways, each community posts a multi-item broadside entitled "Excerpts from Code of Ordinances." The most that can be deduced therefrom is that the residents fear an influx of militant nudists ("no undressing or dressing permitted on beaches, walks, roads or among shrubbery").

If you think that's bad, try this "welcome" sign on for size, which greets you as you enter Seaview, a neighboring community: "Welcome to Seaview. Our walks and beaches are private. No trespassing." A curious prohibition. Considering that one must pass through this town to get to the next one, it is logical that your footsteps will carry you over their hallowed ground. It is contemptible that they even suggest that you do not have this right.

Some of the communities farther west—e.g., Kismet, Saltaire— are not so loony when it comes to shoving ordinances down your throat. They are also more exclusive and have less to offer day-trippers and short-term vacationers. Saltaire, originally founded as "the ideal seashore bungalow colony" back in 1910, has changed considerably since those halcyon days, but has much to commend it even now, if you can afford it, particularly solitude.

Turning from the sublime to the ridiculous, we shall now look more closely at Cherry Grove. This part of the island has been commercialized since 1869, when an entrepreneur added a restaurant and inn to his farmhouse, attracting folks such as P. T. Barnum and Mark Twain. After the hurricane of 1938 washed everything away, Cherry Grove became gay. As it was rebuilt, it was in the image of a new sort of beachgoer: wealthy, New York gays drawn from the burgeoning artistic and entertainment communities. Cherry Grove became their haven. It has remained thus, and a local pundit of longstanding—Nat Fowler by name—proudly writes that Cherry Grove is "the gay summer capital of the world."

It is so gay and so insulated from straight intrusions, even from all the aggrieved bluebloods up Ocean Beach way, that this same writer can claim the Ivory Soap statistic as his sociological measuring stick: "Like Ivory Soap, Cherry Grove is 99 and 44/100 percent pure." A healthy portion of soap suds, it's worth noting, have also spilled over into the neighboring and more moneyed community of Fire Island Pines.

But Cherry Grove remains the bathtub of first choice. Fowler, writing on the history of the town in the *Fire Island Tide*, cites the long Broadway run of Wolcott Gibbs' play *A Season in the Sun* in the early fifties as a real milestone insofar as the play "made the terms 'homosexual' and 'Fire Island' practically synonymous." Today, as ever, the gay community goes about its frolics free of scrutiny or castigation from flag-waving homophobes. And so there is an easy, unfettered air about this party-oriented community, evident in the conversational tone of the local gossip column. Check out this tidbit, about Bingo Night in Cherry Grove: "And do you know who has been bringing in free cookies to the players? Charlie of the Peppermint Stick, that's who."

There is nothing we can add, pro or con, that will change anybody's mind about Cherry Grove. You simply do not come here unless you are a consenting adult who knows what the ropes are. In short, explaining Cherry Grove to a gay would be as redundant as trying to describe Parris Island to a marine.

Somewhere between the two extremes inhabiting this island, there is a happy medium, and that is the town of Ocean Bay Park. Reachable by ferry from the mainland Long Island town of Bay Shore, Ocean Bay Park is literally and figuratively at the center of Fire Island. It tends to draw singles from Manhattan for the weekend, both daytrippers and groupers and correspondingly has more nightlife and zip than the stuffy towns to the west. In contrast to Ocean Beach and Seaview, Ocean Bay Park has a law and order all its own that is observed without the use of signs, reminders and/or arm-bending peer-group pressure. It tends to take the approach that if you are intelligent and discerning enough to visit Fire Island, then you are also responsible enough not to be treated like unruly children when you get there. Enough said.

A few more notes. At the extreme western end of the island—farther west even than the *Fire Island Lighthouse* and the island's westernmost community, Kismet—is *Robert Moses State Park*. There is a bridge over to the park, from the Long Island mainland, and ample parking. People come over for the day to swim, fish and so forth. It's especially popular with New Yorkers on hot summer weekends.

As for getting ferried over to the dozen communities on Fire Island that are serviced by passenger boat, it is beyond the scope or province of this book to offer detailed schedules. Suffice it to say that ferry service is frequent, and you can get there from Bay Shore (serves Kismet, Saltaire, Fair Harbor, Dunewood, Ocean Beach, Seaview, Ocean Bay Park and Point of Woods); Sayville (Sunken Forest, Fire Island Pines and Cherry Grove) and Patchogue (Davis Park, Watch Hill). Detailed schedules are printed in each edition of the *Fire Island Tide*, the island's biweekly news magazine (and a good way to acquaint yourself with the island).

Accommodations

Group rentals are getting harder and harder to get out here and in the nearby Hamptons. The more permanent, older residents—paragons of the burn-the-bridges mentality—have declared war on singles who congregate under one roof, even if they're renting for the entire summer. Ocean Beach, for instance, posts this dictum at its ferry landing: "No group rentals to more than four unrelated persons." So, just hope you can locate a sympathetic community or landlord, and bring your birth certificate, just in case. There are few hotels per se on the island, and most of these communities have been family-oriented for many decades, meaning that the same families rent the same houses year after year. It's like trying to get tickets for the Redskins-Cowboys game.

There is one very distinctive alternative: *Flynn's Hotel*, in Ocean Bay Park. Flynn's is a restaurant/hotel/marina complex that has been in business for over half a century. The hotel is located one sand dune away from a heavenly beach. (The restaurant and marina are on the bay side, barely 300 yards away.) While no one will mistake Flynn's for a major-city Hilton, the rooms are adequate—e.g., they have beds, dressers and clean linen—and the rusticity is addictive, especially after dark, when even a short hike down the walkway necessitates a flashlight. The main building of the hotel used to be the Point O' Woods Coast Guard Station, and dates back to the 1880s. The adjoining buildings are strewn about the sand in the direction of the beach. There is a communal lounge in one of the buildings, with the only TV set in the hotel. The beach itself—well, we could rhapsodize at length, but simply stated, Fire Island offered the most enjoyable swimming in terms of water temperature, cleanliness and absence of beach debris, not to mention natural beauty, that we'd yet had on our sojourn. And Flynn's is eminently affordable. They offer a five day/four night midweek special or a European weekly plan, in addition to single-night rentals. The prices were surprisingly moderate. No better deal exists at any decent beach within a Long Island Railroad ride of New York City.

Restaurants

For those folks who can qualify for long-term rental or outright ownership of one of the limited number of houses on the island, the way to deal with food is to send large hauls of groceries over from the mainland on the daily freight boat. (Groceries are not allowed on the regular ferry, and there are no big supermarkets on Fire Island.) The short-term visitor or daytripper might find himself in a bit of a quandary over food. You are allowed two pieces of luggage on the passenger ferry, so maybe the best thing to do is fill one of them with nonperishable foods . . . peanuts, popcorn, candied apples. . . . In other words, bring your own midway over with you.

Without beating a dead seahorse, however, and all joking aside, it should be repeated that some Fire Island communities do not take kindly to public displays of food consumption, and every single one bans food on the beach. At the height of the Great Pizza Controversy of 1984, the mayor of Ocean Beach sniffed, "If people are going to fight to allow pizza [on the walkways], we may have to go back to eating nothing at all." An exception had been made for pastries, as a result of the Cookie Monster caper seven years earlier. In his defense, it should be noted that the mayor is not the architect of this strict legislation; it has been on the town books, in one form or another, since the 1920s. So watch what you eat and where you eat it, comrades.

As for restaurants, Cherry Grove and Fire Island Pines, not surprisingly, have the best selection. But if you are not staying overnight, it is an expensive water-taxi ride up and back. (Water taxis, also known as lateral ferries, are the only way to get around the island, other than *à pied*.)

Undoubtedly, the restaurants in Ocean Beach had to go through the legalistic equivalent of the Twelve Tasks of Hercules to obtain their permits, and they seem to pass the frustration on to their customers. A simple breakfast at a place called *Morning Call* turned into a nerve-racking test of wills with our waitress. All six of our requests for water and coffee refills were ignored, and after we stiffed the surly college-aged gal on a tip (leaving an explanatory note on our napkin: "A tip is for service. We got no service. You get no tip"), our expensive American cheese omelettes sat heavy in our stomachs.

Ocean Bay Park has a small grocery store/deli, a taco and pizza stand and three bona fide restaurants. *Flynn's* is the best, and though not inexpensive, amply compensates your investment with good food and a nice setting upon the waters of the bay. Around the corner, *Skimmers* is a cut below in price, and also in service and atmosphere. Our waitress—we were on a bad-luck streak—was apparently running late for her water taxi home, and her service consisted of frantic, frequent visits to our table, highlighted by the absurd query, "Would you like some dessert or coffee now?" spoken just seconds after she'd delivered Frisbee-sized cheeseburgers to our table. We held the burgers to our lips like enormous harmonicas and played the blues. Gosh, she didn't even stick around to pick up her tip.

A hot tip for late-afternoon imbibers who have an appetite is Flynn's Happy Hour, where they bring out plate after plate of free hot hors d'oeuvres, the likes of which we've never seen equaled: barbecued ribs, stuffed clams, chicken fingers and so forth. Fill 'er up and hang round until the entertainment begins.

Nightlife

As we've said, it gets dark here at night. Very dark. Not only are there no cars on the island, there are very few streetlights to guide your feet. On a clear night, the moon and stars' illumination will keep you from veering into the shrubbery. But a flashlight is what you really need. For nightlife on this family-dominated island (excepting the relentless gamboling of the gay communities), there is precious little else to choose from.

Yes, Cherry Grove has the most celebrated nightlife, with a heavy emphasis on costume parties that last all night long, softball games where the girls invariably beat the boys and, toward evening's end, the ceremonial removal of the partitions between toilets in nightclub rest rooms. For those whose tastes are more mainstream, the pickings are rather lean. In Ocean Beach, there is *Le Bistro*, with promotional photographs of the entertainment posted outside—mostly solo singers, well-dressed and no doubt well-rehearsed. But given Ocean Beach's propensity for law and order, one stumble or minor impropriety could end in an execution. Yours.

Once again, we must direct you to *Flynn's*. On the weekend, the live rock 'n' roll does not stop until 4 A.M., and is legendary as a singles stomping ground. During the week, Flynn's caters to more of a dinner-boat crowd, with a lightweight band playing show tunes and big-band numbers to a more sedate audience.

FOR FURTHER INFORMATION

We suggest writing to obtain a copy of the *Fire Island Tide* (P.O. Box 8, Davis Park, New York 11772) in order to get a handle on the island. Also, try writing the Sayville Chamber of Commerce, P.O. Box 235, Sayville, New York 11782.

Jones Beach State Park

To those whose lives are circumscribed by the five boroughs of New York City, Jones Beach is not just a beach, it's a godsend. Literally hundreds of thousands trek out here on hot summer weekends. Many Manhattanites ride the Long Island Railroad from Penn Station out to Freeport, then board a bus that spirits them to Jones Beach. They want to get out here, they need to get out here, they *will* get out here, and nothing is going to stop them.

This may be the most heavily visited beach on the East Coast, but there are no motels for miles around, and your food options are mostly limited to hot dogs, clam chowder and ice cream at stand-up concession stands. Jones Beach is endless. There are ten parking fields (not lots), each of them an airline runway-sized spread of flat concrete. There's an outdoor amphitheater out here, as well as a golf course, baseball diamonds, shuffleboard and paddle tennis courts, a pool and picnic areas. Best of all, you can spread a beach blanket under a bright blue sky and watch the waves churn all day, and maybe—just maybe—you'll forget about that grubby, roach-infested studio apartment you call home back in the big filthy city. Like we said, it's a godsend.

Long Beach

Another link in the barrier-island chain, this one is even closer to Manhattan than Jones Beach. There are three towns out here—

Lido Beach, Long Beach and Atlantic Beach—as well as a 3-mile beach and a 5-mile boardwalk.

FOR FURTHER INFORMATION

Long Beach Chamber of Commerce
100 W. Park Avenue
Long Beach, Long Island, New York 11561
(516) 432-6000

Rockaway Beach, Queens

Quite a bit less godlike than Jones Beach, Rockaway is nonetheless much loved by the residents of this, the largest of New York City's five boroughs. You can get here by subway (don't listen to Duke Ellington: take the F train), and the Ramones wrote one of their best songs about it, so it's gotta be cool. Even if some of the fish swim upside down here.

Coney Island, Brooklyn

Coney Island is the most famous beach in New York, the East Coast, America, maybe. One does not "vacation" here. One puts a token in the turnstile, boards a groaning subway full of misfits and steps out, about an hour later, blinking in the sunlight. There's a boardwalk, a legendary amusement park and the inevitable hot dogs. Coney Island is trash with class. It has been immortalized by such writers as Lawrence Ferlinghetti, Lou Reed and Richard Price. Woody Allen recalled it fondly in *Annie Hall*.

To understand the appeal of Coney Island, you must appreciate and love the ways of the city. It's hard to explain to someone who recoils at screeching subway brakes, obnoxious accents and gruff behavior, porky red hot dogs slathered with mustard and relish, roller coasters and "Wonder Wheels," concrete boardwalks and the smell of cotton candy and rancid grease . . . but there is a peculiar attraction to this low-rent bazaar. The beach is nicer than you'd think. Not that you need to hot-foot it over here right away, but Coney Island is *not half-bad*. And if you hail from "the city," it's part of your heritage.

New Jersey: That's "Joisey," as in "Noisy"

Like icing on the Carvel sheet cake of New Jersey, a chain of barrier islands and a white sandy shoreline provide the state with its summer retreat from the heat, beat and concrete of its cities. Well, sort of. They refer to this disjointed coastline as a single entity, "the Jersey Shore," and from Sandy Hook to Cape May, it does manage to have one item in common: the ocean. This distinguishes it from, say, the mountains or the Pine Barrens. Beyond that, the surf rolls over all sorts of diverse turf, from the berserk, carnival-like frenzy of Jersey's boardwalk-spined beaches to the calmer havens of the south shore.

Really, though, when people who are not familiar with New Jersey (those who think of it as a suburb of New York City) hear the term "Jersey Shore," they think "Joisey," as in "noisy," and quickly change the subject. It's not necessarily that they can't believe New Jersey owns a coastline; what is inconceivable is that a civilized person would voluntarily go there for a summer vacation.

But "go" they indeed do, although that verb does not seem adequate, given the numbers. Try "flock," "swarm," "inundate"— anything but "stay away." They shoot out from their suburban hot boxes and stifling inner-city high-rises and shake, rattle and roll their way down the Garden State Parkway to the exit of their choice. Then they proceed to set up a similar sort of camp at the

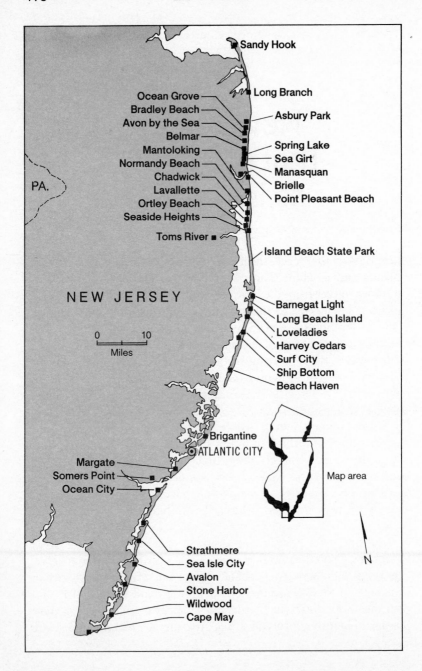

Sandy Hook

Long Branch

Ocean Grove
Bradley Beach
Avon by the Sea
Belmar

Asbury Park

Spring Lake
Sea Girt
Manasquan
Brielle
Point Pleasant Beach

Mantoloking
Normandy Beach
Chadwick
Lavallette
Ortley Beach
Seaside Heights

Toms River

Island Beach State Park

NEW JERSEY

0   10
Miles

Barnegat Light
Long Beach Island
Loveladies
Harvey Cedars
Surf City
Ship Bottom
Beach Haven

PA.

Brigantine
ATLANTIC CITY

Margate
Somers Point
Ocean City

Map area

Strathmere
Sea Isle City
Avalon
Stone Harbor
Wildwood
Cape May

N

shore: mile after mile of cacophonous boardwalk and acres of cinder-block condominiums, flyblown motels, saltbox cottages, mobile-home parks and gaming arcades. The result, on the north Jersey Shore at least, is that once-beautiful barrier islands have been buried in a mind-boggling blanket of alleged summer-vacationing fun. This is the Jersey Shore that most tri-state (New York, Pennsylvania, New Jersey) natives know and love, and that the rest of the nation has largely left alone.

In the popular mind, a Jersey vacation would be the equivalent of banging your head against the wall. But there is another aspect to the Jersey Shore, or at least there are pockets of calm scattered throughout the 120-mile pant leg of land that makes up the coast. Here, less tortured souls can wander, wonder and enjoy themselves without horns honking, bells clanging and babes a-wailing. Such enclaves include Long Beach Island and the area known as "the Cape" (from Sea Isle City to Cape May). These are the places where the knowledgeable Jerseyites (and you, if you're smart) will point their automobiles when the whistle blows and the boss says, "G'wan, git outta heah, dis is yore friggin' vacation!"

One more note: there is a phenomenon on the Jersey Shore that you'll not encounter elsewhere. It is the beach badge. A beach badge is a button that must be purchased and pinned onto your swimwear before you can set foot on a Jersey beach—all of them, excepting Wildwood. Usually, they're sold right on the beach, at the manned points where you enter and are checked. They take this racket seriously, and you stand a good chance of getting caught if you attempt to flout your beach-badge responsibility. The consequences are not as dire as getting caught shoplifting, but the humiliation is every bit as public.

Gateway National Recreation Area (Sandy Hook Unit)

Sandy Hook is the first ocean beach in New Jersey. It extends like a claw above the town of Highlands, as if groping in vain for Coney Island, which lies due north. Sandy Hook is one of four public parks that make up the Gateway National Recreation Area. It is the only one in New Jersey; the others all belong to various New York City boroughs. Considered together, this is one of the most heavily visited national park areas in the country.

Sandy Hook itself is a barrier-beach peninsula. Formerly a productive fishing and clamming ground for the Lenni-Lenape Indian tribe, it is now a government-administered parkland that offers a variety of ecological niches for recreation and study. Sandy Hook is open year-round, and its beach is lifeguarded during the summer months. Admission is free.

Long Branch

Long Branch was, at one time, the summering grounds for three U.S. presidents—Wilson, Grant and Garfield—and a high-class resort for wealthy, well-heeled Philadelphians. Not so now. For even though it is the largest resort town on the north Jersey Shore (pop. 30,000) and among America's very first seaside spas, it sits like a tarnished jewel in a crumbling setting of eroding bluffs and beaches, its glory days but a glittering memory. You can still catch glimpses of its noble history, but in a different light. The statue of President Garfield, for instance, at *Seven Presidents Park* has been spray-painted by so many different vandals that it more resembles some weird urban totem pole than an assassinated leader (who, incidentally, died in Long Branch, two months after being shot in Washington).

The town has an extensive, 7-mile oceanfront, 2 miles of which are covered by boardwalk, but the fingerprints of doom sit nearby: high-rise condos face a beach that has been steadily eroding away, claiming even the streets that parallel it. The nightlife in this town is equally cheerless, consisting of big-city go-go establishments with blinking-light floor shows and exotic dancers. As for food, Long Branch's cuisine was aptly summed up by the restaurant with the biggest sign. It was called Stuff Yer Face. Somehow, hunger deserted us in the face of that invitation.

FOR FURTHER INFORMATION

Greater Long Branch Chamber of Commerce
494 Broadway
Long Branch, New Jersey 07740
(201) 222-0400

Asbury Park

Over ten years ago when the two of us were in college and easily given to impulsive movement, one of us was moved to visit Asbury Park, New Jersey. Against all protests from his Jersey relations, whom he was visiting, this particular beach bum dragged his younger cousins along with him for the day. He had no desire to see the ocean or to smell the salt breeze, nor necessarily to entertain his junior relations. His sole motivation was to pay his respects to the hometown of Bruce Springsteen. He wanted to experience the town that had inspired the Boss—to feel it, see it, touch it, indeed to do everything short of heal it.

In those dreadful days of the early seventies, we were both prone to undue exaltation over any vital sign that bleeped of new life on the rock-music cardiogram. We were eating miserably, yet we found money in our budget to buy records. One of us worked at a record store; the other owned enough albums to stock a record store. We'd abandon our studies and cross several state lines just to see a concert by a favorite artist. You get the picture. After hearing Bruce Springsteen's first album, *Greetings from Asbury Park* (named after the now-legendary fluorescent-orange tourist postcard), one of us was called, as if by the Head Rockin' Siren himself, upon a solo mission, the purpose of which was uncertain though the destination was clear. The beach bum had to stand inside the seed bed of such deeply felt music.

The beach bum can now remember walking with his little cousins along the Asbury Park boardwalk, buying them cotton candy and feigning an excitement equal to their own as they rode the rickety rides that were still running at the amusement park. He can remember, too, staring bug-eyed at the empty hulk of the town: fleabag popcorn stands and idle overgrown putt-putt courses and the red-brick hugeness of a once-grand convention hall that now stood like something that barely survived Hiroshima. And, of course, the beach bum took photographs, because being of college age and therefore moved to expansive emotional swings, he perversely enjoyed the grim subject matter all around him.

Now that the Boss is indeed worthy of his titular nickname, the beach bum would have thought that some of his luster might have rubbed off on his old hometown. The beach bum was wrong. The parlors here are still boarded up. Real grass is now crawling over the fake greenery of the putt-putt courses. The convention hall and casino look unfit to house the "big events" they now advertise: pro wrestling and beer-can swaps. And the town continues its downward spiral onto the slag heap, while the chamber of commerce and the town officials, like vaudevillians in need of a new routine, keep doing the same old song and dance about the "new" Asbury Park, about all the development that is being attracted here, all the new jobs, all the changes that are going to be made.

On a beautiful day in mid-August, all we saw were the boarded-up remnants of yesteryear. Only the stalwart Madame Marie still hangs her shingle. (Of her, Springsteen once sang, "The cops finally busted Madame Marie for telling fortunes better than they do." No one said that Bruce is *always* profound.) The same perfectly attractive beaches and their gleaming blue waters are but sparsely visited. The same procession of old and disoriented people still stalk the rickety boards, though they look more uneasy at the sound of the occasional passing boom box with each passing year. In short, the place has not changed or rebounded at all.

In the face of all that doom, we were barely able to take any pleasure from topping our previous Skee-Ball highs of 370 at an overly easy local arcade. Even there, where the idea is to have fun, the diminutive Italian proprietor, when asked to comment on the demise of his town, launched into a frighteningly hateful diatribe against his fellow man—berating dis guy, dat guy and duh udduh guy, describing a confusing web of raw deals, shady dealings and unmitigated corruption.

And so, we'll stop short of answering the obvious question, raised by the lyrics of Springsteen's most famous song, wherein he warned his listener that "it's a death trap, it's a suicide rap, you better get out while you're young . . . 'cause tramps like us, baby, we were born to run." But we will pose the question nevertheless. Was the Boss referring to his own hometown of Asbury Park? Or to all of New Jersey? (A corollary question: Why, in either case, did the New Jersey State Legislature very nearly select "Born to Run" as the state song? Is this a state with an image problem, or what?)

Despite the gloomy prognosis for Asbury Park, the potential for a phoenix-like rise from the ashes is always there. After all, the joy of every kid in the summer is to go to the beach, and Asbury Park's shorefront and the nearby population centers that could revive it are still there. (New York is 70 miles away, and Philly a mere 60.) The beach itself is as pristine and inviting as it is underused. People should be lining up to buy beach badges ($3 on weekends, $2 weekdays), just as they do when Asbury Park's native son's concert tickets go on sale.

Accommodations

Actually, the Asbury Park area does offer a break in prices, though you get what you pay for, and what you get is Asbury Park. Rooms at the *Pier Six Hotel*, a huge, sprawling house two blocks off the water, start at an unheard-of $18. The *Oceanic Inn*, a more generic sort of motel, offered a double room for $30, with morning coffee and greasy dunking sticks thrown in. And so it goes all over town. There are reasons for the bargain-basement prices, chiefly having to do with the low demand for rooms here. The day after we left, an arsonist torched one of the fleabag transient hotels, and a number of lives were lost.

One more note: Asbury Park has a bad reputation for small crime, even among its citizens. We were needlessly advised to lock our car by the hired hand at the Oceanic, as if, because of our North Carolina license plates, he took us to be rubes from Andy

Griffith's Mayberry. Actually, the most threatening thing we encountered was the jarring sight of a bearded woman feeding pigeons on the sidewalk in front of the motel the next morning. Just another mental patient with no home or hope.

Restaurants

The hot dogs and pizza slabs on the boardwalk are served by people who look like shell-shock victims. At least at the *Howard Johnson's* just off the boardwalk you can predict what you will eat, how long you'll have to wait for it to be served, what Muzak will be playing and so forth.

Nightlife

About the only remaining sign of Bruce Springsteen's legacy is the *Stone Pony*, a club he regularly played when he started out and which is now more frequently played by his imitators. According to a consensus of travel acquaintances, this is the only viable rock 'n' roll club left on the Jersey Shore. There is, if your taste strays in that direction, a place called *Xanadu* mere blocks away. Though well-hidden among the clatter and in the cracks, a gay community of sorts has been developing in Asbury Park, with the result that the town can now boast a few more loud, glitzy nightclubs.

FOR FURTHER INFORMATION

Greater Asbury Park Chamber of Commerce
P.O. Box 649
Asbury and Ocean Avenue
Asbury Park, New Jersey 07712
(201) 775-7676

Ocean Grove
Bradley Beach
Avon-by-the-Sea
Belmar
Spring Lake
Sea Girt
Manasquan
Brielle

Apologies for the laundry list, but this seemed the most efficient way to handle a bunch of largely residential towns strung out along in a row, like beads in a chain, south out of Asbury Park. The farther south you go, the more they improve in terms of prosperity and appearance, though none of them are really vacation destinations of any consequence. But waves do break here, so here goes.

Entering Ocean Grove from Asbury Park, we dashed off on a notepad "starts to improve here," followed by the resigned conclusion "no, more of the same." Being somewhat out of the line of direct fire, Ocean Grove, Bradley Beach and Avon Park are safer than Asbury Park. They have their little boardwalks and old hotels, but recommending that you come here seems rather pointless.

Belmar is the most tourist-oriented of all of these, with a boardwalk, amusement parks and motels at the oceanfront. It is a modestly scaled version of the more extensive boardwalk towns to the north (Asbury Park) and south (Seaside Heights). Belmar is cleaner and calmer than the competition, too—there's just enough to do to have fun without overwhelming the beach. Quite attractive, really.

Spring Lake, Sea Girt and Manasquan each have public beaches, boardwalks and accommodations. These towns are more residential than touristy, however, and the places to stay, particularly on the ocean, tend to be bed-and-breakfasts or venerable, Victorian-type hotels on manicured grounds. None is really geared toward families or singles, although many inland dwellers come for the day, parking on the streets and walking to the beach. Beach badges average about $2 a day, $5 for the weekend.

Brielle, meanwhile, regards itself as so exclusive that it has declared its beaches off-limits to the public. Beach badges can be purchased by residents only. Spring Lake was that way up until a few years ago, when it went public. Now, you're lucky to find a parking place within five blocks of the beach. In a way, the locals' displeasure at the infestation of transients into their neighborhoods is understandable, but there is some debate as to the legality of Brielle's ban on outsiders.

Incidentally, as a side note (or trip), in Spring Lake Heights (inland from Spring Lake, off Route 71) there is a restaurant that gets our highest commendations. Dinner at the *Old Mill Inn* is practically a vacation in itself. Built facing a large pond, with a mill wheel and mill stream rushing past the windows, the Old Mill Inn has a statewide reputation, and deservedly so. The menu emphasizes seafood and Italian cooking, and both food and atmosphere are special.

There are places to go at night, it turns out, too. Here is a list of some of the best fun spots on this stretch of the coast, compiled with the assistance of some of the most discriminating waitresses on the Jersey Shore: *D.J.'s* and *Bar Anticipation* (Belmar); *Parker House* (Sea Girt); *Champagne Porch* (Spring Lake); *Jessie's* (Brielle); *Casablanca*, *Main Street Saloon* and the *Osprey* (Manasquan). But the verdict all over, even when these fine places were being touted, was that the *Stone Pony* in Asbury Park is still the preeminent rock club in these parts. Any joint that has the halo of Bruce Springsteen about it has got to be the place, right?

FOR FURTHER INFORMATION

Ocean Grove Area Chamber of Commerce
P.O. Box 365
Ocean Grove, New Jersey 07756
(201) 774-1391

Point Pleasant Beach

Just over the Barnegat River from Brielle lies the town of Point
Pleasant Beach, an appendage of the larger inland city of Point
Pleasant. "Pleasant" is the operative word here. Point Pleasant
Beach has a large marina, a sandy 2-mile beach and lots of recreational facilities for those who love the water. In the main, the
area tends toward rentals, with a lot of bungalow and shoebox-
style homes arranged in neat rows. But there's also nearly a dozen
motels on or close to the beach and an equal number of guest
homes as well. So you won't go without a place to stay in any
case, and you might even find something to do after dark at the
Village Inn or the *Barber Shop*. Though we did not witness this
ourselves, the wags at the chamber of commerce promise "many
excellent restaurants within a 1 ¼-mile radius, featuring quiet
music and dancing, as well as some lively disco for the young at
heart" (or soft in head). All in all, Point Pleasant Beach is one of
those generic Jersey seaside communities that has found the golden
mean between sun-beaten boardwalk hysteria and the regenera-
tive calm of a wide, breezy beach. And don't forget, every July,
around mid-month, Point Pleasant Beach plays host to the New
Jersey Offshore Grand Prix Power Boat Race. Varoom, varoom!

FOR FURTHER INFORMATION

Greater Point Pleasant Area Chamber of Commerce
517 Arnold Avenue
Point Pleasant Beach, New Jersey 08742
(201) 899-2424

Seaside Heights

By one self-appraisal, Seaside Heights is "the Vacation Capital of
the East Coast." Admittedly, there is more going on here, more

crowds and mayhem, than anywhere else on the Jersey coast save Atlantic City. But East Coast Vacation Capital?

The town belongs to the young. Seemingly every Jersey youth with two quarters to rub together winds up spending his or her evening—and quarters—on the boardwalk. Mom and Dad might be paying for the vacation, but it's their teenage offspring who set the tone out where the waves roll. And the tone is loud, a metallic screech of guitars and cymbals emanating from bars, arcades and ghetto-blasters. It comes blaring out of cranked-up cassette decks through rolled-down car windows. The hoarse-throated entreaties of lubricious rock singers and the frantic squalling of metal guitar armies practically drown out the roar of the surf.

Oh, there's an ocean over there? Yes, there is a beach sitting pretty on the far side of the aqua slides, flying horses, bumper cars, gaming wheels, pizza counters, clam bars, video-game dungeons and beer saloons. Seaside Heights sits at the midpoint of Island Beach, a 20-mile-long barrier peninsula that is now technically a barrier island, ever since the Manasquan River Canal was dredged out up at the north end, severing the peninsula from the mainland. Like a straight pinball shot, Seaside Heights sits directly at the end of the bridge over from the mainland. To the north there is a run of communities that are quieter and more family oriented. To the south lies Island Beach State Park. But for most people coming to the area for the day, weekend or even week (or two), Seaside Heights is the target.

The beach, which runs the entirety of the island, is magnificent, with gleaming, snow-white sand and cool blue surf that runs in long swells and breaks gently on the shore. There are waves enough to attract some surfing action, and there is an annual Surfer Contest that draws blond board bums from all over. Island Beach, looked at solely in its natural state, is an example of the Jersey Shore at its underappreciated finest. The beaches of this oft bad-mouthed state (ignoring the man-made communities that sprawl around them) actually compare favorably with those of the Caribbean and Riviera. If you tend to disbelieve us, stand on the beach at Seaside Heights and look out to sea: the evidence is right before your eyes.

Now, turn and face in the other direction, toward the caprice and cacophony of the boardwalk, and you'll be reminded you're in Jersey all over again—that Jersey, the one of the *r*-less accents, of muscle T-shirts that say things like "Send Rambo to Lebanon," of bands of teen nomads wandering the planks in search of noisy thrills.

Here, on the boardwalk at Seaside Heights, a novel form of economic transaction takes place. There are lots of small booths that stock particular items of varying degrees of usefulness—everything from LPs and tapes to Cabbage Patch Kids, from color TVs to Kewpie dolls. But these goods are not paid for with cash; not directly, anyway. You win them by betting quarters on a wheel of fortune. Put your quarter down in the square with the number you want to bet on; when a few bets have piled up, the guy in the booth will give the pointer a healthy spin. It will come to rest on a number, but it will invariably not be a number that anyone has bet on, and he'll sweep the quarters into a change trough behind the counter. Occasionally, the ticker comes to rest on a number or symbol chosen by some lucky bettor, who will walk away with a nearly free prize. A Quiet Riot album, maybe, or a mirror with the words IRON MAIDEN embossed on it.

It's a good thing folks don't have to buy their groceries this way, we joked. Then we came upon a stall where people were gambling on the wheel of misfortune to win bags of food. And individual items like aluminum foil, a can of coffee, a bag of flour, Pampers. The word "depressed" does not even begin to describe our mood at this juncture.

Not to paint a gloomy, Marxist-prophesied picture of capitalist doom here at Seaside Heights. The boardwalk does bustle with crowds of apparently happy people. Mostly, this is a working-class vacation mecca for tri-state families who rent or own small, boxlike cottages, or pay the motel keepers' overpriced tariffs for a few days.

The communities north of Seaside Heights are another story. These other towns—Ortley Beach, Lavallette, Ocean Beach, Chadwick, Normandy Beach and, finally, Mantoloking—are weaker links in the chain of tourism. Ortley Beach accommodates some of the Seaside Heights spillover, but by Lavallette, the boardwalk lifestyle has slowed considerably. Moving north, the motels are spaced farther apart, ceding ground to summer cottages and year-round homes.

South out of Seaside Heights is the tacked-on community of Seaside Park, a neighborhood of identical saltbox cottages that look as sun-baked and -beaten as any adobe village in the American Southwest. This development stops abruptly at the gates of *Island Beach State Park*, which occupies the rest of the island till it runs out at Barnegat Inlet, a distance of about 8 miles. This well-cared-for park offers two ocean beaches with a half-mile of soft white sand and peerless surf, as well as a nature center. Dune buggies and Jeeps are permitted. The park is extremely popular; by ten in the morning, it was full, and no more cars were being allowed in, so get a head start and beat the crowds. The fee is $4 per car on weekends, $3 on weekdays. Much of Island Beach State Park is given over to ecological research and is a wildlife sanctuary.

In its own way, Seaside Heights is a wildlife sanctuary as well, especially at night. When the summer sun goes down, a thousand neon suns blink on, and the town goes berserk. There are numerous go-go bars and dance clubs along Boulevard Street, the main drag. The primary entertainment is Top Forty disco music, played by deejays at dog-deafening volumes in clubs with pulsing, lit-up dance floors and swirling mirrored balls bouncing points of light off of walls and faces. And the eyes on those faces constantly scan the premises, checking out other faces, trying to establish some sort of beachhead with eyebrow-raising gestures, since the music is so loud that one could only be understood with a bullhorn, if he or she had anything interesting to say to begin with. And the beat goes on.

Not everyone is happy about this. At a quiet wood-and-hanging-plant bar, a 22-year-old kid with a pudding-bowl haircut was nursing a beer while lamenting the death of rock 'n' roll on the Jersey Shore. Rock died, he explained, when the drinking age was raised from 18 to 21. The under-21 set are rockers; their older brothers and sisters are into dance music and pick-up scene charades. When the drinking age was raised, the rock clubs lost their best customers. Clubs closed, and bands either adapted their act to the

Top Forty or perished. (A sobering thought: what becomes of a rocker who's washed up on the Jersey Shore? One would almost rather be a dead clam.)

The only great rock club left on the Jersey coast is the Stone Pony, the kid vouched. It was about the thirtieth such testimonial we'd heard in a few days. Nowadays, all of the sullen-faced, drink-disfranchised youth have little else to do but waste time on board-walk benches and the hoods of their cars, glowering and blasting their surly music into the reluctant ears of passers-by as some sort of revenge. A typical sight: on the boardwalk, three strays were enacting, with Kabuki-like gestures, some sort of violent panto-mime while a Judas Priest tape blared distortedly from their luggage-sized boom box. It did not look like fun.

Meanwhile, Pudding Bowl Haircut was alternately watching the Mets lose on TV and making solemn statements about rock's bygone glory days. The only bar band he liked anymore was an outfit called Yasgur's Farm, which plays note-for-note renditions of the music from the Woodstock Festival. You know, from 1969. When the Mets rallied late in the game, his spirits brightened, and with a few beers in him, he even predicted in an unguarded mo-ment that rock would make a glorious rebound on the Jersey Shore and send that damned dance music reeling into the ropes.

Obliviously, the night pounded on along the Seaside Heights boardwalk, moving to its own relentless rhythms as tides of people surged back and forth, looking for something to do, something to claim their attention for a few seconds. Unchanged in appear-ance since the fifties, Seaside Heights endures as a bury-your-cares mecca for the two-weeks-a-year crowd. They inhale and ex-hale fun with such grisly determination that you realize what has changed since the fifties is not the beach, but the economic pressures brought to bear on American families the other fifty weeks of the year.

Accommodations

Ironically, Seaside Heights paints itself as a beach for budget-minded families, yet its motels were among the most expensive we encountered anywhere and the town is far too touristy, prefab and devoid of historical interest to have any significant number of bed-and-breakfast type options.

Motel room rates double in season—$80 or more a night in June, July and August is not uncommon. The motels themselves, however, are pretty common, in number and appearance. You do not get good value per dollar staying here, but there is always an army of suckers from the metropolitan pipeline who'll cheerfully sign the guest registers. So great is the demand that the motel owners are able to tack on other conditions, such as a two- or three-day minimum stay. Some of them will not even rent to anyone but married couples with children. No singles. "Didja come here to party?" one motel clerk asked suspiciously when we requested a room.

Our hot tip is to stay on the other side of the bridge in the town of Toms River. Rooms are cheaper, the motels are nice or nicer, the neighborhoods are quieter and Seaside Heights is just a short hop away.

Restaurants

When you're raising hell in a place like Seaside Heights, eating becomes merely a biological function. We couldn't bring ourselves to abandon the boardwalk merely to look over a few generic "family restaurants"—you know, the sort that serve fish-stick dinners at prices low enough so Dad can afford to feed the family without taking out a second mortgage. Like all the hungry young beachcombers with the dirty-blond hair and muscle T's and their bikini'd, tattooed, underage girl friends, we marched right up to the boardwalk grease stalls and feasted upon the local specialties: fried fish sandwiches, crab cakes, pizza and calzone, six on the half shell, funnel cake. As they say, when in Rome. . . .

Nightlife

Let's not mince words. Seaside Heights is crass. Its clubs and discos are large, loud and competitive. Most of them are turntable-oriented, and their covers average around $3. Each has its own "Mr. Personality"-type deejay, and competition to draw a crowd is fierce in a shrinking market, with the 18- to 21-year-olds now out of the drink picture. There is a club for every musical after-dark taste, including bad taste.

Chatterbox is the rock 'n' roll club in town. The cover is a dollar or two cheaper than the discos, and Chatterbox has none of their pretentions. The interior is comfortably funky, with basic-black tables, bars, stools, chairs and bouncers. In between video-rock assaults on a large screen, an often danceable Top Forty or "tribute" band doggedly blasts away. Not a bad place.

Panache is more of a disco in the pure, mid-seventies sense, with a kind of European suave about it in the state-of-the-art light and sound systems and attention to decorum. *Razzles* falls somewhere in between Chatterbox and Panache. There's a little rock and a little disco and lots to look at, some of it X-rated. The password here is "hedonism." As we stood on the sidelines, three shirtless male bartenders chased each other around their enclosed, circular bar like demented disco ducks, then stopped to form a line and hump the bar in unison. Occasionally, they mixed drinks. At midnight, there was a floor show. Or rather, an above-the-floor show, as a parade of girls took turns ascending a ramp to a miniature boxing ring suspended over the bar. Inside the ring, the girls went one-on-one with themselves, bumping and grinding and doing risqué things to the beat of Michael Jackson and Donna Summer.

This, friends, is the Jersey Shore nightlife. It's a world of Wet T-shirt Nights and Hot Legs Contests. One place even advertised an Erotic Banana Eating Contest—on Sunday night. (Father, forgive them, they know not what they do.) With nothing left to the imagination, there is something incongruously grim about this involuntary voyeurism. Not that we're milk-drinking Mormons, but . . .

Even after the clubs have closed, the streets are clogged with

cars full of guys with looks of carnal desperation, cruising for
unattached women, giving it one last shot. Heads out the window,
big slabs of arm hanging down, they'd holler such last-ditch lines
as "How's it goin'?" and "Dere's lotsa room in dis car if you wanna
climb in honey, har har har. . . ."

Surrounded by such dialogue, mingled with the sounds of tires
squealing and northern-redneck rebel yells and ZZ Top tapes played
at 180 decibels, it's hard to imagine how we tore ourself away
from Seaside Heights for the ride back over the bridge to Toms
River and our motel, but we did. Must be our journalistic professionalism. Or something.

Information Booth
Sumner Avenue at Boardwalk
Seaside Heights, New Jersey 08751
(201) 793-1393

Toms River-Ocean County Chamber of Commerce
48 Hyers Street
Toms River, New Jersey 08753
(201) 349-0220

Long Beach Island

"Hey, don't listen to dose doom merchants . . . duh ones dat keep
sayin' the beaches are movin' . . . . Whadda they mean duh beaches
are movin'? . . . Looka dis [leans down, picks up a handful of sand,
lets it fall slowly through his fingers]. . . . You see dat sand goin'
anywhere? . . . I don't see it goin' nowhere but right back where
it came from. Where do dey tink it's gonna go anyways,
Iowa? . . . No, you got no worries with dis property. . . ."

The preceding was a fictional monologue that we devised while strolling along the north end of Long Beach Island, just yards away from the Barnegat Lighthouse. In our scenario, an easily imagined Jersey Shore real estate salesman was trying to convince a married couple from Trenton to buy a lot near the water. He was also assuring them there was absolutely no reason for them to be concerned about a sign posted in the sand that read: "Danger—Beach Eroded." The sign itself was being lapped at by waves, while the houses that directly faced the water were abandoned and partly destroyed, apparently by the force of a violent storm.

But across the street, a good 150 feet from where the waves curled and broke, our tireless salesman could confidently point to the nonstop sounds of construction—the buzzing of saws, the hammering of nails into wood, the jokes and shouts of workmen— as evidence that nothing whatsoever could be wrong here. "I mean, would all dese people be buildin' here if dey thought dey wuz gonna wake up one mornin' in duh middle of the Atlantic? Answer me dat."

Except for the made-up dialogue, everything else in the above scenario is exactly as we described it. The sea was encroaching on homes. Severe-looking warning signs had been posted. And across the street, the rhythmic sounds of hammers hitting nails drowned out the barely discernible melody of sand washing out to sea, grain by grain. The construction crew, overhearing our parodic monologue, hooted and laughed. Maybe it genuinely *was* funny to them; after all, they wouldn't be the ones moving in when the house was completed.

Actually, it is not as grim a scenario as might at first appear. A few good souls up at the north end are going to lose their summer homes next time a hurricane plays guess-who's-coming-to-dinner, but most of the rest of this generally uncluttered island is no more vulnerable to the ravages of storm and erosion than any other East Coast barrier island. Maybe less so, since hurricanes rarely visit this far north. The point is one that applies to those who build on any threatened and unprotected stretch of oceanfront, whether on Long Beach Island or Palm Beach, Florida: eventually, Neptune is going to tear your playhouse down.

Having gotten this out of our systems, we can now turn our attention to the far more pleasant task of describing Long Beach Island's considerable charms. Long Beach is an 18-mile-long barrier island at the midpoint of the Jersey Shore. You enter the island via Route 72 (Exit 63 on the Garden State Parkway) at the hectic mid-island town of Ship Bottom. Most of the development is at the extreme ends of the island—Barnegat Light, Loveladies and Harvey Cedars are the "nice" towns at the northern end, while Beach Haven and its plethora of variations (Beach Haven Gardens, Beach Haven Crest, Haven Beach and so on) are clustered to the south.

Long Beach Island is primarily a summering haven for off-islanders. There is one grade school, no high school and precious little wintertime commerce to entice people to stay year-round. No, at summer's end, most folks go back home to suburban New Jersey and leave this place to the wind and the seagulls, returning with fingers crossed around Memorial Day. For those who return here year after year, the rewards go way beyond finding their home unravaged by nor'easters and the beach intact. To them, it must seem almost too good to be true . . . .all this peace and quiet in the middle of New Jersey.

To be sure, nearly every square foot of this realtor's dream is utilized or will be soon, and in some places (at the southernmost tip and also near the bridge) small cities of boxlike migrant worker-style housing and mobile homes have been erected. But more often the island's architecture runs toward neat and even palatial homes on large lots—a testimony to the more affluent type of vacationer that has been coming here since the 1800s. Somehow, it all adds up to peace and quiet.

You do not win Budweiser mirrors for successfully tossing quarters onto margarine plates on Long Beach Island—you purchase hand-carved dressers at one of the area's 80 antique shops. You do not purchase gooey orange sherbet cones and stumble aimlessly down a boardwalk—you take the family to *The Show Place* ice-cream parlor, where they provide live entertainment and a wholesome singalong atmosphere. You do not turn the kids loose at a video-arcade dungeon—you take them to one of several putt-putt courses on the island, where windmills and tire spokes conspire to keep you from making par. For the pièce de résistance, there is the *Surflight Theatre*, an established playhouse in Beach Haven where Broadway musicals are performed most nights in season. And for an encore, there are free concerts in the park on Saturday nights.

But mostly you get up in the morning, don swim apparel and head to the beach. Although one Beach Haven innkeeper's claim—"these are the best beaches in the world"—may have been a little extravagant, tinged with an understandable civic pride, the beaches here boast an active, roiling surf that will please all ocean recreationalists, including surfers. In some places, the waves sink their teeth into the shore with such vigor that a wedding-cake impression is carved into the short porch of sand at the waveline—another reminder that this island is constantly being chomped down on and changed.

As they are nearly everywhere on the Jersey Shore, beach badges are required as long as lifeguards are on duty—daylight hours till around dinnertime. They are purchased either weekly ($2) or seasonally ($6) in each municipality.

Accommodations

In any popular Jersey Shore area, you will pay dearly for the pillow on which you lay your head. Long Beach Island is a popular Jersey Shore area . . . and a cut above the norm, to boot. However, there are options open to you, if you want to come here but are not renting or rich. First thing you'll want to do, especially if you're arriving without reservations, is stop by the chamber of commerce information booth, located in Ship Bottom, just over the bridge from the mainland. From the brochures, price sheets and news sheets, you'll quickly realize that you can find no motels for under $60 a night, and these are just the standard, nothing-fancy roadside variety. Your best bet is to try the bed-and-breakfast inns and guest homes of Beach Haven. Many date back to the 1800s and have been restored in a style that has drawn the seal of approval from the National Historical Register. With a little persistence, you should be able to find an airy room in a distinguished home in a good neighborhood. And you will be saving money. We paid $45 to stay at the *Victoria House*, an ideal spot located by a park one block from the ocean. Next door is the *Amber House*, built by the same man who built Victoria House 100 years ago.

One interesting, perhaps even trend-setting, test case has been brewing over real estate on Long Beach Island. It actually goes beyond real estate, touching upon the class consciousness of New Jersey. The residents of the Loveladies community have defied a court order to provide public access roads to their beaches, insisting that the 12 miles of beach that bound their expensive property are theirs and theirs alone. The truth of the matter is that they don't want outsiders—specifically, daytrippers in jacked-up vans—and they are apparently willing to risk jail and huge lawyers' fees to prove it. Somehow, however, we don't see them up there with such jailed martyrs as Paine, Thoreau or Gandhi.

Restaurants

When used in reference to dining on Long Beach Island, the ad-copy phrase "a casual atmosphere" connotes big tables, fried fisherman's platters, banquet-style rooms or large outdoor decks, and a small army of high chairs. No doubt, many restaurants use this buzz phrase to tip parents off to the predictability and affordability of their menus. The most popular of these places are *Morrison's Seafood*, which has been serving food on the bay side of Beach Haven for 38 years, and *Bill's Seafood*, which has been doing the same up in Surf City for 29 years. BYOB to either—and your baby's, too. A bit more expensive, and peaceful, is the *Owl Tree* in Harvey Cedars, which offers continental cuisine in a Victorian setting.

But a neat sort of middle ground can be found at *Pier 18*—a hodgepodge of fifty-three shops and take-out food stalls, located on Second Street in Beach Haven under one large roof. Pier 18 caters to the tourist's need for fast food with several styles of fare—Mexican, Greek, Italian, Jewish Deli and Sold American, which you consume communally in a dining area shaped like a boat. And you won't get seasick—it's fast food, to be sure, but not just the usual tasteless dreck to stifle the stomach growls.

Nightlife

In New Jersey, they have raised the drinking age to 21 at the same time they have lowered the age of consent to 17. "Nightlife," particularly at the beach, therefore means different things to different age groups. For those over 21, there are drinking establishments with taped music, dance floors and immaculately groomed hired help who need to see two pieces of identification before you can enter. On the underside, you'll find carloads of hot rodders, left out of the bar picture, who cruise the streets, swerving their cars and pickup trucks to the beat of their tape decks.

Lest one be too quick to condemn the southern redneck for his jacked-up Chevy, his Rebel flag and his eagerness to yell "yahoo" at every blessed blinking light, his New Jersey cousin at the shore takes no back seat in the Pointless Antisocial Meanderings Department. Up here, they don't just jack up cars; they jack up *trucks* and drive these godawful machines through the streets, terrifying even the cops. We were treated to a bath—a mixture of standing water and dumpster runoff—and nearly a funeral by one of these geeks, who swerved his truck off the road, and nearly into us, as a "joke." We would have expected this in Seaside Heights, but not Beach Haven. Another 6 inches and our heads would have been ornaments on this prankster's hood.

At the time, we were on our way to *The Ketch*, remarking on the wonderful peace and quiet of lovely Beach Haven. The unplanned ablution necessitated a wardrobe change, and we returned somewhat less idealistic but still hoping for a good time. Thankfully, The Ketch turned out to be more in tune with the feel of the island and not the goons who were tearing around it. The club was large, the bartenders efficient and the crowd well-behaved and -dressed. We drowned our sorrows in kamikazes and beer, and soon were dancing with new acquaintances. On selected weekend nights they have live rock bands. Up island, *Nardi's*, a combination liquor store and roadhouse nightclub, also presents live music.

Occasionally, the drink-deprived 17-to-20-year-old age group is allowed in the clubs for something called a Young People's Night. On one Sunday night in midsummer, 500 "young people" showed up, at $4 a head, to dance to taped music and drink nonalcoholic beverages. Here is an untapped source of revenue in Jersey and every other state—and a solution to the summertime blues for our younger friends.

FOR FURTHER INFORMATION

Long Beach Island/Southern Ocean County Chamber of Commerce
265 Ninth Street
Ship Bottom, New Jersey 08008
(609) 494-7211

Atlantic City

Lord, let me break even. I could use the money.
                                        —GAMBLER'S PRAYER

Atlantic City is located on an island set somewhere between man's conflicting desires to make provident, level-headed use of his income and to throw it away on preposterous speculation. "Bet with your head, not over it" is the advice that the gaming-commission posters offer, but a quick study of the faces on a casino floor will convince you that a lot of folks are drowning in red ink. If you've ever lost a $20 roll of quarters to the slots in the time it takes to smoke a cigarette, and then run up to the change counters with another twenty, figuring, "Hell, I'll just use this money to win on a few lucky pulls, get back to where I was—I'm due to win, you know, then I'll go back to the motel room and watch 'Hogan's

Heroes' reruns," only to lose another roll in no time and find yourself handing over another twenty to the change person, with sweaty palms and a rattled look on your face . . . then multiply the stakes and the compulsions that all the other, less level-headed suckers bring with them, and you'll understand how men and women lose not only their fortunes but their minds in places like Atlantic City.

Several rolls of quarters might seem like spare change to all you high-tax-bracket professionals out there, but to a couple of writers traveling on a budget that the Joads would find austere, this was high stakes. Nevertheless, we headed up to the glitzy hotel casinos of Atlantic City from our budget-minded base in nearby Margate like a couple of overeager rubes out to make a quick killing. With visions of a Niagara Falls of coins tumbling out of a blinking, clanging slot machine—enough money to keep us in imported beer and sole Florentine all the way to Key West—we converted what was left of our dwindling publisher's advance and our modest life's savings and made for the casino floor, dodging cocktail waitresses and high rollers with ten-gallon hats from Texas. A few short hours later, we were phoning home, begging bus fare. Atlantic City was very nearly the last chapter in this book.

But seriously, folks. As it actually happened, our savings were scalded only slightly and neither of us had to be dragged off, kicking and screaming, to Gamblers Anonymous. The ugly truth is that we squandered far more quarters at Skee-Ball arcades along the Jersey Shore than we ever did at the casinos of Atlantic City. We got held up by a few one-armed bandits, but . . . big deal. It's part of the experience, just like coming here to bask in the glorious presence of America's biggest celebrities, all those wonderful famous folk who perform here, gamble here, carry on their shady dealings here, get in trouble with the gaming commission for flouting casino-floor regulations here, and so forth.

Can we talk? We could hardly control our excitement over all the celebrities who were performing in town just during the short time we were in Atlantic City. Diana Ross. Johnny Mathis. The Pointer Sisters. Irene Cara. Grover Washington. Eddie Rabbitt.

Okay, it's not all God-given talent of that magnitude seven nights a week. Moving down the entertainment ladder, in talent if not earnestness, we also spotted: Eddy Arnold. The Lennon Sisters. Bobby Vinton. Lola Falana. Roger Whittaker. The Inkspots. Van Presley (no relation). These are the sorts of people for whom the term "it's a living" has come to assume a tragic veracity.

But we're not done yet. Sliding lower still, we entered a zone where we saw names that we do not recognize and never will recognize. An unusual number of these hack entertainers are duos that go by first names only: Limar and Christian. Scott and Ginger. Angel and Russell. Sunnie and Peggy. Bradley and Ray. Pasqual and Reece.

And in a class by himself, presumably standing on the very floor of hell itself, holding the ladder steady, is someone named Pinky Kravitz. With a name like that, in a town like this, he's just got to be miserable.

One of our favorite spots in A.C. is the boardwalk entrance to Resorts International, which is a veritable showbiz Sistine Chapel, blessed by some of the biggest names in entertainment. Here, you'll see the hands and John Hancocks of the great, the near great and the not great pressed into cement and mounted into the front façade of the building. A random sampling of signatures included Glen Campbell ("Love and peace"), Julio Iglesias ("Love"—what's he got against peace?) and Cher ("Cher"). Seemingly the only biggie who hasn't signed in is the Ayatollah.

But seriously, folks, Atlantic City has become the biggest boom town since Beirut. Ever since the New Jersey State Legislature approved casino gambling for Atlantic City back in 1976, the city has rebounded from the ghost-town decline and destitution of the sixties and early seventies to become the El Dorado of the East. There are ten casinos in operation in Atlantic City, each of which was built at an average cost of $300 million. The casinos have claimed in excess of $5 billion in revenues. Gambling has brought 50,000 new jobs to Atlantic County, and each year brings 26 million visitors to Atlantic City. It is the most visited resort in the country.

And the growth continues. Three more casinos are under construction—and will probably be completed before this book is

published—and many others are on the drawing board. Condominiums and parking garages are sprouting up like toadstools after
a rainstorm. It is a town that is being razed and rebuilt in record
time. Atlantic City is one of the few places in the world where
cranes are not an endangered species. (*Ba-da-bump!*) In the time it
took us to get from the airport to our hotel, the hotel had been
torn down. (*Ba-da-bump!*) The boardwalk has changed so many
times even the gulls are confused. (*Ba-da-bump!*)

But seriously, folks. Out on the boards, a curious thing happened
one afternoon that epitomized the spirit of Atlantic City as it erects
the future and annihilates the past. A fine old hotel from Atlantic
City's gilded age of the twenties, the Shelburne, was being demol-
ished to make way for God-knows-what. A parking lot, in all
probability. The wrecking ball was hoisted above the building's
twelve floors, then released with terrific force. Room by room,
floor by floor, the ball did its damage. Every sixth blow would
exhaust the structure, and another floor would cave in with a
mighty crash, sending massive quantities of concrete, twisted steel,
dust and debris to the ground. Each successful smash would draw
applause and cheers from a crowd that had gathered on the boardwalk to watch the spectacle. Every time the wrecking ball found
its mark, it was as if a jackpot had been hit.

Returning to the casinos, which is where most people spend
their time anyway, day and night, Atlantic City is a 22-hour-a-
day town. The gaming rooms run almost round the clock, closing
between 6 and 8 A.M. to make an accounting of the previous day's
take. The figures are usually astronomical and beyond compre-
hension. In one summer month, the casino at Resorts International
paid out $85 million to its slot players alone. Imagine what they
took in.

It is a fact that the casinos are the consuming preoccupation of
nearly all who visit here, even with a gorgeous beach within a few
steps of the wheels and hands and handles and tables. It is conceivable that eventually the ocean will merely be regarded as a
convenience for the suicidal. For now, though, the beach is an
underused amenity finishing a poor second to gambling. And so,
you'll emerge blinking into the painful light of a sunny summer

afternoon and see a pristine white-sand beach that's scantily populated with swimmers and sunbathers.

Atlantic City is, in the present day, a schizophrenic animal. On the one hand, it's an exceptionally lovely beach, originally founded in the mid-1850s as a health spa, that's protected by its geographical orientation from punishing northeasterly storms and hurricanes like '85's Gloria, and warmed by the waters of the Gulf Stream. Just north of Atlantic City is Brigantine Refuge, a haven for wintering birds and waterfowl. Surrounding the city are great unspoiled expanses of salt marsh and tidal flat. Much of Atlantic County is given over to farmland and looks improbably rustic. Atlantic City, all and all, has a rather remarkable natural setting.

On the other hand, Atlantic City is the new gambling capital of the world. It has already surpassed Las Vegas in terms of dollar income and numbers of visitors. It is a town of incomprehensible wealth and excruciating poverty. The crime rate is the highest in the state of New Jersey. Some of the people involved in these gambling empires belong to organizations that do not carry the Good Housekeeping Seal of Approval. There was a protracted bloodbath in Philadelphia as rival crime families vied for control of Atlantic City once gambling came in. It would be nice to report that there's no Mob presence in Atlantic City, but we all know better.

In the end, though you've heard it before, whether you're gambling or swimming, the best advice you can bring with you to Atlantic City is this: do it with your head, not over it.

Accommodations

We're the wrong duo to be giving advice to anyone about places to stay in a money trap like Atlantic City. Ask Steve and Edie, or Sam and Dave, but not Parke and Alan. The facts are these, and you can run with them. There are ten hotel casinos in Atlantic City. *Harrah's* has two: one up at the marina on the north side, and one in town. *Resorts International* is up on North Carolina

Avenue and the Boardwalk. The *Sands*, the *Claridge*, *Bally's Park Place*, *Caesar's Boardwalk Regency* and the *Atlantis* (formerly *Playboy*—tough break, Hef) are all clustered along the boardwalk between Florida and Kentucky Avenues. The *Tropicana* is a few blocks south (at Iowa and Pacific), and the *Golden Nugget* a few blocks south of that (Albany and Pacific).

The inundation of Atlantic City these days is not surprising, considering the population pool from which it's drawing. Sixty million people live within a 6-hour drive of A.C. New York City, for instance, is 137 miles away, while Philadelphia is only 58 miles away. Buses roll into Atlantic City from points west, north and south all night long. They leave from big cities and small cities, and even from other resort towns on the shore. We would not be surprised to learn that they make stops at convents and mental hospitals to pick up riders.

As part of the bargain, many Atlantic City travel packages include enticements such as free rolls of quarters once you get here, making bus travel an economical way to see the town. Of course, the casinos offer these deals as a loss leader, hoping that once there, you'll gamble away your assets till you're in hock up to your ass. But if you can keep to a sensible budget, this is a great way to experience Atlantic City without paying $150 a night for a room. One is urged not to stretch budget consciousness too far and go looking for accommodations more than a few blocks off the boardwalk. Away from the bright lights, Atlantic City is not exactly Elmtown, U.S.A., to put it delicately. Stray too far and the closest thing to a Golden Nugget you'll have is a lump on the head.

Restaurants

You can eat like a king in Atlantic City, but you also have to be nearly as rich as one. Inside the casinos, there are multiple restaurants to satisfy every taste and whim. There are eight fancy-pants restaurants in the *Tropicana* alone, for instance, including French, northern Italian, oriental, English Court, a garden-

atmosphere coffee shop, a New York theater-district deli, a "sumptuous buffet" and a place called *Slot City* that serves "slots of food."
For the compulsive gambler and glutton, no doubt. And so it goes
down the line.

An interesting bit of food trivia comes to us courtesy of a publication called the *Insider's Guide to Atlantic City*. David Brenner,
the Philadelphia comedian and veteran of countless "Tonight" shows,
likes to wolf down submarine sandwiches at a place called *White
House Subs* on Arctic Avenue. To quote the story: "Just about every
entertainer not on a doctor's diet (and a few that are) drops in for
a sub or cheesesteak, with David Brenner leading the pack. 'I get
a double-meat, double-cheese sub all the time,' 'Kingy' Brenner
tells us. Then he throws a party in his parents' Ventnor apartment,
inviting friends and relatives from New York and Philadelphia."
This is how it goes in swingin' A.C.

One last observation about food and Atlantic City. Eating is not
a particularly relevant pastime in a gambling town. When you're
in Atlantic City, you subsist on a diet of poker chips.

Nightlife

When you tire of gambling, or when it depletes you, there's always
the parade of superbores passing in and out of the hotel showrooms.
Frank (he'll be back). Sammy. Tony. Luciano. In our experience,
whether you're seeing one of the biggest lights on Broadway or
one of its busted bulbs, about the best you can hope for is that
the vulgarity will be kept to a minimum, and that you'll be allowed
to escape with a shred of dignity.

One of the acts we missed when in town nonetheless holds a
curiosity for us still. The name of the act, as advertised, was Nelson
Sardelli and All About Women. Again reverting to printed sources,
this time an entertainment tabloid: "Nelson Sardelli, recently named
Atlantic City's variety entertainer of 1983, combines singing, comedy and a dynamic stage presence to produce what many have
called 'The Ultimate Variety Show.' The lavish costumes and
consummate beauty of 'All About Women,' an eight-woman dance

extravaganza, provides the opening and finale for this entertaining production." For once, we are at a loss for words.

FOR FURTHER INFORMATION

Greater Atlantic City Chamber of Commerce
16 Central Pier
Boardwalk and Tennessee Avenue
Atlantic City, New Jersey 08401
(609) 345-5600

Atlantic City Convention and Visitor's Bureau
16 Central Pier
Atlantic City, New Jersey 08401
(609) 345-7536

Ocean City

Ocean City, New Jersey, bills itself as "America's Greatest Family Resort." Not content to accept such a claim at face value, we contrived to imagine just what this might mean in the present day and came up with some pretty bizarre fantasies. Using other so-called family resorts we'd seen as a yardstick, we envisioned America's Greatest Family Resort as a land of 6-mile-long aqua slides that show inflight videos of Bambi break-dancing, or of restaurants the size of grocery stores, Pac-Man games at all traffic lights, houses made of fried dough with cotton-candy trees in the yard. . . . In short, we came expecting a gargantuan amusement park at the beach, with sand and surf as subthemes.

Luckily, all such fears can be safely set adrift upon the ocean waters. Ocean City is a family resort that lives up to all the good connotations of the term. The reasons for this are securely rooted in the history of the barrier island upon which it is built. Once upon a time not so long ago, Ocean City was a barren (at least through a developer's eyes) stretch of dunes and grass without a bridge to the mainland. Farmers grazed their cattle and pigs here, to keep them safe from mainland marauders. And then came the Methodists. They were shopping around for a site for a camp meeting ground and Christian resort. In 1879, the area known as Peck's Beach was rechristened Ocean City, and an Ocean City Association set about building a bridge and a community. The community was carefully planned along strict Christian principles, with all the necessary paperwork and deeding to ensure that Ocean City would remain untainted and pure in perpetuity. Back then, that meant no alcohol and, more than likely, no fun in the sense that today's kids know it. Nothing has changed in the alcohol department, although you can buy hooch in the "wet" communities over the bridge and bring it back onto the island. But in many other respects, Ocean City has boomed—all within acceptable, family principles, of course—and even the most incorrigible of today's youth will have fun here.

This is a big town. It runs for fifty-nine blocks along the ocean, and is about four avenues deep. A 2 ½-mile boardwalk runs for the first twenty-three blocks and provides a central axis for family wanderings. This is not your average Joisey boardwalk. There is a center yellow line painted onto the boards to assure proper pedestrian traffic flow. The array of fast-food stalls includes such healthful alternatives as "specialty snacks" (bowls of fruit), as well as the regular inch-thick wedges of Sicilian pizza, gummy bears and Swedish fish. The arcades are clean and well-lighted. Even the video games are a cut above the norm, with digital Skee-Ball alleys that play "Yankee Doodle Dandy" when you break 180. Everywhere could be heard the mechanical chatter of the newest arcade games, like the Boxing video game that yells, "Mighty blow, mighty blow, left, right, left, mighty blow, left, get up, get up, seven-eight-nine-ten . . . ding ding," as you dismantle a string of journeymen contenders with villainous names like Piston Hurricane, the Bald Bull and Kid Quick. We watched a 4-year-old boy who was holding an ice pop in one hand nonchalantly vanquish foe after foe with his other. Our own shots at the big-time were over as soon as the quarter tumbled into the slot.

Then there are the other 35 blocks of town, free of boardwalk diversions but still with lots of things for families to do. Among the more common diversions are "sand sculpting" (building sand-castles), which is periodically judged for prizes; shuffleboard (there are 33 local courts); fishing, either from the pier, in the surf or out on the high sea; surfing, which is done from Fifty-ninth Street south; windsurfing, upon the shallow, tranquil waters of the bay; tennis (there are numerous public courts) and, of course, swimming and sunbathing on Ocean City's 8 miles of beach. Don't worry about bringing the children here—its beaches are under the watchful eye of an army of lifeguards that numbers 95 at peak times.

Admittedly, Ocean City has had problems in recent years with beach erosion. It has spent a small fortune pumping sand in from the floor of the bay, but the sea carries it right back out. At high tide along the boardwalk the beach completely disappears and the walls in front of the oceanfront homes look like a boundary for an enormous swimming pool. The beaches at Twenty-eighth and Thirty-fourth Streets are generally regarded as the best within the town limits; they are wider and are not intruded upon by board-walk.

Even with its erosion problems, Ocean City does not suffer as much as one might think. This is a town with a legacy that its visitors know and love and to which they continue through the generations to pay homage. Ocean City is, in fact, almost esoteric in its strict family orientation. There is square dancing at the youth center, religious conventions at the boardwalk pavilion, church-going at listed houses of worship, an annual Baby Parade and, finally, the much-ballyhooed Night in Venice, a watery procession that takes place every July. All the boats in the area are lit up like floats, and thousands turn out to soak up the Fellini-esque carnival atmosphere.

Ocean City will no doubt remain pretty much the same, thanks in large part to the charter that was drawn up at the town's inception. The intention of that charter was "to ensure the original purpose of the party of the first part in securing the whole island as a Christian Seaside Resort." The party of the first part would no doubt be tickled to see how Ocean City has endured as a wholesome resort while gambling and drinking and all sorts of heinous and immoral acts elsewhere are practiced with impunity all along the Jersey Shore.

Accommodations

The prices in Ocean City run on the steep side. An oceanfront room with two beds in a comfortable, multistory motel with a heated pool runs in the $80 to $100 a night range, in season. That figure drops down to $40 or $50 out of season. The best motels, such as the *Sting Ray* and the *Port-O-Call*, are located in the teens along the boardwalk. Though the prices are high, so is demand. Any place that's touted as America's greatest family resort is going to get more business than it can handle, because somehow Dad will find enough green in his wallet to subsidize the trip. Judging from the full toddler attendance at motel poolsides, Ocean City is not hurting for business.

Restaurants

Starting with breakfast, you can do no wrong by going to *T.R. Fenwick's*, located directly on the boardwalk at Twelfth Street. The breakfast buffet here cost us $3.33 and included so many items that are "good for you" (read: fruit) that it was difficult to decide how much to take of the stuff we really wanted to eat (e.g., corned beef hash, fried potatoes, bacon and sausage, English muffins glued together with melted cheese). And we simply did not know where to put the chipped beef.

For dinner, in town, the emphasis is on family seafood houses and hoagie huts, with discount coupons falling out of every piece of locally generated literature. The place most popular with the teen set is *The Chatterbox*, open 24 hours a day, believe it or not, in this family resort. A more genteel gastronomic experience can be had at the *Culinary Garden*, which emphasizes healthy foods prepared with fresh ingredients. The specialty of the house is Pasta à la Culinary Garden, a sumptuous combination of broccoli, crabmeat and fried mushrooms in Alfredo sauce.

If you want a respite from the sedate sanctuary of Ocean City without having to reenter the Land of Screaming Chevvies, head over the bridge into Somers Point and visit *Mac's* restaurant. Mac's is a venerable institution, specializing in Italian and seafood dishes at moderate prices. The food is excellent, from the hearty chowders and shrimp cocktail on through to the mouth-watering desserts, which are homemade and irresistible. Mac's is accessible both from Atlantic City and Ocean City, and if you're staying in the area, is highly recommended.

Nightlife

If it is nightlife you crave in Ocean City, you might best heed the advice of the highway signs and "Follow the Gulls" out of town. This place is bone dry, so you'll have to travel if you wish to tipple. Somers Point is a nice spot to have a relaxed drink or to pick up a bottle. But chances are if you feel the need for a drink or a bottle, you wouldn't have come to Ocean City in the first place. Be that as it may, you will find *Gregory's Bar* (next to *Mac's* restaurant) and *The Waterfront*, both in Somers Point, to be comfortable places to wind down after a day in the sun. Gregory's has the dark, interior-world feel of a city pub and also serves full dinners, while the Waterfront is a bit more high-tech in its stylings and is, more accurately, on the marshfront.

FOR FURTHER INFORMATION

Public Relations Department
City Hall
9th and Asbury
Ocean City, New Jersey 08226
(609) 399-6111

Strathmere
Sea Isle City
Avalon
Stone Harbor

The pristine marshes and inlets south of Ocean City delineate a border for a group of less-traveled seaside communities. These four unfrenzied beach towns cater to a loyal clientele, and don't really beat their chests to attract many more than those who return year after year. They occupy the next two barrier islands down the Jersey coast. Each has a stronger claim toward permanence than any of their neighbors to the north, owing primarily to a strong sand-dune structure—some of the last remaining high dunes left in the state of New Jersey are here—and a firm commitment to sane development.

Strathmere, Sea Isle City, Avalon and Stone Harbor are the kind of places that regulars like to keep to themselves. Each town has a distinct personality and appeal. With the same sort of reverence as their Massachusetts counterparts, those who come here call this area the Cape. By "cape," they're referring to the nub of land that juts out at the lower end of New Jersey, separating the Atlantic Ocean from the Delaware Bay, encompassing Cape May County.

The Cape begins up at Strathmere, where sparsely spaced residences nestle among the reeds and grasses. Many daytrippers park their cars along the side of the road, then hike through openings in the high dunes to the ocean. The next town down, Sea Isle City, is more of a family resort, with 5 miles of wide beaches and low-key activities—e.g., baby parades, lifeguard races, free concerts in the promenade. Sea Isle City has been given the perhaps unfair nickname "Senile City." Apparently, it is so dubbed by the folks who speed through to get to the Wildwoods. In truth, old folks do not flock here in such numbers as to warrant this distinction. (They do, however, flock to Ocean Grove, a town just south of Asbury Park, in numbers sufficient to justify the much more frequently used nickname "Ocean Grave"—ah, Jersey!) All in all, though, Sea Isle City is a quiet place—unexciting, maybe, but not senile. Well, maybe just a little: "Funnel Cakes Are Fun to Eat," reads a huge sign on the boardwalk. We continued southward.

Avalon, named after the mythical resting place of Celtic heroes, is trying hard through strict zoning to preserve that image. In this state, this is a Herculean task, even with the best of intentions. Evidence of growth is everywhere, with seemingly everybody and his cousin from Trenton wanting a slice of Avalon's vanishing quietude. Avalon shares the northern end of Seven Mile Beach with Stone Harbor; together, these two towns span over 100 blocks of burgeoning growth. Avalon's motto is "Cooler by a mile," a reference to the ocean breezes that purportedly keep the thermometer down. Currently there are more rental cottages, apartments and homes than motel courts or teetering condos, but the word is definitely out on this desirable locale. The beach is especially fine— wide and well-patrolled by lifeguards.

Although there is no discernible break between them, Stone Harbor is distinguished from Avalon by its bird sanctuary. Twenty-one acres right in town (between 111th and 116th Streets) are given over to herons, egrets, ibises and whatever else flys through. Binoculars and telescopes are available to study the birds in their habitat. But this is not all there is to Stone Harbor, which has more money and swankier gift shops than its neighboring communities. Let's put it this way: if Avalon is for the upwardly mobile, then Stone Harbor is for those who have already arrived.

Accommodations

Stone Harbor has enough money floating around to keep commercial development off the oceanfront. They don't need such ticky-tack revenue. There are cottages and apartments available for rental through a plethora of private agencies—many more of these than motels, which are infrequent in the area and even more rare on the beach. Nonetheless, there are the *Golden Inn* and the *Beachcomber* in Avalon, which are on the ocean and a block back, respectively. *Shelter Haven*, in Stone Harbor, is two giant steps from the beach, on the bay. Then there's *Villa Maria by the Sea*, a huge, white Victorian structure on the southern edge of Stone Harbor. The Villa Maria harks back to the days of old money along the southern shore and, in the face of all the stylish new wealth that dominates the landscape nowadays, looks more like a rest home. There are worse places, we're certain, to take the final snooze.

Restaurants

Garrity's in Sea Isle City has done big seafood business for years and is a favorite of regulars and day invaders alike. The *Deauville Inn*, however, is the real find in the area. Located directly on the Intracoastal Waterway in Strathmere, the Deauville appeals to locals who seek peace, reasonable prices and good food.

Nightlife

Sea Isle City is, as discussed, sleepy, despite the presence of a place called the *Bongo Room*. Similarly, no one comes to Avalon to get crazy. We looked for a semblance of night activity here, but found nothing worth special mention. Avalon, it seems, is not just a resting place in myth. It's Snoresville at the shore, and that's just how they want it. As for Stone Harbor, well-heeled folks come here to walk around the trendy shopping district and sit at outdoor bars and cafés with names like *Touché*. The latter offers a free happy-hour buffet that features steamed shrimp, so what the heck. . . . Put on that winning smile and your best *Esquire* magazine outfit and pretend to know something about investment banking. Last one on the barstool has to buy the Heinekens.

FOR FURTHER INFORMATION

Stone Harbor Chamber of Commerce
P.O. Box 422
212 96th Street
Stone Harbor, New Jersey 08247
(609) 368-6101

Avalon Chamber of Commerce
30th Street and Ocean Drive
Avalon, New Jersey 08202
(609) 967-3936

Wildwood

Every beach worth its salt proclaims itself to be something, as the philosopher once said, "of that which none greater can be thought." The isle of Wildwood regards itself so highly that it claims not one but several superlatives. It is, according to its own motto, "the world's safest and cleanest free bathing beach." A walk across this wide beach confirms all three claims. It is safe (the beach tapers outward at a gentle incline for a great distance, with no rough surf or undertow and a lifeguard-to-swimmer ratio rivaling Ocean City's). It is clean (the sand is fine and white, and the families that come here are not the sort to toss wads of Burger King wrappers down on the beach). It is free (hooray for Wildwood—there are no beach badges to hassle with; in lieu of fees, "we just thank Mother Nature").

Mother Nature also deserves a pat on the back for bestowing upon Wildwood an erosion-free beach that is 1,000 feet wide in some places. While some might grumble at the prospect of hiking a quarter-mile over hot sand from the boardwalk to the water, this invincible beach is widening still—up to 100 feet a year in some places.

The Wildwood area is more properly referred to in the plural. There are three Wildwoods: Wildwood Crest, North Wildwood and Wildwood proper. The lines of demarcation are a bit fuzzy, and "the Wildwoods" seems to do fine as a catchall. Many years ago, the Wildwoods were a self-described "splendid promenade of health and pleasure." Today, the more homey description of the area as a "friendly family resort" adorns the literature.

The Wildwoods are indeed a magnet for budget-conscious American families. The cost of a motel room is generally less expensive than other resorts on the Jersey coast. Add to the nightly savings of $10 or $20 on a motel room the fact that you don't have to pay to use the beach and you can see where substantial savings begin to mount when you're shepherding a family of five. Wildwood's come-one-come-all philosophy draws vacationers by the hundreds of thousands, and supply has risen to the challenge of meeting the extraordinary demand. Wildwood is a city of motel rooms. There are more than 400 motels, seemingly stamped from the same cookie cutter and given all the predictable names—the *Ebb Tide*, the *Bel Aire*, *Ocean Sands*, the *Sea Gull*, the *Yankee Clipper*. And so forth, until you've exhausted all of the recombinant possibilities of the words "ocean," "beach," "sea," "sand" and "gull."

All of the above can be found in ample supply in the Wildwoods. The beach is endless, both latitudinally and longitudinally, and, with the exception of Seaside Heights, the boardwalk is the noisiest on the Jersey Shore. Extending for 2 ½ miles and encompassing seven amusement parks/piers, the boardwalk at Wildwood is a long, loud stretch of wild wood, but one that doesn't encroach on the more sedentary pleasures of the beach because of the distance separating it from the water.

Wildwood is relatively young, as shore towns go. The area is lacking in much history, except for the fact that there used to be Indians here and they were driven away. (This is practically a given anywhere you travel.) The Indians were Algonquins, and after they were sent packing, the island was used by farmers from the mainland who'd bring their herds over for grazing. The island was then (and is now) known as Five Mile Island. There is not much else to say about Wildwood, except that they had a problem with wild animals—strays from the farmer's flocks who, obeying the tenets of the Bible, were fruitful and multiplied—as recently as 1905.

The herds of tourists that roam Five Mile Island now are ostensibly domesticated. They come from the Northeast and the Midwest, and some even migrate from Canada. Wildwood is not their permanent home, however. Those that come here usually stay for only a week or two, sticking close to their own clan and then returning to their place of origin. There seems to be some rejuvenating biological purpose to their brief relocation; in any case, they return year after year. And when their offspring mature and begin bearing their own young, they very often carry on the annual pilgrimage. Often, several generations can be seen traveling together, despite the mental strain that the incessantly bleating young appear to impose upon their elders.

No, there is not much to chew over in the way of history, when you get down to it. Not much architecturally to distinguish Wildwood, either, unless you fancy row upon row of two-story, L-shaped motels. The Wildwoods are your basic meat-and-potatoes shore vacation, blown up to grand scale. It's an all-American playpen that epitomizes the classic connotations of the word "beach."

Accommodations

The Greater Wildwood Hotel-Motel Association publishes an annual directory of accommodations that's thicker than most pulp novels. There is no scientific way to narrow down the selection—there are 225 pages of listings. Fortunately, the standard deviation among the motels of the Wildwoods is rather low. The great majority of them are your basic two- or three-story structures that half-surround a rectangular heated pool and are done in a color scheme of white, pink and/or turquoise. There will always be children in the pool, making a happy racket. If you're trying to pick a motel, you might as well stick a pin in the directory, or choose one by its name, as you would a race horse—e.g., the *Pink Orchid Motel*, if you're a florist; the *Maple Leaf*, if you're one of our neighbors to the north, or the *Swan Motel*, if you went to college with someone whose last name is Swan, like we did. (Hello, Dennis.)

Restaurants

Hardly a relevant concern in this sort of place. *Neil's Steak and Oyster House* is the closest thing to fine dining you'll find in this boardwalk town—an opinion that's corroborated by the Lions, Rotarians, Kiwanis and Optimists, who *all* meet here. The building in which Neil works his dinnertime magic is a relic that dates from the Time of the Wild Animals—to wit, 1897, which is almost prehistoric in this community's brief memory. Food-wise, there is also a restaurateur by the name of Ed Zaberer, who modestly bills himself as "the host of the coast." His restaurant complex, *Zaberer's*, which is located north of the Wildwoods at the foot of the bridge over to Stone Harbor, is renowned for food at affordable prices. The redoubtable Mr. Zaberer also advertises "Zaberized" drinks, though we have no idea what additives that might involve.

Nightlife

Wildwood might seem a family town by day, but there are lots of single animals prowling the streets at night, after the old folks have nodded off. Given the numbers that come here, there is more of everything in the Wildwoods, including people out looking to have a good time. Thus, there is a thriving bar and club scene, centered along New Jersey Avenue in downtown Wildwood. Here, the disco animal thrives in its natural party habitat: jumbo nightclubs with multiple bars and nominal cover charges, usually with some special nightly promotion that reduces the price of a particular beverage. Shop around, check out the crowds and the cover charges, and cock an ear to the band that's playing, if one is playing. Curiously, in these places, we noticed that a lot of girls dance with each other while the males of the species stare dull-eyed from the rectangular periphery of the dance floor, too intimidated to dance but intrigued enough to salivate from the sidelines. The situation doubtlessly sorts itself out by the end of the evening.

FOR FURTHER INFORMATION

Greater Wildwood Chamber of Commerce
Oak and New Jersey Avenues
Wildwood, New Jersey 08260
(609) 729-4000

Southern Shore Regional Council
Schellenger Avenue and the Boardwalk
Wildwood-by-the-Sea, New Jersey 08260
(609) 522-1409

Cape May

Like a precocious child running away from a home of certifiable
crazies, Cape May is positioned as far from the rest of New Jersey
as is geographically possible. Situated upon the southernmost tip
of land in New Jersey, a peninsula originally known as Cape Island,
Cape May is a world apart from the boardwalk hustle and bustle
to the north. It is alternately referred to as "Victorian Cape May"
and "Historic Cape May," but rarely will you hear it called Cape
May, New Jersey. As if to officially distance itself from this state
or, for that matter, this century, the United States government
has designated the entire town of Cape May as a national landmark.

Cape May is reachable from the north by the Garden State
Parkway, which ends (or, more correctly, begins: Cape May is
Exit 0) a few miles shy of town, petering out near a small assem-
blage of commercial harbor structures, one of which is fronted by
an enormous inflatable Miller High Life bottle. From the south,
you'll enter Cape May over water, via the Cape May-Lewes
Ferry, a smooth, 1 1/2-hour ride across the mouth of the Delaware Bay.

Among the many virtues of this town are its isolation (it's cut
off from the rest of Cape May County, which includes the Wildwoods, by Cold Spring Inlet), the weather (comparatively mild
year-round) and its rich legacy of understated resort life, which

dates from the late 1800s. ("Cape May offers good bathing, yachting and fishing, with driving and hunting in the wooded country
inland from the coast," according to the 1910 *Encyclopaedia Brit-
annica*. The driving's a little hectic these days, but the rest pretty
much holds true.) Somehow, despite the steady influx of summer
visitors, Cape May maintains a firm foothold on its staunchly
Victorian past.

Originally the area was used by the Lenni-Lanape Indians as a
pre-Coppertone summering ground, a seasonal break from their
normally nomadic lifestyle. It was "officially" discovered, however, by Sir Henry Hudson in 1609, though he made no claim for
it at the time. In 1621, a Dutchman named Mey finally staked a
claim to the entire cape, and though his descendants were eventually chased down into Delaware by English colonists who came
south from New England looking for whales, the newcomers were
considerate enough to keep his name afloat. Soon thereafter, Cape
May became a popular seaside resort, one of the first in America,
and ads were placed in newspapers as early as 1766. The steamboat
era of the mid-1800s sidetracked the teeming multitudes to the
fledgling Atlantic City, up the coast a piece. Cape May was therefore able to retain its "country town by the seashore" appeal and
attract a more wealthy following of Manhattan and Philly socialites
who wished to turn the Cape into their own low-key version of
Newport, Rhode Island.

Cape May has endured in its antiquarian Victorian ways, although the town has twice been razed by fire. The fire of 1878
was the ruinous one, leveling 30 acres in the heart of Cape May.
This is truly when the wealth of the town came to the fore, as
Cape May was quickly rebuilt along even more meticulous Victorian lines. You can take a trolley tour of Cape May in July and
August that visits the architectural high points. Today, it looks
much as it did at the turn of the century and continues to enjoy
a respectful following of urban pilgrims from the metropolises of
the East Coast.

The fixation with the past is not meant to imply that there is
no room here for the present. On a busy weekend in the summer,
you'd swear you were smack dab in the middle of the next baby
boom. There are enough crybabies of all ages running around to

form an army, one bent on making you surrender your mind. The cacophony made by three generations wailing in unison for ice cream and lemonade is enough to awaken the Victorian dead. An asphalt boardwalk runs along Cape May's hard, white sand beach, and in season, the parade of people is as incessant as a pilgrimage to a holy shrine.

The town itself is ideally suited to walking, and the surrounding area begs to be explored on bicycle. Especially nice are trips out to the *Cape May Lighthouse* and *Cape May State Park*, the latter being the birdwatching center of the Eastern Flyway. The best times for this are the spring and fall, when the car traffic dwindles and the bird traffic swells.

Most people we met in Cape May who love the place asked us not to say a nice thing about it. They apparently want to stem the mounting tide of visitors. Well, okay then, we'll play along and say nothing more.

Accommodations

Cape May is a year-round resort. It's clamorous in the summer, livable in the winter and most beautiful in the spring and fall, with the birds migrating or returning and the trees turning. Off-season rates are drastically lower than they are in season. With that in mind, you might want to visit here on the near side of Memorial Day or the far side of Labor Day. A comfortable room in a Victorian inn is yours for a song (try humming a few bars of "On the Way to Cape May"). Even in-season prices are reasonable, though, when your dollar is measured on a value scale against such yardsticks as Seaside Heights and Wildwood.

No one should stroll into the tree-lined center of town without first stopping by the *Welcome Center* on Lafayette Street. It is housed in a converted church built in 1853, and dispenses up-to-the-minute information on everything from walking tours to accommodations. The volunteer staffers are helpful, and will even track down vacancies and prices. Starting from the top, *Congress Hall* is the most prestigious of the Victorian summer hotels, an enormous white whale of wood that faces the ocean from a short distance away. Originally built in 1812, then authentically reconstructed after the fire of 1878, this stalwart has been the haven for several American presidents but is yours, with full breakfast, for a price as low as $45 or as high as $73. Over on Jackson Street, six separate Victorian inns sit within two blocks of one another in the quiet shade just a heartbeat away from the action. You can get a room at any of these places for around $45. As for motels, one can have it just about any way he or she wants at the *Sea Crest*, which comprises an older hotel, a modern motel addition and detached cottages out back. Rooms in each section are priced in descending order of modernity, and the complex is across the street from the beach, with restaurants adjacent and the downtown a short stroll away.

Restaurants

Cape May is a small town with a cosmopolitan reputation for everything, including food. The *Mad Batter* sets the gourmet pace here. Located right off the ocean on Jackson Street, in the *Carroll Villa Hotel*, this restaurant serves award-winning cuisine in three different settings: an outdoor veranda, a skylighted dining room and a garden terrace. The menu changes daily, with late-breaking specials posted in colored chalk on the outdoor blackboard.

One block over, on Decatur Street, is *Watson's Merion Inn*, another celebrated restaurant in a historic setting. It has been pleasing discriminating palates here since the turn of the century. And for bargain hunters there's the Early Diner's Special, with entrées priced at $7.95 from 4:30 to 6:30 P.M. By now, we were beginning to realize that there are more "classic Victorian settings" in Cape May than in all of Great Britain. One of the classiest is the *Washington Inn*. Off the beaten track just a little (i.e., you can't hear the ocean), this inn serves delicious dinners in a quiet atmosphere.

For a louder and less expensive meal, try *Carney's* (a saloon with live Irish music and/or oldies bands) or *Harvey's* (which also has live entertainment after dark). And lastly, if you are looking for a fast feed during the day, you might visit the *Akroteria*, an agglomeration of small huts in the round with a wide choice of foodstuffs, most of it healthy.

Nightlife

Musically, the New Jersey Shore as a whole is a large expanse of automation at work—either taped and turntabled disco music or live bands with the collective IQ of a wall outlet. Because of tiny Cape May, however, a flotilla of New Jersey musicians can make enough to pay their rent. It seems that every other restaurant offers some sort of live performers, from well-coiffed eager beavers with satin voices and smooth between-song patter to authentic Irish music. You can hear flat-out rock 'n' roll at *Gloria's* or cool out with jazz at *The Shire*.

If you play your cards right, you might even rub shoulders with a dinosaur of entertainment like Cozy Morley, "the Seashore's Favorite Night Club Comedian," as we did at the *Golden Whale Restaurant and Lounge*. Shortly after we'd polished off the last of our fairly routine fisherman's platters, Cozy waltzed out to, ahem, entertain a crowd whose average member was at least twice our age. A bit of an anomaly for cosmopolitan Cape May, Cozy nonetheless had his finger on the pulse of the geriatric mentality—and, bless our socks, there are more oldsters out there than you think. Cozy was their mouthpiece, welding his shopworn act from the discarded shards of every Catskills comedian who's ever told a joke about a minority group or mother-in-law. His schtick is pure corn, the same stale jokes and dusty singalongs that have kept the geriatric set rolling in the aisles since they were knee-high to a walker. A poor man's Henny Youngman, Cozy gets more mileage out of his tax troubles than Toyotas get to the gallon of gas. "Whoa, yeah [*drum roll, crash of cymbals*] . . . It's a crazy world. . . . Ya gotta be nuts. . . . Hey, I love you people. . . . Where ya from? . . . Camden!!! Hey, I'm from Camden! . . . Didja ever see a Polish firing squad? . . . They stand in a circle. . ." The evening wound down with not one but several singalong renditions of "On the Way to Cape May," with Cozy on ukulele.

Chamber of Commerce of Greater Cape May
P.O. Box 109
Cape May, New Jersey 08204
(609) 884-3488

Cape May County Chamber of Commerce
P.O. Box 74
Cape May Courthouse, New Jersey 08210
(609) 465-7181

Delaware:
Small Wonder

Delaware was the first state in the union. Think about that and try to imagine what a state like Texas would do with such a distinction—branding a mile-long "#1" somewhere on the range is not inconceivable. In Delaware, however, you are not browbeaten with its status. No, this understated state, our second smallest, can be characterized by the following three words: clean, civilized and sane.

If you don't believe us, we'll get a gas-station attendant from Denton, Maryland, to whip your ass. We have a particular one in mind: an overlarge lad in a greasy, improperly buttoned flannel shirt. His belligerence, coming just minutes after we'd crossed the border into Maryland, reminded us that we were not in mannerly Delaware anymore.

For such a diminutive state, Delaware was given a generous coastline. Thirty miles of its shore directly fronts the Atlantic Ocean, while an additional 100 miles faces the protected waters of the Delaware Bay—itself a perfectly agreeable body of water, but a bit outside the scope of this book. Delaware's ocean strand, however, should provide pleasure enough for even the most devout ocean buff. From the historic town of Lewes at the mouth of the Delaware Bay on down to Fenwick Island on the Maryland border, the Delaware shore gives off a thoroughly healthy glow. Even what could be characterized as overdevelopment is not altogether

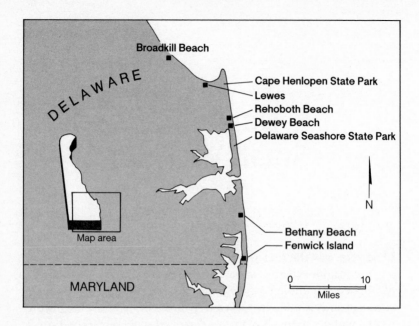

grotesque . . . it's just sort of, uh, slipshod in one or two places.
But the beach, ah yes, the beach is fine, and every single foot of
it is open to the public.

Lewes

The town of Lewes is advantageously located at the mouth of the
Delaware Bay, one of the world's great shipping channels. The
Dutchman Henry Hudson first sailed into the bay in 1609, and
in 1631 Lewes was officially established as a Dutch whaling colony.
The area passed from the Dutch to the British in 1664, with the
Indians having long since been driven out, and Lewes was fought
over by both Maryland and Delaware—a dispute that was ob-
viously resolved in the latter state's favor.

Today, Lewes receives visitors by the ferryful from Cape May,
New Jersey, directly across the bay. The Cape May-Lewes ferry

cuts many miles off the route from New York to Virginia Beach and points south, saving drivers the headache of traveling the inland route I-95, which passes through or near every sooty megalopolis along the northeast corridor.

It should be noted that though Lewes receives ferryfuls of visitors every several hours, not a great percentage of them choose to stick around any longer than it takes to crank up the station wagon and goose it on down U.S. 1 toward Rehoboth and Ocean City. There are reasons for this: the ferry landing is a 5-minute drive from the town's center, and to be truthful, Lewes itself is not Cape May by any stretch of the imagination. However, for those travelers who enjoy the lure of an old seaside community tucked away on a pleasant corner of the coast, this town offers its share of sundry attractions.

The *Lewes Historical Society* conducts walking tours of the town's colonial homes and churches in the summer season. Nature enthusiasts will enjoy adjacent *Cape Henlopen State Park*, a 2,500-acre preserve with pinelands, cranberry bogs, bay and ocean beaches and the celebrated "walking" sand dunes. Additionally, the Lewes area is an angler's paradise, with unlimited opportunities for bay, ocean and "offshore canyon" fishing.

The *Lighthouse Restaurant* at Fisherman's Wharf, by the drawbridge at the center of Lewes, is a triple-threat complex that affords opportunities for fishing, eating and sight-seeing (by boat) from one central location. The restaurant's two dining rooms look out over the Lewes and Rehoboth Canal. From the wharf that adjoins the restaurant, you can take an after-dinner cruise, buy fresh seafood at the dockside market or charter a boat and catch your own.

The atmosphere in Lewes is low-key, with a colonial flavor well preserved by the vigilant townspeople. One supposes that after 375 years, the unhurried, deliberate pace of life in Lewes will survive awhile longer.

Lewes Chamber of Commerce
Kings Highway and Savannah Road
P.O. Box 1
Lewes, Delaware 19958
(302) 645-8073

Delaware Bay

Just north of Lewes, via U.S. 1 and corresponding turnoffs, are a number of bay beaches that are worth exploring if for no other reason than they are off the beaten path. Typically, you drive through cornfields that give way to marshlands, then suddenly you'll round a bend and enter a tiny bayside community centered around a general store. These towns all have the word "beach" in their names—e.g., Broadkill Beach, Slaughter Beach, Primehook Beach, Fowler Beach, Big Stone Beach—but these are not beach towns in the traditional sense of the word. Rather, they are the types of places that folks native to the area like to keep to themselves, and that no one else would think to stumble on or into.

At Broadkill Beach, for instance, an entire family gathered excitedly around their bearded, scarlet-skinned breadwinner while he fought with a fish on his line for a full 5 minutes. Once he landed the thing, they all pulled back from it with whoops and shouts of a different sort. He'd managed somehow to hook a small shark. It was not a particularly menacing specimen, to be sure, but from the shrieks of these kids, you'd think he'd done battle with Jaws . . . and won.

Bay beaches, on the whole, are quiet, unassuming places. The waves are about the size of those you'd get going in a bathtub, and the beaches are small and flat as a table. The natives, however, will swear by them, and more than likely swear *at* the sight of an out-of-state license plate. Under their breath, though—this is Delaware, after all.

Rehoboth Beach

Rehoboth is a rare oasis of civilized values along the stretch of the Eastern Seaboard from New Jersey to North Carolina. Hemmed in by the rodeolike atmosphere of the Jersey Shore to the north (Cape May excepted) and the omnidirectional sprawl of Ocean City, Maryland, to the south, Rehoboth Beach has somehow maintained its composure as a beach resort of taste and decorum. The secret is two simple words: "controlled growth."

It is a policy that has guided the town government through the boom-and-bust years of the sixties and seventies. Whereas much of the Atlantic Coast has been massively rebuilt according to the profit-oriented principles of shortsighted developers, abetted by city councils who see in development a seasonal wagon train filled with tourist loot to be deposited in the town coffers, Rehoboth has kept a cautious reign on expansion. Intelligent zoning has ensured that what commercial development is allowed does not stick out like Mickey Mouse's ears, as it does in so many other beach communities. This is a doubly noteworthy achievement, considering Rehoboth's proximity to Washington, Wilmington and Philadelphia. It is the infestation of rowdy tourists from such urban centers and of thrill-seeking yokels from the more immediate area that can turn your worst nightmare out of *Urban Cowboy*—brawling rednecks and revving engines, witless drinking and blaring music—into a morbid seaside reality.

Rehoboth's many virtues became particularly clear to us after we emerged from some of the noisier battle zones north of here. The biblical word *Rehoboth* means "room enough," and truly Rehoboth Beach was a balm to our abused psyches. Indeed, it has provided solace for distraught souls for nearly a century. Not all of them have been devil-may-care pleasure-seekers, however. The spirit of abstemious Methodism, although no more than a footnote in history, still hovers faintly over Rehoboth Beach, keeping it sane, tame and relatively well-behaved, like an absent guardian whose memory guides you still.

Rehoboth Beach is a relatively young community. By virtue of its inaccessibility in that time before bridges and daily ferries, it was not much visited by white settlers and remained for centuries a clamming and hunting ground for Delaware Indians. That all changed in the late 1800s, when ardent Methodists began eyeing the Delaware coast for an open stretch of beach upon which to establish one of their "Christian seaside resorts," at which, ironically, they seemed to prohibit everything but stiff-backed praying and early bedtime.

In their original charter, the Methodist founding fathers established Rehoboth Beach with the intention of "providing and maintaining a permanent camp meeting ground and Christian seaside resort, where everything inconsistent with Christian morality . . . shall be excluded and prohibited." It is a measure of how far contemporary morality has slid that we can proclaim Rehoboth to be among the best-behaved beaches on the East Coast and yet recall that we witnessed an entire barful of young patrons drunkenly singing "God Bless America" at closing time with something less than patriotic reverence. By way of explanation, they had been downing an aphrodisiacal libation known as Mooney's Iced Tea, which consists of many different types of light and dark liquors, colored with cola, and is as lethal as Marvin Hagler's right hook. Still, the fashion-clad collegians who were festively celebrating summer's end appeared to us as angelic cherubim compared with the sleeveless ruffians we'd grown accustomed to in our travels.

And then there are the beaches of Rehoboth. To paraphrase the American philosopher George Clinton, a good beach begins on the boardwalk and works its way down to the water. Rehoboth's boardwalk wanders these tranquil shores for a distance of 1.1 miles. The restaurants and shops that line the walk are tasteful and toned down, inviting rather than demanding you to stop in. Late in the evening or early in the morning, a boardwalk hike is positively serene. You'll see only gulls and the occasional jogger. Rehoboth Beach is, moreover, blessed by nature to the extent that it is immune to the ravages of storms and steady shoreline erosion. Whatever Mother Nature takes away (as in a devastating 1962 "nor'easter"), she eventually repays with interest.

Summer crowds do pack the beach on fair-weather weekends, and parking can become a problem at such times, but not a major problem. (A crowded beach can be a wonderful thing, as long as it's not crowded with idiots.) Besides, an extensive, well-planned and -maintained system of state parks along the Delaware shore readily accommodates the spillover. To the south of Rehoboth lies the *Delaware Seashore State Park*—7 miles of untrammeled beach, with facilities for swimming, fishing, camping, boating, picnicking and so forth.

Just north of Rehoboth Beach is another smaller state park at *Gordon's Pond*—a large saltwater pond that's a haven in winter for migrating geese. The town of Rehoboth Beach is itself well-seeded with parks—fifteen of them, to be exact—and a liberal number of lakes and ponds. It is an extraordinarily pleasant town to walk around; you'll find yourself gazing longingly at some attractive house, fantasizing its renovation and your relocation there.

All in all, the natural attractiveness of the area and the determination of its residents to put its best face forward combine to make Rehoboth Beach one of the East Coast's real red-letter communities. It's the sort of place that we are urged, with pleading looks and importuning voices, *not* to tell people about. But how can we resist? In the end, the sort of people who belong here will find it anyway. The rest, meantime, will slither away, most likely to Ocean City. As Aristotle hypothesized, water seeks its own level. Especially at the beach.

Accommodations

Unless you're on the severest of budgets (e.g., you're sleeping in your car), you're urged to splurge a little and stay at the *Henlopen Hotel*. The Henlopen is an opulent hotel-restaurant-patio complex right on the beach. This is the third Henlopen Hotel to occupy this site, the first having been built in 1879. Even though the present Henlopen is only 11 years old, some sense of the gracious Old World elegance of its precursors survives to this day. In summer, rooms range from $80 to $105 a night.

Alternatively, there are motels and bed-and-breakfast inns around—the former out on the highway, the latter in town. But there's nothing to beat the sound of the surf close by, if you can manage it.

Restaurants

In keeping with the cultured look and comportment of the town, Rehoboth Beach's restaurants are a cut above typical seaside fare. The *Blue Moon* is widely acclaimed as Rehoboth's finest restaurant, attracting an upscale cosmopolitan crowd. No fisherman's netting and mounted marlins on the walls here—the Blue Moon is all vaulted stainless-steel ceilings, mood lighting and modern artwork. The Blue Moon is especially popular with Rehoboth Beach's growing gay population. Little by little, Rehoboth is gathering steam as the gay enclave of choice along the mid-Atlantic coast, between the already established havens of Provincetown and Key West. There is currently a degree of controversy over this within the community.

More informal dining and drinking can be found at the *Front Page* and *Fran O'Brien's*, two popular restaurant-bars that are meeting places for those into casual chic. The Front Page has a polished copper bar and a daily "Editorial Hour" from 4 to 6 P.M. that offers "cheap drinks and free opinions." Fran O'Brien's is set back on a residential street, unobtrusive and cozy. Plenty of people know about it, though, and "meet me at Frannie's" is a favorite plan for an evening rendezvous.

Nightlife

Rehoboth Beach's best nightspots are located along its main drag, Rehoboth Avenue. We started slowly, kicking off our evenings here with a visit to the arcades where the boardwalk meets Rehoboth Avenue. Bearing in mind that we could play eight games of Skee-Ball for the price of one imported beer, we spent the equivalent of a six-pack, quarter by quarter, on our favorite pastime. For our efforts, we won rubber noisemakers, a tin whistle, lensless plastic glasses and a pocketful of miniature Superballs, which we bounced down the boardwalk.

Having exhausted our hoard of Superballs, it was time to bounce from bar to bar. The town's two busiest bars offer widely divergent experiences. The *Country Squire* is a lively place for dressing down and devolving. A deejay spun scratchy favorites from yesteryear and conducted a running trivia quiz. Correct answers were rewarded with anything from a neon beer sign to free shooters (shots of alcohol, usually taken straight up). Gradually, the frayed edges of the working class were brought to the fore by the deejay, who mounted a verbal offensive against tourists. About the third time the entire bar toasted their native Delaware-hood with a raucous roar, we left, feeling conspicuous in our silence. This meant we missed the tie-a-knot-in-a-maraschino-cherry-with-your-tongue contest (no relation to the erotic-banana-eating contest), but it was time to move on.

Up the street, we ventured into *A Summer Place*, scene of the Mooney's Iced Tea swampfest described in the main essay. Summer Place draws a young, pampered crowd. It was, to be frank about it, extremely gratifying to be around a crowd without a collective chip on its shoulder. And so well-dressed! Guys in drawstring slacks and pastel polo shirts with upturned collars; girls in their summer dresses. . . . Ah, paradise.

FOR FURTHER INFORMATION

Rehoboth Beach Chamber of Commerce
P.O. Box 216
73 Rehoboth Avenue
Rehoboth Beach, Delaware 19971
(302) 227-2233

Dewey Beach

Delaware's oldest and youngest communities are both located along its brief coast, within 10 miles of each other. Lewes is the stately great-grandad, settled continuously since the 1600s, and Dewey Beach is the young whelp, an outgrowth of Rehoboth Beach that has been incorporated only recently. Dewey Beach has caved in to the sort of unchecked growth that Rehoboth has so studiously avoided. The result is a goulash of buildings clustered haphazardly along U.S. 1. There is not much land to work with here—just south of Rehoboth the peninsula narrows to a thin strip between bay and beach. Thus, Dewey Beach is an eruption of construction that is somewhat unsightly but is indisputably livelier than Rehoboth Beach.

Dewey Beach is big on summer rentals, especially with the Washington, D.C., young-professional set, those movers and shakers who have not completely succumbed to Yuppie sellout. The entire town, in fact, is like a ramshackle frat house, and seemingly every car sports this slogan on its bumper: "Dewey Beach—A Way of Life." Not surprisingly, one of the hottest tickets in town when we were there was a group called Otis Day and the Nights. You know, the soul revue featured in *Animal House*. Yes, here in Dewey Beach you'll find the sort of noisy rock 'n' roll bars that Rehoboth eschews. The *Bottle and Cork*, in particular, is a shot of loud fun amid the more placid environs of the Delaware coast. Rock 'n' roll and beer mingle in sudsy communion. Just down the road, the *Rusty Rudder* draws more of a sit-down than a fall-down crowd. You can even pull up and dock your boat here. Just the sort of Margueritaville that Jimmy Buffett might write a song about.

FOR FURTHER INFORMATION

Town Hall
Dewey Beach, Delaware 19971
(302) 227-6363

Bethany-Fenwick

Bethany Beach, South Bethany and Fenwick Island are three discrete communities that by virtue of their proximity are generally spoken of in the same breath. They bill themselves, somewhat misleadingly, as "the Quiet Resorts." If by this they mean there isn't an awful lot to do after the sun goes down, then yes, they are quiet. But the encroachment of shore-and-sky-obscuring condominiums, such as a seemingly endless development in South Bethany called the *Sea Colony*, makes for a pretty maddening racket, visually speaking. And there is enough traffic and clutter along U.S. 1 through here to make you recheck the dictionary definition of "quiet." (Fenwick Island, if you wish to get more disputatious, isn't even an island, really.)

Actually, Bethany-Fenwick falls somewhere between Rehoboth Beach and Dewey Beach on the noise meter. The area tends toward the rental of summer cottages, houses and condos. Actually, it's not all monstrous. The Fenwick area has some solid old homes tucked away behind the dunes. If you drive on its back streets, you will find some equally solid citizens taking solid strolls down the middle of them. No matter how slow you are going (and the speed limit is 25) they will veer exaggeratedly into the reeds at the sound of your car engine. It appears to be more of an editorial comment than a safety precaution, however.

The beach has been subjected to some erosion in recent years; on a busy summer day, it can resemble one giant beach towel as folks crowd together. Several nearby parks and preserves enhance the profile of the area and temper the congestion. The southern end of *Delaware Seashore State Park* nearly touches Bethany Beach; *Assawoman Wildlife Area* lies just east of Bethany-Fenwick, and *Fenwick Island State Park* runs from South Bethany to the town of Fenwick Island, with public beaches on the ocean side and crabbing and fishing on the bay side.

The state beaches are worth singling out for praise. They are officially and collectively known as the Delaware Seashore State Park. There are intermittent beach-access points, recognizable by their huge asphalt parking lots and the abandoned concrete gun towers behind them—the remnants of our East Coast defenses in World War II. For $4 you get a place to park (good all day at all lots), a clear path through the dunes and free license to roam once you hit the beach. There are showers and facilities at the parking lots and concession stands at several of the larger lots. And there are lifeguards.

More important, there is no commercial buildup looming behind you. The beaches are beautiful and, considering the huge number of people who use them, surprisingly free of debris. And the waves are moderately large—perfect for body surfing. Aside from this, the most excitement you can hope for is when the biplanes fly past dragging advertising ribbons behind them—"½ Price Shooters Tonite at JB'S!!!!"—or when the young lady who has so discreetly isolated herself from the swarm around the lifeguard stand proceeds to remove the top of her bathing suit in order to bake away her winter bra lines. One grandfatherly sort we saw could scarcely contain himself when a shapely female did just this, though he pretended all the while he was just looking for seashells.

For the most part, the Delaware Seashore State Park is used by discriminating daytrippers who are well aware of (and prepared for) the late-Sunday traffic backup on Route 50. Without traffic, these beaches are a 2 ½-hour drive from Washington D.C., and many find the trip to be well worth it.

FOR FURTHER INFORMATION

Bethany-Fenwick Area Chamber of Commerce
P.O. Box 502
Bethany Beach, Delaware 19930
(302) 539-8129

Maryland—
Up for Crabs

Maryland is one of the weirdest shaped states in the union. It looks like an Oklahoma that was accidentally dropped in a blender and then rescued before being totally puréed. A finger of Maryland reaches out and touches the Allegheny Mountains in the west, a foot stands atop Washington, D.C., and the other foot wades into the water of the Chesapeake Bay, wriggling its big toe in the Atlantic Ocean. And so Maryland gets its peek at the sea, between Delaware and Virginia.

If you are beach bound, you will find yourself on that right foot, straddling the bay and ocean. Because it is so removed from the mainland, this area—known simply as the Eastern Shore—has a personality all its own. It's slower paced than the industrial web of Baltimore, and is water oriented as well as agricultural. Though most of the people out here on the Eastern Shore face west for their inspiration and livelihood, toward the crab-filled Chesapeake (the bay that H. L. Mencken once called "an immense protein factory"), there is a 30-mile ocean coastline here as well.

At the northern extreme sits Ocean City, where mainland Maryland comes to rear its beach-seeking head. On any given weekend from Memorial Day to Labor Day, the backroads of the Eastern Shore are bottled up with an army of cars on retreat from the greater Baltimore-Washington megalopolis. There is something frantic about this automotive procession, and the frenzy is carried all the way into town. Ocean City has a gold-rush boomtown feel

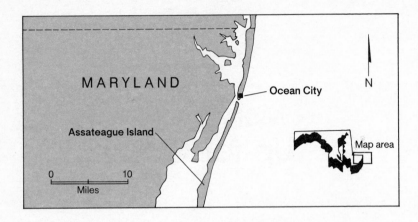

to it. If the visitors' frazzled nerves can be blamed on the utterly inadequate road system that brings them here from the west, then the natives' short fuse might have to do with the specter of a disappearing shoreline. Almost yearly, sand has to be pumped in to fill the beach here. But then, learning to live with the vagaries of water is part and parcel of living in the state of Maryland.

Within minutes of Ocean City, if you head south on Route 611, you can see another, quieter side of the Maryland shore. As soon as you've crossed the bridge out of Ocean City, you are thrust into a golden landscape of cornfields and farmland and horses and cows. Fresh produce is sold by the side of the road. The sky is deep blue, the air is clean and no jacked-up dune buggy is buggering your tailgate. Yes, this, too, is Maryland. Most of Assateague is designated as National Seashore and so remains remarkably unspoiled. Though its share of the coast is small, Maryland offers beaches at both ends of the spectrum.

Ocean City

Some beach towns are so filled with the spirit of self-promotion as to border on the evangelical. To measure this sort of frenzy, one need only check the amount of literature that has to do with the selling, renting or leasing of its real estate. In this regard, Ocean City, Maryland, is a major publishing house.

If you write its chamber of commerce for any kind of information, you will get more fan mail than Bullwinkle *and* his famous flounder. There is, in fact, something cartoon-like about Ocean City, something almost funny about the desperation among all the cinder-block and concrete. Perhaps the dimensions of Ocean City's particular brand of lunacy can best be illustrated with a few unofficial statistics, culled from the aforementioned fan mail: here lie 145 streets, forming the rungs of the narrow ladder of land upon which Ocean City is precariously situated. Along these streets are packed a Hong Kong's worth of high-rises, a Miami's worth of motels and a cuckoo's nest of condominiums. All of this is penetrated by a lone coastal highway (Route 528) that runs the length of the town and is known affectionately, by visitors and natives alike, as "Six Lanes of Death."

To be more precise, in the 1985 business directory there are listings for 114 motels and hotels (with 60 or more rooms in most), 620 apartment complexes, 63 real estate agencies, more condominium developments than one can keep track of (like rabbits, they multiply even as we speak), 137 gift shops, 143 restaurants, 58 fast-food franchises, 48 "amusement outlets" for the kiddies, 18 ice-cream parlors, not to mention acres of parking lots and 2 airports to fly you in and out of this mad fantasyland. But perhaps the most telling statistics of all are the ones they neglect to include in the directory: there appear to be no sand dunes, no patches of sea grass and 10 miles of beach that has to be constantly replenished.

Ocean City has been singled out by many shoreline ecologists for some of the most dire predictions of doom. You'd never guess that Ocean City was so vulnerable by looking at the beach on an average summer day—at least below Thirtieth Street, where most of the motels and boardwalk businesses are located. The strand is actually quite wide there. But it's an artificially nurtured stretch of pearly white sand, not unlike Miami Beach's, and a sure sign that something is ultimately amiss is the one posted beside the northernmost inlet (an inlet, incidentally, created by a devastating hurricane in 1933): "An Army Corps of Engineers Rehabilitation Project." In the fall of last year, Hurricane Gloria literally reduced the Ocean City boardwalks to kindling. Miraculously, this was the worst of the damage.

Regardless of its instability, the same loyal constituency flocks to Ocean City year after year. Mostly, they are the young and the restless, sprung from the twin suburban webs of Baltimore and Washington. Weekends witness a mass, highway-jamming exodus of cars and decal-covered pleasure vans packed to the roofs with near-naked bodies, station wagons teeming with testy family members, lonesome rockers on leave from their second-shift jobs at the packing plant and the normal high school gaggle of pretty girls and pretty sorry-looking guys. The adult types make their reservations ahead of time and, to heighten the sense of expectation, spend countless winter hours extolling the summer charms of the place. Then they all get in their cars at the same time, as if on cue ("Gentlemen, start your engines"), and clog Route 50 up tighter than an AM radio playlist.

Our first glimpse of Ocean City—after creeping into town near the rear of the traffic cortege and searching long and hard for a legal parking space, that is—was a windowful of T-shirts with a decidedly heavy-metal bent: "Iron Maiden," "Judas Priest," "Twisted Sister," complete with these bands' Neanderthal logos. But when we set foot on the boardwalk, we beheld a veritable nation of well-scrubbed families: on bikes, on foot, buried up to their necks in sand. In short, they were everywhere. No, the crazed biker-chic motif was offset by the sight of all these happy families.

To be sure, there is a slab of raunch to be found in Ocean City, but it is a cancer of a more benign sort. Perhaps this is due to the commingling of disparate groups, with the solid citizens beating the raunch hands by virtue of numbers alone. We have a lingering image of the town that cemented this impression. On our final stroll down the boardwalk, we beheld a pair of strange young men. One was a dangerous-looking lad of indeterminate age (old enough, however, to be liberally tatooed), a wisp of a mustache on his face to go along with his vacuous, been-awake-all-night glare. His partner was the fattest teenager east of the Mississippi, a black kid with a baby face and a body the size of a Plymouth. He performed a series of defiant gyrations that he conceived to be break-dancing while the white lad's boom box sprayed an ear-splitting rap song. Fat Albert's twitching took his humongous body directly into the path of passing families. Instead of the anger he meant to elicit from the throng, however, the people paid him and his urchin friend absolutely no mind, treating their behavior almost as part of the nearby Ripley's Believe It or Not Museum. In other words, they chose not to believe it, or even to notice.

Speaking of leaving Ocean City, the bottlenecks of traffic on either side of the Chesapeake Bay Bridge are not merely frequent, they're legendary. In fact, a small party cult has been spawned by the delays, which are fully anticipated, part of the experience. The standstill on the Labor Day weekend after our visit was measured by the Highway Patrol as 18 miles. And they no doubt still extol the charms of Ocean City when they get there.

Accommodations

As far as availability, the prodigious statistics have already been given. As far as affordability, most overnight rooms fall in the $50 to $60 range. Weekly rates are prominently displayed on all of the literature, leading one to suspect that most folks plan on the latter. Enough people come to Ocean City in season to make a vacant room difficult to find, as hard as that is to believe. If you are arriving unprepared, you might want to visit the chamber of commerce office out on Route 50, 3 miles west of town. We could see endless rows of brochures through the front window, like socks and ties in a men's shop, but alas, at seven o'clock on a Saturday morning, the chamber was not open. Motels are most plentiful below Thirtieth Street, on the main drag. Here you will find, if there can be said to be one, the center of town. As stated, the beach is widest here, and you don't have to drive all over hell to find the fun.

Restaurants

You can go to the family chowder houses or eat a king's ransom worth of fried fisherman's platters or chomp on a meatball sub at one saloon after another. We went where all the smart cowboys go—Roy Rogers Family Restaurant. Here, amid the concretized landscape of Ocean City, we found a bit of America the way it used to be: teenage help in cowboy hats, red-and-white checked Western shirts and gentleman's string ties doing their best to resurrect the legend of the Old West in this sad frontier town by the sea. "Howdy, podnuh. What kin I getcha?" Perhaps a roast beef sandwich and a Coke. "Need a roast beef, podnuh!" "It's in the corral, podnuh!" And so on. Yes, Mr. Double R has done something real special with his chain. His burgers and salad bar are enough to make a traveler's eyes water with gratitude, and will put the color back in the cheeks of even the most famished saddle tramp. In his own squint-eyed way, the man is a genius.

If roast beef is not exactly what you trekked to the ocean to feast on, you'll find the aforementioned chowder houses and family seafood restaurants in an obedient line upon the beach. It won't make a lot of difference which one you duck into. Perhaps the heavyweight hunger-crampers could try *Paul Revere's Smorgasbord*, which has an all-you-can-eat spread.

Nightlife

More facts and figures: there are 33 bars and saloons in Ocean City. Rock 'n' rollers will want to walk out to the *Gang Plank*, straddle the *Brass Rail* or sidle up to *Samantha's*. Most of the rest of the juke joints in this shoot-'em-up town are the sort of high-pressure good-times places, with names like *Brass Balls*, the *Bearded Clam* and the *Cork Bar*, that give all drinkers a bad name. Should you wish to retreat to your room before you forget which motel is which, you can visit one of 15 beer-and-wine shops or 5 county-run liquor stores in the Ocean City area. Not to mention all those 7-Eleven clerks who are just dying to bag your six-pack.

Ocean City Public Relations Department
Box 158
4001 Coastal Highway
Ocean City, Maryland 21842
(301) 289-2800

Assateague Island

Assateague is a 37-mile-long barrier island that belongs to two
states, Maryland and Virginia. Maryland gets the lion's share, but
only a fraction of that is accessible to the public. Most of Assateague
is designated National Seashore and is inaccessible to cars and off-
limits to Jeeps. But Maryland has thoughtfully provided a state
park along a 2-mile section of the island up at the northern end,
which adjoins a 2-mile public beach run by the National Park
Service.

If these jurisdictional distinctions are unclear, what it boils down
to is that 4 miles of beach and several campgrounds are open to
the public. Here, one can enjoy the splendid wildness of Assateague's beaches and even pitch a tent, if one is so moved. The
state park campground offers 311 sites, and there are "primitive"
campsites on the National Park side of the line on both the bay
and the beach. Despite all this space, the campgrounds are often
packed full in the summer.

There is a lifeguard-protected beach on the federal property
called North Beach, and this is the most popular spot in the park.
The hard-top road runs out south of here in a parking area, though
it continues for 14 miles as a "back trail" accessible to Jeeps and
oversand vehicles (a park-service permit is required). There are
plenty of activities on the bay side as well, such as canoeing in the
shallow waters of Chincoteague Bay. All in all, Assateague Island—with its wild-pony population, its flocks of shore birds and
its untrammeled expanses of white sand and low dunes—is a hum-

bling reminder of the beauty of an unspoiled beach. We took a refreshing dip here in cool September waters, the beach nearly empty of any signs of life except for scurrying gulls. Ironically, Assateague, at its northernmost end, practically kisses Ocean City, whose beach has been vulgarized and virtually destroyed. Only the narrow Ocean City Inlet separates the two, though they are spiritually light-years apart.

FOR FURTHER INFORMATION

Superintendent, National Park Service
Route 2, Box 294
Berlin, Maryland 21811
(301) 641-4111.

Virginia: Checking Out the Chesapeake

The state of Virginia is known as the Old Dominion. It is a name as full of itself as a powdered wig on a barrister, suggesting an illustrious past we shouldn't even have to ask about. It is indeed a state of great breadth . . . and of great contradictions. Virginia played an integral part in the formation of the American nation, and it played an equally integral part in its dissolution and ghastly Civil War. The state is divided by water and a myriad of land forms into zones of great diversity. Even within its short coastline there is division and dichotomy. If we exclude the seemingly endless inner shoreline of the Chesapeake Bay (which we will, for the stated purpose of this book), then Virginia can be said to own two distinct coastal regions.

First, there is the upper portion, known as Virginia's Eastern Shore. The Eastern Shore seems almost an afterthought, a sliver of land that was truly unknown to the outside world until the movie *Misty of Chincoteague* made every Barbie Doll owner in the United States suddenly covetous of a wild pony. Of course, the construction of the Chesapeake Bay Bridge and Tunnel in the sixties, which routed north-south traffic through the formerly uncongested peninsula, hasn't helped to preserve its anonymity. Still, the Eastern Shore is relatively unspoiled and its side roads will lead you to the very edge of nowhere. A healthy chunk of Assateague Island belongs to Virginia, and there are countless inlets on the peninsula waiting to be discovered and explored. The town of Chincoteague,

through which you pass to get to Assateague, is where visitors lay over when in the area.

This is in direct contrast to Virginia's second ocean region, an area known as Tidewater, which in recent decades has become one of the largest urban areas in the country, not to mention one of the most visited beach resorts. The whole Norfolk-Suffolk-Newport News-Virginia Beach polyglot covers an obscenely large area—hundreds of square miles—and takes up a sizable chunk of the state's southeastern corner, butting right up against the North Carolina border.

Within this sprawl zone is the city of Norfolk—until very recently, the largest city in Virginia. Now, the dubious title of Most Populous City has passed a few dozen miles to the east, to Virginia

Beach. Since the two cities are neighbors, the issue of their respective populations is almost hair-splitting—more a function of where the city limits signs are, since the concrete bunker neighborhoods merge into a big overwhelming oneness of endless Tidewater-dom. The real distinction is that Norfolk is a navy town, and Virginia Beach is a beach town. On Virginia Beach, the high-rises grow like cornstalks and tacky chic reigns supreme in the summertime. Not only is Virginia Beach the largest city in the state, it is still one of the fastest growing. The Good Book addressed this phenomenon thousands of years ago . . . something about building your house on sand. But what the hey. There's plenty of sand to go around out here. Miles and miles of it.

The Eastern Shore and Tidewater regions are connected by the Chesapeake Bay Bridge and Tunnel. It is a 17 1/2-mile marvel that'll carry you over and under the waters of the deep blue sea for a fee of $9 per car. One minute you are in the wilds of Cape Charles on the Eastern Shore, then you are out in the middle of the Atlantic, and finally you are wheeling your way into congested Tidewater. Just another touch of extremes from your friends in the Old Dominion.

Chincoteague
Assateague Island

Sunlight sparkles across the Atlantic.
Graceful fishing boats gently slice through the stillness of the Chesapeake. Wild ponies stir. Bird sanctuaries come alive amid bursts of song and color. And in quiet towns and villages along a peninsula that stretches for 70 unspoiled miles, time seems to pass with an unhurried ease.
It is dawn on Virginia's Eastern Shore.

If you believe the sort of ornate bunk that is written in travel brochures, then you might be inclined to think from the above that the only difference between Virginia's Eastern Shore and the French Riviera is the accents of the natives. Not so. Virginia's

Eastern Shore is a lonely nub of sand and rock that hangs, like a stalactite, to the bottom of Maryland's Eastern Shore. Up until the early sixties, most Virginians didn't even know that this desolate, watery reach of land was part of the Old Dominion.

Unless you are an avid duck hunter or a working waterman, you probably have no knowledge of the Eastern Shore outside of Assateague and Chincoteague. But those two names are commanding an ever-growing reputation among easterners who are looking for some of that "unhurried ease." And so nowadays the weather-beaten oystermen and crabbers who live out here are not just saluting the flag of Virginia. They have expanded the gesture, somewhat reluctantly, to include license plates from every state in the union.

Undoubtedly, the people most affected by this Charge of the Lite-Beer Brigade are the residents of the tiny island of Chincoteague. Only 7 miles long and 1 ½ miles wide, protected like a babe from the mighty Atlantic by the surrounding arm of Assateague Island, Chincoteague has been converted, rather suddenly, from an outpost of rugged watermen into "Virginia's only resort island." There are obvious reasons for the turnaround, among them the opening of the Chesapeake Bay Bridge and Tunnel, which brings a steady volume of north-south traffic over U.S. 13 through the heart of the Eastern Shore. Then there is Assateague Island. When a bridge was built from Chincoteague to Assateague in 1962, the traffic began to trickle over. When Assateague officially became a National Seashore in 1965, the trickle turned into a stream. And with forces promoting the commercial development of Chincoteague in the wake of this new attention in the years since, the community is fighting to save a way of life that had been happily unmolested since the late 1600s.

Assateague Island is a place of great beauty, and we have Lyndon Baines Johnson to thank for its preservation as a National Seashore. With its pristine beaches (the only ocean beaches on Virginia's Eastern Shore accessible by car) and undisturbed marshlands, and the wild ponies that roam over both, Assateague is a national treasure. Two million people visit Assateague annually, though most of them frolic up on the Maryland end. One of the big draws down on the Virginia side is the wild ponies. There is no lack of theories as to how they got here, and no definitive answers. Did they swim ashore from a wrecked Spanish galleon? Did English colonists drive them out here because they were destroying crops on the mainland? Was it pirates who put them ashore?

In any case, they are not nearly as wild as they look. As a matter of fact, some of them are tamer than the family cocker spaniel. A group of four, looking for a handout and a friendly pat on the nose, surrounded our car as we attempted to drive out of a parking lot on Assateague. With the patience of Job and expressions that said, "We've got all day, guys," they positioned themselves in such a manner as to make our forward progress impossible. There were two up by the front bumper, resting their heads on the hood, and two alongside—one each by the driver and passenger windows, poking their heads in. It was a Mexican standoff. When they eventually realized we had no store-bought goodies to lay on them, they ambled away. But they wouldn't budge for 20 minutes. It was one of the most memorable moments in our travels.

Every year, the last Wednesday and Thursday in July are the designated Pony Penning Days. There is a roundup of ponies on the Virginia side of Assateague Island, and the herd is driven across the channel from Assateague to Chincoteague, where they are auctioned off by the local volunteer fire department. The event, which grows yearly in popularity, draws upward of 30,000, and the average bid is $225. In their own way, the wild ponies helped put Chincoteague on the map, by way of the celebrated children's novel (and subsequent movie) *Misty of Chincoteague*, by Marguerite Henry. It is telling that, years later, the movie was still playing at the only movie house in town.

The ponies of Chincoteague may be wild, but the town itself is being tamed by a lot of out-of-towners with dollar signs for eyes. You know you are getting near Chincoteague when, just before crossing the bridge onto the island, you are besieged by almost 3 miles of billboards stuck into what must have been (and what still would be) a breathtaking marshland. We counted 81 signs, and not a one of them was pleasant to look at. This low-rent greeting halts, briefly, in the village of Chincoteague itself, then picks up again on the far side, when you hit Beach Road, the route out to Assateague Island. Ironically, the most egregious offender in this hideous hodgepodge turns out to be a lifetime resident. His free-enterprise brainstorm was a water slide—a huge serpentine structure like something you'd see up in Ocean City. But this one is like nothing you've ever laid eyes on. It's fronted by a plastic, lighthouse-sized "bathing beauty" who's holding an American flag. The sign on the road bears this hollow taunt: "We're Wet Enough, Are U [sic] Wild Enough?"

Still, in all fairness, it should be pointed out that the great majority of islanders have not buckled under to pressure to turn Chincoteague into another Ocean City. There is a defiant quality to these people, most of them descended from pure Anglo-Saxon stock and set in their watery ways, that says they are not going to yield their claim to this land without a struggle. In the past, they have tended to keep to themselves. Like Maine Down Easters or true blue Nantucketers, they are people of the sea, as hard in their exteriors as the oysters they pluck from these waters and damned wary of folks from the mainland. But the current drift of the island toward the uncharted waters of development is bringing the native Chincoteaguers out of their, uh, shells.

History has proven Chincoteaguers to be adaptable creatures. When Union troops occupied the island during the Civil War, they quickly sided with the North. When city slickers began craving the native "salt oysters," regular ferries from Chincoteague carted the critters off to the mainland by the bushel (with lemons and cocktail sauce, presumably, following in smaller rowboats). And then the oyster harvest dwindled, even as a bridge was being built from the mainland to the island in the 1920s.

Now, Chincoteague is at a different sort of crossroads. With the bridge over to Assateague making its stunning beaches accessible to all, Chincoteague is threatened by a surfeit of prosperity, as peculiar as that may sound. Civilization is banging at the gates. . . . Will they let them in? Could they stop them even if they wanted? Is that hideous "bathing beauty" a harbinger of what the future holds for this island community? The axe of responsible growth, it seems, has fallen on Chincoteague.

Accommodations

If you come here looking for birds in their wild habitat, as many do in the spring and fall (260 species have been counted on Assateague), you might first spot the *Sea Hawk Motel* by mistake. Affixed to the top of its sign on Beach Road is an enormous plaster hawk skewered on a stick, a fleeting symbol, perhaps, for most of the ragtag string of businesses on this thoroughfare. But if you are smart, you will continue to flap your wings down the road, around the traffic circle toward the Assateague Island bridge. Then you'll swoop down on the *Driftwood Motor Lodge*. Its motto is "Elegance at Nature's Door," and the elegance it offers is just the right kind— understated natural-wood architecture, comfortable rooms, a beautiful view of an unbillboarded marshland and a convenient location. (It's the closest on the island to the beaches of Assateague.) A double room in season runs about $55, but drops to $35 in mid-September. Fall, incidentally, is one of the best times of year to come here, for swimming and birdwatching, or for relaxation and contemplation. Closer to town, on the bay side, is the *Island Motor Inn*, cut from the same tasteful cloth.

Restaurants

You can tell, just from a brief perusal of the names, logos and interiors of Chincoteague's restaurants, what separates the old salts from the new-money invaders. The former frequent the old, slightly run-down but stalwart-looking establishments in the vicinity of the bridge over from the mainland. They congregate at places like the *Chincoteague Inn* to milk the last drop of beer and conversation and pound down fresh clams, oysters and fish. At the Chincoteague Inn, a half-dozen oysters or cherrystone clams go for $2, no entrée costs more than $6, and the emphasis is on, well, no emphasis at all.

Pulling away from the harbor a bit, you begin to find restaurants that do emphasize something—if not exactly continental cuisine, then at least a certain suburban flair for hanging plants, exposed wood and a price structure more in tune with the mainland visitors who dine here. Of the newer, classier joints, the *Landmark Crab House* is by far the most appealing, offering a waterfront dining room and lounge and an extensive menu specializing in local seafood.

Nightlife

After the Chincoteague oysters have been tucked into their beds, the town and the island soon follow suit. The decided lack of nightlife is not surprising when you consider that the normal day for a working island resident begins before the sun comes up. The bar at the *Landmark Crab House* serves a good drink, and some of the other restaurants around town, like the *Pony Pines* and *Bill's Seafood Restaurant*, dispense spirits as well. The *Misty Harbour*, on Beach Road, is about the only nightclub, per se. On the night we checked it out, they were charging $3 for a band that sounded roughly like Lynyrd Skynyrd, at least from the vantage point of the parking lot, which was, admittedly, overflowing. Ocean City is 1 1/2 hours away over winding, dark roads—definitely not worth the trouble. The bridge onto Assateague Island is open till 10 P.M., so a moonlight drive and beach walk are not altogether out of the question, and quite possibly the most attractive option.

FOR FURTHER INFORMATION

Chincoteague Chamber of Commerce
P.O. Box 258
Chincoteague Island, Virginia 23336
(804) 336-6161

Chincoteague National Wildlife Refuge
P.O. Box 62
Chincoteague, Virginia 23336
(804) 336-6122

Virginia Beach

Our arrival in Virginia Beach, after a long day of driving, should have ended with the waving of a checkered flag. Perhaps the disheveled kid who was loitering outside a McDonald's on the beach, heckling passersby, could have done the honors. For the two of us, who had just endured a citizens' Grand Prix to the beach on a racetrack called the Virginia Beach-Norfolk Expressway, the only thing that would have made any sense amid the heat and the dust and the 80 mph speed we were bullied into driving would have been some kind of signal that the race was over.

Suddenly, you're here. Near the beach, the expressway fizzles to an end, distributing its traffic among several numbered streets. Then, mere blocks later, they all dead-end into Atlantic Avenue, which runs along the ocean. There is a Great Wall of hotels and such between Atlantic Avenue and the Atlantic Ocean that runs for nearly forty blocks. And that, friends, is pretty much it for Virginia Beach. For the millions of people who come here on vacation—as opposed to the hundreds of thousands who call it home—Virginia Beach begins and ends on Atlantic Avenue, between Second and Thirty-eighth Streets. This strip is demarcated by a concrete boardwalk along the beach, which runs for about 3 1/2 miles.

Statistics tell an interesting story about Virginia Beach. It is the largest city in the state of Virginia, but its 300,000 citizens are spread out over nearly 300 square miles. The city is visited annually by 2 million tourists, who climb all over one another in a sweaty heap, sharing what amounts to eighty square blocks. (Admittedly, tourists don't all come at once.) The result is an overcrowding perhaps unequaled on the beaches of the East Coast. We've been told horror stories by former residents of incredible liberties taken with private property by invading Huns. There are tales recounted by those with homes near the beach of finding cars parked in their front yard—not on the street, but *on the lawn*—and of coming home to discover strangers showering off with their garden hose. The traffic snarls are legendary, what with hordes streaming in from the south and west on the Virginia Beach-

Norfolk Expressway and from the north over the Chesapeake Bay Bridge and Tunnel.

Virginia Beach, after all, is the only ocean beach in Virginia, excepting the portion of Assateague Island that belongs to the Old Dominion. When you consider that a state the size of Virginia, which is located at the midpoint of the Atlantic Coast, must find a way to make do with forty blocks of beach, you will begin to understand why this town has given new meaning to the word "bottleneck."

Here's what you'll see when you get here—once you're able to find a place to park your car, that is. If you can locate a walkway to the beach between the skyscraper resorts, you'll cross a pedestrian expressway—i.e., boardwalk—en route. The boardwalk has separate lanes for walkers and bicyclists. The latter is further subdivided by a solid yellow line so that bike traffic can safely move in both directions. The beach itself is surprisingly narrow, as Virginia Beach proves itself to be yet another East Coast beach town with an erosion problem. The strand is of an acceptable width down around the lower-numbered streets, but narrows precipitously as you move northward. There are three-block intervals along the way where beach-replenishment projects are in progress.

There are no dunes in Virginia Beach, as they have been bulldozed down to make room for all the formidable hotel-motel-condo edifices. It's a short hike and a sudden drop from the boardwalk to the water's edge. The ocean is shallow for a good distance out. This must be one reason why it is a popular family beach—even toddlers would have trouble drowning in these depths.

The sun sets earlier on Virginia Beach than it does on the rest of the East Coast. Not because it's in a different time zone, but because Old Sol passes behind the concrete horizon of the hotel tops at around four or five. And so the beach, in broad daylight, is shrouded in shadows. You will also notice a peculiar sight in the heavens every 10 minutes or so. Navy jets, on maneuvers from one of several local bases, pass overhead, in formation. They say you get used to it, but we'll bet you a sonic boom you don't.

You can always avert your eyes. There are more eye-catching sights on the ground anyway. If you are a healthy U.S. male, you'll be happier than Elvis Presley with a platterful of peanut butter and jelly sandwiches. There are miles of nubiles in daring bikinis on Virginia Beach. In between all the wiggling asses and casual mammarian bouncing, a guy could find enough flesh for fantasy to keep himself going all winter long. Most of the guys we saw on the beach, no doubt accustomed to the flesh parade, were involved in various group athletic endeavors, however.

Surfing is big on Virginia Beach; indeed, the city has provided board bums with four all-day surfing areas along the oceanfront, and the rest of the public beaches are fair game before 10 A.M. and after 5 P.M. All this generosity doesn't mean the surfers still don't overstep their boundaries on occasion. We saw a Virginia Beach patrolman, rolling up on what looked like a riding lawn mower, politely request that one group who'd strayed too far confine themselves to their designated area. The cop's next order of business was to reprimand a bunch of scofflaws who were drinking beer on the beach. When they saw him coming, they broke up their touch football game and dashed, en masse, into the water. He summoned them out and gave a patient lecture about bottles and booze on the beach, to which they nodded, like good scouts, in earnest agreement. Virginia Beach, we decided, does have a human dimension, despite the anonymous press of the crowds.

Maybe Virginia Beach is not so beatific nowadays as it was to one of its earliest explorers, who wrote: "Heaven and Earth never agreed better to frame a place for man's habitations than Virginia." But the beach can be a pleasant place to be, especially in the early fall (anytime after Labor Day) or on a rare uncrowded summer weekday. And, residentially, Virginia Beach is surprisingly serene. Away from the beach, mile after mile of quiet neighborhoods roll westward, with well-kept two-story homes on tree-shaded lots. And what do they do for a living, the 300,000 people who live in Virginia Beach, not to mention the approximately one million in the extended area known as Tidewater, which encompasses Virginia Beach, Norfolk and Newport News? Seemingly incongruous industries overlap here. There are four military bases, which employ large numbers. Tourism, of course, is big business. And agriculture, oddly enough, contributes significantly to the city's economy. There are 44,000 acres of land under cultivation within the Virginia Beach city limits!

Farms, jets and surfboards—if you can somehow accommodate all three in your consciousness, you'll begin to get an idea of what Virginia Beach is all about. And you can't leave out history. Despite the impact of the modern age and rapid growth upon the area, there are inescapable reminders of its historic stature as the seat of colonial life in America. The first landing party in the New World came ashore at Virginia Beach on April 26, 1607. After exploring the Chesapeake Bay, and encountering hostile Indians, the settlers founded the colony of Jamestown on a small island in the bay, some distance from Virginia Beach. Of their first night's run-in with the Chesapeake Indians, one diarist wrote: "At night when we were going aboard, there came the savages. Creeping upon all fours from the Hills like bears, with their Bows in their mouths: Charged us very desperately in the face, hurt Captain Gabriall Archer in both his hands, and a saylor in two places of the body very dangerous."

Two of the most frequently visited sights in Virginia Beach are the *Adam Thoroughgood House* (purportedly the first brick house in America, circa 1636) and the *Lynnhaven House* (a well-preserved brick farmer's dwelling, circa 1730). Other things to see include the *Old Cape Henry Lighthouse* (up where the beach makes a left turn along the mouth of the Chesapeake; circa 1791) and two museums of the sea—one old (the *Virginia Beach Maritime Museum*, circa 1903) and one brand-new (the *Virginia Museum of Marine Sciences*, an enormous complex of aquariums, exhibits, outdoor preserves and so on). Just above the Cape Henry Lighthouse is the *Seashore State Park*, a 3,000-acre wooded park with 20 miles of biking and hiking trails and 300 campsites along the Chesapeake Bay, plus swimming beaches and boat-launching ramps.

Jamestown and Williamsburg are close by, and there are all sorts of places in the vicinity where battles and landings are commemorated. Highway markers constantly remind you that you're in "Historyland." But perhaps a more telling symbol of Virginia Beach in the present day is a park called *Mt. Trashmore*. Here, along the Virginia Beach-Norfolk Expressway, visible from the highway, a literal mountain of refuse rises from the ground. Soil and garbage have been compacted and stacked to create a public playground, complete with skateboard bowls and soapbox derby ramps. There are even two lakes on the premises. (Question: Given the nature of the park, what are the lakes filled with?) Somehow, Mt. Trashmore seems an almost too-perfect metaphor for the growing Virginia Beach-Tidewater metropolitan area, and one which needs no further editorial comment from us.

Accommodations

As it is in huge beach towns from Wildwood to Miami, there are too many choices and too few distinctions to be made among them. And so a handpicked list is of relatively little value. The latest figures indicate that there are over 9,000 rooms for rent in Virginia Beach, yet so popular is this area that the neon "no vacancy" signs begin glowing by high noon. Virginia Beach's hotels and motels run the length of Atlantic Avenue and Pacific Avenue (one block back). Expect to pay a minimum of $60 in season and as much as twice that at some of the resort hotels that rise above it all on the oceanfront. There are economy motels to be found adjacent to the high-priced spreads—places such as *MacThrift* and *Econo-Lodge*—and these can ease the vacation budget somewhat. Also, the wise traveler will pay close attention to the fluctuations in price before Memorial Day and after Labor Day. The air and the ocean are still warm, the crowds have thinned out and the prices drop. We have a favorite motel on the dry side of Atlantic Avenue called the *Carriage Inn*. Its prices are among the most competitive on the beach; the decor is tasteful, in the Old Virginia "lamplighter" mode; the rooms are large and decently furnished and it's all set a few steps back from the bustle. For a complete directory of Virginia Beach accommodations, write the Tourist Bureau, P.O. Box 533, Virginia Beach, Virginia 23451.

Restaurants

This is Chesapeake Bay country, so you're going to come up with a haul of seafood anywhere you toss your dinnertime net. Virginia Beach caters to the tourist's taste buds, so beware of mediocrity.

Some of the assembly-line "all-you-can-eat" joints serve great quantities of fried seafood, but the quality is in inverse proportion to the size of the platters. You can wind up with a plate of shrimp the size of thumbnails that taste like chicken livers. A frozen breaded crabcake, complete with ice crystals, was served to us at one place. A *nice* place too, not just a greasy spoon. And within a whiff of the Chesapeake Bay!

There are seemingly more "Captains" serving seafood in Virginia Beach than there are in the U.S. Navy. Two of the more highly touted ones are *Captain Kidd's* and *Capt. George's*. Both serve all-you-can-eat seafood buffets that rise above our generic criticisms of this method of preparation. Kidd's is on Atlantic Avenue, by the ocean, and George sizzles his shrimp and so forth on Laskin Avenue, a short distance inland. If you want to dine in a spare-no-expense type of environment, seat yourself at *The Captain's Table*. Located in the *Beach Quarters Hotel*, with a dining room overlooking the ocean, the Captain's Table serves continental cuisine in an elegant, intimate atmosphere. It has been around for many years, and has the reputation as the Tidewater area's "most romantic restaurant."

No less intimate is *The Lighthouse*, a larger restaurant broken up into a number of small dining rooms. The motif is nautical, the emphasis more strictly on seafood. The Lighthouse is on the oceanfront, down at Rudee Inlet. A more down-home, regional approach to cooking, complete with such curiosities as sweet potato biscuits, can be found at *Blue Pete's Seafood Restaurant*, another popular area eatery of long standing. Blue Pete's is set in rural Virginia Beach—and yes, parts of Virginia Beach are rural. Lastly, *Steinhilber's Thalia Acres Inn* is an institution to those in the know in Virginia Beach. There is an Old World feeling about Steinie's (as the regulars call it), evident in its many original seafood preparations. They have oyster roasts on the grounds, in season.

Nightlife

Here, as everywhere, loud disco and "video music" rule your wallet and overload your brain. Ours was a futile search for a happy medium between the false pretensions to glamour of the Top Forty nightclubs and the low-rent environs of the typical bar-cum-pool-hall. We paid a $2 cover on a Monday night at the door of a club that resembled, both outside and inside, a Tyrannosaurus Rex's jaw. We were told, after paying the cover, that we would have to tuck our LaCoste shirts into our pants, and that we could do so inside. We didn't even stay long enough to tuck our shirts in. One look around was sufficient for us. We were hit with a blast of obnoxious music, and took in the room—a sea of Perfect Haircuts, heads that were scanning the room like lighthouse beacons, noise too loud to permit conversation. We immediately crossed the street and played thirty-six holes of Jungle Golf.

If you care to delve into the fecund night life here, which is largely oriented toward deejays and singles (in both connotations of the word), pick up the free local entertainment magazine, *PortFolio*, when you hit the area. It will tell you all you need to know.

FOR FURTHER INFORMATION

Virginia Beach Visitors Center
19th and Pacific Avenue
Virginia Beach, Virginia 23451
(804) 425-7511

Norfolk Convention and Visitors Bureau
Monticello Arcade
Norfolk, Virginia 23510
(804) 441-5266

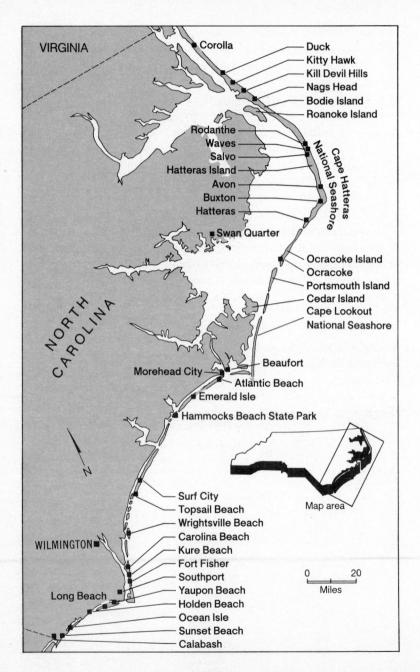

VIRGINIA

Corolla

Duck
Kitty Hawk
Kill Devil Hills
Nags Head
Bodie Island
Roanoke Island

Rodanthe
Waves
Salvo
Hatteras Island
Avon
Buxton
Hatteras

Cape Hatteras National Seashore

Swan Quarter

Ocracoke Island
Ocracoke
Portsmouth Island
Cedar Island
Cape Lookout
National Seashore

NORTH
CAROLINA

Morehead City   Beaufort
Atlantic Beach
Emerald Isle
Hammocks Beach State Park

Map area

N

Surf City
Topsail Beach
Wrightsville Beach
Carolina Beach
Kure Beach
Fort Fisher
Southport
Yaupon Beach
Holden Beach
Ocean Isle
Sunset Beach
Calabash

WILMINGTON

Long Beach

0   20
Miles

260

North Carolina:
Variety Vacationland

The phrasemakers have been calling North Carolina "Variety Vacationland" for decades. For once, the hyperbole is apt. The state is 543 miles wide, from its westernmost mountains to the outermost bulge of the Outer Banks. The highest peak east of the Mississippi, Mt. Mitchell, stands 6,684 feet tall in the heart of the North Carolina mountains. More than a mile below that, through the rolling foothills of the Piedmont and the golf courses and peach orchards of the Sandhills, the eastern third of the state irons itself out to near flatness. Here, on the sun-baked, sandy-soiled Coastal Plain, tobacco and corn are grown for miles and miles. Keep driving. You'll get to the beach before the day is over. We promise.

Ah, you're here. The only problem is, you've got 300 miles of beach to choose from. Along with New Jersey and Florida, North Carolina is the most beach-blessed state on the eastern perimeter. Everyone has heard of the Outer Banks—the barrier-island chain that runs from the Virginia border on down to Cape Lookout. But this should not overshadow the fact that there are plenty of beaches below the Outer Banks, too, each with an indigenous Carolina character of its own. These are a bit harder to get a bead on. Mostly, they're frequented by native Carolinians who know and love them. They are far removed from the peering eyes of the rest of the world. And so they are pure, untrammeled backwaters compared to the noise and commotion of tourist bazaars like Virginia Beach and Myrtle Beach, which act as manic bookends to the North Carolina coastline.

Southern and northern ocean currents meet off the coast of Cape Hatteras, making for great fishing and good surf. The metaphor serves as an illuminating comment on North Carolina in general. You might say the best of both worlds come together here. The progressive-minded intellect of the North meets the generous hospitality and rich manners of the South in a state that has been smiled upon as providentially as any in the country.

The Outer Banks

The Outer Banks conjure up all kinds of associations: history (the first attempt to colonize the New World was made on Roanoke Island in 1585); shipwrecks (the seas off the Outer Banks are known as the Graveyard of the Atlantic); piracy (Blackbeard and his ilk terrorized the coast); hurricanes (the islands regularly get chewed up and moved around by seasonal storms); fishing (the game fishing and surfcasting are unexcelled); and regional lore (the denizens of the Outer Banks are a colorful lot who've been "doing their own thing" for centuries).

Seventy-two miles of open beach along the Outer Banks have been set aside as Cape Hatteras National Seashore, and another 58 miles have been designated Cape Lookout National Seashore. These are not the sort of beaches that attract boardwalk rats, arcade animals, cheap-thrill seekers and other urban terrorists. These unspoiled stretches of shoreline, most of them on Hatteras Island, are cerebral and breathtaking. Fields of sea oats sway atop barrier dunes, beyond which lie some of the loveliest beaches, and best swimming, on the Atlantic Coast.

Nature hasn't been altogether kind to the Outer Banks, however, and from time to time she's been downright nasty. The Outer Banks are, after all, extremely vulnerable. They are something of a geographical oddity, an elbow-shaped, 110-mile strip of barrier islands that protrude into the Atlantic at an average distance of 16 miles from the mainland. They sit smack along the path that hurricanes take traveling up from the tropics. Between the full-fledged hurricanes of early fall and the gale-force winter "nor'-easters," the Outer Banks have taken more than their share of meteorological abuse. Many a storm has cut a swath right through the islands; Hatteras Island itself was created in September 1846 when an unkindly hurricane severed it from the rest of the Outer Banks. Some of the more recent infamous visitors have been Hazel (1954), Diana (1984) and Gloria (1985).

The severity of its storms, coupled with the perilous currents off Cape Hatteras and the treacherous shallows of the outlying sandbars known as Diamond Shoals, have earned the area the sobriquet "Graveyard of the Atlantic." Here, the sea has claimed 600 ships in 400 years; the more famous shipwrecks have become part of the dubiously colorful lore of the region. So have its light-houses, which have been warning ships away from the Carolina coast since the mid-1800s. There are three of them: the *Bodie Island Light* (on Oregon Inlet, south of Nags Head); the *Cape Hatteras Lighthouse* (at 208 feet, the tallest on the Atlantic Coast); and a smaller one on Ocracoke Island. Though none of the lighthouses are open to the public for climbing, there are museums at both Bodie Island and Hatteras.

Though wind and tide may rage at times, the weather is fairly calm and usually hot during peak summer months. The water at Nags Head is cooler than it is at Hatteras or Ocracoke, because this section of the banks does not jut out as close to the Gulf Stream as the others do. In June, the ocean is chilly; July and August are warmer. And it's still bathwater by Yankee stan-dards.

For a place that has been steadily becoming one of mid-America's favorite vacation getaways, much of the Outer Banks retains its native attractiveness. In their unadulterated state, these islands are a compelling sight. They have been stabilized from wind and water erosion by means of man-made barrier dunes that have been an-chored by sea oats and erosion fences. There are salt marshes on the Pamlico Sound, whose lazy, tepid and shallow waters are thick with cord grass and teem with marine life. The National Park Service conducts nature walks that begin at the visitors' centers on Ocracoke, Hatteras, Roanoke and Bodie Islands. One can also learn about the coastal and marine environment at the *Dare Marine Resources Center* in Manteo.

To oversimplify the Outer Banks, it is possible to find solitude and relaxation on Ocracoke and parts of Hatteras, but whatever you do, don't come to Nags Head looking to make your Great Escape. At the height of the summer season, expect to find crowds, ofttimes frightful heat and a substantial stretch of beachfront that has been blighted by a surfeit of concrete. Unprotected by National Seashore status, Nags Head is overrun by squat, sun-bleached cottages; newer high-rise condominiums; and endless rows of telephone poles.

One supposes that the witless development of this section of the fragile barrier islands will continue until the next whopper of a hurricane comes along and blows the whole show six leagues under— condos, junk-food joints, Foos-ball parlors and all. Some scientists speculate that the Outer Banks are slowly but inexorably being pushed inland by time and tide. Perhaps, in some far-off millennium, the Outer Banks will become joined to the mainland. In the meantime, the greatest pleasure they afford is that of a world apart.

Duck

About 6 miles above Kitty Hawk, where U.S. 158 makes an abrupt turn onto the mainland, a spur road continues north to the little hamlet of Duck. Just a few years ago, there wasn't a whole lot to Duck—just a few arts and crafts galleries, specializing in artfully carved ducks, and a smattering of private homes. Nowadays, Duck is booming. Well, *quacking*, at least. The road has been extended all the way from Duck to Corolla, an intriguing dot on the map at the far northern end of the Outer Banks. And here comes traffic. And here come rich folk who find Nags Head too crowded. And before too long, Duck is too crowded. At a 1985 meeting where the citizens of Duck were trying to decide for or against incorporation, one perspicacious native posed the question, "Gee, what is Duck getting out of this?" It's getting reamed by unwanted growth, by the sound of it. Same old story.

Kitty Hawk
Kill Devil Hills
Nags Head

"Speak softly of our Outer Banks of North Carolina," advises a travel brochure from the local chamber of commerce. "For once you've shared our secrets, you may decide to tell only your best friend." Judging from the traffic jams on Route 12 in the vicinity of Nags Head on most summer days, someone's either got a pretty big mouth or more "friends" than Willie Nelson. The approximately 20-mile stretch from Kitty Hawk to the bridge over Oregon Inlet, with Kill Devil Hills and Nags Head in the middle, is utterly crammed with private cottages and burgeoning development. There are some 30 real estate agencies pricking the beach with For Sale signs, and more than 50 hotels and motels in the Nags Head area alone. A secret? Hardly.

'Twas not always so. Not too many decades ago, the main islands of the Outer Banks—Bodie, Hatteras and Ocracoke—were not covered by two-lane blacktop but by a rusty metal track. One hopscotched over to Hatteras on an infrequent ferry. (A ferry is still the only way to get to Ocracoke.) The Outer Banks were, at one time, a sanctuary from civilization, a wild, unspoiled chain of barrier islands completely divorced from the mainland. Nags Head was the first to fall to the entrepreneurs, and is by far the most built-up area on the Outer Banks, no doubt because this is where the islands come closest to joining the mainland.

Nags Head is the gateway to the Outer Banks. U.S. 64 brings eastbound traffic from the North Carolina mainland into South Nags Head, via Roanoke Island. (The town of Manteo, on Roanoke Island, is the home of Andy Griffith, renowned TV sheriff of Mayberry, North Carolina.) Many travelers approach Nags Head from the north, via U.S. 158, which is a straight shot down from the Tidewater area of Virginia. Oddly enough, Nags Head is closer to New York City (433 miles) than it is to the mountains on the other side of the state.

The name Nags Head stems from the practice, in days of old, of walking a nag, or mule, up and down the beach in the dark of night with a lantern tied around its neck. This would send a false signal to ships at sea that would draw them into shore, where they would wreck upon the shoals. The islanders would then plunder the shipwreck for its bounty. Nice guys. These days, you needn't worry about being led astray down here—the southern hospitality is genuine.

We have, over the years, watched Nags Head pass from semi-obscurity to nationwide notoriety. And while it pains us to report that Nags Head has been marred by seedy overdevelopment—down go the sea oats, up goes the "time-sharing community"—its tourist-crammed tumult is still a far cry from the neon deca-dence of Atlantic City. Basically, Nags Head is visited annually by an army of middle-class "just folks," from mid-America and the Carolinas. Their wants are simple: 4 hours of daily frolic on a hot beach; a boxlike motel room to return to, with a wheezing air conditioner and a color TV set; and a number of fish-camp-style restaurants where one needn't make a down payment to feed a family of five. All of the above can be found in abundant supply. For all these reasons, Nags Head draws huge numbers from the states of Pennsylvania and Ohio, and lately has been catching the overflow from Virginia Beach's inundation. Nags Head, in short, is a great place to play license-plate tag.

Nags Head even has its share of scenic wonders and tourist diversions. *Jockey's Ridge*, for instance, is, at 100-plus feet, the larg-est natural sand dune on the East Coast. Hiking to the top of this huge heap is a popular activity for those vacationers who haven't yet been rendered insensate from one too many fried fisherman's platters. It's not as easy as it looks. If you make it to the top, you might see an even more arduous form of recreation, hang-gliding, being practiced. Jockey's Ridge is the hang-gliding capital of the East Coast. Hang-gliding and kite-flying both thrive here, and one can choose from a number of specialty shops to get outfitted with a glider or a kite.

Those less inclined to exertion may prefer to visit the *Wright Brothers Memorial* or wander around historic *Fort Raleigh*, on Roa-noke Island. Let us first recap the brilliant career of Orville and Wilbur. Kitty Hawk was the place where, on December 17, 1903, a pair of bicycle repairmen-cum-inventors from Ohio named Orville and Wilbur Wright launched the world into the air age. Wilbur's 850-foot cruise in the brothers' prototype "flying machine" was mankind's first successful powered flight. (Another renowned inventor, Thomas Edison, perfected his wireless telephone on the same beach a year earlier.) The Wrights' aeronautic feat is commemorated by a 60-foot granite pylon at the top of Kill Devil Hill, the brothers' launching pad. The nearby visitors' center houses exhibits and replicas of the Wrights' gliders. Worth a visit on a rainy day; after all, these guys *really* had the Wright Stuff.

As for Roanoke Island, it was here that the first English settlement in America was established. Dispatched from the motherland by Sir Walter Raleigh in 1585, an expedition of men founded Fort Raleigh; two years later, a second shipload of colonists located the fort but could find no trace of its inhabitants. Their unexplained disappearance remains a great question mark in American history. A nightly outdoor pageant, *The Lost Colony*, tells the story. But a daytime visit to the Fort Raleigh National Historic Site should also be part of your agenda.

Finally, it should be noted that Nags Head—and indeed the entire Outer Banks—is an angler's paradise. Whatever your preference—surfcasting at dawn, pier fishing in the cooler evening hours, trolling a line from a rowboat on the sound side, or chartering a deep-sea fishing expedition—the list of catches is wide and varied year-round. Bluefish and Spanish mackerel are the most frequent summer surf fish; more exotic catches include the pompano and channel bass. (The world's record channel bass was caught on the Outer Banks.) There are piers at Kitty Hawk, Kill Devil Hills and Nags Head. Gulf Stream and inlet fishing trips can be arranged at the *Oregon Inlet Fishing Center*.

Accommodations

There is no lack of places to stay in Nags Head and Kill Devil Hills. Even so, it is best to book far in advance for July and August. One can choose from among a string of luxury high-rise hotels, both new and old, clustered along the beach in "downtown" Nags Head, or go for one of the smaller, less expensive motels that line the beach for nearly 15 miles. In the latter category, we found the *Tanglewood Motel* to be a pleasant place to drop anchor. Located up in Kill Devil Hills, away from the commercial morass of Nags Head, the Tanglewood is comfortable and well-kept. A lot of Nags Head's older hotels were luxury palaces back in the sixties; now, they're the elder statesmen of the oceanfront. The venerable *Carolinian* gets the nod in this category, though the *John Yancey* and the *Quality Inn Sea Oatel* also have a charm that antedates most of the competition and harks back to a less harried time on the Outer Banks.

Restaurants

After passing all kinds of arid new developments with names like *Admiral's View* and *Whispering Sands*, whose names evoke more than they deliver, we passed . . . *A Restaurant By George*. Yes, that's the name of the place. This new-ish Nags Head restaurant bucks the assembly-line fish-camp stereotype of the Carolina coast with a splendid selection of steak, seafood and fowl. Some of the finest seafood on the Outer Banks can be had at *Spencer's Seafood Safari*, on the Nags Head Causeway. They've been at it for 35 years, and have won the Critic's Choice Award as one of America's outstanding seafood restaurants.

For the most part, however, this is the land where the "all-you-can-eat" mentality prevails. Gourmets, beware. The Outer Banks can be deadly on the digestive system. Platters and baskets of fried seafood are the order of the day. Of course, this fazed us not the least whit. Our advice: when in Nags Head, do as the nags do. Pick up a squeeze bottle of tartar sauce in one hand, grab the catsup in the other and start squirting. One word of warning—the oysters and scallops are not local, and so are best avoided. The oysters always taste like pencil erasers in these kinds of places anyway. If you think it will make a difference, you can ask to have your seafood broiled. These are not French-trained chefs, however. Besides being more expensive, if they consent to do it at all, broiled seafood often comes out fused to the platter and tasting like rubber. Don't worry. To wash it all down, you'll be given pitchers of iced tea so presweetened it'll drive you into insulin shock.

If, perchance, you should tire of all the red webbed plastic baskets full of fried flounder and hush puppies, try the North Carolina-style barbecue at *Midgett's*, or head to *Papagayo* in Kill Devil Hills for a great Mexican dinner and a frozen Margarita or two. Papagayo is attached to the *Croatan Inn*, which is one of the better hotels in Kill Devil Hills and worthy of investigation in its own right.

Nightlife

We know what the families are up to down here, because we came with ours many years ago. Let's put it this way. Bring an extra deck of playing cards and maybe that old Monopoly game with half the pieces missing that's been sitting up in the attic for many years. Basically, for the family-oriented, nightlife in Nags Head means a few rounds of miniature golf after dinner and maybe a run to the 7-Eleven later on for ginger ale and Oreos.

Those of a rowdier bent can find places to go to exorcise the nighttime demons. The premier place for noisy fun on the Outer Banks is the *Atlantis*, on the beach in mid-Nags Head. A steady stream of cover bands keeps the energy level up, and the crowd— a mix of college kids working in town for the summer and burly locals—manages to make a big-time ruckus, particularly on weekends. You never know what you'll find going on here. We chanced to wander in the night of a wet T-shirt contest. The next day, through an even greater coincidence, we gave a ride home to the winner of the contest, who was thumbing by the side of the road.

Beyond the Atlantis, there are smaller roadhouses where one can join in the keg-tapping, juke-joint revelry, or one can head to the hotel lounges for a dressier good time. Both the *Carolinian* and the *Holiday Inn* have lively clubs on the premises, and regardless of whether a live band or a deejay is making the music, they draw a decent crowd.

Dare County Tourist Bureau
P.O. Box 399
Manteo, North Carolina 27954
(919) 473-2138

Outer Banks Chamber of Commerce
P.O. Box 90
Kitty Hawk, North Carolina 27949
(919) 261-3801

Hatteras Island

Thank God for the federal government. One can only sail a prayer toward the heavens for the miracle of the Cape Hatteras National Seashore—72 miles of untouched shoreline. Nature is, of course, free to pulverize at will, and does so with aplomb, opening or closing inlets (the average lifespan of an inlet is 100 years) and stripping or widening the beach. But ever since the provident intervention of the National Park Service in 1953, much of the Outer Banks has remained off-limits to man's folly.

This is a good thing, because many a realtor has scrutinized the undefiled expanses on the Outer Banks and seen not fields of waving sea oats but acres of unharvested dollars. One chagrined North Carolina realtor was quoted as saying that the protected shoreline—which includes the southern tip of Bodie Island and most of Hatteras and Ocracoke, except for the eight villages scattered among them—looked like "lots of nothing" to him. Cluck, cluck. Just think of the lots that could be divided and subdivided and sold off; the water slides and surf shops and burger stands we're missing; the 18-hole golf courses and Kubla Khan-dominiums that could bring new prosperity to the Outer Banks.

In truth, the man has a point. There is something monotonous about mile after mile of the same barrier-island scenery. For most of its length, Hatteras Island—which accounts for more than 50 of the 72 miles of National Seashore—is pretty unexciting to look at. The island is, for most of its length, so narrow that no trees or vegetation, beyond the hardiest sea grasses and squat shrubs, can survive the constant attack of wind and salt spray. So Hatteras, which is barely a quarter of a mile wide in some places, is not "scenic" in the classic sense. There are some high dunes up around the northern end of the island, which give it the look of a scaled-down Cape Cod, but mostly you're watching hot sand, short dunes, patchy grass and a few wind-blown shrubs whiz by the car windows. So what's the big deal?

The big deal is—well, there are several of them. First, there are the beaches. Serene, empty stretches of brown sand, rolling surf and warm waters. These beaches can impart an indescribable pleasure to those who, in the words of an atypically philosophical National Park Service brochure, "can still enjoy that vanishing state of being called solitude." Then there are the environmental benefits of a hands-off policy. A prime beneficiary is the delicate salt-marsh ecosystem—incubator and crib to so much marine life. It is additionally comforting, to man and crab alike, to have 72 miles of beach unblemished by Mountain Dew bottles. Finally, if one really thinks that the island is going to waste in its natural state, he or she is referred to the villages of the Outer Banks, to witness the rampant uglification that follows whenever the lid to the Pandora's box of free enterprise is lifted.

The first villages you encounter as you head down Hatteras Island are a cluster of three with the evocative names of Rodanthe, Waves and Salvo. We remember how these towns looked in the sixties: maybe a gas station, a tackle shop, a few whitewashed homes fighting a losing battle with sand abrasion and a post office the size of a bedroom closet. First came paved roads; then, late in the sixties, the state erected the Herbert C. Bonner Bridge, linking Hatteras with Nags Head and eliminating the state-run ferries, which were a much more pleasant way of making the passage. More recently, bigger crowds have been trickling down in this direction, buying lots, putting up second homes. As Nags Head has come to take the look of a used hanky, all eyes are upon Hatteras. Fortunately, they can only do damage within the town limits, but already Rodanthe, Waves and Salvo are wearing the tawdry look of a miscostumed clown.

The towns are overrun with cheap attractions: Bumper Boats, Go-Kart Tracks, Can Am Racers, Honest Bill's (he sells pizza and subs, near as we could tell), Lazy Shirts and the Froggy Dog restaurant are but a few of the businesses that sit in the shadow of a mammoth water slide. A huge, gaudy palace called the Kona Kai Resort has appeared here in recent years, and it looks as inappropriate on the Outer Banks as a Holiday Inn on the rim of the Grand Canyon. A plague of vacation houses, all cut from an identical blueprint (natural wood, steep-roofed, built on stilts) sit on shadeless, sun-baked lots, crowded together and facing each other at odd angles. Though these "developments" are given evocative names like Sea Isle Hills and the street signs are carved in the shape of fish (you too can live on Porpoise Lane), there's no escaping the fact that these towns no longer have charm.

As this is getting entirely too depressing, we shall turn to the much cheerier subject of the 80 percent of the island that bears no such scars. The north end of Hatteras, from Rodanthe to the Bonner Bridge, is the *Pea Island Wildlife Refuge*. Pea Island falls under the jurisdiction of the U.S. Fish and Wildlife Service and offers protection, first and foremost, to birds. Established in 1938 as a refuge for the snow goose and other migratory waterfowl, Pea Island has become a home and resting place for 265 species of birds. Most of the refuge is open for exploration, and there are bird observation platforms scattered about. Jeeps are a no-no, though.

Three-quarters of the way down the island, near the town of Buxton, the *Cape Hatteras Lighthouse* rises out of the ground. There are, near the light, a park service visitors' center, a museum of the sea, and a popular, guarded beach. The lighthouse is the most recognizable symbol on the Outer Banks. Built in 1870, it has been warning ships away from the treacherous shoals of Cape Hatteras for more than a century. The familiar black-and-white spiral decorates a lighthouse that is 208 feet tall, takes 265 steps to climb and burns with 250,000 candlepower.

There has been a decade-long crusade to save the lighthouse, which has been under attack from within and without. The encroachments of an advancing ocean made it seem certain that the structure would topple in a matter of years. Expensive attempts have been made to fortify the structure and the beach in front of it, with jetties, pumped-in sand and banks of sandbags. Though we can remember a summer when the waves were angrily lapping against the base of the lighthouse, it seemed, in 1985, to be pretty secure, and the sea was in retreat. The real threat to the lighthouse at the moment is internal. Vertical cracks have been found running up the interior walls, and a 40-pound chunk of cast iron came loose from a window frame and fell to the ground. At one time, you could climb to the very top and then walk out onto a platform that encircled the light for a stunning view of the Outer Banks in all directions. Now, it is completely closed to the public.

But the lighthouse still affords a spectacular photo opportunity, and there are plenty of other things to do here. The park service conducts nature walks and lecture programs; check at the visitors' center for schedules. The beach here is big with surfers, and the ocean provides excellent, long breakers for body and board surfing. Back at the lighthouse, one can take a self-guided hike along the three-quarter-mile *Buxton Woods Nature Trail*, which winds through a genuine maritime forest of pine and oak. The island is nearly 4 miles wide at this point, offering sufficient distance from the sea to allow trees to survive. A word to the wise: bring insect repellent.

Cape Hatteras itself—the bend in the elbow of the Outer Banks— is right by the lighthouse. The cape is famous for two things: shipwrecks and fishing. Most of the 600 ships that have gone down have been victims of the shallow sandbars known as Diamond Shoals, which extend for 10 miles out from Cape Hatteras. The hazard is that two primary north-south shipping lanes pass close by the shoals, which are constantly shifting. Successful passage, even today, means precise navigation through narrow channels. Many ships have been casualties of war, as in World War II, when German subs lay in wait off the Cape to pick off U.S. tankers. Ship remains are scattered all over the Outer Banks—on the shoals, buried in sand, and along the shore.

As for fishing, some will make a convincing argument that the best fishing on the East Coast can be found off the Outer Banks. Hatteras Island, in particular, is world-renowned for its runs of channel bass and giant blues, and for its unsurpassed surfcasting. The reason for this seafood bonanza has to do with the fact that two powerful and opposing currents collide off Cape Hatteras. One is cold (the Virginia Littoral Drift) and one is warm (the Gulf Stream). Where they come together, the seas are filled with both northern and southern species of fish. Add to this the fact that Cape Hatteras is the closest the Gulf Stream passes to land north of mid-Florida, and you'll understand why Hatteras is known as "Game-fish Junction."

Hatteras has much to offer and much isolated space to enjoy it in. Despite our disparaging remarks about some of the villages here, it should be noted that the towns of Buxton and Hatteras, at the middle and south end of the island, respectively, look much as they always have—weather-beaten, comfortably funky fishermen's shacks. Though there are an alarming number of "Lots for Sale," one reckons that the prickly Hatteras natives won't cede their way of life, or the look of their communities, without an honest fight. Once a Hatterasman, always a Hatterasman. It's in the blood.

Accommodations

There are real estate agents, rental agents and private and public campgrounds galore. You can buy a home for a lifetime, rent a cottage for two weeks or pitch a tent for one night. The *Cape Point Campground* offers tent camping by the sea, and there are park service campgrounds at Frisco and Salvo; all cost $8 per night and fill up quickly in the summer. As for motels, most of them are old-fashioned "motor courts" in varying states of repair. To our tastes, a trio of fifties court-style motel/cottages at the north edge of Buxton best epitomize the traditional beach vacation. By name, they are the *Cape Hatteras Court*, the *Outer Banks Motel* and the *Lighthouse View Motel*. All three are lined up in a row, on the beach, as you round a curve into, uh, downtown Buxton (several bait shops, a few gas stations, a dress shop, several grocery marts and a handful of restaurants . . . you're in and out of town before you know it). All three motels offer comparable (i.e., low-key, relaxed, easygoing) accommodations and competitive rates. You can almost hear the screen door slam on a whitewashed cottage as a gaggle of tots run up the cement walkway and bound the stairs to the beach. Ah, memories.

Restaurants

The *Channel Bass Restaurant*, in the town of Hatteras, is a top choice for seafood on the island. In addition to the fish that is the restaurant's delicious namesake, one can order any number of seafood delights, singly or in combination. A Captain's Seafood Plate ($14.95) will assuage the hardiest appetite, and most folks could make do with the Mate's Seafood Plate, scaled down slightly in price ($11.95) and selection. Up in Buxton, the *Diamond Shoals Restaurant* serves all-you-can-eat seafood dinners to those for whom enough is too little. It's a favorite of local fishermen, so . . . enough said. Breakfasts here are exceptional and large. One array of breakfast foods, the Cape Point, was coming out on platters the size of desk tops. Farther up, in Waves, the *Soundside Restaurant* is family-owned and offers a nightly seafood buffet. Of course, the fishing is so good on Hatteras there's no excuse for not catching your own dinner.

Nightlife

Dare County (of which Hatteras Island is a part) has local option on demon alcohol, and the good folk of Hatteras have voted nay. Nightlife here revolves around wholesome family cookouts on the beach, and one pictures excited youngsters eagerly lowering impaled marshmallows within searing distance of a bed of glowing coals. On a less evocative note, a sign outside a shop in Avon indicates that one can now rent TVs, movies and VCRs on the Outer Banks. Hooray! Actually, there was a time when this sort of diversion was exactly what people came to the island to escape. The native Hatteras rowdies who can't get no satisfaction on their own turf have found another local option. They make for the ferryboat to Ocracoke to rave, break-dance and stumble-foot around the bars of that island, where beer is legal. Reports of the weekend evening exodus, and the 4 A.M. returns, are legendary.

Outer Banks Chamber of Commerce
P.O. Box 90
Kitty Hawk, North Carolina 27949
(919) 261-3801

Cape Hatteras National Seashore
Route 1, Box 675
Manteo, North Carolina 27954
(919) 473-2111

Dare County Tourist Bureau
P.O. Box 399
Manteo, North Carolina 27954
(919) 473-2138

Ocracoke

Ocracoke Island is the southernmost sliver on the Cape Hatteras
National Seashore. Even the name sounds distant, like an echo or
a foghorn way out at sea. The island is 15 miles long, and except
for the wedge of land at the south end on which the village of
Ocracoke resides, it is protected by the federal government.

Ocracoke is a special place, one that leaves a haunting jumble
of glimpses and remembrances. You must fight the urge to write
bad poetry about the island, confining your newfound sensitivity
to sand and sea and sky to a few snapshots of the sun rising through
a curtain of mist and sea oats. There are few islands as undefiled
as Ocracoke anymore.

This is not to say that the island is completely untouched by
the hand of man. Ocracoke is accessible by ferries at both ends.
Those from Hatteras Island land up at the deserted northern end,
and the ferries from Cedar Island (to the south) and Swan Quarter
(a swampy crossroads on the mainland) dock near the village. As
a result of the car traffic dumped on the island, one does spy the

odd discarded pop bottle by the side of the road. But the vast majority of Ocracoke is eerily untouched and uncorrupted.

The cheapest and commonest approach to Ocracoke is via the state-run ferry over from Hatteras. The price is right (it is free), and the service is smooth, efficient and regular, operating twice hourly for most of the day. The ferry takes you on a spectacular 40-minute passage past sandbars and small islands occupied only by flocks of gangly seabirds. The feel of salt spray blowing in your face and the cawing of gulls that trail the boat, hoping for a hand-out, make this a memorable commute. The village of Ocracoke is a 14-mile drive down Route 12 from the ferry landing. With the Pamlico Sound on one side and the Atlantic Ocean on the other, and few signs of life other than gulls and the occasional car, you'll have no complaints.

Ocracoke is about as removed from the mainland world as you can get. It was not even shown on maps, for the longest time, in mainland textbooks. Yet it offers enough vacation activities to sat-isfy even the most demanding shore lover. First of all, there are 14 miles of beaches. Take your pick of the numerous beach-access turnoffs. There is one protected beach located about 2 miles north of the village, where guards man their perches throughout the summer season.

There is only one drawback to Ocracoke's beaches, but it is something that no bleach-blond Adonis with a whistle and a tan can protect you from. We are referring to the plague of predatory green horseflies that occasionally attack the beaches. These are twice the size of your average housefly, and their stings are like being jabbed with little syringes. They can drive a sane man batty in no time. No insect repellent on earth will ward off their painful assaults. Although the smallest consolation can be taken in the fact that they are slow and easily slapped, who wants to spend an afternoon accumulating a patty of bloody fly guts all over their hands? The best advice we got was to grease down with suntan oil (lotion won't work), which creates enough of a seal between your skin and their mouths to repel them. That hurdle overcome, you can now turn your attention to Ocracoke's beautiful surf. In summer, the water temperature is always on the toasty side, often hitting the upper seventies.

Under the auspices of the National Park Service, a number of educational activities are conducted on Ocracoke—such things as nature hikes, bird walks, lighthouse watches and strolls along the harborside. The visitors' center, located near the village ferry landings, keeps detailed listings of the park service programs, many of which are slanted toward Ocracoke and Outer Banks history.

Ocracoke is as full of history as it is horseflies. Most accounts begin somewhere in the mid-1500s, when ships used to wreck offshore as commonly as cars collide on the Cross-Bronx Expressway. One European vessel spilled a cargo of live horses, which swam ashore and prospered in a wild state for centuries. Because they tend to deplete the island's grasses, Ocracoke's wild ponies are now kept in a corral at the north end of the island. The public can view them from a platform by the side of the road.

During the bleak days of piracy, Ocracoke was home sweet home for the dreaded Blackbeard (a.k.a. Edwin Teach). This woolly bully took a North Carolina girl as his fourteenth wife (and we mean "took" her). They lived among the coves on the sound side near the south end of Ocracoke. Some of the unsavory lore of these pirates—our nation's first biker gang—can be found on Ocracoke, if you're into that sort of thing, although it has always amused us how such a legacy can, over the years, come to be regarded as vaguely romantic. "Jolly" Roger? Rape, pillaging, murder, plundering . . . these things are jovial?

Ocracoke was not even a separate island until an 1846 storm severed it from Hatteras Island. But the most interesting bit of Ocracoke history has to do with World War II, when German submarines regularly sank merchant ships and tankers off the North Carolina coast. Lifelong residents can still describe the burning wreckage, the oil spills, the dead bodies that washed up on the sand. There are photographs at the visitors' center. As a result of Ocracoke's strategic placement, a harbor was scooped out at the southern end and dredged-up sand was used to fill in the shallows adjacent to it. Thus, the village of Ocracoke was built on land that used to be under water, and the tiny town surrounds a man-made harbor, the Silver Lake Marina.

Tourist interest in Ocracoke has grown considerably in recent years, and the little village is bursting at its seams. But by virtue of its isolation and confinement to one corner of the island, Ocracoke will never become a condo outpost for the superrich. Instead, the island is a national treasure, and its village is inhabited by a modest population of 650 hospitable souls who make a decent living serving the human cargo that continues to wash ashore.

Accommodations

Although the village of Ocracoke is as small and unassuming as a rhinestone in a dog collar, there is enough lodging to go around. Most of the inns and motels are clustered near the harbor, around which the village is laid out. Of these harborside haunts, the *Berkeley Center Country Inn* looked to be the most enticing. Buffered from the village by short evergreen trees and a sprawling, manicured lawn, the Berkeley boasts a large spread for an inn with only seven rooms.

In contrast to the Berkeley's genteel profile, a motel called *The Anchorage*, the tallest and most modern structure on the island, sticks out above the tree line like a red-brick sore thumb. At four stories, it dominates the Ocracoke skyline, and has become a point of contention among those natives who don't want to see their island go the way of Nags Head.

The finest lodging house on the island is the *Island Inn*. It is located away from the harbor, on a side street just off of Route 12. Formerly a combination island schoolhouse and naval officers' club, the main building is a rambling white two-story structure that was built in 1901 from pieces of shipwreck. A new wing was built across the way in 1981, yet the historic flavor of the inn has not been compromised. Large and rickety but curiously unobtrusive, the Island Inn is an Ocracoke institution worthy of its name. The stairs in the main house are creaky, the paintings in the lobby are slightly eccentric and the place looks from the outside like a backcountry church. But the rooms are comfortable, the rates are reasonable, in and out of season, and there is more character to the Island Inn than any ten brick motels.

If you're really traveling economy class, there's always the *National Park Service Campground* midway up the island. Despite the heat, the intense solar exposure and the kamikaze raids of the green horseflies, the campground is usually full to capacity all summer long, and sites are booked eight weeks in advance, we are told.

Restaurants

Ocracoke is a horn of plenty for the tired, huddled and famished masses who come here on ferryboats from the mainland. It's a 2 ½-hour ride from Cedar Island or Swan Quarter, and it takes at least that long to drive the length of Hatteras and pop over on that ferry—ample time for visions of fried clams and breaded flounder to dance wildly inside their heads.

But if you really want to break out of the mainland mold and try something special, you are advised to seek out either of the island's two gourmet restaurants. *The Back Porch Restaurant and Bake Shop* is the newest entrant in the anti-fried fish league. Located on a side street as you head north out of town, the Back Porch is a wooden house made to look rustic and upscale, with a screened-in porch, ceiling fans, wooden chairs on the veranda, varnished wood bar. It tries hard to excel, and has succeeded at it. But the question it still tries to answer is, will the intractable locals and the out-of-town yokels ever warm to the wonders of gourmet cooking as opposed to deep-fat frying? Try the baked fish of the day to get a handle on this place's culinary approach, which tends toward French, then gamble on something exotic like Melanie Shrimp Verde. The fresh-from-the-oven bread is excellent, as are the desserts.

The *Island Inn Dining Room* is also worth a visit, for the food and the birds. Dominated by an aviary that runs along the front of the building, the dining room does not serve stuffed cockatoo or Parakeet Helper, but you can order Ocracoke Island cuisine, as liberally interpreted and embellished by Larry Williams and Foy Shaw, the owners of the inn. Williams was born on the island and has supplemented his native know-how with an expertise culled from many off-island sabbaticals. The list of entrées might include, for example, a curried shrimp dish or a sweet and spicy Cajun chicken casserole. A favorite scallop dish comes from an old family recipe. Whatever else you order, you should start off with a shrimp-salad appetizer and polish off your meal with a huge wedge of Mississippi mud pie. Then crawl back to your room and watch cable TV through chocolate-glazed eyes.

Nightlife

"No Fools/No Fun" seems to be the official motto of this island, as regards its nightlife. We saw it emblazoned on a baker's dozen worth of car bumpers. We tried to imagine these sputtering wrecks taxiing home, weaving unsteadily after a hard night of partying in the local bars.

This motto, however, is not fair to the predominantly peaceful bent of Ocracoke and is, in fact, only half correct. We had no fun, that much is true. But we did see any number of people, all of them guys, who could easily have passed a fool's audition. Like the lost remnants of Blackbeard's gang, they crab-walked drunkenly through the bars, looking for women to dance with, tables to fall over and out-of-town writers in clean white slacks to stare at.

But let us name the bars and leave the fools be. There are three or four places in town, other than the restaurants, where one can wander in at night for a cold beer. And a brew is all you'll get, too—liquor by the drink is a local option in North Carolina, and has not been adopted here.

On Their Banks is a comfortable, screened-in establishment that serves sandwiches as well as beer. It's located smack dab in the middle of Ocracoke Village, among the gaggle of motels nearest the harbor. The real action, however, is at *Maria's* and the *3/4 Time Pub*. Maria's has a stage, a dance floor, a bar and a dining area. Its chief competitor, the 3/4 Time Pub, sits directly across the street. Together, they are the nucleus of Ocracoke's nightlife. Both are within walking distance of town. Although both clubs offer live music, on the nights we visited we were not convinced that either of the bands was actually living. It would have been less painful had we not been hit up for a cover charge. Usually, you pass the hat—and let it pass—for bands as bad as the two we heard.

We crisscrossed the street a few times, finally settling on Maria's. But after the local band mangled a Bruce Springsteen tune and then segued into a southern-rock oldie ("Keep On Smiling"—difficult, under the circumstances), we had to leave. Over at the 3/4 Time Pub, we stood outside amid the sand and the burrs and listened to a version of "Summertime Blues" that gave them to us. We opened the door of the club, but before we had a chance to so much as glance around the room, three fingers were jabbed in our faces—presumably indicating a $3 cover charge. By way of reply, we gave back one and returned to our inn to watch a televised baseball game.

Truthfully, Ocracoke does not need a nightlife. Because Hatteras Island is completely dry, however, Ocracoke has inherited the ravenous spillover from that more populated island. They drink on Ocracoke and then somehow aim their cars back toward the 2 and 4 A.M. ferries, or else just simply pull their No Fools/No Funmobiles behind a dune and pass out.

FOR FURTHER INFORMATION

Outer Banks Chamber of Commerce
P.O. Box 90
Kitty Hawk, North Carolina 27949
(919) 261-3801

National Park Service Visitors Center
Ocracoke, North Carolina 27960
(919) 928-4531

Cape Lookout National Seashore

In another boldly pro-environmental move, the barrier islands south of Ocracoke were set aside by the feds as National Seashore. Lately, Cape Lookout has been upgraded to a National Park. The three islands in the Cape Lookout group—Portsmouth Island, Core Banks and Shackleford Banks—run for a distance of 58 miles, from Ocracoke Inlet to Bogue Inlet. They are accessible by ferries that carry passengers for $10 and cars for $50. On the islands, there are primitive campsites and rental cabins.

Cape Lookout is for self-professed adventurers. There are few buildings on these islands, save for the pink houses of Portsmouth, now a ghost town. Portsmouth used to be an inhabited community that was the site of a coast guard station. There is a still-functioning lighthouse on the island, but it's hard to tell just what else is operational here. It's harder still to predict just what sort of usage is envisioned for Portsmouth Island and the others in years to come. Currently, public ferries leave from the towns of Atlantic, Davis and Harker's Island. Charter trips over from Ocracoke are available as well. And you can always make the trip in your own boat.

FOR FURTHER INFORMATION

Cape Lookout National Seashore
P.O. Box 690
Beaufort, North Carolina
(919) 728-2121

Atlantic Beach

It simply can't be avoided—this one is about hurricanes and human nature. As the itinerary would deem it, Atlantic Beach was our stop when the emergency weather bulletins began appearing across the bottom of the TV screen. The announcements cut ominously into the late-afternoon "Munsters" reruns that were by now part of our daily ritual. (You didn't expect us to spend eight hours a day in the sun, did you?) A glance through parted motel-room draperies revealed nothing but blue skies, bright sun and, because the room rates had just fallen to their post-Labor Day levels, loads of happy late-season vacationers.

Unconvinced of any imminent peril, as the hurricane was stalled over the ocean 200 miles southeast of us, we returned our attention to the tube—the Three Stooges were up next. For the moment, all seemed right with the world, or at least with Atlantic Beach, North Carolina. The Stooges' antics were soon interrupted by a weather bulletin, however, and suddenly we recalled something we'd seen the night before of which we'd taken little notice.

We had been in a convenience store across the road, poking through postcards and picking up some beer, when the portly proprietress casually mentioned that a big storm was headed our way. She used the word "hurricane," but it came out "hair-ih-kin," as it often does in these parts, so we paid her no mind. But outside, a steady trickle of cars lined up at her gas pumps, and she suggested that we, too, might want to top our tank should there be an Eleventh Hour evacuation. Although she was outwardly laughing at everyone for their predictably touristlike panic, there was the unmistakable look of the grim reaper about her fleshy face.

We purchased our postcards and beer and beat it out of the store. What makes these people think they know more than the weatherman does, we wondered. Swollen ankles? A twinge in the elbow? It was a clear, beautiful, moonlit Carolina night. A hurricane? No way.

But the next afternoon a sudden sense of forboding caused us to switch to the local all-weather station. A Southern-accented voice intoned a gloomy message while a camera panned across an array of instruments imparting vital barometric statistics and tide levels. The voice kept repeating the phrase "hurricane prepared-ness." This was serious. While the sun was still in the sky, we took a final swim in the balmy, though curiously agitated, waters of Atlantic Beach, and then we fled the island, hightailing it over the drawbridge into Morehead City. On some summer days, traffic is backed up so far the bridge takes an hour to cross; we imagined the massive snarl that would occur should everyone on the island attempt to evacuate en masse. Safely on the mainland, we drove west, gobbling up the blacktop of Route 70. The month was September, the year 1984. Hurricane Diana was slowly stalking the East Coast, uncertain as to where she would come ashore.

Truthfully, a part of us wanted to stay, titillated by the idea of "sitting one through," of exposing ourselves to the unutterable fury of nature. However, as the hot humid air gained in intensity and the afternoon light took on an eerie blue glow, we reasoned that we could more safely learn of Diana's onslaught from a television set on higher ground.

Bogue Banks—the island upon which Atlantic Beach is located—lies on a nearly perfect east-west axis, practically offering itself as a welcome mat to brutalizing northeasterly storms and hurricanes. It seemed to us that Diana's fist of fury, headed straight for the southern North Carolina coast, would simply chop this lovely 29-mile barrier island in half, as though it were a two-by-four at a karate exhibition.

Luckily, Diana hit south of Atlantic Beach, landing at the town of Southport, and—as Hurricane Gloria would prove a year later—was not as catastrophically destructive as first predicted. After a five-day break on the mainland, during which time we waited with mounting impatience for the storm to pass and roads to reopen, we returned to Atlantic Beach. We beat a small army of insurance claims adjusters to the Carolina coast, where their ranks filled local hotels—an odd new form of tourism. Atlantic Beach looked much as we'd left it, as did the entire island of Bogue Banks—which also includes the communities of Salter Path, Emerald Isle and Indian Beach.

This area is more commonly known as the Crystal Coast—a handle hung upon it in recent years by the chamber of commerce, with no real antecedents in history or folklore. In short, it doesn't mean much of anything. But it doesn't have to—this is North Carolina, where the beaches are, almost by definition, better. And the Crystal Coast, for 29 unbroken miles, is a beach fancier's dream.

Most of the island, with the exception of the commercial congestion at the foot of the causeway over from Morehead City, basks quietly in its own beatitude. There is room here. The large hotels south of the causeway are spaced well apart. A healthy covering of brush and vegetation holds the dunes in place, and most of the buildings are set back from the beach, behind the dunes. Even the island's lone water slide is unobtrusively built like an ant farm into the backside of a huge dune.

In addition to swimming on 29 miles of beaches, folks come here to fish from the surf and the eight piers on the island. There is also a touch of history. *Fort Macon State Park*, up at the northern end of the island, commemorates this key Civil War fort on 365 acres that also include a public beach. Just over the bridge lies Morehead City, and over a second bridge, the port town of Beaufort. Having both civilization and great stretches of unspoiled shore at close hand, the Atlantic Beach area is hard to beat. Since they're doing so well with their beaches down here, we'll let them call the place whatever they want—even the Crystal Coast.

Accommodations

Although Bogue Banks stretches for 29 miles from Bogue Inlet to Beaufort Inlet, most visitors congregate toward the northeastern end of the island. They pour over the bridge from Morehead City and are deposited in the heart of Atlantic Beach. South of the convenience store-biker bar pandemonium of this area is a series of convention-sized hotels, and between the *Ramada Inn* and *Holiday Inn* are a couple of formidable old favorites. The *John Yancey* has been around for twenty years. Located in the Pine Knoll Shores section of Atlantic Beach, the Yancey has an 1,100-foot private beach and plenty of spacious oceanfront rooms. There's an unpretentious elegance about the place, which wears its age well. You'll find it easy to fall into conversations with people here, especially if you come down for free doughnuts and coffee in the morning.

Just down from the Yancey is *The Atlantis*, itself a commodious, quiet place to stay if you've come to enjoy the surf. Both are recommended. Though there are stretches taken up by private beach houses and the ever-encroaching condo, much of the rest of the island is refreshingly undeveloped.

Restaurants

For the barbecue nut, North Carolina happens to be the place where pig pickin' is king. This is true even on the coast, where there is a barbecue joint for every fish house. *Smithfield's Chicken 'n' Bar-B-Q*, located on the island in the tiny town of Salter Path, is inexpensive and popular with families. The *Channel Marker Restaurant*, on the causeway in Atlantic Beach, is where you will find the island's freshest seafood.

Generally, though, the best restaurants are in Morehead City and Beaufort. *Mrs. Willis' Restaurant* is a wonderful place to start . . . and finish . . . and come back to. The barbecue is prepared according to a family recipe that dates back to 1949, but the restaurant also offers a variety of home-cooked southern meals that are almost too inexpensive to believe. This is something of a local institution—a convention of bald-headed people had dined there the day before—and everybody seems to know everybody else. The *Sanitary Fish Market and Restaurant*, also in Morehead City, has a statewide reputation for its seafood, and has been around since 1938. Located on the Morehead City waterfront, the Sanitary is both a restaurant and fresh-fish market. It's also the largest seafood restaurant (capacity 650) on the North Carolina coast. Over in Beaufort, the *Beaufort House Restaurant* sits proudly in the neatly restored town center; gourmet seafood specialties are served by waitresses in colonial garb. And you get to look out over Beaufort's beautiful harbor.

Nightlife

Duty bound and determined, as usual, to have a good time or die trying, we sampled the nightlife of Atlantic Beach on several successive evenings. Mostly, we found it indigestible. Nonetheless, we are passing along a recipe for a concoction that winds up being prepared on a weekly basis down here at the circle, where the bridge deposits traffic into a scuzzy morass of taverns, nightclubs, poolhalls and ale houses. This two-block locale is the one unsightly nick in the Crystal Coast. Then again, if you drive a monster

Harley, you'll probably like it, and might even come back for seconds.

"Recipe for Trouble"

Mix 20 pickup trucks full of ornery coastal rednecks with a steady trickle of Marines on leave from nearby Camp Lejeune on a payday weekend. Fold in a few bike-gang members and stir till blended. Toss in several tattooed girls younger than they look, and spice it up with some attractive high school-age jailbait. Heat this mixture in the summer sun for 8 hours at 90 degrees or more. Move the concoction out of the sun and into a dimly lit tavern, distributing evenly around pool tables, bar area, rest-room entrances and parking lots. Slowly steam in beer for the next 6 hours, then shake vigorously to the rhythm of a heavy-metal band with a name like Warhead. Now add generous handfuls of drugs, preferably Quaaludes, although baggies of marijuana will do just as well. *Voilà!* By one in the morning, the final product should be an ugly knife fight between guys with two first names over a pool game or a girl. Garnish with whatever syringes or guns are later discovered by authorities in a nearby motel room. This recipe will serve an entire community all too often.

FOR FURTHER INFORMATION

Carteret County Chamber of Commerce
P.O. Box 1198
Morehead City, North Carolina 28557
(919) 726-6831

Hammocks Beach State Park

Once a day, from June through Labor Day, a passenger ferry travels between the mainland at Swansboro and a small, unspoiled island just south of Bogue Banks. The ferry is free, but capacity is limited and reservations are suggested—call (919) 326-4881. The 2½-mile trip, which crosses a salt marsh, takes 25 minutes to complete. Once on the island (its proper name is Bear Island), you are still a half-mile hike from the beach, but the isolation you'll find out here is ample reward. There are showers and facilities at Hammocks Beach, but otherwise nothing but high dunes and wilderness. Signs from the main highway (Route 24) direct you to the ferry landing. A day spent wandering Hammocks Beach State Park will leave you feeling like a modern-day Robinson Crusoe.

Topsail Beach

Very little of the American East Coast can honestly be described as out-of-the-way, hidden, a world apart and so forth, despite the frequency with which such phrases are bandied about by those whose jobs it is to attract throngs to the beach. Plainly, if a beach is truly off the beaten path and desired to remain that way, people wouldn't print up 40,000 color brochures advertising their isolation. The beaches of southeastern North Carolina, however, are an exception to this rule. Probably because of their distance from the major population centers of the Northeast, they remain free of locustlike tourist infestations. They're not undiscovered, but they are uncrowded.

Topsail Beach rests at the southern end of a 25-mile-long barrier island. Two other small towns, Surf City and Del Mar Beach, share the island. You'll find little commerce here: each town has a pier, a gas station, a small grocery mart and, maybe, a motel. Your dining choices are severely limited as well—unless your idea of eating high on the hog is an ice-cream stand called the *Jif Freeze*. (Actually, there is a perfectly acceptable seafood restaurant in Topsail Beach called *The Breezeway*.) Surf City, North Carolina, has very little to do with the mythical town of the Jan and Dean hit, with its "two girls for every boy." Topsail Beach is a little larger. It can boast a 65-unit motel, restaurant and pier complex known as the *Jolly Roger*. Mostly, though, the island consists of privately owned beach homes, which are rented by the week or month through local real estate offices.

The typical carload that crosses the Intracoastal and follows Route 50 till it runs out in Topsail Beach is a family of four or five from one of the inland cities of North Carolina's Piedmont. They've probably been coming here for many years, and they'll probably rent the same house summer after summer for a week or two. Their haven will be a modest beach cottage built of wood, painted in some improbable pastel and lifted off the ground by stilts. Most of these places are the proud property of off-island owners, who make show of their pride with a plaque nailed above the front door, upon which is engraved a name, hometown and a wacky nickname for their seaside retreat—for example, "The Johnsons/Winston-Salem/'Gritty Britches.' "

The island is divvied between two relatively unpopulated North Carolina counties, Onslow and Pender. With the exception of a large Marine base, Camp Lejeune, there is little on the mainland other than swamps, brackish water and thick forests of scrub pine. Still, Morehead City (to the north) and Wilmington (to the south) are only an hour away, so there are oases of civilization within driving distance. Chances are, however, that you'll come here to escape citified distractions, and this little island is as good a beach as any to get away from it all.

FOR FURTHER INFORMATION

Greater Wilmington Chamber of Commerce
P.O. Box 330
514 Market Street
Wilmington, North Carolina 28402
(919) 762-2611

Wrightsville Beach
Wilmington

Joe: Hey, Moe, how many developers does it take to make one island retreat?

Moe: Well, I know that one, Joe. It takes three: two to hold down the island and one to screw in the condos.

But even as Moe and Joe speak, true island retreats are becoming scarcer than whale's teeth along the East Coast. Some are simply a euphemism for "retreat" in the sense of what you do after you've lost a battle. Along the coast of North Carolina, the war of shoreline attrition is in its relative infancy, although with undeveloped coastal land so scarce in northern states, it has been waged with increasing vigor in recent years. At Wrightsville Beach, they may as well begin hoisting the white flag of surrender. Long before the condo craze sent America scurrying to the shoreline, checkbook in hand, Wrightsville had already been caught, held down and had the condos screwed in.

Wrightsville Beach is a three-in-one name. It refers to the beach, which has been alarmingly eroded; to the town of 1,700 permanent residents, which swells when the summer season gets under way; and to the island itself, which is located 10 miles east of Wilmington, North Carolina's foremost port city. Although it is as tightly packed with residences as any suburban subdevelopment and the prevailing architectural style is Early Savings Bank, it is not the mode of architecture on the island that is being disputed. What is distressing about Wrightsville Beach is how little is left of it in some places. Barely 3 miles long and only 150 yards wide in spots, Wrightsville is one of the smallest barrier islands on the Carolina coast. And it's getting smaller. Despite efforts to pump in sand, the ocean has advanced to claim the beach right up to the frontal dune. According to one writer's account of the Carolina coast, what is left is a "solid wall" of sand that's battered with full force by the sea.

All ends of the compass have been fairly well filled out on Wrightsville Beach. The roads run out to the northern and southern tips of the island, and homes occupy most every available square foot of sand from beach to bay. Most of the private homes have been built safely back from the beach. It's the dormitory-sized hotels, like the *Blockade Runner* and the *Sheraton* and the *Surf "Motelminium"* (Moe: "Hey Joe, whaddya get when you cross a motel with a condominium?"), whose future may be a little more precarious. The island narrows dramatically at the northern end—in fact, Wrightsville Beach, viewed aerially, is an isosceles triangle—which is where the heaviest commercial development is concentrated, and where it least belongs.

To be fair, the commercial flotsam that usually accumulates in and around a beach community has not been allowed to float onto Wrightsville Beach. Instead, it lines the 10 miles of Route 76 that lead to the island from the city of Wilmington. Here, a kornukopia of krazy kix awaits the kiddies and their kooky adult kronies. To wit, shopping malls with six-screen cinemas, hamburger and fried chicken franchises of every imaginable denomination, a Jungle Rapids Water Slide, "private" chocolate-brown cinder-block nightclubs with no windows, lots of little motels (poor relations to the queenly high-rises on the oceanfront) . . . but really, this is not entirely ocean-inspired. It's just the same plain old zoneless, mindless suburban growth that happens everywhere in America where people gather together to live, worship, drive and eat the cheeseburger of their choice.

There is a lot of history kicking around in Wilmington's attic. It was here, in 1765, that the patriots protested the Stamp Act, and a major battle in the Revolutionary War was fought at *Moore's Creek*, just north of town. At nearby *Fort Fisher*, a key Confederate fort fell to Union troops, signaling a turning point in the Civil War. The battleship *U.S.S. North Carolina* is permanently docked here now, serving as a museum and a memorial to World War II war dead. The *North Carolina* saw action in every major battle in the Pacific and was, for years, regarded as the greatest battleship in the American fleet. It's visited by a million people a year.

Wilmington has figured prominently in times of war because of its strategic position at the mouth of the Cape Fear River. It is and has always been North Carolina's largest deepwater port. Extensive renovation and development along the waterfront, à la Baltimore's harborfront restoration, is in progress. At *Chandler's Wharf*, on South Water Street, a complex of three restaurants and twenty shops lines the banks of the river.

Wilmington's profile has risen even higher in recent years as the movie industry has moved in. Studios, back lots and soundstages have been built here by movie moguls like Dino de Laurentiis.

With films being shot in-state by the likes of de Laurentiis, Steven Spielberg, Stephen King and Michael Cimino as we were passing through in the summer of '85, Wilmington is looking to become the Hollywood of the East.

And there's still more to do here, like visit *Orton* and *Poplar Grove Plantations*, both of which are open to the public. There are remnants of gracious antebellum living everywhere—in the magnificent homes and formal gardens on these plantations (both a short drive out of town) and elsewhere in Wilmington. Finally, don't miss Wilmington in the springtime, when the azaleas are in bloom.

But back to the beach again, driving through the congested corridor of Route 76. Things quiet down, in all respects, as you near Wrightsville Beach. As you traverse the final leg of the causeway, the last real development you'll see is something called the Moorings. It serves double duty as a sentry and a symbol for the community. These tall condos of gray wood look exactly like a living Cubist concept of housing. So careful to avoid the stigma of condomania, these dwellings almost sneak by without your noticing them. Which is just as well—you probably couldn't afford them.

Still, these are not uncongenial folks out here on Wrightsville Beach. Rare is the true Tar Heel who is. In point of fact, one jolly pedestrian who resembled Fred MacMurray reduced us to guilty silence with an unsolicited wave of hello as we drove past him. Seconds before, we had been laughing at the man's calf-length madras Bermudas. Nor are these folks filthy rich; those people congregate on enclaves like Figure 8 Island and Bald Head Island. No, Wrightsville Beach is built for comfort, not exclusivity.

Accommodations

Two major hotels, *Sheraton* and *Holiday Inn*, are on (the former) or near (the latter) the ocean at Wrightsville Beach. There are privately owned motels on the beach (*The Blockade Runner*) and the bay (*The Edgewater*) that will not drain the budget quite so dearly. Beyond this, the island is mostly rentals of variously hybridized hotel-motel-condo-apartment-efficiency-cottage-type deals. Your best bet may be to stay in the Wilmington suburbs, near the state university (where Routes 17 and 74 meet). The motels are cheap out here, and the beach is within striking distance. If you head out to Wrightsville Beach early enough in the morning, finding a parking space for your car and beach towel should be no problem. Several of the economy motel chains are clustered out here—e.g., *Days Inn*, *Econo Lodge*—at prices even a college kid can afford. But truthfully, if you want to stay on the beach, with sand at your back door and the roar of the surf audible from your bedroom window, you're better off heading north or south of Wrightsville Beach.

Restaurants

The Bridge Tender is the first choice of many who head down this way. Located on the sound side of Wrightsville Beach, just off the causeway, the Bridge Tender is renowned for serving the finest and freshest seafood on the Carolina coast. A superb seafood meal can also be had in the more modest surroundings of a real working pier at the *Crystal Pier and Restaurant*.

As it turned out, we divided our time between fine food in Wrightsville Beach and fast food in Wilmington. One night's experience of the latter was an education in the phenomenon of the multi-item salad bar, usually found at a family steakhouse. There were almost more gleaming metal troughs than you could imagine types of food to put in them. What could possibly be in a 54-item salad bar—pine cones? Spam? Fish tails?

Nightlife

A family-oriented island, Wrightsville does not abound in nightlife. That is best sought out in Wilmington, where there are a couple of clubs near the university. Most of the action is at *The Mad Monk*, the most raucous nightspot in the area, and *The Patio*, which is tamer only because it's smaller. Both book live bands on the weekends and sometimes weeknights.

Out on the beach, the bar scene can be rougher, especially when a lot of servicemen from the several military installations in the area are turned loose with their weekend passes. Their presence is particularly felt at the gaggle of bars near the pier at the center of town. About the island's only no-man's-land, this area has been given over to metered public parking and, on weekends, not a few jacked-up Camaros and PT-boats-on-wheels.

FOR FURTHER INFORMATION

Greater Wilmington Chamber of Commerce
P.O. Box 330
514 Market Street
Wilmington, North Carolina 28402
(919) 762-2611

Pleasure Island:
Carolina Beach
Kure Beach
Wilmington Beach
Handy Beach

Carolina Beach is the most populous (and popular) community on the 7 1/2-mile-long barrier island known as Pleasure Island. Pleasure Island is located about 15 miles due south of Wilmington on Route 421. It is a merest snip across land, at a place called Snow's Cut, that allows the Pleasure Islanders to properly call their home an island. But an island it is, a rifle-shaped jut of land that hangs on a due north-south axis, bounded by the Atlantic Ocean and the Cape Fear River and severed from the mainland at the aforementioned cut by the Intracoastal Waterway.

Pleasure Island, which includes Kure and Handy Beaches, in addition to Carolina Beach, is thick with history. Seemingly all of the colonizing nations of western Europe dropped anchor on Cape

Fear at the southern end of the island. France hired an Italian, Giovanni da Verrazano, to find some real estate in the New World. Verrazano poked around the Cape Fear region in the 1520s, then left without establishing a claim. Spain was next, sticking around long enough to change the river's name to "Jordan" from the original Indian name, "Sapona." The mid-1600s saw the British settle here unsuccessfully and give the river three more names, the last of which, Cape Fear, stuck.

The British abandoned the area and did not return to settle in earnest until the early eighteenth century. Unfortunately, their reappearance signaled the decline and fall of the beleaguered Cape Fear Indians, who would not return to the area at all. Beset on all sides, by enemy tribes as well as the archenemy New World colonists, the Cape Fear tribe lost its last squaw in 1808.

The story does not end here. Because of the advantageous nature of Cape Fear as a port of entry, the river has witnessed more scenes of violence than MTV. Fifty years of Indian wars gave way to a period of terrorism at the hands of pirates. Among them was Blackbeard, the ratty-haired raider of many a lost ark. Blackbeard's plunderings, allegedly conducted with impunity from high state officials (who received an early form of kickbacks), continued until the exasperated governor of Virginia sent two sloops down to roust the vermin from the seas. A bloody battle near the island of Ocracoke resulted in Blackbeard's death in November 1718.

Blackbeard's spirit lives on in the form of real estate developers and construction barons who are ravaging the coast of North Carolina with much the same aplomb. There is a construction boom afoot on coastal North Carolina, and Carolina Beach is one of the areas under the most rapid development. In recent years, the arrival en masse of new condo projects has given Carolina Beach sort of a reverse facelift. Ironically, a lot of all this brand-new real estate was being auctioned off at bargain-basement prices.

One thing's for certain: few, if any, such constructions are more than 30 years old. That's how long it's been since Hurricane Hazel leveled the North Carolina coast, back on October 15, 1954. On that day, entire islands were cleared of all private and commercial property as if by a giant wrecking ball from the heavens. Of course, memories are short and regard for the environment, and its hazards, is slight, and so the slapdash shorefront development rumbles on unabated through the eighties.

A painful reminder of the past blew through on September 13, 1984, in the form of Hurricane Diana. This 24-hour refresher course in meteorological firepower cost residents of the state an estimated $30 to $60 million in damages. Considering the visible consequences of the hurricane in the Wilmington/Carolina Beach area—massive trees uprooted, roofs ripped off houses, piers chewed to kindling, radio and water towers toppled—the fact that there were no casualties directly attributable to the storm was nothing short of miraculous.

The hurricane took particular umbrage with McDonald's, whose cheap plastic signs were unvaryingly pocked with holes and tilted at precarious angles. A huge McDonald's billboard was toppled; Ronald McDonald's billboard-spanning grin now lay on the ground, disembodied, looking for all the world like something Andy Warhol would put on a canvas. They weren't grinning in Carolina Beach, though, in the wake of the storm. Yachts had been sunk, every building under construction was damaged and Route 132 through town was impassible because of flooding. By now, Carolina Beach has recovered—having successfully weathered another hurricane, 1985's Gloria—and is every bit as cocksure and condo-crazy as it was before the storm. But the island's experience should serve warning to every beach community along the East Coast: it could happen again anytime.

All talk of hurricanes aside, Carolina Beach is a popular retreat for native North Carolinians. It is highly touted as a family beach. As such, Carolina Beach and its neighboring communities are rather narrowly oriented toward the basic beach pastimes—swimming, fishing, sunbathing, eating three times a day, playing Trivial Pursuit at night. It is very down-home, very neighborly. The beach, which has been rumored for many years to be eroding, seemed to us to be wide and secure, with a healthy dune structure.

The Carolina Beach area is popular with anglers—big runs of blues in the spring and all sorts of game fish farther out at sea. Deep-sea fishing expeditions and charter boats are plentiful, and there are a dozen marinas, from Carolina Beach down to Calabash, for those who arrive with their own. There are three piers on

Pleasure Island as well, and the state has thoughtfully provided many public access walkways to the beach.

If there is a theme being worked out here, it is between that of low-key, family-style charm and encroaching modernization. On the oceanfront, you'll find small, family-owned grocery stores and motels; one block inland, a corridor of fast-food stands. Kure and the other smaller beaches seem thus far immune to the plague. Carolina has succumbed, but has not yet been irreparably damaged. And don't get us wrong—Pleasure Island is by and large a pleasurable island to visit and vacation on.

Accommodations

There are more hotels and motels on Pleasure Island than most of the other barrier islands in the immediate vicinity, and maybe more than on any North Carolina beach outside of Nags Head. By our count, there are at least a dozen and a half decent motels in Carolina Beach and environs, such as the *Sea Ranch Motel*. A 19-story condo/hotel convention center is in the works for Carolina Beach. Here, as anywhere, if you plan to come for a week or longer, renting a house or cottage makes the most sense. A listing of agents who handle such rentals can be had from the chamber of commerce.

Restaurants

Avoid the ubiquitous fast-food chains, whose convenience and predictability is tempting, and look for the family-owned restaurants. Here, you'll likely find good, honest home-style cooking and service. When you go out on the Carolina coast, bear in mind that fried seafood baskets and platters, served with hushpuppies and slaw, are a specialty. In Kure Beach, you might try *Big Daddy's*; in Carolina Beach, *The Harbor Master*. These restaurants brook no gourmet pretensions but their solid servings of seafood will keep you sated till the next dinner bell.

Nightlife

Carolina Beach draws fewer itinerant troublemakers than some of the beaches directly north, which are right in the line of fire of the many military bases and redneck strongholds of mid-coast Carolina. No, there's not a lot to do in Carolina Beach at night. You might drift into *The Silver Dollar*, on the Carolina Beach boardwalk, to have a beer and check out the band. Best bet, if you're seriously in need of a night out, would be to run up to Wilmington, about 15 minutes away, where you'll have a few more options.

FOR FURTHER INFORMATION

Pleasure Island Chamber of Commerce
Drawer A
Carolina Beach, North Carolina 28428
(919) 458-8434

Bald Head Island

Bald Head Island sits in the mouth of the Cape Fear River, looking, from the map, as if it might tear itself loose and float out to sea. The island has been described as a subtropical paradise; most of us will never get the chance to find out, as it is a very ritzy resort indeed, accessible only by boat or plane. An 18-hole seaside golf course is the island's main drawing card. It's affixed to an inn and restaurant complex. A pricy place to drop anchor, but if you got it, may as well flaunt it here.

Figure 8 Island

While staying with a sportswriter friend down the road in Savannah, Georgia, about a month after we'd left North Carolina, we had a chance encounter at an outdoor café with a well-known Atlantic Coast Conference basketball coach. He was more interested in asking us about beaches than in answering questions about basketball, and he had a good offensive game. One exchange went like this:

Coach: "Have y'all ever been to Bald Head Island?"

Us (in unison): "Nope."

Coach: "Y'all aren't going to have much of a book."

Thanks, sport. Well, we can top that. Not only have we never been to Figure 8 Island, we'd never *heard* of it until long after our travels were over. We still don't know much about it—it doesn't even show up on maps of the state. We do understand that it's only for the wealthy, that it's somewhere in the Wilmington-Cape Fear vicinity and that it's occupied by Gatsby-esque private mansions. You can't get on the island without a pass from a resident, and there's no commercial development. We included it only as an excuse to recount our conversation with the coach.

Southport

Southport is a small (pop. 3,000) fishing and tourist village at the mouth of the Cape Fear River, along the southern banks. Situated at the point where two substantial stretches of the North Carolina coast—the 47 miles in Brunswick County and the segment from Carolina Beach north to Swansboro—meet in near perpendicularity, Southport is an important crossroads and gateway. The *Southport-Fort Fisher Ferry* ($3 per car, five trips daily) crosses the Cape Fear, landing on the southern end of Pleasure Island; the 45-minute trip can save nearly 60 miles of driving. Southport is also adjacent to Oak Island, whose beaches are popular with families, and Bald Head Island, the semiprivate island resort.

Southport itself holds attractions like *Fort Johnston*, the first fort built in North Carolina, and *Price's Creek Lighthouse*, an 1849 edifice at the ferry landing. While Southport is notable for being the northernmost extremity in the range where the palm tree grows, the city's pride and joy are its oak trees, some of which are said to be hundreds of years old. "Live Oak" is as universal a street name in these parts as "Elm" and "Maple" are up north. Farther inland from Southport is an area called Green Swamp that holds the peculiar distinction of being the only native habitat in the world for such fabled carnivorous plants as the Venus flytrap, the pitcher plant and the sundew.

Unfortunately, Southport took quite a lashing at the hands of 1984's Hurricane Diana. The storm first touched land here, and initial reports claimed the city had been wiped out. Southport did take a pounding—300 of its prize oak trees were uprooted, and seemingly the entire town was under water—but it managed to put itself back together pretty quickly. We hope that this charming little city doesn't have to peer into the eye of a hurricane again any time soon.

FOR FURTHER INFORMATION

Southport-Oak Island Chamber of Commerce
Route 6
Box 52
Southport, North Carolina 28461
(919) 457-6964

Oak Island:
Long Beach
Yaupon Beach
Caswell Beach

Oak Island is entered on its eastern end over a high, humpback bridge along Route 133. Heavily forested right up to the shoreline in many places, it looks to be a good place to find a bit of peace and quiet. Caswell Beach is quite residential, with a permanent population that works at the Coast Guard facility there. On this end of the island, you'll also find the *Oak Island Lighthouse* and the remains of *Fort Caswell*, which dates from the nineteenth century. The grounds and buildings are now, curiously, owned by the North Carolina Baptist Assembly and are off-limits to the public.

Yaupon and Long Beach draw more vacation transients and summer-home owners, though there is also a not-insubstantial number of year-rounders here. Down at this end of the island, which accounts for about ²/₃ of the island's 14-mile length, the atmosphere is more play- and pleasure-oriented. Still, it is more relaxed and sparsely settled than a lot of neighboring islands.

Accommodations

Along the island's main road, which runs parallel to the shore about four blocks back, are a number of pleasant, shaded motels. There is precious little commercial development right on the ocean-front, although you can scare up a motel or two on the beach, like the 59-unit *Ocean Crest Motel*. Here, as on the other islands in Brunswick County, people rent houses for blocks of time. Unlike the other islands in Brunswick County, a lot of people own homes and occupy them twelve months a year as well. Despite all, this is some of the most untrammeled beachscape this side of Hatteras. Oak Islanders like to refer to their beach as "North Carolina's best-kept secret," but there is a helpful chamber of commerce information center that will readily dispense hard facts to you; it's located just over the bridge onto the island.

Restaurants

This was going to be a rave about a barbecue joint, but it closed somewhere between the time we ate there and the next summer, which is when we ran into an acquaintance who lives near Long Beach who said it was there no longer. If nothing else, this serves as an object lesson about the transience of business along the beachfront. For the record, it was known as Garland's Barbeque; one hopes that they're making barbecue still, somewhere, somehow. As for seafood, one can find adequate portions fried in the famed Calabash style at places like *Jones' Seafood House*.

Nightlife

Beach music lives here. One nightspot, *The Gallery* in Long Beach, advertised "shag music" on its marquee. The shag is a wild spin-a-rama of a dance that is done only to beach music and will tie you in knots if you don't do it right. It takes talent; if you master it, you can dance difficult steps and twirl your partner while casually sipping a beer with your free hand.

And do you know what beach music is? It's another book, that's what it is. But for the time being, just shut your eyes and think "sweet soul music," with a steady lilt and, often, male falsetto voices. Think Drifters. Tams. Showmen. Chairman of the Board. Maurice Williams and the Zodiacs. All right; enough for now. The lesson will resume under NORTH MYRTLE BEACH, SOUTH CAROLINA. As for Long Beach, there are four or five serious party spots strung out among the procession of restaurants and gas stations and garages that lead into Long Beach, after the bridge turnoff. Among them are the aforementioned Gallery, the *Beach Club* and *Flaming Star*.

FOR FURTHER INFORMATION

Southport-Oak Island Chamber of Commerce
Box 52
Route 5
Southport, North Carolina 28461
(919) 457-6964

South Brunswick Islands:
Holden Beach
Ocean Isle
Sunset Beach

Holden Beach is the northernmost of what are known as the South Brunswick Islands; the other two inhabited and reachable islands in this string are Ocean Isle and Sunset Beach. Holden Beach is a thriving family beach, chockablock with late-model rental homes on stilts and older, squat, single-story cinder-block homes that bear the scars of age. Holden Beach is long, flat, comfortable, slow-paced: your basic North Carolina beach town. There are water slides on both sides of the bridge over to Holden Beach, to give you an idea of the type of fun that awaits you. The bridge itself is not one of those grand, winding structures such as lead onto Hatteras Island, Oak Island or Atlantic Beach; rather, it is a one-lane drawbridge that spans the Intracoastal Waterway. A stop-light regulates the flow of traffic so that cars move in one direction at a time. Believe it or not, this is high-tech compared to Ocean Isle and Sunset Beach. Despite an assault of billboards on the mainland side of the bridge, Holden Beach is a fairly tranquil place.

Ocean Isle is the next barrier island down from Holden Beach. The farther down you go, the smaller the islands get. Ocean Isle is only 6 miles long. For better or worse, they've managed to cram a lot onto it. Telephone lines crisscross the island like mosquito netting. Houses are going up all over. A new bridge is being built, to replace the one-lane antique that heretofore has kept a lid on the tourist influx. One unique feature to the island is the series of Venice-like canals that fork in on the Intracoastal Waterway side of the island, affording many residents backyard dockage for their boats. Ocean Isle remains a pretty island with a lot of the homey charm of down-east North Carolina. Given the portents of all sorts of impending development, Ocean Isle would do well to haul in the reins a bit.

Sunset Beach is the smallest of all the South Brunswick Islands and the least crowded. A one-lane pontoon bridge that must swing outward whenever a boat approaches ensures Sunset Beach's relative isolation. Sunset Beach is aptly named: the sunsets are spectacular, particularly when they glint off the wet sand flats at low tide. Sunset Beach is just a small teardrop of an island hidden in the southeasternmost corner of the state. Well hidden.

Calabash

When talk turns to seafood, all eyes turn to Calabash. This remarkable little village with a population of 128 might just be the seafood capital of the East Coast—except that few on the East Coast know of it outside of North and South Carolina. No matter. There are 32 seafood restaurants in Calabash, and they serve over 1 ¼ million seafood dinners annually. The town is wall-to-wall restaurants, many of which lay false claim to being the "original" Calabash seafood restaurant.

Though the word "original" is rather loosely thrown around here, like so many shrimp shells, the differences among the restaurants are so minor as to reduce the argument over which is best to hair-splitting insignificance. The "secret" to Calabash cooking is to lightly batter and fry the seafood—fish fillets (mostly flounder), shrimp, oysters, scallops, crab cakes and so on. The real secret to the popularity of Calabash and its restaurants, however, has to do with the size of the portions doled out on the plate, which could sate the heaviest, hungriest he-man's appetite.

So far-flung is Calabash's reputation that the town name has become an adjective for this particular style of seafood preparation. You will find restaurants that advertise "Calabash-style seafood" up and down the North and South Carolina coasts. You'll even find the same phrase adorning restaurant marquees in the Blue Ridge Mountains. But there's no beating the real thing, if only for the experience of being there in the noisy, bustling dining rooms in summertime, knowing that whatever else you've done wrong in your life, you're in seafood heaven right now.

FOR FURTHER INFORMATION

South Brunswick Islands Chamber of Commerce
P.O. Box 1380
U.S. 17
Shallotte, North Carolina 28459
(919) 754-6644

South Carolina: Palmetto Power

We admit that we're biased. One of us grew up in North Carolina, the other in Georgia, and South Carolina was kind of a mutual joke. In particular, it seems doomed to play second fiddle to its larger, geographically more diverse and economically more prosperous sister state to the north. Although South Carolina flourished like no other colony during antebellum times, when cotton was king, she was never Reconstructed exactly as she was before the fall of the South.

North Carolinians will tell you they have a larger and more fertile land area, more and better universities, better mountains and better coast and better culture. They have furniture and textiles, moonshine and clogging and they have superior barbecue. And finally, they do not dream of the eventual resurrection of Dixie.

When both of us were attending college in North Carolina, a drive through South Carolina was unthinkable, as if the state were one big Bates Motel operated by psychopathic rednecks. In hindsight, this was, of course, simply regional chauvinism with little basis in fact. At the time, however, South Carolina's reputation for gratuitous mayhem seemed awfully real, borne out by a couple of life-threatening joyrides to which one of us was subjected while hitchhiking through the state. And the city of Greenville, a.k.a. "the Buckle of the Bible Belt"—well, never mind about the city of Greenville.

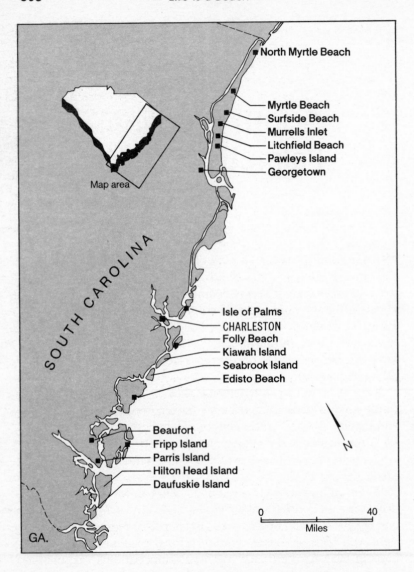

So anyway, with every citizen in South Carolina hating our guts by now, we will concede that the South Carolina coast was a glorious surprise. These may be the most underrated and best-tended beaches on the Eastern Seaboard. For a state of relatively modest dimensions (measured alongside its neighbors), South Carolina did not get the short end of the coastal stick. It not only got 280 miles of it, but it received what amounts to two coastlines.

First, there is the wall-to-wall frivolity of the Grand Strand, a hunk of jet-age real estate packed to the gills with vacationers from all over the country. Long a favored honeymoon spot, Myrtle Beach now enjoys a more general reputation with all kinds of vacationers. Myrtle Beach is a large city that exists for no other reason than recreation. Think about it—how many of those can you count on the East Coast?

South Carolina's second coast starts with the venerable old town of Charleston, and includes the posh resort-island developments that run right down to the Georgia border. This part of the South Carolina coast is generically known as the "lowcountry." Sounds mysterious—redolent of long, hazy days, palmetto trees, salt marshes, deserted beaches, exotic birds, odd customs and folkways that prevail in a world undefiled by creeping modernity. The lowcountry is a sliced and diced series of islands, forests and wetlands that recall what seems like the ancient past. One sees ghosts of it still—the once-thriving port of Charles Town (established in 1670), the original rice and indigo plantations where the southern aristocracy lived coolly even in sweltering heat, the funky smell of swamps and the lost Confederacy.

Charleston, Hilton Head, Kiawah, Seabrook, Fripp—these places today attract a nouveau aristocracy of golden-skinned Yuppies, pink-socked golfers and villa-owning retirees. Tennis stars, golf pros, Arab sheiks, bank execs, textile barons, corporate consultants—these are the sort of folks you're likely to see taking their Izods for a walk along the shores. Among these backcountry roads and hidden stretches of beach, however, you are also likely to find enough titillation for your wanderlust to draw you back again and again. And you'll praise God that there are still a few regions left in this country that retain a sense of place.

North Myrtle Beach

Is it possible to have too much of a good thing? If so, then the Grand Strand of South Carolina—encompassing Myrtle Beach, plus the numerous communities to the north and south—must rank as the overdose capital of the East Coast. Nowhere else do so many assemble for the express purpose of enjoying sun and sand, suds and sin, sports and swelter, shagging and shucking.

The statistics are staggering. The Grand Strand extends for 60 miles, from the North Carolina border down to the city of Georgetown. Ten million people a year visit the Strand. There are an estimated 45,000 motel rooms along the Strand and 12,000 campsites. Eating down here requires the decision-making skills of a corporation president, as there are more than 600 restaurants in the area. Myrtle Beach is a growing golf and tennis resort, with three dozen golf courses and 200 tennis courts. No wonder Myrtle Beach refers to itself as "the East Coast's primary vacation destination." Only Atlantic City, along the East Coast, draws more people, but the feverish activity of addictive personalities at indoor gaming tables is not a beach vacation in the purest sense. So Myrtle Beach gets the nod: this is where you come in the summertime when you want to unroll your beach towel in the sun.

A distinction should be made between North Myrtle Beach (the subject of this entry) and Myrtle Beach proper (the next entry). North Myrtle is an amalgamation of five towns: Cherry Grove, Ocean Drive, Atlantic Beach, Crescent Beach and Windy Hill, in north-to-south order. All but Atlantic Beach have formally merged into the single township of North Myrtle Beach, although the residents like to boast that each community retains its own character. The differences, if you are driving south along U.S. 17 or Ocean Boulevard are slight, however, and the road unrolls in an unbroken stretch of motels, restaurants, shopping centers, outlet stores, fireworks and novelty shops, water slides and miniature golf courses with jungle themes. U.S. 17, more commonly known through here as Kings Highway, is not a fun route to drive nor is it a regal experience; it is akin to Ocean City, Maryland's "six lanes of death."

North Myrtle presents myriad options for a big evening. You can belly up for an all-you-can-eat seafood feast, restore your circulation with an after-dinner game of jungle golf among honking geese and meandering rabbits and then return home with a carload of fireworks—and not have had to travel more than a couple hundred yards! If you have any life left in you, you can go out and shag till 4 A.M. to the sounds of a beach-music band. By then, you'll be ready to apply for your South Carolina citizenship. Or go home a weary Yankee, lacking what it takes to cut it in the southern part of heaven.

So much for our southern chauvinism. The fact is, most of the Grand Strand's business comes from South Carolina and the neighboring states of Dixie—Tennessee, North Carolina, Georgia—although a disproportionate share also hail from the state of Ohio. Sudden exposure to southern culture can be confusing to uninitiated Yankees; sometimes you feel like you've entered a foreign country. Way down here on the Strand, and as you get deeper into Dixie, the southern accents get so thick they almost sound British.

First-timers are advised (by us) to stay in North Myrtle rather than Myrtle Beach for the simple reason that the beach is better and healthier. Along the North Myrtle strand—Ocean Drive, in particular—the beach is as much as an eighth of a mile wide at low tide. This is in contrast to Myrtle Beach, where severe erosion has left the town with an ocean that breaks treacherously close to the foundations of its high-rise condos and hotels.

Despite the homogeneity of North Myrtle Beach's five communities, there are a few differences worth noting. Ocean Drive (a.k.a. "OD") is the largest in terms of population, size and reputation, and also has the best nightclubs. The greatest clustering of motels and accommodations, particularly at the oceanfront, is along Ocean Boulevard in the neighboring communities of Ocean Drive and Crescent Beach. There are three golf courses on the ocean side of U.S. 17 in the Ocean Drive-Cherry Grove vicinity, and three more golf courses skirt the Intracoastal Waterway on the far side of 17 down toward Crescent Beach. The Grand Strand Jetport is just west of 17 in Windy Hill. And the stuff-yer-face stretch of 17 known as Restaurant Row is just south of Windy Hill, in what is technically north (as opposed to North) Myrtle Beach.

But these distinctions are trifling, considering that we're discussing an area only about sixty blocks long. The similarities are more striking than the differences, and they pale next to those that set it apart from Mother Myrtle, just a few miles south. In North Myrtle Beach, you'll be swept up in the impersonal and aggravating bustle of traffic, then get hit with a dose of southern hospitality when you least expect it.

The Grand Strand is actually more youthful than one might suppose—the resort development there began in earnest in the 1960s. But manners are timeless, and the solicitous good nature of the southern character has been passed down for generations. It is precisely this sort of Carolina charm that leaves an impression of "y'all come" friendliness on all who visit here. Ten million people a year, and still climbing.

Accommodations

The greatest selection of accommodations on the Grand Strand is available in Myrtle Beach proper, along Ocean Boulevard, while the emphasis in North Myrtle seems to be on restaurants. Actually, there are even more motels than restaurants on the Strand; 700 establishments provide a place to sleep or . . . whatever. Nevertheless, since on an average summer weekend the Myrtle Beaches play host to 350,000 people, reservations should be booked ahead. Buying a condominium or partial ownership of one through a time-sharing arrangement is theoretically a way of hooking into the Grand Strand for the long term—although the ocean seems intent on reclaiming a lot of beachfront real estate in Myrtle Beach particularly, making such an investment appear to us to be an act of lunacy.

In any case, if you pass through here, you'll doubtlessly find yourself besieged with offers of free gifts "just for visiting" one of the many present or planned high-rise communities going up. It's a good way to score a clock radio, a multifunction watch or twenty silver dollars, although disengaging yourself from the huckster making the sales pitch can be as difficult as removing your arms from the jaws of a hungry shark. We were accosted on several occasions in restaurant parking lots as we tried to find our way back to the car.

As far as choosing a hotel or motel, a sentimental favorite is the *Cabana Terrace*, on North Ocean Boulevard in Cherry Grove. For one of us, many years ago, the Cabana Terrace was the site of a "beach weekend," where seemingly the entire high school relocated itself for a raucous rite of passage. "Beach weekend" is an estimable tradition in the high schools and colleges of the Carolinas. On a designated weekend every spring, a given high school's senior class, and whatever underclassmen were cool enough to pass muster, would make a mad break for the beach at the tolling of the final bell on Friday afternoon. Then the fun begins: . . . all sorts of unmentionable acts . . . ten people to a room . . . hangover stories that will be told and retold into old age . . . overnight deliverance from the ranks of virginity . . . trouble with the law and frantic calls home . . . the whole gauntlet of experiences that accompany an adolescent's coming of age, compressed into one May weekend. North Myrtle Beach has played host to many a beach weekend, and endures as a place where the young and the restless come to party. Not to besmirch the reputation of the Cabana Terrace; it is an elegant oceanfront hotel, and surely would not have abided us had our behavior been too untoward. But it is not possible to pass it by without shedding a fond tear for the teenage rabble-rousing rituals of yesteryear, which (we hope) survive even now under the neon glow of North Myrtle.

Restaurants

Big-time chowing down thrives here on the Strand. With 600 restaurants to chew from, one might be legitimately paralyzed into indecision. Actually, there are a few useful guidelines. By far the greatest concentration of quality restaurants can be found along U.S. 17, along the northern edge of Myrtle Beach proper, an area known as *Restaurant Row*, and along the Windy Hill and Crescent

Beach areas of North Myrtle Beach. A dinner for two at the typical Grand Strand restaurant will neither be family-restaurant inexpensive nor the wallet-gouging experience of a true gourmet restaurant. Likewise, the food is neither plain nor fancy; you won't go home in gastrointestinal distress, but you won't be smacking your lips and toasting the chef, either.

The choices are boundless, and one should begin by deciding on a type of cuisine. One can then make a final choice from whatever category, be it seafood or soul food. Here are a few suggestions:

For seafood, perhaps *The Outrigger* or *Steere's Calabash Seafood*. Both prepare seafood in the popular Calabash style, and you can choose from fixed-quantity platters or all-you-can-eat specials at both places. With the exception of the steamed spiced shrimp at The Outrigger, which are recommended, the preparation never strays toward the exotic, but you won't go home hungry. The *Sea Captain's House*, with restaurants in both Myrtle Beach and Murrells Inlet (to the south), tends toward a more elaborate seafood menu—Low-Country Crab Casserole, Neptune Shellfish Salad—and enjoys a wide reputation for excellence. Similarly, *Riceplanter's*, which is kin to *Planter's Back Porch* in Murrells Inlet (and is discussed in greater detail there) is a highly regarded exception to the general rule that true gourmet cooking is as rare as loggerhead turtles out here on the Grand Strand. The accent is on South Carolina low-country cooking, which is similar to New Orleans and bayou-country cuisine.

Cagney's and *Slug's Choice* are two restaurants that do a land-office business; the interior furnishings fairly drip rattan opulence and the food is almost as impressive. The bars at both places seem designed for casual social interchanges, with backgammon tables, plush upholstered chairs, palm fronds and ceiling fans setting a relaxed day's-end atmosphere. Slug's Choice has a sister restaurant, *Slug's Rib*, which specializes in prime rib. Just up the road, *Gabby's Rib* dishes out the messy kind of rib—generally not recommended for first dates or job interviews, but a very satisfying feed in familiar company. Across the road, *Christy's* offers a more upscale dining experience, featuring lobster, prime rib, stuffed flounder and such.

Enough? One more point: if you go out for lunch or dinner in

South Carolina on a Sunday, you can eat, but you won't drink, and you might not be merry. There is no alcohol served all day Sunday, and this ban begins at the stroke of midnight on Saturday night. They call them blue laws, probably because they make everyone—restaurant and club owners, residents and visitors alike—feel blue all over.

Nightlife

North Myrtle Beach is the home of the shag, a dance that originated and was popularized here in the fifties. It's a modified jitterbug, with lots of quick steps and fast spins. It has never become extinct. Many fad dances have come and gone, yet none has displaced the shag from the memory banks. To this day, there are shag-dancing competitions and beach-music clubs all over the Carolinas, even far inland. There is even a Shag Preservation Society.

The shag is danced to beach music. Beach music songs are hand-picked rhythm-and-blues records with a kind of calypsolike bounce. "Under the Boardwalk" by the Drifters is a good example: you can practically feel the palms swaying in the breeze and envision love-struck couples promenading arm in arm at the shore's edge. With its roots in the fifties, beach music is a rare oasis of carefree contentment that harks back to simpler times. Pressing cares seem to vanish within the casual swirl of a comfortably packed dance floor, the band blowing some shaggable tune such as "Stay," "I've Been Hurt," "Give Me Just a Little More Time," "Double Shot of My Baby's Love"—classics all, and most of them unfamiliar or forgotten beyond the range of the Carolinas.

The shag and beach music thrive at such oceanfront beer-blast palaces as *The Galleon* and *Crazy Zack's* in Ocean Drive. We got a quart bucket of beer at the latter for a buck and a quarter! Don't worry, you'll sweat it all out on the dance floor. Out on U.S. 17, the beach-music club of choice is *Studebaker's*, which advertises "wild women" and "wilder men," and is jam-packed on weekends. The interior is decorated with old signs and logos from the Wonder Bread years of the fifties and sixties. The music they play takes you back there, too. Beach music is also the calling card at the

Coquina Club in the *Best Western Motel* on Ocean Boulevard in Myrtle Beach proper. And it's got the official endorsement of those who bestow accolades upon the world of beach music, having won the Showclub of the Year Award from Beach Music Awards, Inc., in 1983. (It *is* another world down here. . . .)

If you have no idea what you want to dance to, the *2001* "entertainment complex" is a good place to go to sample a little bit of everything: Top Forty, beach music, disco, live music—all blasting simultaneously from different areas and dance floors. Perhaps believing that a discothèque has to have some note of Studio 54 exclusivity about it, 2001 offers valet parking and charges a fairly stiff cover (in the neighborhood of $5) most of the time. So come here prepared to spend the whole evening. Practically across the highway is *The Afterdeck*, whose several outdoor patios overlook the Intracoastal Waterway. People dress smartly here in the primary preppie colors: golfing green, Easter-egg pink, canary yellow. The speakers are hidden in palm trees outdoors and hung high overhead inside; and the living-room-style furnishings make a perfect rookery for casual courting. Down the road is *Xanadu*, a glittery disco that plays Xenon to 2001's Studio 54. The blinking columns of light and sensory overload will make you feel as if you're on some sort of disco spaceship.

Any and all of these places must observe South Carolina liquor laws, which are arcane, to say the least. This means that your drink must be mixed from a sealed, airline-sized liquor bottle, and that all alcohol sales must cease at midnight Saturday night for a period of 24 hours. Incredible as it may seem, Saturday night is over at midnight in Myrtle Beach. So start early (like around noon) or stock your own freezer if you want to keep the night alive.

FOR FURTHER INFORMATION

North Myrtle Beach Chamber of Commerce
P.O. Box 754
U.S. 17
North Myrtle Beach, South Carolina 29582
(803) 249-3519

Myrtle Beach

At some point in their lives, if only for one cathartic visit, every human being who lives within a day's drive of Myrtle Beach will come here. This is a given, like death, taxes and underage beer drinkers. Some people, however, actually frequent the place. To these incorrigible souls, Myrtle Beach has, over the course of their lifetimes, taken on all the luster of a Magic Kingdom. It is Christmas in July for the tots. It is Wassail Night for high schoolers. And for those who never outgrew it, Myrtle has become a honky-tonk Shangri-La, an ongoing trip back in time to their lost youth.

It should be obvious that Myrtle Beach is not for every vacationer. It is, in fact, the sort of place that more meditative people warn you against. From as far north as Delaware and as far south as Florida, well-meaning folks were telling us, "Ah, you don't want to go to Myrtle Beach." So often were we told this that it became something of a mantra for us on the mid-Atlantic leg of our journey. To be truthful, we had tended to avoid the place ourselves over the years in deference to more placid sandscapes. However, the beach is our beat, so we dove, rather gamely, into the mayhem of Myrtle.

What can we say? Myrtle Beach was anything but the Black Hole of Calcutta we were warned it would be. In fact, the town—all 108 streets worth of it—can be a whole mess of fun, a rowdy combination of Disneyland and Gomorrah. The beach itself is nothing to write home about, unless you're writing to say, "Stay away—there is no beach." At high tide in front of our motel in the heart of town, the beach was all but nonexistent. What few feet of sand there were between the breakers and the asphalt were filled with strange deltas of washed-up detritus: cigarette butts, plastic straws, discarded arcade junk. The buildings, in effect, *are* the sand dunes.

At high tide, when Myrtle's beach benignly disappears, the sunbathers seem content to lie under the palmetto trees that are the signature of this resort (and the state tree of South Carolina) or else sit atop the hard hills of dirt in front of the parking lots, barely 6 feet from the ocean's lapping tongue. Alternatively, they lose themselves in the maze of amusements that are another lure of this fantasy land.

First, there are all the distractions you'd expect to find in a resort town of this size—a water slide, a roller coaster, a contraption known as the Astro Needle that stands 300 feet tall and a number of parking-lot-sized amusement arcades. Of the latter, we preferred the *Electric Circus* arcade over the *Fun Plaza*. At the former, Skee-Ball was only 10 cents a pop, and you could easily win prizes such as a crab keychain. Although Fun Plaza offered more variety—a photography booth, acres of Skee-Ball and ancient baseball and bowling games—everything cost a quarter and the games seemed unduly stacked in the house's favor.

Above and beyond the usual distractions, though, there is a plethora of the unusual to entertain and befuddle the vacationer stranded by high tide. Actually, a small industry has been spawned around this theme. If you wander in the right direction, you will think you have stumbled into the very aorta of the unusual. In the space of one block, you are transported into a Twilight Zone of weird attractions. First and foremost among these is the *Ripley's Believe It or Not Museum*. It costs $4.25 to view a display of bizarre artifacts, and although this particular museum's holdings are on the lean side (there are ten Ripley museums in the United States to spread the collection among), the breadth of Robert Ripley's eccentric imagination is amply displayed. Equally well-known is the *Guinness Book of World Records Museum*, located nearby. The world's longest wig was draped several times around a naked mannequin in the display window. What else could be in there? we wondered. The world's largest toenail?

Next door to Guinness is the *Hollywood Illusion*. For $3.95, the wonders of modern deception allow you to "participate in an eighteenth-century séance with Groucho and Harpo." We were warned off this one by a local waitress, though we trust that good sense would have warned us away at the door in any case. And then there is, of course, the *Myrtle Beach National Wax Museum*, where you can "watch history, religion, adventure, horror come to life!" (That is, if none of those categories seems redundant to you.) History, for example, spans the period "from the birth of mankind through the Civil War." (Bear in mind that this is Dixie.) Religion "introduces you to a beautiful Eve as she commits the Original Sin with Adam trying to hide his nakedness from the sight of God." And so on.

The nature buff might enjoy the *Shark Museum*, located in a complex called *The Gay Dolphin*. (No comments from the peanut gallery.) The music buff will enjoy a visit to one of two walk-in recording studios—"Walk in a nobody, walk out a star"—that allow you to sing along to a prerecorded instrumental track and have your efforts pressed onto vinyl at $7.95 per song. The choices were between the bluegrass standard "Rocky Top" and Michael Jackson's then-reigning hit "Beat It." We worked up a punk-rock vocal arrangement of "Rocky Top," but chickened out at the studio door. Sid Vicious will never know what he missed.

Yes, there is something for every buff in the book here in Myrtle Beach. A quick summary of the history of the area will perhaps explain how it got this way. Originally, all of what is now Horry County was settled by indentured servants who were glad to take anything they could get—which is precisely what they got. Bounded by an impenetrable swamp to the west (which you can smell when the night breeze is blowing in a seaward direction) and isolated from the wealthier areas to the south, what is now Myrtle Beach was not incorporated until 1938, was leveled by Hurricane Hazel in 1954, and was not officially even a city until 1957. What is here now is a builder's market that just missed being kissed by hurricanes in 1984 and 1985 (although it received some minor petting and was evacuated twice).

Myrtle Beach is not offensive in the way that Ocean City, Maryland, or Hampton Beach, New Hampshire, can be. A steady year-round population of over 18,000, a moneyed golfing crowd and a sense of southern manners even in a commercial morass keep this leg of the Grand Strand from teetering too grievously in that direction. Still, it is a pretty sloppy place, unless your tastes run to crowded highways, teeming arcades, Confederate flags and small, packed, receding beaches. Likable as it is, for whatever reasons, you're really better off staying not in Myrtle Beach proper but in the immediate vicinity—either due north or south of here.

Accommodations

All this has been pretty thoroughly covered under NORTH MYRTLE BEACH, since the distinction and the boundaries are so fine. A few additional words are in order, however. Room rates drop considerably in the spring and fall, as do the crowds. The room we stayed in at mid-September, which was right on the ocean in the heart of Myrtle Beach, cost us $22. The same room went for $76 a night in July. Accommodations start right at the top with the *Sheraton*, which stands like a fortress at the northern end of town, and work their way down to groupings of two- and three-story generic motor courts with names such as *Sea Crest*, *Sea Oats*, *Sea Banks* . . . fill in the blank. One's as good as another. Most have swimming pools. All of them kind of look and feel as if they've passed their prime. But they'll gladly take credit cards, and every room's full in season, you can be certain. Even at $60 and up.

Restaurants

To get a handle on the restaurant scene around here, perhaps it is best first to ponder the names of two local clothing outlets— *The Ample Lady* and *The Big and Tall Shop*. Everywhere you walk in this town, you are besieged by signs imploring you to eat. And not merely to eat, but to stuff yourself with unholy quantities of food. Outside and inside the arcades, the fast-food signs depict lurid and gaudy representations of foot-long hot dogs with chocolate-brown residue (presumably chili) piled on top, double-decker burgers with weird orange cream (melting American cheese?) falling out sideways, "corn on the cobb [*sic*]" and so on and so forth. Every window in town seems to slide sideways, with an arm extending a brown bag of searing french fries to a gaggle of hungry tots. Ice cream, ice cream everywhere, and not a drop to . . . ah, never mind.

A short drive out to Kings Highway reveals more. In Myrtle Beach, it seems that gluttony is a bargain. Practically every sign boasts an "All You Can Eat" or "All You Care to Eat" (no distinction) special. Fried seafood is most frequently proffered. Dinner-hour debauchery is encouraged here, but 12 kilos of fried flounder and a bucket of hushpuppies are no bargain when, hours later, they begin threatening an encore. *Morrison's Cafeteria*, a chain with franchises in shopping malls throughout the Southeast, served us a perfectly square meal, as it did hundreds of our fellow (senior) citizens. It was fine indeed, and all we cared to eat.

Nightlife

There is a touch of Jersey in the night—touch, as in touching you up for a cover charge in order to listen to taped disco music under the splintered glow of a revolving mirrored ball. It's too loud to talk even to your friends in these places, so you shamble around with a beer like a gerbil in a cage until you either find an unoccupied place to stand or another gerbil to dance with. These places have been covered in detail under NORTH MYRTLE BEACH, but to re-iterate, the main theme of our excursions was down with disco, up with beach music, and whatever happened to rock 'n' roll? Even in the worst Top Forty/disco haunts, however, boys and girls find a way to mingle unabashedly in a self-created southern sorority atmosphere that has little to do with the "doom-doom squelch" disco voodoo being blared overhead. "Y'wanna dance?" "Mmmm . . . okee-dokie . . . but not this song" is a typical snip-pet; we got turned down on grounds of bad music more than once.

An interesting musical side trip and sociological study was pro-vided us in a place called *The Bowery*, in the heart of Myrtle's oceanside arcade district. At the Bowery, guys the size of the trucks they drive drink beer in amazingly swift gulps under the ubiquitous furls of the Confederate flag. A live band went through the motions of old-time southern rock 'n' roll, while the biggest, shaggiest guy in the world roared with Neanderthal yowls of approval at the next table, sloshing beer around like a keg somebody forgot to turn off. Though our eyes were darting around nervously, no one else even seemed to notice: this was par for the very bizarre course. As we were leaving, we saw the sign above the door, which said: "If you like this place, keep your mouth shut. If you didn't like this place, tell everybody you know." You can see that we're not keeping our mouths shut.

FOR FURTHER INFORMATION

Myrtle Beach Area Chamber of Commerce
1301 North Kings Highway
P.O. Box 2115
Myrtle Beach, South Carolina 29577
(803) 626-7444

Surfside Beach
Garden City Beach
Murrells Inlet

South of Myrtle Beach, down the U.S. 17/Kings Highway corridor, are three seaside communities that serve as quieter companion pieces to the stentorian symphony up the road. To get there, you temporarily leave the subtropical man-made fantasyland of Myrtle Beach and veer past an air force base. Given the high population density in the area, the presence of an air force base in the middle of it all merits inclusion in the Ripley's Believe It Or Not tour. Soon, however, you are hurtling through an obstacle course of malls, McDonald's, 7-Elevens and K marts—the usual encirclement of chains that divide American towns as easily as they conquer them, and seem to serve as our modern-day greenbelts. Quickly, if you follow the proper directional signs, you can turn left out of this mess and enter the secluded family vacation community of Surfside Beach.

Dominated by a *Holiday Inn* at the north end and a midtown fishing pier, this summer residential area is a nice alternative to the clatter of Myrtle Beach, yet is close enough so you don't lose access to its food, fun and nightlife. Some of the houses are flat boxes, indicating deeper "Roots" than Myrtle (could these have belonged to the original indentured servants?), some are nice, un-assuming two-story affairs, and some look like drive-in banks, wooden octagons on stilts.

The beach is not much wider here than it is at Myrtle, even with much of the primary sand-dune structure intact. The *Surfside Beach Pier* has a quiet little oceanfront restaurant and beer bar that is very low-key compared to the only other vital sign of nightlife—*The Country Junction*, which calls itself "the Grand Strand's Nash-ville Connection." Located out on U.S. 17, the Country Junction offers live country music by local and national talent. (Boxcar Willie was performing the night we drove past.)

If you want to avoid the highway altogether, you can drive along Ocean Boulevard. Without much further ado, you will shortly arrive in Garden City Beach, a more upscale retreat. Wooden condominiums are springing up on both sides of the boulevard here. They are christened with names such as Atlantic Winds and Captain's Walk III—beach buzzwords that the developers hope will complete the illusion of solitude that was begun in their bro-chures. Condos seem to be overtaking this former hutlike com-munity, though some of the weather-beaten smaller dwellings still cling to the sand. All over the East Coast, we got the feeling that the condo building boom was not being matched by a condo buying boom, and Garden City Beach was no different. A long banner, listing prices, hung from the side of one impressive (and impres-sively empty) tall building, a tapered, all-white affair that looked like something Mies van der Rohe might have left on his drawing table. But it is peaceful and quiet in Garden City, and most of the dunes are intact, so maybe it's just a matter of time before an inundation begins—hopefully, on a modest scale.

Back on U.S. 17, a few miles farther south is the town of Mur-rells Inlet, at the midpoint of the Grand Strand. If you chance to come here, it will definitely not be for the sun or surf. The inlet is actually a wedge of marshland bordered by what is, in effect, a fishing community. Deep-sea fishing boats are located along the marsh on Business 17, ready to go out at the drop of a hook, line or credit card. Murrells Inlet is also the celebrated seafood mecca of the Grand Strand, a more discriminating and low-key alternative to Myrtle's Restaurant Row or the North Carolina border town of Calabash. There is none of the stuff-yer-face nonsense here, although there are plenty of restaurants to choose from.

People gravitate to Murrells Inlet because it is an old stolid fishing village with the feel of the backwoods and a history that dates back to the Revolutionary War. Detective-fiction writer Mickey Spillane makes his home among the secluded creeks here. Perhaps he was drawn by the legendary "ghost lights" that have reputedly appeared offshore for generations, or maybe he just wanted a safe place to count his residuals from the Miller Lite commercials.

To get a feel for the vaunted Murrells Inlet cuisine, we visited the highly touted *Planter's Back Porch*, located at U.S. 17 and Wachesaw Road. Under the shade of pecan and oak trees, this restaurant serves up atmosphere as well as seafood. If you have not made reservations ahead of time, you will probably have to "set a spell" on a front-porch rocking chair. There is a back bar and a bricked terrace and an outdoor gazebolike spring house. The interior is as light as a bird cage, painted yellow, with ceiling fans overhead and pert, polite southern gals hauling the food around.

The entrées are all splendid and southern-accented, but the shrimp Creole was especially good. One of their more popular offerings is the Back Porch Inlet Dinner, kind of a package deal where, for $13.50, you receive an appetizer, soup, salad, seafood entrée and a baked potato. Speaking of spuds, they are one of the calling cards here at Planter's Back Porch. A local specialty, the pine rosin baked potato is prepared by tossing a spud into a bubbling vat of pine rosin. When it has simmered long enough therein, it floats to the surface, then is removed and wrapped in butcher's paper. The result is a piping hot, almost mashed potato on the inside that tastes slightly sweet and incomparably good.

FOR FURTHER INFORMATION

South Grand Strand Chamber of Commerce
P.O. Box 650
U.S. 17
Murrells Inlet, South Carolina 29576
(803) 651-1010

Litchfield Beach

South of Myrtle Beach, where the clutter comes to an end and U.S. 17 passes through rows of tall pines, the subtler aspects of life in the low country come to the fore. Litchfield Beach is a small community with a quiet shoreline that's pretty much given over to the gulls and the fiddler crabs. Out here, the loudest thing around is the silence—a stunning contrast to the commotion not 20 miles away.

It is this tranquility that draws people to the *Litchfield Inn and Country Club*. Virtually the only commercial lodging establishment on this stretch of the shore, the Litchfield Inn is a "hotel condominium" that offers accommodations in a choice of a seven-story oceanfront tower, a two-story inn or a detached lodge. The "country club" part of the Litchfield complex includes an 18-hole golf course and indoor and outdoor tennis courts.

There are also a lot of rental homes that run the length of the beach, with elevated boardwalks that lead over the extensive barrier dunes to the beach. Regardless of what arrangements you have made for staying here, rest and relaxation are guaranteed. And any attack of cabin fever can be treated with a short drive to Myrtle Beach.

Litchfield Beach is also near *Brookgreen Gardens*, the largest outdoor sculpture garden in America, with a collection of 400 works by nearly 200 native sculptors. Admission to the gardens and grounds is $3. Directly across from Brookgreen on U.S. 17 is *Huntington Beach State Park*, a year-round recreational park with a swimming beach, a salt-marsh boardwalk and a large castle called Atalaya, built as a winter home by the wealthy industrialist who founded Brookgreen and donated these parklands to the state.

FOR FURTHER INFORMATION

South Grand Strand Chamber of Commerce
P.O. Box 650
U.S. 17
Murrells Inlet, South Carolina 29576
(803) 651-1010

Pawley's Island

Continuing down U.S. 17, one passes through Pawley's Island, a former plantation owners' resort and one of the oldest vacation retreats along the Atlantic Coast. The southern gentlemen who steered the fortunes of their rice, cotton and indigo plantations would come here to unwind (as if life on the plantation were such a hardship for the master of the house). Vestiges of that storied past abound on Pawley's Island, in the old inns and churches, and in the accoutrements of the low-country lifestyle: hurricane lamps, sweet-grass baskets, weathered shutters and handwoven rope hammocks.

The "Original Pawley's Island Rope Hammock," some say, is the most comfortable hammock of all, having been perfected here by a riverboat pilot and his brother-in-law in the late 1800s. Their knotless hammock—no bumps, so you sleep better—is still being made the old way. People come to the *Hammock Shop* for miles around to buy them.

FOR FURTHER INFORMATION

South Grand Strand Chamber of Commerce
P.O. Box 650
U.S. 17
Murrells Inlet, South Carolina 29576
(803) 651-1010

Debidue Beach
Georgetown

The Grand Strand suddenly gets empty south of Pawley's Island. There's a little black line off the large red line of U.S. 17 that leads to a black dot at water's edge called Debidue Beach. Those folks whose job it is to crank out the printed goods on Myrtle Beach often do not even include this hidden niblet on their maps. That's because there's no tourism here, just remote backwater salt-

air dead-fish emptiness. Just south of the Debidue turnoff, U.S.
17 swings west into Georgetown—the third oldest city in South
Carolina, the effective southern boundary of the Grand Strand,
and too far inland to be of much concern to this book. And so,
we headed south, paralleling 60 miles of unoccupied islands and
wildlife refuge. Next stop, Charleston.

FOR FURTHER INFORMATION

Georgetown County Chamber of Commerce
P.O. Box 1443
Georgetown, South Carolina 29440
(803) 546-8436

Charleston

So where is Charleston? Where is the city of tall spires and antebellum mansions, of debutante cotillions and an old-boy aristocracy that reigns still, of gracious southern living elevated to a
high art? That was the Charleston we came looking for, but on
our initial plunges through the city we were disappointed and
bewildered. We crossed a number of high, narrow and seemingly
endless bridges, which transported us from one zone of prefab
commerce to another, all of which were more hysterical than historical: miles of malls, all the usual fast-food pit stops, modern
subdevelopments. To us, Charleston seemed on first impression
just another American city blighted by the slime mold of quick-
stop franchises.

Ah, we judged too soon. Like the pearl that must be pried from
the shell that surrounds it, you must work to find the "real"
Charleston. Old Charleston, we discovered, lives up to all the
claims made for it. Indeed, even the most glowing accolades pale
next to the experience of being there, especially at night, when
you can take in the stillness of the deserted streets, the grandeur
of the architecture, the tangy salt breezes that blow off the river.
In its own mind, Charleston exists outside of time, before the Civil

War destroyed the South, when the courtly manners and gentility of the southern ruling class set the tone for life in the city and on the plantation. Though the plantation system has been dashed, and the gross hypocrisies of slavery with it, the blueprint for gracious living survives in Old Charleston, underneath spreading oak trees.

Old Charleston is built on a fist-shaped protrusion of land, bounded on the west by the Ashley River, on the east by the Cooper River and on the south by their confluence into the Atlantic Ocean. Looking southeast over water from the Battery, one can faintly see tiny Fort Sumter Island off in the distance. *Fort Sumter* is where, on April 12, 1861, the first shots of the Civil War were fired. Confederate soldiers stationed in Charleston Harbor fired on Union troops occupying Fort Sumter in defiance of the Rebel army. And thus began the War Between the States, the bloodiest civil war in human history. Boats leaving from the *Municipal Arena* in Old Charleston make the trip to Fort Sumter several times a day; round-trip fare is $6.

Though the South was beaten in body, it has never yielded in spirit. For a primer in the irreverent wit and outrageous manners of high-tiered southern society, the movie *Dear Charleston* is a must-see. It is shown ten times a day at the *Preservation Society Visitors' Center* (147 King Street) and at the *Old Exchange Building* (122 E. Bay Street). A less ironic orientation film, *The Charleston Adventure*, runs continuously at the *Visitors' Information Center* (85 Calhoun Street). The Visitors' Information Center is also a good place to begin a walking tour of the historic district. There is plenty of public parking here, and the displays and brochures will get you off on the right foot. Limber up for some serious walking, because there's plenty to take in. There are seventy-three surviving pre-Revolutionary buildings in Charleston alone—nothing short of a miracle, considering that the town has been ravaged and razed by fire, earthquake, hurricane and civil war. Approximately ten historic homes and buildings, an equal number of churches, museums and galleries, and plantations and gardens, plus three forts, are open to the public. There are, as a kind of ballpark figure, in excess of 3,000 designated "historic buildings" within Charleston.

You might start with the two house museums operated by the

Historic Charleston Foundation. The *Nathaniel Russell Home* (51 Meeting Street) and the *Edmondston-Alston House* (21 East Battery) are open daily year-round for a fee of $3. Even if you're taking in the costly sights, allow plenty of time for freestyle strolling around the streets of Old Charleston. The people and neighborhoods, the sights, sounds and smells, make this city a museum of living southern folkways, as full of native quirks and character as New Orleans. From the bustling open-air market on the aptly named Market Street to the splendorous old homes that line the Battery along the riverfront, Old Charleston begs to be explored and savored. On one charmed late-summer night, we looked out over the river from the Battery. The moon was high and full, an offshore breeze carried a mossy, pungent scent, a high school marching band could be heard drilling in the distance and ghosts of the Old South seemed to rumble around us in the night—peeking through curtained bay windows, disappearing down dark alleys, haunting the abbeys of towering churches.

Throughout your perambulations, let the stately spire of *St. Michael's Episcopal Church*, which dates from 1761, be your compass point. Towering above the city rooftops from the intersection of Meeting and Broad Streets, this steeple is just imposing enough to give even the most indifferent heathen a moment's pause. From here, you can fan outward beyond Old Charleston and visit its gardens, parks and plantations. *Middleton Place*, along the Ashley River northwest of Charleston, is a good place to start, or stop. These extensive acres of azaleas, camellias, magnolias and crepe myrtles are the oldest landscaped gardens in America. The strolling is easy, but the admission is steep: $7 for adults.

If you're on any kind of budget, pick and choose your destinations carefully when coming to Charleston. Everything costs dearly, and when you begin adding up the tariffs charged at the doors of the various buildings and gardens, you could wind up sight-seeing yourself into the poorhouse. (Perhaps they'll throw you into the *Provost Dungeon* at the Exchange Building.) It probably never occurred to the well-meaning but hopelessly antiquarian dowagers of Charleston society that money need limit anyone in the pursuit of the finer things in life. But for those not born into old money, and not yet making piles of new money, take this caveat with you when planning your visit: Charleston is classy, and class carries a price tag.

An average of 2 ½ million people visit Charleston every year. The most popular time to come is during the annual Spoleto Festival, an arts-and-culture extravaganza inaugurated in the spring of 1977 that has been drawing huge numbers, and growing as an event, ever since. It's the party of the year in Charleston. Typically, it spans the last week in May and first week in June.

Accommodations

There are hotels and inns on the peninsula where Old Charleston is situated. Look to pay $50 to $100 a night for the privilege of this proximity. You might try the *Mills House Hotel* (where you'll get a lot of expensive attention) or the *Heart of Charleston Motor Inn* (less opulent, but commodious and more affordable). A plethora of inns is scattered about the historic district. *Planter's Inn* is known for gracious accommodations and an exceptional restaurant, *Silk's*. You really can't go wrong choosing an inn here in Old Charleston—each tries to outdo the other in the thoroughness and authenticity of its restorations and Old World furnishings. A few that come highly recommended include the *Indigo Inn*, the *Vendue Inn* and the *Kings Courtyard Inn*. If cost is a limiting factor, inexpensive motels can be found in North Charleston or along U.S. 17, west of the Ashley River.

Restaurants

One can find pretty much anything he or she wants in Charleston, from cheap home-cooked low-country meals to the upper limits of nouvelle cuisine. Part of the fun of Charleston is that it's a walking town, so you'll do just as well making your own discoveries on the streets as following a guidebook. Charleston is full of cozy hideaways cloistered down narrow side streets. The town is a very match to the wick of romance, and we vowed to return here with our respective *amours* at some later date. (That is, if they were still speaking to us, or if we were still capable of speech, after a season spent on the beach. Postscript: they were not, and we were not.)

Dinners at some of the fancier Charleston restaurants—the *Colony House*, the *Cotton Exchange*, the *Philippe Million Restaurant*—can run from entrées priced under $10 to six-course prix-fixe dinners in the $25 to $40 range. We opted for *Henry's*, a locally popular restaurant that offers atmosphere without affectation. With its wooden booths and nautical knickknacks hung about, ceiling fans stirring the air, we knew we'd stumbled into a den of unpretentious southern hospitality. And the food! *Mon dieu* . . . a huge piece of fresh flounder, stuffed with a mixture of crabmeat, breading and chopped olives, and topped with tiny Carolina shrimp. And a dish called Chicken Plimpton, served in the pot in which it was cooked, which was falling off the bone. The best part, if the attentive service and down-home atmosphere aren't enough, is that a bill for two came in under $20.

Nightlife

They're not doing the Charleston in Charleston anymore, at least not in any of the nightspots our feet wandered into, but you can dance to anything from rock to Dixieland. There are a number of bars and clubs along Market Street from which to pick and choose. You can hear a new-wave band in one club, then cross the street and find an audience in coats and ties listening to a Dixieland quartet. Charleston, which we thought to be a bashful town, on the basis of the muffled conversations and decorous manners we'd observed (Speak up! we kept thinking to ourselves, as we attempted to eavesdrop around town), does know how to let its hair down. Most of the letting down (and picking up) in Old Charleston goes on at the *No-Name Bar*, on the Vendue Range near the river. Everyone—women especially—was dressed to the nines. We even saw a few tens. Dressing down in Old Charleston, we quickly learned, was not cool or common. Women sipped tall drinks through straws and gyrated demurely under the flashing lights of a high-tech dance floor. Like all good southern belles, they are able to intimate wickedness without surrendering one *soupçon* of modesty.

"Are you coming here tomorrow night?" we heard one belle bubble
to another. "Us girls are just going to have us a ball."

FOR FURTHER INFORMATION

Charleston Trident Chamber of Commerce
85 Calhoun Street
P.O. Box 975
Charleston, South Carolina 29402
(803) 722-8338

Charleston County Park, Recreation and Tourist Commission
P.O. Box 834
Charleston, South Carolina 29402
(803) 895-7108

Isle of Palms

Twelve miles northeast of Charleston a road runs out to Isle of
Palms, a beach resort on narrow Sullivan's Island. The beach at
Isle of Palms, like that at nearby Folly Beach, has been troubled
with erosion, though it does not look so desperate as Folly. The
Wild Dunes Beach and Racquet Club is located here; it's another sports-
man's resort complex for the fun-hungry who can afford it. The
first-rate facilities, and the premium that those who visit pay for
them ($105 and up per day), have rescued Isle of Palms from the
sagging, flyblown look of Folly Beach.

Folly Beach

If Folly Beach were a hospital patient, it would be on the critical
list. Severe erosion has brought the ocean pounding at the back

doors of squat, weather-beaten cinder-block homes, and no amount of fortification has yet been able to halt the sea's steady march. The town of Folly Beach, as a municipality, isn't faring any better.

Folly Beach is the nearest ocean beach to Charleston, 11 miles away. At one time, a trolley used to run between Folly Beach and Charleston, and ragtime bands provided lively entertainment in the pavilion, which burned to the ground many years ago. There is no such lighthearted, good-time jazz playing now; at the main crossroads near the town center are any number of forbidding taverns with no windows and letters missing. One can almost hear the gravel spitting out from under tires, and the inevitable rebel yell.

There is a restaurant, the *Atlantic House*, whose dining room looks out over the water. A huge *Holiday Inn* complex has opened along the oceanfront, which suggests that some sort of regeneration may be in the offing for Folly Beach. But if the ocean keeps up its relentless attack, the word "folly" could assume a greater significance in the not too distant future.

Kiawah Island

Many moons ago, when the land was primeval and the Indians aboriginal, the Kiawah tribe inhabited the low country of South Carolina. They walked here, the story goes, from Siberia, crossing the Bering Strait thousands of years before it was an international crime to do so. They were nomads, hunters, wanderers who had no homeland . . . until, that is, they reached this region. Humbled by their new paradise by the sea, they ceased their wandering, set about fishing and farming, and by the time the white man arrived without reservations, the Kiawah were so content that they "cheerfully shared their land" with him (or so the guidebooks cheerfully revise).

The rest is, as they say, history. What Indians disease did not kill, serfdom more or less enslaved, and soon enough, the Kiawah tribe was forced to return to their glorious nomadic tradition—

which is to say they ran like hell into the hill country. All they left behind was their name.

Kiawah Island is blessed in so many ways that it is difficult to know how to begin describing it without sounding like we were paid off. Perhaps it is best to start with something as simple as a stop sign. Although this last item might go unnoticed in the real world on the mainland (hell, where we come from they are flagrantly ignored), here on Kiawah Island, the stop signs are carved out of wood and painted burgundy. To ignore its request is to set yourself up as a hopelessly ill-mannered lout. It's the same with the speed-limit signs. On Kiawah Island, the speed limit is 23, 33 or 43 miles per hour. On the mainland, when a driver sees a "35 mph" sign, he usually goes 45 miles per hour, as part of the understood, inflated speed scale. Here, on Kiawah, you simply go 33 miles per hour, no questions asked. In fact, it is almost an honor to drive 33 miles per hour.

Of course, these are the least of Kiawah's appeals, but they do illustrate the meticulous attention that is paid across the board to detail—in particular, the larger issues governing development on a previously unmolested barrier island. Perhaps because of its late start and the proenvironmental bent of the times, Kiawah was spared the worst aspects of uncontrolled resort growth. Outside of one isolated outcropping of small private homes (belonging to folks who refused to sell) and the ruins of an ancient plantation (its fields now overgrown, the walls of the house crumbling), the island was not touched by a serious shovel until 1974. There was no bridge, no paved roads. At that time, the entire 10,000 acres of Kiawah Island, except for those private tracts, were purchased by the same company.

Many of the members of the "team" that developed Kiawah had done the same sort of pioneering development work at Sea Pines Plantation on Hilton Head Island. Sea Pines was a resort built according to a new blueprint, under the directives of a maverick named Charles Fraser. The idea was to construct a resort that would provide for human recreation without disturbing the natural environment, and possibly even improving living conditions for all the little critters and big trees.

Backed by money from all over the world—the largest investor was the oil-rich country of Kuwait—and proceeding from a stated commitment to do things correctly, the Kiawah Island visionaries did not even break ground until an exhaustive sixteen-month study determined the environmental impact of a resort upon the ecology of the island. The result was a game plan that even earned the grudging respect of environmental groups. From the beginning, there was a dedication to the preservation of the island's rich wilderness and wildlife that continues to this day. It is a governing philosophy that is so pure, it is almost suspect—you don't expect these things of resort developers, whose slash-and-burn mentality has desecrated so much shoreline.

But, the proof is on the drawing board: only 3,500 of the island's 10,000 acres are scheduled for development, and the remainder is not just a lot of marshland, either. A healthy chunk has been set aside for the 23 species of mammals, 30 species of reptiles and 200 species of birds that call the island home. Three endangered species—the Atlantic loggerhead turtle, the brown pelican and the alligator—are even staging a second-half comeback in the waters and wetlands surrounding Kiawah, leading to the wholly unexpected conclusion that one route to species preservation may be controlled human development of the sort practiced on Kiawah Island. Egrets, herons and ospreys fill the air and splash in the water as abundantly as their new neighbor, the golf ball. Fish leap unbothered above the surface of the fairway's lagoon watertraps as if it were the first day of creation. Twelve miles of bike paths take you into the heart of the wilderness, and Jeep safaris probe even deeper.

If that were not enough, the beaches are some of the best on the East Coast. There are 10 miles of sand fronting the Atlantic, and they have been growing for almost 100 years—ever since jetties were built up the coast at the mouth of Charleston's harbor.

The construction of all the villas, inns, homes and restaurants has been as conscientious as the overall environmental planning. "Oceanfront" construction here would mean "ocean view" on any other beach. That is to say, all habitations are built a safe distance behind the barrier-dune structure. Long, elevated walkways lead to the beach from a number of access points. The architecture itself has been praised by journals and professionals. The villas on the oceanfront are all understated wood contours, blended into a background of woods and shrubs, low-lying enough that you scarcely notice any interruption in the natural landscape. Most of the private lots are scattered and hidden in the woodlands, so that every owner and visitor will feel the solitude that drove them to seek Kiawah in the first place.

For some vacationers, this sort of purposeful isolation might be somewhat off-putting, since it smacks of exclusivity. There is that undeniable element to the scene here—evident in the well-manned security force, the several Checkpoint Charlies at which one must display proper identification, and the upper echelons of human wealth that circulate here, running up unthinkable vacation tabs. However, Kiawah Island isn't just a well-tended wilderness hangout for the wealthy. It is a family-oriented resort, open to all. While it is far from inexpensive, you can actually throw away a lot more money at beaches of far less luster.

Unlike its competition in this new and seemingly endless barrier-island market, Kiawah even has a public beach, located before you get to the first security gate on the southern end of the island. And again, most of the services on the island are available to the public; reservations, however, are recommended in advance of your arrival. The list of things that are inconspicuously fitted onto Kiawah's island reads like a vacationer's Nirvana: golf courses (one designed by Jack Nicklaus, one by Gary Player), Jeep trails and bike paths, racquet and tennis clubs, canoeing routes, fishing trips, several gargantuan outdoor swimming pools, a 150-room inn, rental condominiums in several island "villages," 6 restaurants, 4 bars and a spa.

But we'd like, in closing, to add something else to the list, after the part about "4 bars and a spa": "plus 2 beach bums who, after months of wandering their nation's eastern shoreline, decided to end their trip here and set up a Panama hat franchise." That is to say, we would have liked to add that postscript, but alas, we needed to push on down to Florida. And so we bid a sad goodbye to this East Coast Eden.

Accommodations

A simple listing of rates would not be entirely fair without first describing the product. To say you are staying overnight on Kiawah Island is like saying like you are grabbing some grub at The Four Seasons. You do not so much sleep between clean cotton sheets here as you are swaddled inside the glossy pages of *Architectural Digest*. Care and attention to detail have gone into every dwelling, walkway and sign on the island. Built of native wood and scaled down to blend in with the abundant wilderness, the dwelling places here come in two sizes—rooms at the inn or villas in the woods. As mentioned, there are 150 rooms in the centrally located inn complex, and they seem to draw vacationing and honeymooning couples.

The villas are a different story. Most are privately owned and used as tax write-offs and/or part-time homes. When not otherwise occupied, the villas are rented by the day or week. Generally rented to families, the villas are built according to similar Kiawah specifications, but each is furnished according to the tastes of the owners—which generally run along Laura Ashley/Country Rustic Chic lines. The beds in the master bedrooms could sleep a family of five. The carpeting is more comfortable than some of the motel beds we'd slept in. In short, with a walk-in bathtub, a washer, dryer, dishwasher, microwave oven, full kitchen, two porches and a hall of mirrors, we were, shall we say, living above our station. Not that it took much getting used to.

A room at the Kiawah Inn, during the peak season, which runs from March 28 to October 31, ranges from $95 to $130 a day. The price spectrum is much wider for the villas, which are, at the modest end, listed as "One Bedroom/Non-Oceanfront," and at the extreme end, "Four Bedroom/Oceanfront." In season, you will pay from $130 to $350 a day for a villa at Kiawah.

Restaurants

The dining rooms on Kiawah Island tend toward elegance. One requires jackets; all require a certain devil-may-care attitude toward money. Due to the fact there is no competition here, there is no point in going into detail about your options. Basically, if you stay on the island, you'll dine here—and dine well, of course. Besides, you will be made familiar enough with them upon your arrival. The alternative is to buck up for a half-hour drive into Charleston. Drive carefully through those dark woods, though—they seem to be the sort of roads and woods in which a ghost story can come to life.

Nightlife

If you have come to Kiawah strictly for the nightlife, you have paid a pretty stiff cover charge. For most people who visit, nightlife is a low-priority item on the vacation agenda. The fact that there is any sort of after-dark activity at all is just icing on the cake, as far as we were concerned. After a day of golf, tennis, bicycling, walking, Jeeping, swimming and exposing pink flesh to the sun, most night activity begins and ends with dinner. Those incorrigible sorts who aren't sawing Z's by ten o'clock can usually be found sipping after-dinner drinks at the *Indigo House Lounge* in the East Village or working off their second wind at the *Topsider Lounge* in the West Village—both a short hop away from their room at the inn.

At the former, an acoustic guitarist was strumming and taking requests in an atmosphere that seemed one quiet drink away from beddy-bye. The conversation was as polite as the occasional applause. At the latter, though, the party continued past midnight as the business world let its hair down to the sounds of a four-piece band that was playing everything from Louis Armstrong to "Louie, Louie." Groups of newfound friends and business connections unwound after their work- or golf-filled day, making chat in between wild rug-cutting flings to the beat of pop-jazz.

Kiawah Island
P.O. Box 12910
Charleston, South Carolina 29412
(803) 768-2121

Seabrook Island

Next door to and sharing a main entrance road with Kiawah Island, Seabrook is like her reclusive little sister. The island is named for William Seabrook, a wealthy cotton planter who used it as his personal hunting preserve. The Seabrook Island resort opened for business in 1971. Seabrook offers a family vacation package comparable to Kiawah's, on a scale of more modest dimensions, primarily in terms of acreage. Seabrook Island covers 4,000 acres, half of which are developed, while the rest is woodland and marsh. There are 3½ miles of beaches, molded by the same forces that created Kiawah. The endangered brown pelican has one of its largest rookeries in a shallow sandbank just offshore from the island's Beach Club.

As usual, there's golfing (36 holes), boating, fishing, tennis (19 courts), and so on. All the things you come to expect from a high-class Southern barrier-island resort development. The motto on Seabrook's highway billboard says it all: "Come for a Week/Stay for a Lifetime." And bring about a million dollars with you, if you plan on doing the latter.

Seabrook Island
P.O. Box 32099
Charleston, South Carolina 29417
(803) 768-1000

Edisto Island

Edisto Island is the remotest and most undeveloped island accessible by car along the South Carolina barrier-island chain. Long-fibered cotton was grown here in antebellum times; nowadays, tomatoes and cucumbers are farmed. Visitors to Edisto must cruise down a state-road back alley, Route 174, for nearly 30 miles off the major north-south artery, U.S. 17. Vacated plantations line the road.

Because of its remoteness, one would think that the developer's hand of doom would not have touched this place, but alas, 'tis a sad story. There are 700 cottages, some dating back to the twenties, crowded along Edisto Beach's main street at the water's edge. To attract buyers with the promise of oceanfront real estate, the barrier dunes were bulldozed away. It's a little bit like knocking down a dam and then wondering afterward why there was a flood.

Practically next door to the town of Edisto Beach is a 1,225-acre state park with a mile-long beach, plus a salt marsh and subtropical forest. There are 75 marsh-view campsites, all first come, first serve. Less primitive accommodations can be found over at *Oristo*, a 300-acre family resort on the southern tip of the island that comes with all the trimmings: tennis, golf and private cottages.

Beaufort

Not only is the name of this low-country seaport mispronounced "*Bew*-fert," but its appeal as a vacation stop has been misrepresented as well. Every available source of travel information pertaining to this part of the coast went to exaggerated lengths to single out Beaufort for praise. The mildest of these blurbs referred to it with the almost meaningless travel-writing cliché, "a picturesque old port town." The most extravagant hailed it as "the Crown Jewel of the Cotton Kingdom." As evidence, its boosters point to the natural harbor, the restored colonial and antebellum architecture and the whole-scale resurrection of the "glory years" of the Confederacy.

Whether a heritage of cotton plantations and slavery needs to be resurrected at all is not really the point here. (Although we did find ourselves wondering how the sizable black population feels about such revisionist shenanigans.) The real point remains that Beaufort is not even what they say it is.

First of all, it is a hot and humid town, set away from the ocean on land that was probably at one time a swamp. Second, it is anything but "suspended in time," as the brochures proclaim, despite the fact that the entire downtown area was declared a National Historic Landmark in 1974. No, with a population of 10,000 and three military installations located within 10 miles of here, Beaufort is very much a part of the slipshod modern world. In fact, in order to find one's way to the alleged historical district, a visitor is required to drive through a nightmarish reminder of present-day civilization that rings Beaufort's outer environs. "Lessee, uh, there's a K mart, three steak houses, one taco hut, a cement shopping mall, a Wendy's, a McDonald's, a lawn-mower repair shop. . . . Heck, we must be coming up to a new town." There are even several combination pool hall-motel complexes, suggesting a Marine's night out that we dare not ponder the particulars of.

To be fair, Beaufort is not hell on earth, but when you are promised a crown jewel, you don't want or expect dime-store costume baubles. In truth, Beaufort is a sleepy southern coastal town of sun-baked clapboard homes and a few of the aforementioned historic mansions; of Spanish moss dangling from grandfather oak trees; untended, spooky cemeteries, and a legacy from a very dark time in history that should be allowed to continue to sleep. . . . Goodnight and sweet dreams.

FOR FURTHER INFORMATION

Beaufort Chamber of Commerce
P.O. Box 910
1006 Bay Street
Beaufort, South Carolina 29902
(803) 524-3163

Harbor Island

Harbor Island is ever so slightly larger than its neighbor to the south, Fripp Island, which it practically bumps up against. Resort development mischief is afoot here, but fortunately most of the island is given over to *Hunting Island State Park*. It's one of the most frequented parks in the state. In addition to 3 miles of beach, there are lagoons, lighthouses and a boardwalk over marshland. There are facilities, exhibits and concessions on the island, and 200 sites upon which to put up a tent, not to mention a fight against mosquitoes.

Fripp Island

When you first glance at a map of the lower coast of South Carolina, it almost looks like something created by a Veg-O-Matic. Outside of Maine, it is rare to find so many unattached slivers of land strewn so close together in the water. Most of these unevenly sliced 'n' diced islands—even the ones that lack a true oceanfront, stymied by another island—are advertised on gargantuan billboards that dot the low-country backroads for miles in every possible direction. One billboard says, "Share Our Secret." Another beckons you to "Escape With Us." Still another boasts that its new model residences are "Barely Feet from the Ocean," as if that would inspire you to build a permanent home there. The billboard for Fripp Island simply says, "The Uncrowded One."

Located 19 miles southeast of Beaufort, huddled neatly in the ocean with the Marines' Parris Island training base directly west of it, Fripp Island has been uncrowded for a long, long time. So uncrowded and isolated was the island considered in colonial times that it was given away like a souvenir ashtray to Captain Johannes Fripp as an award for his efforts at keeping the surrounding coastline safe from Spanish marauders.

Until the recent trend toward private resort communities came along, the island had remained uncrowded by human beings. Even today as you enter the front security gate, a sign issues the following warning: "$1,000 Fine for Feeding or Molesting the Alligators." Apparently, this sign is aimed at cretinous children with bags of cheese popcorn or swarthy poachers with concealed weapons. Who else, pray tell, would want to molest an alligator?

Lest the gators deter you from enjoying a carefree vacation, however, a quick drive around the island will reassure you that you have not stumbled into Mutual of Omaha's Wild Kingdom. Though you will see an occasional raccoon scurry into the brush (but more often splattered on the roadbed) or an impressive-sized deer bound across a well-manicured front yard, most of Fripp Island's 3000 acres is either virgin marshland or under the less wild rule of tasteful but fairly dense residential and recreational development. The wilderness effect given off by the occasional animal darting among oak and palmetto trees is mainly due to the fact that that particular lot has not been sold yet. The telltale surveyor's stake can be seen with its orange flag driven into the earth. Fripp Island is uncrowded now, but maybe not for long.

Perhaps that is simply nitpicking at its billboard motto, because Fripp Island does offer an attractive setting and decent services for its residents and visitors: a 3-mile beach, tennis and racquetball courts, an 18-hole golf course, a marina, an inn and a healthy number of pleasant villas. It also is a fair compromise for those not economically ready for Kiawah or Hilton Head, where a game of golf costs a Fripp Island mortgage.

Although only a third the size of Kiawah, Fripp Island is similar in that it's owned by a single development company. One of the stated goals of this consortium is to protect and preserve the ecological riches of the island. In fairness to them, they have avoided dense commercialism—there is one convenience store on the island, one restaurant and one bar (with a great beach-music jukebox). One drawback is that the beach seems to be vanishing right under the pilings of the bar-restaurant, especially at high tide, which was making alarming incursions into the grass-covered primary dunes.

Perhaps beach "renourishment" (pumping in sand) will keep the sea at bay. In the meantime, Fripp Island is a pretty place, so uncrowded at the time of our visit as to be eerie. The tidal marshes are photogenically full of happy, swooping birds. The deer still lope unabashedly past the lawn sprinklers. And somewhere among the mud and reeds a group of alligators sits around, secure in the knowledge that they will not be turned into ladies' pocketbooks or cheese-popcorn addicts. However, were Captain Fripp to come ashore today, he might be—to paraphrase this resort's bumper sticker—"Fripped out" by all the changes he'd witness.

Accommodations

Similar to Kiawah, Fripp rents its unsold or unoccupied villas by the day or week. In the summer, prices range from a low of $60 for a double guest room near the centrally located beach club to a high of $165 a day (or $825 a week) for a two-bedroom oceanfront villa. In between the two extremes, you can stay on high ground near the tennis courts in a perfectly fine two-bedroom villa for $95 a day (or $475 a week). Off-season rates are quite a bit lower. The resort is open year-round.

Restaurants

For all intents and purposes, there are two restaurants on Fripp Island: the *Beach Club Restaurant* (in the main *Beach Club* complex) and the *Marina Restaurant and Lounge* (on the marina at Old House Creek). The former is a bit fancier; the emphasis at the latter is almost exclusively on seafood, perhaps making it the more germane choice. If you're in the area for longer than two hours, you can try both. Despite the brochure's urging that "reservations are recommended," both were, closer to the billboard's promise, uncrowded.

Nightlife

The *Sandbar Lounge*, located upstairs in the *Beach Club*, is where whatever is happening, is happening. That could mean nothing. It could mean a free pig-pickin' spread, as it did on the night of our arrival, and generous glasses of 50-cent draft. Sometimes, when the summer is in full swing, there is entertainment. Our entertainment was a raccoon, which unabashedly waited at the bar door for a handout.

FOR FURTHER INFORMATION

Fripp Island
Fripp Island, South Carolina 29920
(803) 838-2411

Calliwachee Island

Somewhere out in the ocean between Fripp and Hilton Head Islands is yet another southern sea island under development. Calliwachee Island, say the billboards, is "The One Close By." As the area is fast approaching the saturation point in terms of how much development it can support—a couple of these island developments are rumored to be catastrophic financial flops—one wonders just how well a newcomer will fare in this crowded market . . . no matter how green a golf course, how well-surfaced a tennis court, how charming an oceanfront villa they can construct. Stay tuned. Or if you're "close by," drop in and see for yourself. (Send us a card.)

Hilton Head Island

Hilton Head is no ordinary island. For one thing, few signs or billboards assault the eyes once you've stepped ashore (the mainland approach is another story), and strict building codes prevent storefronts from leering at approaching motorists. Resort development has been hushed away from the main route, U.S. 278, that cuts through the island. And instead of towns or small communities, the island has been blocked off into discrete "plantations," each tended by a development consortium, yet all adhering to the charter of regulations established before the first shovelful of sand was turned over in 1956. Within these plantations, there are more golf holes than you can wave a putter at, and these are some of the best courses in the country.

If you haven't guessed, Hilton Head is one of the premier resort islands on the East Coast. Maybe you don't have to be dirty rich to come here, but it won't hurt. *Brown's Guide to Georgia* has dubbed it "a playground for America's upper, upper middle class." Take off one of those uppers and you can still afford to vacation here. Take off both, and you might not want to push it beyond a weekend in the off-season. If you are in some sub-middle class/caste-category and find yourself on Hilton Head, chances are you're carrying someone else's bags into one of the hotel lobbies.

Regardless of your ways and means, Hilton Head is a splendid place to be any time of year, offering varied recreational opportunities in a spectacular subtropical island setting. Over the years, development has proceeded gradually, according to a kind of gentleman's agreement that honors the preservation of nature inasmuch as is possible, and hews to high standards of taste architecturally. Lately, as Hilton Head's reputation has spread far and wide, development has proceeded on a grander scale, accelerating beyond what the island's original owner and development guru, Charles Fraser, perhaps had in mind. But it is still a paradise that is largely preserved and governed by conscientious planning.

Hilton Head Island occupies approximately 27,000 acres of land and fronts the Atlantic for 12 miles. In terms of land area, it is the largest true barrier island south of Long Island. The island was named for Captain William Hilton, a British explorer who discovered it in 1633, aboard his ship *Adventure*. Cotton, rice and indigo were grown on plantations here in the 1700s. Hilton Head played a major role in the Civil War. Early in the war, the Confederate fort located here, *Fort Walker*, fell to the Union army. The North used Hilton Head as a massive naval encampment and established its "Department of the South" here. Hilton Head also served as a base from which the North could blockade the key southern cities of Charleston (90 miles away) and Savannah (30 miles away).

Nowadays, Fort Walker has been supplanted by fortifications of another sort. Inside these arsenals are stocked all the amenities of the good life—name-brand liquors, fine foods, king-sized beds, color televisions and a small army of foot soldiers looking to attend to your every need. The word "fort" does not appear in the plantations' names, which instead suggest oases of pleasure—e.g., Palmetto Dunes, Port Royal, Sea Pines Plantation.

The latter place is the keystone in the Hilton Head mythology. Sea Pines was the first resort plantation to be developed on Hilton Head, and it has set the tone for all subsequent construction. Hilton Head owes its good looks to the visionary developer Charles Fraser. Back in the fifties, the island was owned by Fraser's father and several of his partners in the lumbering business. Young Charles himself worked occasionally on the timbering crews out on Hilton Head. Eventually, however, he saw another, far greater cash crop for Hilton Head: tourists.

Unlike most developers of that time, Fraser was motivated as much by ecological altruism as by the usual acquisitive greed. He desired to spare his beloved Hilton Head the sort of "visual pollution" that had turned many a pristine beach into scorched earth. "I may never make any money," he told his mother, "but I want to create something beautiful."

Of course, he has gone on to make millions from Hilton Head, but he did honor his promise to preserve and protect the environment while sculpting a recreational Shangri-la for the wealthy. The key to his strategy was total control. From the beginning, Sea Pines Plantation was constructed according to a deed of rights, signed by all who built homes here, that allowed Fraser the final say over every aspect of architecture, beach access and land use. He made his roads wind around large old trees, and chopped down a prize oak only after two automobiles had crashed into it. Even now, with Hilton Head sliced up like a pie into six plantations and a raft of developers on board, a central charter ensures that Fraser's standards will be observed in perpetuity.

Hilton Head was predicated upon proenvironmental principles, but it was popularized by the game of golf. Fraser, something of a golf historian, built a top-flight course called *Harbour Town* on his Sea Pines Plantation, and Arnold Palmer put Hilton Head on the map by winning the first Heritage Golf Classic ever held here. Because it was Palmer's first tournament victory after a year-long slump, it made national news, and the Heritage Classic, played every April, has since become one of the premier stops on the PGA tour.

Golf remains one of the principal reasons people come to Hilton Head, although the island attracts a generous cross-section of families, retirees and conventioneers as well. But that little dot-pocked golf ball is still the central icon. Our composite portrait of the typical Hilton Header would be a corporate vice-president, golf fanatic, in his mid-fifties, with a big bright golfer's hat on his head and a still-mighty swing. As for his wife—well, it's hard to say about these golf widows, since they're left behind closed doors so much of the time, stoically idling the hours away until hubby plays out the eighteenth hole.

Hilton Head offers 18 courses spread out over its 42 square miles. The island, which is 12 miles long and up to 5 miles wide in some places, boasts courses designed by top course architects such as George Fazio and Robert Trent Jones. One of the most challenging courses in the country is still the first one built here: the Harbour Town Golf Links, on Sea Pines Plantation. But there are top-rated courses all over the island. Tennis players also get their due on Hilton Head. There are 15 racquet clubs and more than 200 courts scattered around the island, and such stars as Evonne Goolagong and Rod Laver maintain residences here.

As if golf and tennis weren't diversion enough, there are 12 miles of wide, sandy beaches and opportunities for outdoor activities from birdwatching to surfcasting. At low tide, the beach is flat and wide and hard enough that you can pedal a bicycle almost the entire length of the island. At high tide, at least on some parts of the island, the waves do seem to wander awfully close to the dune grass, but this is par for the coast.

Hilton Head is about as nice a low-country vacation spot as you will find. Here, decked out in tennis whites and golfing greens, folks throw themselves into the good life with all-American bravado. Granted, paradise on earth—unlike the reward of untold riches proffered in the afterlife—is an exclusionary thing. You won't find rural blacks from the other side of the bridge batting balls around the tennis court, nor will you find hard-laboring John Doe and his blue-collar buddies barreling about the links in a golf cart. For that matter, singles don't come here in great numbers, either. Not because they can't afford to, but because this is predominantly a playground for corporate sports nuts and their families, and a resting place for moneyed retirees.

Still, 700,000 people manage to make their way here every year, and the numbers are rising. Hilton Head is now an incorporated township, with a permanent population of 14,000. All this is great news for those who want to see the island prosper, bad news for those already living here who wish to see further growth curtailed. There are a fair number who fall into the latter camp. They live in nice villas overlooking quiet ponds and lagoons, and they paid dearly for their retreats. They do not want their peace defiled by the loud intrusions of thousands of yo-yos who don't behave well in public.

This is a difficult, perhaps unresolvable debate. In the meantime, Hilton Head appears to be in very capable hands. The large consortiums that manage the plantations have made certain that the owls hoot and the gators prowl, free of human interference. Architecture performs in concert with nature. Acreage has been set aside as wilderness preserves. No Hardee's or McDonald's will offend with garish arches; they will repose meekly in huts of unfinished, weathered wood, like obedient serfs.

For those who are able to afford Hilton Head, this boot-shaped island, with all its kicks, may be the closest they come to Fantasy Island. Particularly if you're a golfer, Hilton Head will be your fairway to fun.

Accommodations

Hilton Head has been portioned off into a half-dozen "plantations," which divvy up the oceanfront along the south and east faces of the island. *Sea Pines Plantation* is the largest, the oldest and the choicest of these. If you are planning a vacation on Hilton Head, you can stay in one of the large hotels on the plantations. These include a *Hyatt*, a *Marriott* and a *Holiday Inn*, as well as smaller operations such as the *Adventure Inn* and the *Sea Crest Motel*. Or, you can rent a privately owned villa.

The latter choice may be more attractive, particularly if you are bringing the family and staying a few days. If several couples or families are traveling together and splitting expenses, the cost advantages are greater still. Consider what you are getting, compared to a hotel room: an entire furnished household, complete with kitchen facilities, screened-in porches and balconies, and more room, peace and privacy than you might have dreamed possible. These villas can be booked for one night or much longer. We stayed at a villa in the *Palmetto Dunes Plantation*, and had a resort vacation worth writing home (or a book) about. With tennis courts operated under the auspices of Rod Laver and a golf course designed by the likes of Fazio and Jones only a stone's throw away, how could it miss? Palmetto Dunes is also the site of the *Hyatt Hotel* and the *Mariner's Inn*.

One more note: Palmetto Dunes and all the other plantations are a bit tricky for finding your way around. Jumping from plantation to plantation is not easy—and you will do some plantation-hopping if you're staying in one place, dining in another, dancing elsewhere, and so on. Even within the plantations, the roads can be hard to figure—crazy figure 8's and loop roads that defy logic.

Restaurants

With over 90 restaurants to choose from on the island, you could spend an entire summer at a different one every night. Of course, not all of these merit culinary kudos—chances are you've already been to a *Western Sizzlin' Steak House*—but all the major chain hotels have gourmet restaurants on their premises. Most specialize in continental cuisine (very pricy) and brag about their European chefs.

Chances are you'll want to eat locally caught seafood when you're down here. If so, venture to *Fisherman's Lagoon*, a favorite of many who know the island, or *Hudson's*, a complex of restaurants and a fishermen's marina. Located near the end of Squire Pope Road, Hudson's has a long history as a seafood market and marina and, more recently, as a restaurant. *Hudson's Restaurant*, founded in 1968, has done so well that a companion eatery, *Hudson's Landing*, was built next door. Combined, they have a total seating capacity of 750 people—and you'd still better make a reservation. The attraction is the seafood, which is unloaded off of trawlers right at dockside. Steamed shrimp and oysters make for good nibbling, and the list of entrées ranges from broiled fresh fish to more elaborate presentations—such as sea trout baked in a sauce of sherry, cream, cheese and shrimp. Hudson's maintains a remarkable consistency in the quality and presentation of its food, given the volume of business.

We must also mention *Porky's Southern Style Barbeque*. Being barbecue connoisseurs, we visited Porky's to compare South Carolina barbecue with North Carolina's, with which we'd had many years' familiarity. South Carolina's is more coarsely chopped and drier. It is also covered with a vinegar-and-tomato-based sauce. While North Carolina barbecue wins our taste test hands down, we cannot dispute the appeal of barbecue in any form. Porky's serves the classic South Carolina barbecue dinner, which includes chopped barbecue, a side dish of Brunswick stew, french fries, cole slaw, toast, pickle and a nice hunk of onion. You can't beat it.

Nightlife

Most of the nightlife on Hilton Head goes on in the lounges of the big hotels. Some of the popular nightspots are *Robber's Row*, in the *Holiday Inn*; *Club Indigo*, at the *Hyatt*; and the *Mockingbird Lounge*, at *Marriott's*. Disco show bands and beach-music revivalists are the order of the day. Our favorite island hotspot is *Jim's Paradise*, at the *Sea Pines Circle*. Amid the casual, crony-ish varnished-pine bar and hanging plants, a deejay spins a variety of old and new records and takes requests. The small dance floor starts to fill up around mid-evening. Honorable mention goes to *The Post Office*, which books live acts.

As the nightlife is fairly low-key overall, and verges on the mundane in the lounges, your after-dark activity should at least once commence before daybreak, after 8 hours' sleep, with a hike around one of the three nature preserves on the island. Something like 260 species of birds stop through here annually, and the marshes, swamps, forests and wetlands make for a fascinating study. Come to think of it, the beaches look pretty enchanting with morning's red sun rising up—more enchanting by far than the sight of a red-faced disco singer warbling "I've Got the Music in Me" late into the night.

FOR FURTHER INFORMATION

Hilton Head Island Visitors' and Convention Bureau
P.O. Box 5647
Hilton Head Island, South Carolina 29938
(803) 785-3673

Daufuskie Island

Daufuskie Island is among the last remaining members of an endangered, and soon to be extinct, species. Unprotected from the real estate developer by any form of law—local, state or federal—this remote island, located between Hilton Head and Savannah, may be the last privately owned barrier island along the East Coast to feel the jaws of a bulldozer.

Like Kiawah Island up the coast, Daufuskie somehow managed, until recently, to remain in pristine, almost primeval, isolation. There was, however, one notable difference between the two paradises, at least insofar as human beings were concerned. Whereas Kiawah was virtually free of inhabitants at the time of its development as a resort, Daufuskie was quite nearly a separate kingdom. Inhabited by slave-descended blacks, Daufuskie Island was once home for upward of 2,000 people, even as late as the 1950s. Cut off from the mainland, this proud clan managed to sustain an adequate living from the 5,000 acres of land at their disposal and the surrounding, boundless sea.

About fifteen years ago, however, the proverbial do-gooder—in this case, the writer Pat Conroy—came along, and in the process of doing good by the inhabitants, he, in the long run perhaps, done them wrong. He put them on the map, as it were. His book, *The Water Is Wide*, was made into the movie *Conrack*. It dealt with Conroy's own experiences of teaching the Daufuskie inhabitants all about the joys and wonders and glories of the mainland we all know as America. The movie starred Jon Voight as a sort of rural White Shadow, and somewhere in the process of translating the island to the page and the page to the screen, fatal inaccuracies boldly crept into the plot. The once fairly stable community was portrayed as deprived in every conceivable way, slightly childish and even primitive, a sort of Appalachia-by-the-sea. The book and movie were popular, and the natives never saw any of the loot. Or so their side of the story goes.

Be that as it may, the fact remains that all the media hoopla brought the island the sort of attention that any community in the world can do without. At first, Daufuskie was treated as a semi-quaint curiosity—sort of like Cherokee, North Carolina, in the early days—and later, after the poverty level increased with rising land values, it became a realtor's "wet" dream. As regards its curio status, it is told that the earliest tourists, and even a few today, expected their boat excursions from Hilton Head or Savannah to reveal buck-naked natives with spears and blow guns. Of the realtors' sudden interest in the place, tales abound of the army of pink-skinned Ulysses who crossed the wide waters from yon Hilton Head (all of four miles) bearing trinkets and ready cash to exchange for waterfront property.

In short, the inhabitants were taken to the cleaners in the land grab. Now, only fifty or so of the original clan still live on the island. And the island awaits the bulldozers. The last piece of waterfront property was sold in late 1984.

If there can be said to be a silver lining to this tale, it might be found in the following facts:

1. The development has not yet started full-scale.
2. It is prohibitively expensive to build a causeway or a bridge to this tiny outpost.
3. The developers promise to build wisely and to preserve the historical sites, ecology, and so on, as was done at Kiawah.

The dark clouds around the silver linings may be said to be these:

1. The resort is bound to be quite exclusive.
2. The original inhabitants of the island, if jobs do become available to them, will no doubt become glorified manservants again.

Georgia: Confederacy of Dunces or the Brains of the New South?

Georgia is the largest state east of the Mississippi River. This is just the sort of statistic a downtrodden populace loves to hand out to give itself an inflated sense of worth. And Georgia has had its share of downtrodden days. Remember when it was unflatteringly known as the Cracker State? We are talking Reconstruction here (the state's more distinguished colonial history is covered under Savannah). Reconstruction was a time of regional stasis that was only beginning to lift when the Great Depression hit. Of course, Georgia fully earned and deserved the Cracker State sobriquet, given its whiplash-inducing recoil at the thought of entering the Twentieth Century: poll taxes, burning crosses, "states' rights" parties, populist stump-thumping politicos, lynching posses and so forth. In short, the Georgia of not-so-long-ago was a far cry from the Georgia of here-and-now, the one that's proudly known as the Empire State of the South.

It took the city of Atlanta to lift the state out of its antebellum tar pit. Even though the average small-town Georgian would argue this fact until he was red in the neck, it is true that until Atlanta became the boom town of the New South, the state of Georgia spent an inordinate amount of time cursing and bellyaching about General Sherman, praising and deifying the likes of Lester Maddox and trying to nab northerners for speeding. (The town of Ludowici, 30 miles southwest of Savannah, is the most nefarious speed trap in the history of mankind.)

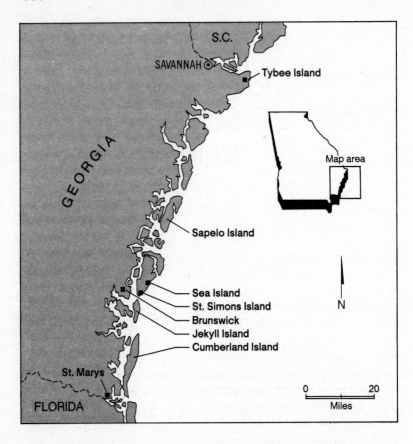

Today, Atlanta continues to grow, and the rest of the state has been dragged into semiprosperity on its corporate coattails. It did not hurt the state's self-image at all to have one of its citizens elected President in 1976. ("Hah, ahm Jimmuh Cahtuh an' Ah woan tah be yuh Presuhdint. . . .") Other names, of course, have helped to earn the state its due respect from the rest of the world—Martin Luther King, Andrew Young, not to mention the Mouth of the South, Ted Turner.

The Georgia coastline has played a part in the state's positive PR blitz as well. Once known as the Golden Isles of Guale by the covetous Spaniards, the Georgia coastline is a series of barrier islands strung out like cotton balls for over 100 miles. Georgia's sea islands have been developed wisely, which is to say that they've been left pretty much undeveloped. There are reasons for this that have nothing to do with private-sector benevolence. Much of the land is salt marsh—protected areas that serve as incubators for the creatures of the sea. Add to this the fact that no direct interstate route connects the coastline with Atlanta and few bridges connect the islands to the mainland, and you are virtually assured of the sea islands' continued isolation.

However, you will find ample territory to cover on a vacation. From the historic port town of Savannah to the "Golden Isles" of Jekyll and St. Simons Islands, on down to Cumberland Island National Seashore on the Florida border, you can pretend to be a true twentieth-century explorer. Just keep it under 55 if you're anywhere near Ludowici. And have yesselves some fun, y'all.

Savannah

A survey of Savannah's history and a tour of the town will lead you to the conclusion that there are two Savannahs: the old Savannah . . . and the old Savannah. Savannah has managed to resurrect its colonial and antebellum past and, in the process, has made itself a tourist destination on a par with Charleston, South Carolina. As the Georgia Semiquincentenary Commission put it in a slogan that sounds more like a philosophy, "The Past Is the Present."

Located on a bluff overlooking the Savannah River 18 miles inland, Savannah has 250 years of history to celebrate. Georgia began here. Crucial battles in both the Revolutionary and Civil Wars were fought here. King Cotton was coronated here. The Girl Scouts of America were founded here.

The story of Savannah begins with the arrival of General James Edward Oglethorpe and 120 colonists on February 12, 1733. Oglethorpe was a young Parliamentarian who proposed a novel notion for emptying out England's debtor prisons. His proposal would relieve the country of the cost of supporting an indigent population and, at the same time, liberate the debtors from their pitiful Catch-

22 situation. The solution? Send them to the New World to found a colony. And thus was born Georgia.

As the colonists would soon find out, they were exchanging one set of prison walls for another. Part of the bargain was that Georgia would serve as a buffer between the northern colonies and Spanish-controlled Florida to the south. The entire city of Savannah was walled in to protect its citizens from attacks by the Spanish.

Savannah, a strategic port city, and its nearby fortifications have been under siege from both foreigners and countrymen: in 1742, by the Spanish; in 1778, by the British, and in 1862, by the Union army. One wonders if debtor's prison wouldn't have been a safer fate after all. The three forts close by Savannah—*Fort Screven*, *Fort Pulaski* and *Fort Jackson*—are all open to the public.

War was hard on the city. The British occupied Savannah for much of the Revolutionary War. The Civil War brought about its near devastation, as Savannah was Sherman's final destination on the infamous "march to the sea." Wisely, the citizens of Savannah surrendered to Sherman rather than risk the holocaustal destruction he had wreaked upon Atlanta. General Sherman presented the city of Savannah to President Lincoln as a Christmas gift in the year 1864.

But fires and natural disasters would further rack this embattled city, and the collapse of the cotton economy in the 1890s nearly did her in. For the next half-century, Savannah's spirits plummeted. But one thing Savannah never lost—either to war or the wrecking ball—was the architectural evidence of her glory days. General Oglethorpe, in addition to being a humanitarian leader and a military genius, was a civil-engineering whiz as well. He laid out the city of Savannah according to a blueprint of his own devising. His design called for the symmetrical arrangement of lots around public parks or "squares." The result was America's first planned city, and it remains an object of study by urban planners.

A 2½-square-mile area has been designated a Historical Landmark District by the U.S. government. It is the largest such district in the nation. Oglethorpe's squares survive, as do many buildings and homes from the 1700s and 1800s. More than 1,100 buildings, in fact, have been restored and preserved since the formation of the Historic Foundation in the 1950s. The women who founded this organization have bullishly battled real estate scalawags and have raised the city's self-esteem. Nowadays, preservation is big business. Millions visit here every year to tour the *Historic District* and the *Victorian District*, and to browse the waterfront, where a sizable commercial rejuvenation is under way. Tours are offered by the *Historical Savannah Foundation*, as well as by private tour companies. The city can be explored by trolley, boat, bicycle, horse-drawn carriage or on foot. But seeing it is a must; presumably that's why you came here. (You didn't come, it's safe to say, to breathe the bad air spewed out by the city's paper-processing plants or to drink its muddy tap water.)

Recycling the past has brought new life to Savannah, but it's not the sort of city to rest on its laurels . . . or its crepe myrtles, weeping willows or oak trees. Savannah, with a natural deep-river harbor, is the tenth largest seaport in the United States, and the import-export cargoes that pass through here are assessed in the hundreds of millions. The huge oceangoing vessels can be watched from the cobblestones of River Street. This particular vantage point, where past and present coexist in close proximity, seems an apt emblem for the city of Savannah.

Accommodations

In Savannah, you can put on the ritz in one of several ways. Downtown, along the waterfront and scattered around the Historic District, are a number of inns in renovated houses. There is Old World charm to burn (oops, bad choice of words) in these seventeen or so inns, many of which—the *East Bay Inn*, for instance—are appointed with period antiques, brass beds, large drawing rooms and private baths. You'll pay $60 and up for the privilege of an overnight ticket back to the courtly colonial era.

If you prefer more modern surroundings, a row of large, new hotels skirts the Historic District. The *Hyatt Regency* is the most centrally located of these, being situated at the midpoint of the riverfront renovation with entrances onto both Bay and River Streets. And it has those glass-walled elevators that small-town tourists love to go back home and rant and rave about to the kinfolk. A selective directory of accommodations can be had from the *Savannah Area Convention and Visitors' Bureau*. Write ahead, or drop by here when you hit town.

Restaurants

After a hard day of pounding the bricks and cobblestones, you're going to have an appetite. You have come to the right town. Savannah is a city of great ethnic diversity—everyone from West Africans to Irish Catholics and French Huguenots have settled here, and the food in this melting pot reflects that mix. There are ethnic-holiday celebrations in Savannah during the year, such as an Oktoberfest and a major St. Patrick's Day blowout. German and Irish cooking, respectively, can be sampled to the bursting point, along with pool-sized quantities of beer. The festivities are centered along the riverfront streets, which have become the year-round heart of the city's social life.

Down to specific restaurants. For southern cooking, *Johnny Harris'* restaurant cannot be beat. Founded in 1924, and featuring a spacious art deco dining room that looks like a planetarium, Johnny Harris' is where Savannahans go for down-home ribs and barbecue, as well as seafood dishes such as crabmeat au gratin en casserole. Don't pass up the onion soup or the crab soup, either.

The *17 Hundred 90 Restaurant* and the *Chart House* are the classiest operations in Savannah. The former is set in a restored warehouse on River Street; the latter, in a restored Georgian townhouse on East President Street. Both offer steak and seafood fare in the $10 to $15 range. For pizza, sandwiches and burgers, and cold draft to wash it all down with, try *Spanky's* or the *Crystal Beer Parlor*. Seafood fanatics who like the preparation kept good and simple are referred to *Williams Seafood Restaurant* and *Palmer's Seafood House* (the latter is on nearby Wilmington Island).

Now, may we be permitted an unmitigated rave? We had, on this trip, consumed seafood in such quantity that we began to sprout gills. We had tasted it all—the good, the bad, the ugly, the inedible and the unmentionable. We had even begun trading off non-seafood eating privileges on occasion, observing fishless days much like Catholics observe meatless days.

With no particular longing for seafood or much appetite, we went to the much-commended *River House* and enjoyed what was, quite simply, the best meal of the trip. For starters, we had fried calamari (squid). We were then asked to pick our own fish out of ice-filled copper pans in the windows of the restaurant. They were filleted before us. The pompano was broiled and served with a hollandaise sauce, and the swordfish was grilled. Our meal was preceded by a frozen peach daiquiri (remember, Georgia is the peach state), accompanied by a California wine, and rounded out with flaming mugs of Irish coffee. We left several steps closer to heaven.

The River House is managed by a lifelong Savannahan whose family also owns another restaurant, *The Shrimp Factory*, with an equally intriguing menu of dishes (e.g., Pine Bark Stew). Both places are located on River Street.

Nightlife

Rather than bore you with tales of our own desultory peregrinations around the city, we defer this section to a friend of ours who was living here at the time of our visit. Like the true southern gentleman he is, he offered to draw up a list of Savannah's nightspots, which he scratched on the back of an envelope for our benefit over drinks at the *Night Flight Café*. We saw no reason to alter or add to it:

SAVANNAH'S TOP BARS

by John Dunlap

1. *Night Flight Café*, River Street. Best live music in town. Intimate, like The Cavern [the Liverpool club where the Beatles got their start].

2. *Spanky's*—two locations, with River Street the older one. Most famous for its St. Patrick's Day celebrations.

3. *Studebaker's*. Lots of dance music. About the only place that goes heavy on beach music, oldies,

4. *Bennigan's*, Abercorn Street. Good atmosphere.

5. *Mainsail*, Victory Drive. About the only other place with decent live music.

6. *Dooley's*, River Street. Free live music.

7. *Malone's*. Goes for younger crowd. Obnoxious amount of disco music.

8. *Night Lights*, Abercorn Street. Probably the most popular disco place, but was better when it used to be Remmington's and had live music. Opted for the money and disco.

FOR FURTHER INFORMATION

Savannah Area Convention and Visitors' Bureau
301 West Broad Street
Savannah, Georgia 31499
(912) 233-6651

Tybee Island

Tybee Island is Savannah's nearest beach. Located 18 miles east of town on U.S. 80, Tybee is a worn but charming beach town for the city folk to escape to in the summer. Its cottages and motels have age on them, but they wear it well. (Why does a squat, paint-flecked motel look quaint in Georgia and decrepit in Jersey?) Tybee has not fallen prey to creeping gentrification and its 5 miles of beaches remain accessible to the general population—mostly Savannahan daytrippers, although half a dozen or so motels support a small vacation industry. There are few attractions other than the beach, although there is one small museum here with a collection that includes historical exhibits, dolls and, perversely, a shrunken head.

The fine, silty sand makes for a beach that's flat, hard and wide at low tide—a characteristic of the Georgia-South Carolina coast in general, but especially pronounced here. The ocean is bath-water warm in the summer months, and is comfortable to swim in from April through October. And the air has been saluted for centuries for its beneficial properties to sufferers of hay fever and asthma.

FOR FURTHER INFORMATION

Tybee Island Chamber of Commerce
P.O. Box 491
Tybee Island, Georgia 31328
(912) 786-4077

Sapelo Island

There is a string of uninhabited or barely inhabited sea islands that runs from Savannah to St. Simons Island. These include Skidaway Island (which is developed, with a state park), Ossabaw, St. Catherine's, Sapelo, Wolf and Little St. Simons Islands (all undeveloped). Sapelo Island is maintained by the state as a wildlife refuge and estuarine sanctuary, and the University of Georgia has established its marine institute there. Though there are no public facilities on Sapelo or roads over from the mainland, the *Department of Natural Resources of the State of Georgia* conducts boat trips and tours of the island on Wednesday and Saturday mornings only. The boat trip is followed by a bus tour and does not include any stops for food or picnicking. The cost is a reasonable $2, but the expeditions are limited to twenty-eight and reservations must be made well in advance. Write the Department of Natural Resources, Coastal Resources Division, 1200 Glynn Avenue, Brunswick,

Georgia 31523, or call (912) 264-7218. If you have any interest in marshes and coastal wetlands and desire to see a barrier island that looks much as it did before this country was settled, a sojourn to Sapelo Island offers a unique opportunity.

Brunswick

Brunswick is the old port city for which Brunswick stew—a thick soup of pork, corn and other vegetables—was named. It is the seat for a county called Glynn, and home of the marshes celebrated in the rapturous poems of Sidney Lanier. It is also the home of several paper- and pulp-processing plants, the smoke and fumes from which combine with the more natural swampy funk from the marshes to produce an odor not unlike that of Brunswick stew that has been left out on the counter too long. The accommodations you will find here range from *Days Inns* on down. One of the restaurants recommended at the welcome center was *Kentucky Fried Chicken*. And if you are not moved or amused by religious phone-in television shows, then the nightlife you will find here can be on the rough side. Wouldn't you be a bit ornery or, at the other extreme, deeply religious if you had your nose in Brunswick stew all day, every day?

The best thing about Brunswick is that the entrance to the St. Simons Island Causeway can be found here. The minimal toll that is charged to use it is money well spent.

FOR FURTHER INFORMATION

Brunswick–Golden Isles Chamber of Commerce
P.O. Box 250
Brunswick, Georgia 31521
(912) 265-0620

St. Simons Island

Glooms of the live oaks, beautiful-braided and woven . . .

So begins "The Marshes of Glynn," the much-celebrated poem by Sidney Lanier (1842–1881). This Georgia-born laureate's words are as familiar to Georgia schoolchildren as Shakespeare's. Lanier lived long enough among the Golden Isles of Georgia's southern coast to absorb their beauty into his soul and sustain his vision through fifteen agonizing, and eventually fatal, years of consumption. Though he wrote the famous poem from afar, while convalescing in Baltimore, his descriptions of the area are stunningly accurate today, even with the looming smoke of Brunswick and the taint of condominiums. Perhaps, then, to do justice to St. Simons Island, the largest of the Golden Isles over which Mr. Lanier's cherished marshes are dispersed, it is best to defer to his words. Here, you will find the same haunted beauty that infuses the island, a place that can be as deep and dark as a tangled forest, or as bright as a shrimp boat heading into the sun.

> *Affable live oak, leaning low*
> *Thus—with your favor—soft, with a reverent hand,*
> *(Not lightly touching your person, Lord of the land!)*
> *Bending your beauty aside, with a step I stand*
> *On the firm-packed sand,*
> *Free by a world of marsh that borders on a world of sea.*

You cannot visit St. Simons without being impressed, if not overwhelmed, by the vegetation. True to the poet's words, oak trees proliferate in such numbers here that they grow almost to the ocean's edge. Though usually not the most affable of God's botanical umbrellas, these oaks somehow seem less haunting when you can step out from under one of their canopies and within a few strides be tramping on the firm-packed sand, looking for seashells. Of course, if you explore the entirety of this island's 2-by-14-mile expanse, you are likely to be affected in the opposite way, resurrecting in your mind's eye the ghosts of the original Guale

Indian inhabitants, or the French explorers, or the Spanish con-
quistadors, or the British, or the slaves and their descendants—
all of whom trod here, lived and died here. You can follow their
ghosts across the graveyards and through the legends that shift in
the gloom of the saw palmettos and Spanish moss.

> *Sinuous southward and sinuous northward the shimmering band*
> *Of the sand-beach fastens the fringe of the marsh to the folds of*
> *the land.*

When the tide shifts and the water rises here, it approaches fast,
obliterating the offshore sandbars and ascending on the land with
a forceful vengeance. When a northeastern gale or a full moon
provokes it, the tide can be downright frightening, especially from
the vantage point of the causeway that runs to the island through
the very heart of the marshes of Glynn County. Truly, it is then
that the sea and the marsh and the sand merge into one.

> *Oh, what is abroad in the marsh and the terminal sea?*

As stated, several different groups of people have, at various
times, visited, conquered and inhabited St. Simons Island. One
can imagine each of these groups looking out to sea and wondering
whose sails would be the next to arrive. Once here, nobody seems
to want to leave this mysterious and beautiful place without a
struggle. In recent years, there has been a new kind of invader.
It is called money, and its conquistador, if given a name, would
be something like Sir Ponce de la Condominium-of-wood. The
vanquished people are the usual victims: the poor and the long-
time natives who can't afford the higher taxes that are dragged like
a shrimper's net behind the boat of overdevelopment. The island
is not too far gone at the present time. In fact, compared to many
places we have seen, it is downright idyllic. But the race is on,
and the year-round population has risen to 10,000 (as compared
to neighboring Jekyll Island's 800).

The latest neighborhood to feel the squeeze is the predominantly
black one on the western, marsh side of the island. It is a former

millworker's community that has heretofore been left alone to stew in its own legends, customs and labors since the latter days of slavery. Curiously enough, it is called Jew Town, and has unabashedly been known by that name as far back as the town library's newspaper accounts go. No doubt, the name will thankfully die even as the condos sadly uproot another island's native people and send them looking for new homes . . . off the island. What is the saying . . . it takes money to make money? Well, it's not too popular down in Jew Town these days.

> *Oh, like the greatness of God is the greatness within*
> *The range of the marshes, the liberal marshes of Glynn.*

Ah, but be not disheartened, readers, a burn-the-bridges movement is afoot, as the newcomers begin to realize the enormity of their land grant called St. Simons. History was forever changed here when the Spanish tried to drive out the British. That ended at the Battle of Bloody Marsh in 1742, the first decisive military battle fought in the New World. It may not be the last decisive battle fought on this island, however. Perhaps the people who come here looking for Hilton Head South will be repelled by the menacing gloom of the stately oaks or the creep-show hair of the Spanish moss.

> *As a silver-wrought garment that clings to and follows the firm sweet*
> *limbs of a girl.*

This was only thrown in to show that Sidney was never so ill that he couldn't occasionally mix the sweet weakness of the flesh into his metaphors. St. Simons Island is definitely not as pious nor as imposing as a saint. Be ready to be swayed.

> *Vanishing, swerving, evermore curving again to sight. . . .*

That's quite enough, Sidney.

Accommodations

If you visit the beach at St. Simons Island, you cannot avoid the *King and Prince Hotel*. In fact, one of the main stretches of ocean-front beach on the island is known unofficially as King and Prince Beach, even though the hotel does not own or police the sandy expanse. Presumably, the hotel has been here so long that everyone just assumes it does. So, you may as well stay at the beach's namesake. It is a venerable establishment, with the red-roofed atmosphere of a hacienda and set directly on the ocean. No other hotel on St. Simons is so situated.

In recent years, a great deal of renovation and expansion has been undertaken. A new addition to the main building has provided 55 new oceanfront rooms. The cocktail tavern takes up two floors of a miniature tower and the once-great lobby is now an entranceway worthy of a king, a prince, a duchess, a duke of earl or a simple wayfaring stranger. Although there are a few other accommodations available on the island, the King and Prince is the only one that makes you feel like an honored guest and not just another bimbo with a credit card.

Restaurants

One of the restaurants that came highly recommended here served the same bland seafood that can be found for half the price at any cafeteria. If you want to pay top dollar for a meal, you are again referred to the *King and Prince*. Dinner is solid surf-and-turf fare, with the prime-rib-and-Lowenbrau crowd battling those who can't get enough fresh seafood. Breakfast is a similarly regal affair; particularly worthy of culinary investigation are the omelettes. Ours were filled with shrimp, asparagus spears, mushrooms and onions and topped with a cheese sauce. Through the windows of the spacious dining room, you can see the shrimp boats passing along the horizon, heading back to port with the prize for tomorrow's platter.

For lunch or dinner, try any of these three less expensive places, all located at the center of town. *Queens*, the oldest family restaurant on the island, has dinner specials for under $4. A radio was playing country music, the food was good, solid, blue-plate-special stuff, and the place was full of real natives, not polyester off-island Roy Clark lookalikes. *Brogens*, though more of a bar, serves great sandwiches in a friendly atmosphere. And, lest we forget the *Rib Cage*, where, if you are truly curious, you can order a bowl of authentic Brunswick stew, as well as hearty barbecue sandwiches and plates.

Nightlife

Usually, to say a place has a civilized nightlife is like saying, "She's got a great personality and is lots of fun," when you mean she weighs 450 pounds. At the beach, "a civilized nightlife" is a euphemism for one drink at a hotel lounge, a short chat about the fate of some team or other with the bartender and a six-pack of beer on ice back in the motel room, sipped while watching a made-for-TV movie about a handicapped athlete. St. Simons Island has a civilized nightlife, but not quite that civilized. It has sort of a healthy, localized flavor that is accommodating to the stranger, though not built for or around him.

Most newcomers are steered to the *Emmeline and Hessie Seafood Restaurant*, which is technically not *on* St. Simons Island. It is an architecture student's idea of a Michelob Light commercial, set on the marsh on the marina side of the bridge onto the island. It has tall ceilings, exposed beams and a sort of Aspen ski lodge atmosphere, with more hanging plants than the National Arboretum. Indeed, it probably is as good a place to start as any, but after two beers, you begin to feel like you don't wear the right kinds of shirts to hang around here. (At least we did.) Much of the crowd is attached to their yachts, docked for the evening at the adjoining "Boat-el." If you come here, order a dozen raw oysters to down with your beer.

For a more substantial slice of St. Simons, try *Richard's*, a bar and discothèque in one of the shopping centers. It strives for the unification of two different worlds, putting the pool tables in back and a dance floor up front. Most people come here to talk and dance. The disco lights look like a makeup mirror run amok, but Richard's is popular with the islanders—estranged mustache men, pretty divorcées and clumps of happy, well-groomed natives. Top Forty is the tone of the tapes, and many songs are repeated several times in an evening, in case you missed them the first time around. The *Horse's Head Pub* is located nearby. It claimed to offer the only live rock 'n' roll on the island. A heavy-metal group called King Rat was playing the week of our visit. We didn't even have to roll down the car windows to know we would not be stopping in.

Toward the center of town, *Blanche's Courtyard*, though primarily known as a restaurant, has live music on the weekends. If you can figure out which door to enter, you will be entertained by ragtime music . . . you know, songs from yesteryear, strummed and plinked by guys in matching striped jackets. Late at night (actually, any time is good), *Brogen's* is the best place in town to be. A loud and congenial knot of regulars gravitates here. The central focus of the place, aside from its affordable beer and good taste in tapes, is a shuffleboard game—a fantastic pastime, as we came to learn, the object of which is to bop each other's metal discs around on a popcorn-salt-covered alley . . . ah, never mind. See for yourself.

FOR FURTHER INFORMATION

St. Simons Island Chamber of Commerce
Neptune Park
St. Simons Island, Georgia 31522
(912) 638-9014

Sea Island

Sea Island is the barrier island that closely borders St. Simons to the east. This can be looked at in one of two ways: it protects St. Simons from the ocean, and it steals most of her beachfront. Though the two islands are often linked in conversation, the only true link between them is the thinnest of roads, which cuts through a marsh. In every other way, they are worlds apart.

Sea Island is a land of old and aging money. Developed in 1926 as one of the South's first millionaires' hideaways, it somehow became known early on as the Cottage Colony, a nickname that has inexplicably stuck with it through the years. Most of the homes here are the size of the Alamo. They may, in fact, have been built with the Alamo in mind, for the architectural style runs toward the Spanish hacienda mold, with many homes painted a tropical pink color, giving Sea Island a breezy casualness that conceals the serious money that went into developing it. Sea Island Drive is the palm tree-lined boulevard that cuts the only path through the forty blocks of residences. Each intersecting street is announced by a sign that looks like a royal family's shield.

New homes are being built on an extra ten-block cul-de-sac that borders on an unpredictable marsh, but the most valuable and exclusive properties are the private palaces that front the ocean. The owners of these mansions pay for their seclusion with more than just money. After a heavy rainfall, the island becomes an oversaturated sponge, and deep pools of water sit on the side streets, rendering them impassable even by a Lincoln Continental.

The *Cloister Hotel* is the one big commercial enterprise on Sea Island, but for some reason it was not built along the beautiful beach. Instead, this internationally renowned resort faces away from the ocean. You can play tennis or sip tall drinks here, but if you want to play golf, you'll have to leave the exclusive Cloister compound. The *Sea Island Golf Course*, like the *Sea Island Gun Club*, is located on St. Simons Island. Figure that one out.

FOR FURTHER INFORMATION

St. Simons Island Chamber of Commerce
Neptune Park
St. Simons Island, Georgia 31522
(912) 638-9014

Jekyll Island

In the cold light of an uncrowded day, Jekyll Island looks more like a millionaires' ghost town than a beach resort. Jekyll Island is state-owned, and great stretches of its 9 ½ miles of beach remain undeveloped. The overall effect is of a certain swampy lassitude. The island is overrun with teeming greenery and hooting birds. Man is almost an afterthought, suffering to get comfortable in the heat and humidity.

First there came the millionaires, rich Yankee industrialists looking for a little slice of Tahiti on the East Coast where they could warm up in the winter. Round about 1886, an informal fraternity of America's biggest tycoons—including such names as Rockefeller, Vanderbilt, Morgan, Pulitzer, Goodyear and Blimp—purchased the island with the intention of establishing a winter retreat. The Jekyll Island Club became a Who's Who of American money, an old-boy network without equal. Here, they could abandon the frigid north for a subtropical Georgian sea island, access to which they strictly controlled per their desire for total privacy.

The money boys wound up packing, never to return, with the sighting of enemy warships in the waters around Jekyll Island at the outset of World War II. At the time of their exodus, the millionaires of Jekyll Island controlled one-sixth of the nation's wealth. What they left behind is now known as *Millionaire's Village*, and a guided tour of their pleasure palaces can be taken for $4. Eight of the thirty-two millionaire's "cottages" are open for inspection. Of particular interest are the Rockefeller home—just a little twenty-five-room shack, you understand—and the home of plumbing magnate Robert Crane, who, in tribute to his particular empire, installed seventeen bathrooms on the premises.

The Jekyll Island Club sold their island, treehouses and all, to the state of Georgia for a paltry $675,000. (It's not as if they needed the money, you see.) Since the time of that sale, in 1947, the state has been a careful watchdog over growth and development on the island. First and foremost, its intention is to give native Georgians a beach of their own, so that they don't go dumping their vacation dollars all over the state of Florida. Golf is a big inducement to come here. There are three 18-hole courses on the island, making Jekyll the largest golf resort in the state of Georgia. (Small beans, however, compared to South Carolina's resort islands.)

The millionaires are gone, and a full-time population of 800 now lives on the island. Their small, single-story brick homes are no match for the sort of dwelling a J. P. Morgan type would throw up with his loose change, but the island has a pleasant middle-class feel to it. It is somehow fitting that Jekyll Island is back in the hands of just-folks from Georgia and not northern robber barons. Correspondingly, a vacation here promises a no-thrills bout of beach and quietude amid the teeming flora and fauna of the dank subtropics.

Accommodations

There are a handful of motels that are in various stages of being converted to condominiums. *The Wanderer* remains a non-condo. It has been around these parts forever, and quite literally "wanders" for about a quarter mile along Beachview Road. *Hilton*, *Holiday Inn* and *Ramada Inn* are all represented here. A number of motel room-cum-private villas reside up at the northern end of the island, but we spent a night at one of these in the most malodorous environment either of us has ever drawn a breath in. The living room gave off a stench that grew stronger with the humidity, prompting us to leave a message to the housekeeping staff on the bathroom mirror in shaving cream: "This place smells like raw sewage."

Accommodations run in the $50 to $60 range in season, with some discounting in the off-season. Depending on how profitable a season they're having, you might be able to score a real deal in a slow summer. Discount coupons for hotels and motels on Jekyll Island, as well as on St. Simons Island, can be had at the *Brunswick U.S.A. Welcome Center* along I-95 just north of Brunswick, or at the visitors' center just before the St. Simons Island Causeway. Despite the bargain prices, we were not impressed overall with the quality and maintenance of the Jekyll Island accommodations, which needed more than just a touching-up with a paintbrush. We left Jekyll Island with the feeling of having marinated in an atmosphere that was decayed, wilted, mildewed and stinky.

Restaurants

Banal motel-restaurant food. The less said, the better.

Nightlife

All of the nightlife is in the hotel/motel lounges. The *Mariner's Cove* lounge at *The Wanderer* books a lot of beach-music originals and is probably the best place to go for dancing. The lounges at *The Buccaneer*, a 210-unit motel, and the *Holiday Inn* can draw a crowd when the music's good. The *Ramada Inn* is home to the *Mr. Hyde Lounge*. (Mr. Hyde is a bit of wordplay on the Robert Louis Stevenson tale *Dr. Jekyll and Mr. Hyde* that doesn't really work, since the Jekyll for whom this island was named was Sir Joseph Jekyll, the main benefactor behind the colony of Georgia.) The bar scene was more of a pesky Hyde than a kindly Jekyll, with lots of loutish locals pawing one another into the wee hours. A better time can be had on St. Simons Island, a mere stone's throw across water, but about a dozen miles by road—and light-years away in manners.

FOR FURTHER INFORMATION

Jekyll Island Tourist Bureau
1 Beachview Drive
Jekyll Island, Georgia 31520
(912) 635-3400

Cumberland Island

Okay campers, this one's for you. Cumberland Island is hardly worth the trouble it takes to get here unless you plan to stick around for a few days to enjoy its isolation from the perspective of a campsite. Cumberland is the largest and southernmost of Georgia's barrier islands, and the longest undeveloped beach on the East Coast. Its beach runs for 20 miles, and the island is 3 miles wide. All 37,000 acres of Cumberland Island are forever off-limits to commercial development.

Reachable only by a passenger ferry that leaves twice daily from the historic river town of St. Marys, Cumberland Island is about as primitive as it gets along the East Coast these days. Although there were visitors and even inhabitants here before the National Park Service instituted the ferry service (the Carnegies built two mansions, one still intact, one in ruins), the island was declared a National Seashore just in time to prevent it from becoming a national golf course. Cumberland might have become another Hilton Head, were it not for the interest-group pressure of conservationists and environmentalists. In fact, in 1968, the bard behind Hilton Head, Charles Fraser, purchased a 3,000-acre tract from three dissident heirs to the Carnegie fortune, to whom the island had fallen, and intended to develop a resort with the enchantingly misleading name Cumberland Oaks. The name was misleading in that many of the Cumberland oaks would have been felled to make way for a golf course.

In any case, he was enjoined to sell, and finally capitulated, so that Cumberland Island remains untamed and free of golf carts. The island is covered with live oaks, palmettos, magnolias and slash pines, which form a forest haven for over 300 species of birds. Alligators roam the marshes and lagoons, and wild horses, pigs and deer have the run of the place. As such, a visit to Cumberland Island can turn into quite an adventure—not your usual sanitized camp trip, with electric hookups for the Winnebago to back up to. Reservations for both campsites and ferry passage should be made in advance. There is only one camping area on the island with any facilities, and that has a sixteen-site/sixty-person limit. Additionally, there are four back-country camping areas that involve hikes of up to 11 miles. If you go for this sort of thing, you won't need us to tell you what to bring along.

The ferry costs $6.25 per person, and your car, of course, stays on the mainland.

FOR FURTHER INFORMATION

Cumberland Island National Seashore
P.O. Box 806
St. Marys, Georgia 31558
(912) 882-5334

Florida:
Orange You Glad
It's Here?

If someone, the CIA maybe, were to snip off the corner of the country known as Florida and allow it to float off into the Caribbean, we Americans might as well strike the word "vacation" from our vocabulary at the same time. Florida is sunshine and beaches, palm trees and coral reefs, Panama hats and flip-flops, bright-hued citrus fruit and rainbow-colored fish. Florida means sandcastles to children, Spring Break to college kids, a two-week reprieve to Mom and Dad and retirement to the old folks.

Florida. The very word seems to warm up a room.

America's love affair with the Sunshine State is a relatively recent thing, in terms of our nation's history. Florida's potential as a vacation paradise was first realized by a man named Henry Flagler, a wealthy industrialist who laid railroad track all over the state. His master stroke was the Florida East Coast Line, which was begun in 1883 and ran from Jacksonville to Key West. Along the way, in towns such as St. Augustine and Palm Beach, Flagler left his architectural imprint in the form of palatial luxury hotels and a private mansion, Whitehall, that is the San Simeon of the East.

In any historical account of Florida, you'll see Flagler's name turn up as often as Ponce de León's. Ponce, as every schoolchild knows, was the man who discovered Florida in 1513. Then the

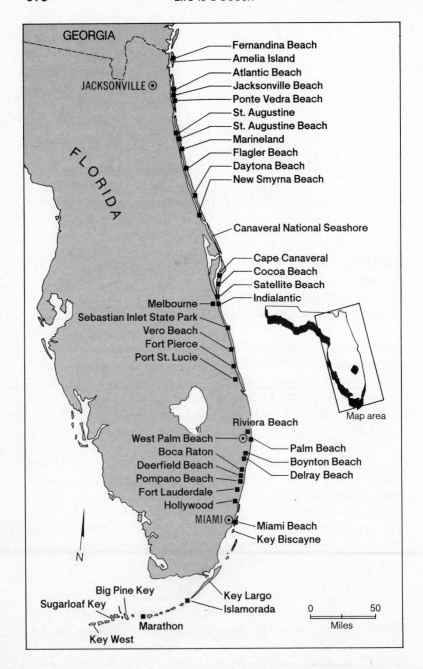

GEORGIA

JACKSONVILLE ⊙

FLORIDA

Fernandina Beach
Amelia Island
Atlantic Beach
Jacksonville Beach
Ponte Vedra Beach
St. Augustine
St. Augustine Beach
Marineland
Flagler Beach
Daytona Beach
New Smyrna Beach

Canaveral National Seashore

Cape Canaveral
Cocoa Beach
Satellite Beach
Indialantic

Melbourne
Sebastian Inlet State Park
Vero Beach
Fort Pierce
Port St. Lucie

Map area

Riviera Beach
West Palm Beach ⊙
Palm Beach
Boca Raton
Boynton Beach
Deerfield Beach
Delray Beach
Pompano Beach
Fort Lauderdale
Hollywood
MIAMI ⊙
Miami Beach
Key Biscayne

N

Big Pine Key
Sugarloaf Key
Key Largo
Islamorada
Marathon
Key West

0   50
Miles

Spanish governor of Puerto Rico, the idealistic explorer believed he would find a Fountain of Youth in this uncharted territory. Far from finding eternal life in Florida, he was killed during his second expedition here.

Florida finally landed in the lap of the English after being batted around like a badminton shuttlecock between Spain and Britain. At the time of its formal admission into the union in 1845, the reluctant Floridians—who were calling for independence—branded this inspirational state motto upon their flag: "Leave Us Alone!"

Today's Floridians are a far more hospitable breed. Florida, in a real sense, is as much a melting pot as Manhattan. People come from all over the nation to live here, retire here, play here and die here. And in the humid heat, you do melt—like a candy bar on a hot sidewalk. If you're at the beach, you can always dash into the water to cool off. The beaches of Florida's east coast are kissed by nearly 3,000 yearly hours of sun, and get a great big bear hug from the Gulf Stream as well. And there is a lot of beach down here—more than any other state in the nation, when you figure the East Coast and the Gulf Coast together. Florida is, after all, a 447-mile peninsula, with the Atlantic Ocean running down one side and the Gulf of Mexico running up the other. That translates, when you take into account the winding shore around all the bays and inlets, into a whopping *8,462 miles* of coastline.

Anita Bryant is not the only one who wants a piece of the Florida sunshine tree. Those 8,462 miles of beach attract 36 million visitors a year. Those 36 million tourists spend a yearly $18 billion having fun. And like the rockets out of Cape Canaveral, Florida's prosperity keeps going up. We could go on wowing you with statistics, but it's a long way from Fernandina Beach to Key West, so let's get right down to the beaches.

Fernandina Beach

Fernandina Beach is a charming, well-preserved city of 8,000 at the northern end of Amelia Island, Florida's northernmost barrier island. By deduction, that would make Fernandina the first beach in Florida for those heading down the coast. Fernandina Beach can, in fact, boast of many other "firsts" and "onlys." Perhaps most notably, Fernandina—and indeed, all of Amelia Island—is the only place in the United States to have been under the rule of eight different flags.

Besides France, Spain, England and the United States, in that order, there are a couple of off-the-wall flags that flew over this strategically situated island. Among them is the Green Cross of Florida—an off-brand that was hoisted over Fort San Carlos in June 1817. That was followed by the Mexican rebel flag, which was raised by an insurgent pirate with a bad sense of direction. Best of all was the ascension of the flag of "the Patriots of Amelia Island," a splinter group of U.S. sympathizers who successfully overthrew the Spanish on March 17, 1812. Their blue-and-white standard fluttered in the breeze for all of one day. All of this is enough to make today's Third World appear stable by comparison, but except for the interim during which the Civil War was fought and the flag of the Confederacy flew over Fort Clinch for less than a year, the Stars and Stripes have graced the Amelia Islanders since 1821.

The post-Civil War years were a real boom period for Fernandina Beach. The first cross-country railroad in Florida originated here and ran clear through to Cedar Key on the Gulf of Mexico. The railroad, and the federal occupation of Fernandina in the aftermath of the Civil War, brought prosperity to the town. Two luxury hotels were built by the railroad, drawing wealthy guests from New York City and the North. Along Centre Street, huge Victorian mansions were built by shipping magnates who made their homes and fortunes in this bustling port city.

Fernandina Beach faded in popularity in the early years of the twentieth century, as the rich abandoned it for more exotic locales, but the city enjoyed a commercial rebound in the second decade with the founding of the modern shrimp industry. Here, the first offshore shrimp trawlers shoved off in 1913. The shrimpers still dock at *City Marina*, which has the signal honor of being Florida's only marine welcome station. Boaters can stop here for free orange juice, maps and so forth.

Lately, the town fathers have been embarking on an ambitious restoration of the historic downtown district. It's been one of the easier such projects, as the buildings have been well maintained all along. The thirty-block *Centre Street Historic District* features many examples of elegant Victoriana in what would seem an unlikely location—between the Georgia border and the city of Jacksonville in the swampy middens of eastern Florida. The theme of preservation and renewal has been extended to the shopping district, where storefronts have been re-created in the style of the previous century. Best of all, the town is not merely a cosmetic, dollhouse revival of glory days. Fernandina Beach is a real working community of shrimpers and fishermen. What with its architectural past, its maritime present and the first glimpse of Florida's fabled shoreline, Fernandina Beach is worth a visit. Maybe not a long one, but certainly a stopover.

Accommodations

There are a fair number of bed-and-breakfast inns along the beach and huddled in the historic district. The *Bailey House* has lately been turned into such an establishment. Built in 1895 by an agent for a steamship company, it was one of the most elaborately constructed homes of its day, with many turrets, gables and bays outside and period antiques, brass beds and carved furniture inside.

For a complete list of inns and motels, write the chamber of commerce or, if in the area, drop by. It's located in what used to be the train depot, along Centre Street near the waterfront. You can also elect to camp at *Fort Clinch State Park*, the site of a never-completed pre-Civil War fort on Cumberland Sound. The park has numerous campsites and is only a short distance from the beaches and the town center.

Restaurants

For the best local seafood, take your pick of the *1735 House* (on the beach), *The Crab Trap* or *Snug Harbor* (both in the historic district). Roasted oysters and broiled rock shrimp are specialties here.

Nightlife

High on your list of must-visits if you pass through Fernandina is *The Palace*, which is the oldest bar in Florida. It was built in 1878, thrived in the Gay Nineties and is not doing too badly in the Eighties, by the look of things. Little has changed, in fact. A piano player pumps out singalong standards on a rickety upright eighty-eight, and frosty mugs are slid down the hand-carved oak bar by an amiable tap man. Grizzled veterans of uncountable tavern nights huddle in clutches, deformed by alcohol into the preposterous shapes of twisted balloons. One ruddy-faced salt elbowing up to the bar wore a hat with plumage so ludicrous it would have embarrassed a Barbary Coast pirate, and to the brim of this creation was pinned what looked like a card with his name on it. In case he forgot? we wondered. The way things used to be is the way things are in the Palace Saloon. By the way, do not leave without eating an order of steamed Fernandina shrimp.

FOR FURTHER INFORMATION

Fernandina Beach Chamber of Commerce
P.O. Box 472
Fernandina Beach, Florida 32034
(904) 261-3248

Amelia Island Plantation

Amelia Island is a unique environment. The island sits at the edge of the northern range for palm trees and other tropical flora, and is simultaneously the southernmost extremity for sea pines and plants that thrive in more temperate climes. The overlap makes for a fascinating zone of vegetation. Birds, too: over 260 species drop in en route to nests north or south. The endangered alligator makes a home here as well, though the reptiles must be removed once they've reached the adult stage because people tend to treat them more like lovable pooches than child-eating carnivores. Thus, they are relocated to a more secluded environment. (Would you ever have guessed that these fearsome reptiles are lured to the surface and into nets with a bait of *marshmallows*?)

Somewhere on Amelia Island, it is believed, is a huge buried treasure of gold. Amelia has some of the most notorious names in sea thievery in her past, including Jean Lafitte, Blackbeard and Captain Kidd, so buried treasure is a tempting speculation, drawing bounty hunters with Geiger-counter metal detectors hoping for a miracle. The truth, if it's gold you're looking for, is there's probably more to be found around the wrists and necks of the men and women who come to Amelia Island Plantation.

If Kiawah Island, South Carolina, is the filet mignon of resort plantations along the south Atlantic coast, then Amelia Island is at least the broiled lobster. Together, they are a prize surf-and-turf combination. Amelia Island very nearly could have turned out looking more like hell's half-acre than the peerless pearl of the East Coast. The Union Carbide Corporation originally held title to the land upon which the plantation sits (after the Timaquan Indians and the flags of eight nations, of course). The chemical firm intended to strip-mine the land for potassium. Fortunately, the 900 acres upon which Amelia Island was built was sold to developer Charles Fraser. Fraser locked horns with President Johnson over the issue of developing his barrier islands. As it turned out, Fraser's plantations were constructed with careful consideration for the natural environment, while Johnson would preside over a massive defoliation of the jungles of Vietnam.

The 900-acre Amelia Island tract was developed in prescient anticipation of a class of people with novel vacation desires. These were people of means who wished for privacy and recreation in a sylvan natural setting at the sea's edge. Not gaudy monstrosities rising out of tree-strafed sand lots, but tasteful condominium dwellings that blended with nature and were hidden in the cooling shade of oak trees and palmettos. And there had to be the very best golf courses and tennis courts, as well as top-quality instructors. Amelia Island Plantation has three 9-hole golf courses, all designed by master course architect Pete Dye. Tennis-wise, you can follow the bouncing ball right to Chris Evert Lloyd's condo. Chris and husband John Lloyd make their year-round home here, and Chris' brother, Drew Evert, is the resident pro.

You pay, of course, to keep such exclusive company. Amelia Island tends to draw a clientele of retirees, conventioneers and honeymooners. The first group has made a killing, the second is making a killing and the last are about to. We are talking about the kind of money that makes money obsolete: all transactions are made via a charge card that is issued upon your arrival. Goods and services are run up on a computerized account and paid for with plastic at the end of your stay. Even tips are automatically figured into your bill "for your convenience."

This is how it is done at Amelia Island Plantation, as well as many other such resorts we visited. Saves all that messing around with folding money, which is such a bother, you know?

Accommodations

If you have to ask how much you'll pay here, you should probably be thinking more along the lines of Myrtle Beach. Still, as we've tried to stress, cost is relative to quality, and the difference between a $120-a-night villa at a place like Amelia and an $80 shoebox motel room in an overcrowded honky-tonk beach ghetto is greater than $40. On Amelia Island Plantation, you can choose from an ocean-front room in the *Amelia Island Inn* or a privately owned condominium apartment. The latter are spread out all over the property and range in size from one to four bedrooms. Some face the ocean, and some are set back on the inland side of Route A1A. They fall in the $100- to $200-a-night range, depending on size, location and season. Michael Jackson chose to stay here when the Jacksons played Jacksonville (no relation) back in 1984, about a week before our less-heralded arrival. Jackson went straight to the top: a "pool villa," which features an indoor pool in addition to the usual lavish appointments.

Restaurants

Amelia Island Plantation has a number of restaurants on the premises where you can drop a bundle of money with the flick of a Bic pen. The *Duneside Club* is "oceanfront and elegant"; jackets are required. *The Verandah* is more relaxed, with an all-American menu of seafood, beef and chicken—a bring-the-family kind of place. The *Beach Club Steak House* is high-toned and casual, featuring steak and prime rib. Here, too, is the lounge where the after-dinner entertainment takes place. In addition, there are snack bars and an ice-cream parlor scattered about the plantation. Room service is another alternative, even if you've camped out in some far-off villa. Lastly, there's always nearby Fernandina Beach, which has some good restaurants, or Jacksonville, which has some even better ones.

Nightlife

For all intents and purposes, there is none, save for the rather low-key goings-on at the *Beach Club Lounge*. Here, you'll sip frozen tropical drinks, sit in high-back wicker chairs and make goo-goo eyes at your paramour while the band plays some Andrews Sisters or Lionel Ritchie songs in the background. If you're over 35, you're probably already asleep by the time the band strikes up the first tune, in anticipation of an early-morning tee-off. If you find yourself exquisitely bored, twiddling thumbs while watching your peach daiquiri turn to orange slush, then you probably shouldn't have come here in the first place.

But really, Amelia Island is about daytime recreation and nighttime relaxation. Golf. Tennis. Year-round swimming on 4 miles of perfect beach. Biking and hiking. Fishing in the ocean, inland waterways or, better yet, in one of the stocked lagoons on the grounds. Let's get reflective here: a ride along sun-dappled bikeways out to the marsh at *Drummond Point* or to the *Sunken Forest* just behind the barrier dunes will yield more in the way of personal gratification than another desultory evening spent in a citified discothèque environment.

FOR FURTHER INFORMATION

Amelia Island Plantation
Amelia Island, Florida 32034
(800) 874-6878

Jacksonville

Jacksonville sits just over the Florida state line in an area of the country more often sped through than sought out by vacationers. In years past, if travelers stopped in the Jacksonville vicinity at all, it was only overnight, as it makes a convenient layover on the long run to or from Fort Lauderdale and Miami. This is all changing somewhat, as Jacksonville is a southern city on the upswing, becoming a place deserving of tourist attention in its own right.

Statistically, Jacksonville stands alone by dint of a curious distinction: it has the largest incorporated land area of any city in the United States. Although this fact is etched in black and white into the record books, it is with some incredulity that we report that Jacksonville's city limits encircle 841 square miles. Translated into road language, this means that you pass a green sign on I-95 that reads "Jacksonville City Limits," then you drive for another 15 minutes before you see the first sign of civilization—a billboard for McDonald's. In quick succession, though, you thereupon pass an international airport, some sparsely settled outlying suburbs and then—boom!—you are suddenly in the heart of Jacksonville. Taking up a mere corner of its prodigious square mileage, downtown Jacksonville clings to the banks of the busy St. Johns River. The city's proud new skyline is reflected in the slow-moving waters of the St. Johns, making for a fine photo opportunity and lending Jacksonville a chic cosmopolitan sheen.

Jacksonville is the classic resurgent southern city. Having taken its knocks over the years for being merely a sun-baked haven for navy boys, shirtless rock 'n' rollers and insurance salesmen whose companies put them on hold here to wait out a promotion, Jacksonville is no longer a void. The downtown waterfront area has undergone the same Rouse-architected facelift that revived Baltimore's harbor area, and the skyscrapers are growing behind it like a bumper crop of concrete and steel. And there are things to do: a zoo to stroll in, the Busch beer plant to tour (yes, with free samples), art museums to browse and even an "ArtBeat" phone number to dial for info on current cultural events. There is a massive interstate system that lassoes the frenzy. With a half-million people and more coming all the time, an average yearly temperature of 78 degrees, palm and palmetto trees and beautiful beaches nearby, Jacksonville is a junior-varsity Los Angeles. Of course, this also means that the highways are more like raceways, with the addition of water hazards to spice up the driving experience. Our best advice is that which is given to every novice in LA—if you miss your exit, hold on tight to the steering wheel and go with the flow. Eventually, you'll hit the beach.

Jacksonville's beaches are located 12 miles from the downtown area, which translates to a 20-minute drive on one of three major thoroughfares. These beaches are a prism of possibilities—from the northern naval bombshell of Mayport (best avoided) to beautiful, unspoiled Catherine Abbey Hanna Park, and south through the middle-class residential communities of Atlantic Beach and Neptune Beach, the commercial hubbub of Jacksonville Beach (a.k.a. Jax Beach), the old-money manses of Ponte Vedra, the new-money palaces of Sawgrass and, finally, miles and miles of untouched wilds and dunes known as South Ponte Vedra. Let's see . . . what more could there possibly be? Like the city they very nearly adjoin, all of these seashell-strewn beach towns are true diamonds in the rough. "So *this* is Jacksonville?" we kept remarking, startled to find a city so different from the one we'd expected.

Two of the above-mentioned beaches deserve to be singled out for further comment. First, seldom will you find a park as nicely laid out as *Catherine Abbey Hanna Park*. Located just south of Mayport on A1A, this 450-acre oceanfront park features a half-mile beach that is pleasing to the eye. Here are sand dunes so healthy that trees grow out of them. There are hiking trails, a stocked freshwater lake and 300 campsites set in the shade of an Everglades-like forest. Admission is 25 cents per person; never has two bits been so well spent.

The second area that begs more description is Jacksonville Beach. It's a straight shot out of Jacksonville to Jacksonville Beach, which is the hub of vacation activity and the only town in the area that can be called densely commercialized. Most of the commercialism is a benign, unfocused hodgepodge of leather shops, seashell sellers (say that three times quickly), small delicatessens, liquor stores with attached cinder-block lounges, and a 2,000-seat pavilion lording over it all, with flags from every state in the union waving overhead. Amid all this are some unsightly blemishes—mainly boarded-up bucket-of-blood saloons and a few that are still open for business, with the usual array of two-wheel choppers lined up out front. This developmental dichotomy—we had the feeling that Jacksonville Beach was in the midst of a transition upward—leads to such curious spectacles as a biker and a businessman or a Yuppie and a punk sharing the same sidewalk, shoulder to shoulder. The same sight in a New Jersey Shore town would have filled us with unutterable dread, but here it only served to underscore the casual, unstylized atmosphere of the northern Florida coast.

Accommodations

Nearly all the surrounding communities are residential, leaving Jacksonville Beach as the center of the tourist trade on this stretch of the coast. Most of the major chains are represented, including *Holiday Inn*, *Howard Johnson's* and the budget-priced *Friendship Inn*. Holiday Inn, in particular, assumes a high profile along the Florida coast; we'd noticed it only sporadically heretofore. The Friendship Inn chain is well worth looking into. When available, you can save $10 or $20 a night over the name-brand competition, and the accommodations, if not glamorous, are always adequate.

Sea Turtle Inn in nearby Atlantic Beach towers above the competition in Jax Beach, offering plush rooms at moderate rates in a high-rise right on the ocean. There is a relaxed air of professionalism here that goes well with the beautiful beach in front of it.

Indeed, we felt like we were back on Hilton Head Island or Litchfield Beach, not butting up against a city of 350,000.

Restaurants

The reputation of Jacksonville's cuisine, like the cultural scene, has been on the rise. It's nothing to rival, say, Charleston, but is improving yearly. If you want a truly fine dinner, you'll have to head back into town, for the pickin's at the beachfront are pretty slender. If you do brave the freeways, you'll find plenty to choose from in the downtown and greater Jacksonville areas. Seafood specialties are served in a Victorian mansion at the *Hilltop Club* in Orange Park (a southwest Jacksonville suburb). A great array of fresh seafood is served at *The Sailmaker* in downtown Jacksonville. You can choose from eight to ten types of fish daily, and have it fried, broiled or mesquite-grilled. *Pier 6 Oyster House and Seafood Restaurant*, on Jacksonville's south side, tends toward Maine lobster and seafood platters. As an appetizer, you can order local Appachiola oysters at only 10 cents per.

One of the best places on the beach is the restaurant at the *Sea Turtle Inn*, with a wide seafood menu including such local catches as red snapper and grouper, but alas, no sea turtle. Nice atmosphere, to boot. Across the street is the *Ragtime Tavern*, a motif bar and restaurant with the main riff being New Orleans. Its lunch specials are a good way to gauge your taste for this particular style. If you're hooked, go all out and have an honest-to-goodness Louisiana-style dinner at the *Cajun Catfish* in Jax Beach.

Nightlife

Around Jacksonville, you see a classic dichotomy of archetypes between surfers (blond, tan, fit) and bikers (beer guts, hair everywhere, surly). The nightlife scene kind of cleaves along these lines. The upscale disco-dance clubs attract the healthier-looking hunks and lithesome beach lovelies, and the roadhouse lounges draw the residue.

There is a long-standing tradition of rabble-rousing rock 'n' roll in Jacksonville. In the mid-seventies, some of the most stalwart of the southern rock bands to spring up in the wake of the Allman Brothers—e.g., Lynyrd Skynyrd, the Outlaws—hailed from Jacksonville. They reveled in the proud regionalism of their southern roots and came on like gangs of thugs, mean and ornery and full of rotgut whiskey. There was more smoke than fire here, however, and when the smoke cleared, what was left was a raft of roughneck clichés grounded in the Hell's Angels philosophy: good old boys with hair down to their waists, no shirts, busted-up boots and an attitude that said, "I'll kick your ass if you look at me or my old lady. I'll kick your ass if you ain't southern. Hell, I'll kick your ass for any old reason."

You can still find the last flickers of that world in the nondescript cinder-block roadhouses and blighted-area poolhalls that line the beach boulevards. Your cues will be: 1) an absence of windows, 2) an abundance of Harleys and 3) a cinder parking lot. If you would like to emerge at the end of the evening with your physiognomy intact, you may wish to look elsewhere for entertainment. Actually, we had a swinging time at the *Holiday Inn's Top Cat Lounge*, a penthouse disco that mixed decent rock 'n' roll records in with the expected Top Forty smashes. The deejay even took our request for an obscure Pretenders song. And that's a far cry from being poked in the eye with a pool cue.

Other than a smorgasbord of movies, the nightlife seemed salaciously slanted toward "adult entertainment." We did find an innocuous folksinger playing at *Shucker's Beach Club*, a combination raw bar, nightclub and restaurant in Jacksonville Beach. The latter proved a comfortable place to stare at a beer bottle and/or an unattached member of the opposite sex. On certain theme nights, they even provide incentives to mingle: the best minglers win free dinners from the restaurant, and no doubt collect in other ways as well.

Last of all, we stumbled on a rock 'n' roll tavern, the *Crystle* [sic] *Palace*, that pretty much escaped the roughneck stereotype (i.e., tennis shoes were as welcome as biker boots). It had the unkempt rowdiness of a good rock 'n' roll bar: dim lights, thick smoke and loud, loud music.

FOR FURTHER INFORMATION

Convention and Visitors' Bureau of Jacksonville and Its Beaches
206 Hogan Street
Jacksonville, Florida 32202
(904) 353-9736

Jacksonville Area Beaches Chamber of Commerce
P.O. Box 50427
413 Pablo Avenue
Jacksonville Beach, Florida 32250
(904) 249-3868

St. Augustine

"St. Augustine is *not* a college town, and it is *not* a tourist town," we were told over the din of prerecorded music at a hotel discothèque on a crowded Friday night. Since we had not suggested that it was either of those things, we began to wonder. Using our new friend's unsolicited "is nots" as a starting point, we set out to determine just what St. Augustine, the oldest continuously settled city in America, is all about.

It turns out that our source was right on one count and wrong on another. St. Augustine most definitely is not a college town. Tiny Flagler College is located here, in a Spanish Renaissance-style building that used to be the Ponce de León Hotel back in the gilded age of Florida's east coast. But one minor institution of higher learning does not a college town make—even a small town of 13,000.

To deny that St. Augustine is a tourist town, however, is sheer folly. The defensiveness is understandable: to call a place a "tourist town" is to imply that it has no life of its own beyond bedding and bilking the transient hordes. Thus, the long lines of cars down the streets and across the bridges are not seen as dollars flowing into the community but as a traffic-snarling nuisance that compromises their quality of life. But think: without them, St. Augustine would be a dry, dead little town indeed.

Yes, St. Augustine is a tourist town, for better or worse. Given its battle-scarred, war-torn four centuries of history, tourism seems a fortuitous fate after all. St. Augustine is referred to in tourist literature as "the City of the Centuries." The white colonial presence dates back to 1513, when Ponce de León landed somewhere in the vicinity of St. Augustine, in effect "discovering" the state of Florida. But half a dozen subsequent attempts by the Spanish to settle the area proved fruitless, and it was the French who established the first permanent settlement. King Philip II of Spain empowered the explorer Menendez to redress this situation, and with guns and trumpets blaring, Menendez landed at St. Augustine on September 8, 1565, with 600 colonists, who routed the French from the territory.

Their troubles, it turned out, were only beginning. The Spanish were besieged by the British and by pirates in the 1600s and 1700s, and Spain ceded Florida to British rule in 1763. This interlude lasted for a scant twenty years, during which the American Revolution was fought. Florida remained loyal to the British Crown, not to the colonies. The war's outcome angered the Floridian loyalists, and Florida reverted to Spanish rule in 1783. After all that, Spain sold Florida back to the United States, which took possession of the territory in 1821. So long, Spain.

Not that the dove of peace was ready to smile upon the St. Augustinians and their sun-kissed land. The city was in a condition of apathy and decay at the time of its Americanization, and found itself beset in ensuing decades by catastrophe after catastrophe: a yellow-fever epidemic, a calamitous winter freeze that decimated the orange groves and a bloody war with the Seminole Indians that culminated in an ambush massacre of an entire regiment of troops. Then came the Civil War. For most of its duration, St. Augustine was under Union occupation.

A lot of blood has been spilled in the streets of St. Augustine. Indeed, when one inquires into the "glorious" past of a town like St. Augustine, one finds only hardship and an almost inconceivable record of violence and cruelty. It was only after railroad and resort magnate Henry Flagler took an interest in the east coast of Florida, and St. Augustine in particular, that the city began to enjoy any sort of genteel life at all. The era of gracious living came to St. Augustine in the early decades of this century, when wealthy northerners would trek down to stay at one of Flagler's palatial hotels and to enjoy the warm air, scented with orange blossoms and shaded by palms.

Nowadays, St. Augustine is a peaceful haven in which you can study the relics and embattlements of the past without having to worry about whizzing cannonballs, smoking muskets or flaming tomahawks. The number of museums and restorations is, frankly, overwhelming. The city's active preservation society has restored buildings and houses along St. George Street in the downtown district, and the chamber of commerce, in its detailed and helpful visitors' guide, lists no fewer than eighty-eight attractions within the city limits.

Where do you start? Well, St. Augustine can be toured by sight-seeing trolleys, which take in something like fifty points of interest. These trolley tours include drop-off privileges—which means you can disembark at will and reboard a later trolley at no extra charge—but they do not include admission fees to the attractions themselves, some of which are fairly steep. The city is also eminently walkable; with a comfortable pair of shoes and a good map, you can see most of what needs to be seen at your own pace. A lot of places can be left out of your itinerary.

In St. Augustine, as in any tourist town, there are authentic spots of historical and architectural interest. Then there are gyp joints. Take the purported *Fountain of Youth*, which is not really the spring that Ponce de León was alleged to have discovered, but "a well symbolizing the traditional search for the Fountain of Youth." Three dollars is a lot to pay for a sip of the city's brownish, fishy-smelling water, and the planetarium and Indian burial grounds also on the premises are not enough to make this a worthwhile attraction.

There are a lot of "oldest" buildings in town as well, many of dubious dollar value. The *Oldest Schoolhouse*, *Oldest Jail*, *Oldest Drug-store*—snoozy stops along the sort of bullhorn tour many folks seem to go ga-ga for. At the Oldest Store, for instance, a "fabulous collection of yesterday's mementoes will make you realize how far we have come since the days of the steam-powered tractor, Grand-pa's red underwear and the Gibson Girl corset." We'll bet you a pair of Grandpa's red underwear that you'll be yawning inside of five minutes.

Some of the sights are administered by the St. Augustine Historical Society. These at least have the cloak of legitimacy about them, and won't snake your pocketbook quite so severely as the ones under private ownership. The best stops, in fact, cost the least. It only costs 50 cents, for instance, to enter the venerable *Castillo de San Marco*. The building of this enormous, impregnable fortress (it has never been captured) began in 1672 by the Spanish, in response to the constant attacks upon the town and their treasure fleets. As there was virtually no stone to be found in this sandy locale, they constructed their fortress from coquina—the rocklike substance built up from the calcified remains of many billions of butterfly clams into a coral-type mass. The coquina was quarried by a chain gang of convicts and Indian slaves, and the fort, which took fifteen years to complete, proved to be an ineradicable defense that frustrated all adversaries. Coquina turned out to be far *better* than rock and concrete, in fact.

Coquina was used to build most of the public buildings and private homes in St. Augustine, as well as another fort, Mantanzas, on adjacent Anastasia Island. In the late 1800s, Henry Flagler built his three resort hotels—the Ponce de León, the Alcazar and the Cordova—out of coquina. As previously mentioned, the Ponce de León now belongs to Flagler College, and its courtyard is open to the public. The Alcazar is now City Hall in the front and the *Lightner Museum* in the back; the latter houses a vast collection of Victorian antiques. And the Cordova, an impressive structure built in imposing Venetian Renaissance style, is now the *Flagler Memorial Presbyterian Church*. All are well worth seeing; Flagler was the Conrad Hilton of his day.

Near the Castillo de San Marco, which is now a National Monument, is the *Nombre de Dios Mission*, where, in 1565, the first parish mass in North America was conducted. Since St. Augustine was founded before the British colonies at Jamestown and Plymouth Rock, the mass at Nombre de Dios ("Name of God") can be regarded as "the first community act of Christian religion in what is now the United States." The grounds surrounding the mission are beautiful and serene. A 208-foot-tall stainless-steel cross commemorates the site where the first cross was planted on Florida soil. There is no fixed admission fee, but a voluntary donation is suggested.

Beyond all this, we urge you to stroll down St. George Street, in the heart of the restored district. Maps and info galore can be had at the *St. Augustine Visitors' Information Center*, which is an excellent place to begin. Again, there are a lot of places of genuine historical interest in St. Augustine amid bogus tourist fare. There are wax museums and alligator farms aplenty for those who are inclined toward the latter.

St. Augustine is a beach-and-boating town as well as a showcase for history, though the former activities tend to take a back seat to the procession of antiquity before the tourist's glazed eyes. There is heavy boat traffic along the Intracoastal Waterway through here. And across A1A over the Bridge of Lions lies St. Augustine Beach. During our visit, the beach was experiencing erosion problems, and our oceanfront motel room was very nearly an indoor pool. The waves broke against a seawall, and a chain-link fence ensured that no swimming would be done. But St. John's County, of which St. Augustine is the county seat, fronts nearly 43 miles of coast, from Ponta Vedra Beach to Summer Haven, and much of it is quite isolated and unbuilt-on. Anastasia State Park, which is part of St. Augustine Beach, offers the best swimming opportunities in the immediate area.

Getting back to the original assertion—that St. Augustine is not a tourist town—consider these facts: St. Augustine is annually visited by 1.2 million people, who pump $100 million a year into this small town's economy. Case closed.

Accommodations

St. Augustine is ruled by the chain motels and hotels. Basically, then, you should begin by picking a location. There are three areas in which accommodations are clustered: along San Marco Avenue and Avenida Menendez (actually, they're one and the same street), which run by Matanzas Bay in the downtown historic district; along Anastasia Boulevard, over the Bridge of Lions at the north end of Anastasia Island, in the direction of the beach; and along A1A on the oceanfront in St. Augustine Beach. If you want to see the sights and soak up history, stay downtown. If you want to be near the ocean, stay in St. Augie's Beach. But with the rampant erosion we witnessed, St. Augustine Beach would not be our first choice for that sort of Florida vacation. In short, stay downtown. All the sights are within walking distance. Prices in season tend to be rather high, but after Labor Day, you couldn't pay much more than $30 a night if you wanted to. We got a great deal at the *Ramada Inn*. Thanks to the American dollar's strength abroad, tourism in general has been down in Florida in recent years, and price cutting has become quite common. So shop for a bargain, and check the motel marquees and visitors' center bins for rock-bottom price quotes. Lastly, there are always the popular budget motel chains—*Scottish Inn*, *Econo Lodge*, *Days Inn*—which are a thrifty alternative to the costly elder-statesman motel chains.

Restaurants

Located in an exquisitely furnished two-story house in downtown St. Augustine, *The Raintree* will make you forget you're mere feet from busy San Marco Avenue. The menu is continental, with such dishes as Veal O'Connor (topped with shrimp and hollandaise sauce), Brandy Peppersteak (smothered in a rich cream sauce) and Lobster Thermidor being several of the house specialties. Once you've been here, you'll likely return with every visit to St. Augustine.

The city also boasts an excellent gourmet Italian restaurant, *Aldo's*, and a number of good seafood houses. The best of these might be *Cap's Seafood Restaurant*, 3 miles north of town on A1A. Try the pompano amandine: pompano, the filet mignon of fish, is native to these waters. Also, order the St. Augustine shrimp on any menu, as they are renowned for their size and sweetness.

Nightlife

The disaffected, tourist-spurning under-30 population of St. Augustine likes to regard their city as Greenwich Village South—a place where handicrafts and folk art and occult wisdom thrive amid a beaming New Age consciousness. Correspondingly, you find a lot of coffeehouses and jazz dens and intimate porchside wine bars in St. Augustine. And no action. Ever hopeful, though, we walked into what was reputed to be "*the* downtown nightspot for Top Forty, pop, new wave and disco dancing fun!" at 10:30 on a balmy Thursday night, and found the place deserted. So we made for *Scarlett O'Hara's*, a wood-and-fern lounge in a two-story house where a middle-age combo was playing jazz, and it was wall to wall. Scarlett O'Hara's is clearly very popular.

Over on St. George Street, there is a spate of English pub-type places. Two of the more frequented among them are the *St. George Tavern* and the *White Lion Tavern*. If you walk down the street, you may chance to hear live music emanating from one of the tavern windows—anything from a weepy folksinger to the grinding guitars of a rock band.

But by and large, for the sort of cheap thrills that were the mainstay of this odyssey of ours, we had to travel to St. Augustine Beach. There is nightlife to be found here in some of the hotel discothèques and at a place called *Passport*. Passport is generally packed with a young crowd who bop merrily to the Top Forty. The bar and the dance floor are big, and so are the generous and inexpensive glasses of draft poured here.

Still, even the best places in St. Augustine and its beach have a tincture of restraint. The bars here shut down at 1 A.M., as opposed to 3 and 4 A.M. in Jacksonville and Daytona Beach to the north and south. On our return to Passport our second night in town, the marquee advertised a "lady's legs contest." Such events are ipso facto embarrassing, but this one lacked even the remotest compensatory titillation. The winner, by the way, wore a bag over her head.

Next stop: *Sister Sally's* lounge in the *Holiday Inn*. We caught the tail end of a fashion show that vainly struggled to affect a certain cosmopolitan glamour. The atmosphere was plush, and the

well-dressed crowd circulated with a proper cocktail-party de-
meanor. The gossip we'd heard and the advertising seemed to
suggest that liaisons could be forged here, but our social mal-
adroitness in disco settings thwarted us once again. Worse, some
local halfwit somehow got the bizarre idea that we were attempting
to "force" a girl to dance with us, and challenged us to a fight.
Most fights in bars start because someone is looking for trouble;
any old excuse will do. Our adversary actually thought he was
being chivalrous. "If you want to fight, you know where to look
me up," he muttered mysteriously before stumbling off. We left
Sister Sally's, and St. Augustine, scratching our heads.

FOR FURTHER INFORMATION

St. Augustine and St. Johns County Chamber of Commerce
P.O. Drawer O
Lightner Building
75 King Street
St. Augustine, Florida 32085
(904) 829-5681

Visitor Information Center
10 Castillo Drive
St. Augustine, Florida 32084

Marineland

The incorporated township of Marineland (pop. 8) is home to the
world's most popular marine-oriented tourist attraction. The porpoise of Marineland (pardon the pun) is to provide an entertainment
spectacle starring creatures from the deep: an underwater "Ed
Sullivan Show," as it were. The porpoises and sea lions are the
standup comedians and gymnasts; the electric eels are the magi-
cians, throbbing like neon signs. A multidimensional film, *Sea
Dream*, immerses you in the violent underwater world of sharks,
barracudas and stingrays.

An adult ticket to Marineland, good for all shows and exhibits, costs $6. Located 20 miles south of St. Augustine and 40 miles north of Daytona Beach, Marineland would make a feasible day trip from either city. There is a *Quality Inn* at Marineland, however, if you want to stay overnight.

As long as you're in the area, or even if you're just passing through, *Washington Oaks State Gardens* offers thrills of a more sublime nature. Nature is indeed sublime on the 390 acres of this lovely park, deeded to the state by its former owners. Located several miles south of Marineland, Washington Oaks looks like all of coastal Florida did before our European forebears arrived. There is great variety within a brief distance here. As you move inland from the water's edge, you pass from exposed coquina rock on the beach to coastal scrub (stunted, wind-warped vegetation) to a coastal hammock community (live oak, magnolia, hickory) and finally to a tidal marsh bordering the Matanzas River. A short nature trail winds through the hammock and along the river. The park's man-made gardens are beautiful as well, with colorful flowers and exotic plants such as the giant elephant's ear. Dirt pathways wind through the oaks, their limbs overhung with Spanish moss, past a spring-fed pond and beautiful patches of roses, camellias and azaleas. All in all, we found Washington Oaks to be one of the most peaceful spots on Florida's east coast.

Daytona Beach

A beautiful local woman, a haircutter by trade, was sitting at the bar of a popular native hangout, checking out the scene with a gangster lean. She tilted her head and spoke sideways, pushing her hip-length hair aside as if it was a motel-room curtain. "Excuse me for not looking directly at you when I speak," she explained, "but my girl friend was supposed to meet a guy here and I can't find . . . There she is!" She smiled and waved toward the back of the place, then turned her attention back to the matter at hand.

"Oh yes, you want to know why Daytona is called the World's Most Famous Beach. Well, first of all you tell them that we have the most beautiful girls on the East Coast, and then if that's not enough, you can say that no place else in the world will let you drive your car right up to the water."

The conversation hung there as we digested this information, then suddenly a song from the jukebox sliced through the chatter of the happy-hour throng. One beat, two beats, an onslaught of drums and then a voice giving words to the undeniable credo of Daytona Beach: "Whoa-oh-ah, girls just wanna have fuh-hun, girls just wanna have fun. . . ." The lovely haircutter excused herself from the bar and ran across the room to greet her friend. From afar, she could be seen laughing and joking with an entire town full of admirers for the rest of the evening.

Let's face it, Phil Donahue has inspired us to deal with the truth. Every subject, no matter how sore or seamy, must be faced head on, with no averted eyes, no apologies and no quarter. What follows may sound like a sexist rant, but it is the gospel truth, so help us God. The truth is, Daytona Beach has got the girls.

They are everywhere. Girls riding mopeds on the sand. Girls in gold slippers walking poodles that wear more clothes than they do. Girls on bicycles, oblivious under Walkman headphones, beaming Mona Lisa smiles. Girls at night, dressed to maim. Girls dancing together to the latest tunes, because the boys are somber in cowboy hats and surfer shades. Girls in cowgirl hats and shit-kicker boots. Girls in mini-dresses and high heels. Girls in leather pants and headbands. Always in packs. Girls, pretty ones, even in the sad topless go-go lounges. Girls under bright blinking dance-floor lights, laughing at themselves. Girls, girls, girls. Oh boy.

When it comes to girls, the Beach Boys are going to have to do a lot more than sing on the Fourth of July to convince us it gets any better than this in California. They may wish they all could be California girls, but on the East Coast, Daytona Beach will do just fine.

That such a culture would exist here is no real mystery. The beach is 23 miles long, 18 miles of which can be driven on. The water and air temperature are warm all year round. There are thousands of motel rooms begging to be trashed by young customers. The local merchants seem to encourage a young crowd to come here, with special packages for the legendary Spring Break months of February and March. They also encourage them to party, as if they needed any urging, by leaving the bars and clubs open till three or four in the morning, seven nights a week. Because it is such a buyer's market, very few of the clubs charge a stiff cover. To a pair of travel-weary, disco-whipped veterans of many months on the road, Daytona Beach was almost too good to be true.

Families come here, too. The operative spirit seems to be that there's room enough for everybody. And then, of course, there are the girls. Did we mention them?

Daytona Beach is equally well-known for cars, which can be found both on the beach and at the raceway. The beach, in fact, *was* the raceway until the late fifties, when the *International Raceway* was constructed a few miles inland. Neighboring Ormond Beach (a lookalike cousin to Daytona) is called the Birthplace of Speed. It was so dubbed in the innocent predrug days when speed meant cars. Several land-speed records were set and broken on the sand here.

Although the speed limit on the beach is now down to 10 mph, cars still cruise the 500-yard width of Daytona Beach at low tide. People park right on the beach, too, in an orderly row. At high tide, the car bumpers flirt with the waves, while their owners flirt with each other. Horns are honked. Guys yell things. Girls laugh. And so the world of Daytona Beach goes round and round.

As everyone knows, this is no town for the poet or the priest, nor for the inveterate loner. There are dog races, car races, jai alai matches—in short, *speed*. There's beer to be drunk, music to be danced to, hell to raise, people to meet. Daytona is like a large party where everyone is invited, come as you are. We just thought everyone needed to know the rest of the story—you know, about the girls.

Accommodations

To say Florida has an off-season is a bit of a misnomer—the sun shines here all year long. But the motel rates fluctuate dramatically in the buyer's favor from Labor Day to the end of December. Rooms in early October in Daytona Beach—with a sky as blue and a sun as warm as you could hope to find—were going for as low as $12. This works out great, because the town is still alive and the lifeguards are still on duty. Of course, it is not the same as the legendary Spring Break or the racing days of February and March, when a room is hard to find at any price. But even then, prices never really leap toward the outrageous; $60 and $70 for a double room seems about standard during the high season. The choices, of course, are endless, from 20-unit neon-palm-tree motels to 200-unit monoliths. We got an unbeatable two-night package deal on a double room at the *Castaway Beach Motel*—a huge complex with an on-premises restaurant, a country-&-western nightclub, multiple pools and, yes, an ocean out back.

Restaurants

For a place that possesses all of the subtlety of a Wild West frontier town, Daytona Beach has a surprisingly solid reputation for quality dining. *Klaus' Cuisine*, for instance, is run by the guy who captained the U.S. team at the 1980 International Olympic Culinary Exhibition (this is the one we did not boycott). *Chez Paul* bills itself as Daytona's First Authentic Fondue Room, which is good, because if there's one thing that steams us, it's an inauthentic fondue room. *Chez Bruchez* is a time-honored French restaurant of forty years standing.

The rest of the town, however, appears to be one big beefsteak and lobster land. Many nautical motifs and tons of fried fish. One example of what you will find here is *T-Bone's Steak and Bar-B-Q* in the Castaway Beach Motel. It offers a blue ribbon to any person who can eat a 50-ounce porterhouse steak and then wash it down with a 46-ounce margarita. A blue ribbon. Bbbburp. They should offer the person a Blue Cross/Blue Shield policy. It's good hearty eatin', folks, but really. . . . For a slight change-up, *Hog Heaven* offers a decent and inexpensive barbecue plate that will have you snorting fire and pawing the ground with the best of them. In any event, bring a big appetite to this town, because the philosophy toward food is summed up by the name of one of the more popular local seafood eateries: *Down the Hatch.*

Nightlife

One of the most enduring acts on the Daytona Beach scene is that enormously popular performer . . . the Atlantic Ocean. He (she?) has been giving nightly performances for years that have literally kept many hundreds of fans driving along the lip of the stage all evening long. There is no cover charge, of course, but the safety factor might keep more timid funseekers at bay. The speed limit is supposed to be 10 mph, and alcohol is legally forbidden on the beach. Still, twenty-five people are run over each year, most of them at night.

For a more relaxing and equally rewarding moonlight drive, you might try crossing the Halifax River and heading toward Ormond Beach along its western bank, on Riverside Drive. The palm-lined boulevard and pleasant breeze off the river is too much like a dream of California to deny.

All that's well and good, but now to the main event. This town is one enormous party. Most of the bars and clubs remain open into the wee hours and reopen mere hours after closing. The selection is enough to make your head swim. Although there is more to see and do than we could partake of in one weekend, the best bet for a healthy slice of the night is to park your car near the 600 block of North Atlantic Avenue and pound the surrounding pavement. Within two blocks, you will run the gamut of the Daytona scene—two honky-tonk country-&-western bars, a disco lounge, a video-rock club, a live oldies revue, a popular no-cover dance club and, finally, a comfortable oyster and alcohol bar you'd love to take home with you.

The last of these, the *Oyster Pub*, was our hands-down favorite. It's a locals bar with real heart. It has a decent jukebox (vintage Stones, Beatles, Troggs, Motown), a big-screen TV, friendly bartenders and a happily buzzing clientele. You may want to start your evening here, comb the neighborhood and then return for a nightcap. The same people will still be hanging round.

The Beachcomber, right around the corner from the Oyster Pub, is a well-known and well-worn gathering place, and definitely worth ducking into. It has a dance floor and beer is reasonably priced, but the real lure is that it charges no cover and people are plentiful. The *Club Mocambo* is another well-worn lounge, but we were prevented from ducking into it by a phony baloney dress code. A Medusa-like woman aimed a pocket flashlight beam at our pants legs and deemed them unsuitable for the Mocambo's smoke-filled, red-lit interior. "It says no jeans. . . . Can't you read the sign?" she crowed. Little Eva performs her one hit ("The Loco-motion") several times a summer here.

Honky-tonk is another popular form of music in this town. To the uninitiated, it is country music with a mule kick. There are several clubs that feature live honky-tonk bands. *Finky's* claims to be Florida's answer to Gilley's. (We did not ask the mechanical bull if this was so.) Finally, for live rock 'n' roll, the two places that were repeatedly recommended to us were *The Other Place* (in Ormond Beach) and *PJ's* (in Daytona). The former leans toward heavy metal and Led Zeppelin reincarnations; the latter is a little bit off the beaten path and only for the truly adventurous rock 'n' roll renegade.

FOR FURTHER INFORMATION

Daytona Beach Area Chamber of Commerce
P.O. Box 2775
Daytona Beach, Florida 32015
(904) 255-0981

Daytona Beach Shores Chamber of Commerce
3616 South Atlantic Avenue
Suite A
Daytona Beach Shores, Florida 32019
(904) 761-7163

New Smyrna Beach

Not to be outdone by Daytona Beach's claim to being "the World's Most Famous Beach," the slogan slingers of New Smyrna Beach have retorted with their own superlative. New Smyrna Beach is "the World's Safest Bathing Beach." By elevating their humble coastal community to such Olympian heights, they intended, no doubt, to conjure some of their more illustrious neighbor's vacation magic. It is an appealing claim, and one we'd heard before (in New Jersey, wasn't it?). "Safety" is a tough thing to argue with, especially at the seashore, what with all those nasty riptides and hungry sharks and broken Bud bottles posing a constant threat to one's well-being. But since the subject has been raised, we think it only fair to issue a short synopsis of New Smyrna Beach to the rest of the world.

Two possible interpretations of their slogan immediately spring to mind: it is a safe beach because nobody comes here; or, it is a safe beach because nobody can find it. The town of New Smyrna Beach is, in fact, located miles inland on U.S. 1, amid a string of Jiffy Marts, Quik Piks, Handy Dandys and coin-operated car washes that bake in the sun like packaged honey buns being reheated in a diner microwave. In short, it is not unlike many towns from Maine to Florida that have been—like U.S. 1 itself—passed over by time and the more modern four-lane contours of I-95, barely a whisper to the west.

The beach that's attached to New Smyrna is a hard turn and a 10-minute drive off the main road. Things improve a bit when you get there (a few condos, some boats along a causeway), but the same lost-in-time quality prevails on the beachfront. For instance, we won big at the local Skee-Ball arcade, but our prizes were buttons with sayings like, "Let's Make the Scene," "Up, Up and Away" and "Flower Is Power." We also won a peace-sign necklace, but the peace sign hung upside down from a droopy length of cord. You can't find merchandise like this anywhere else in the world—because, for better or worse, the rest of the world is living in the eighties.

As we headed down to look at "the World's Safest Bathing Beach," a zeppelin-sized semi truck pulled alongside and then passed us, air-braking dramatically in order to negotiate the tricky cement entrance ramp onto the beach. Not only can a person drive for 8 miles along the World's Safest Bathing Beach, but he can do so in his very own 10-ton rig. Breaker, breaker, good buddy, I think I just ran me over some of them bathers, ten or four of them maybe, good buddy.

No, New Smyrna Beach is a town that must have felt some sort of civic peer pressure, because of its location (15 minutes from Daytona Beach, an hour from Cape Canaveral and Disney World), to come up with a slogan, however farfetched. People either retire here to quiet adult condominiums along the water or they stop overnight only when they are more road-weary than Wile E. Coyote. Look at it this way—if you come to a town with "beach" in its name, should you have to ask "Where's the beach?"

FOR FURTHER INFORMATION

New Smyrna Beach/Edgewater Chamber of Commerce
P.O. Box 129
New Smyrna Beach, Florida 32069
(904) 428-2449

Canaveral National Seashore

Between New Smyrna Beach and Cape Canaveral lie 25 miles of uncrowded and unspoiled beaches. Canaveral National Seashore adjoins the Kennedy Space Center, occupying 57,000 acres of Florida coast and wetlands. Canaveral is accessible at either end, but there is no road connecting the two public beaches: Apollo, at the north end (via A1A) or Playalinda (via FL 406 and FL 402). Facilities are primitive, particularly at Apollo, though there are small visitors' centers at both ends. The beach is desolate and striking. Saw palmettos and Spanish bayonet rustle at the edge of sandy cliffs that drop down to a narrow beach. The surf is neither as high nor as rough as Cocoa Beach, nor is it as flat and gently sloping as Daytona Beach. Fishing, swimming, shell collecting and nature hikes are all possible here. If you can abide a little rusticity, the rewards are plentiful out here on one of the most serene stretches of Florida's east coast.

Cocoa Beach

The closest place to the moon in this world is Cocoa Beach. It is here that the space program began, here that the Apollo missions to the moon were launched, and here also that our nation's space shuttles have been brainstormed and sent into orbit. For this reason, Cocoa Beach and environs—which include Merritt Island and Cape Canaveral, as well as Titusville, Rockledge and Cocoa on the mainland—is popularly known as the Space Coast.

Cocoa Beach has been booming ever since President Kennedy ignited the country with astronaut fever back in the early sixties. The luster and pizazz of the space program helped bring to life an area that was known largely for its grapefruit and oranges. With the burgeoning budget of the National Aeronautics and Space Administration under the Democrats came a new influx of professionals into the area: engineers, designers, technicians and assistants.

Hemmed in by the Kennedy Space Center and Cape Canaveral to the north and by Patrick Air Force Base to the south, Cocoa Beach has the nondescript personality of a military town. Retirees have also been settling here in recent years—the oceanfront is seemingly one unbroken condominium. Figure in too the fact that the local chamber of commerce has been touting Cocoa Beach as a vacation mecca—NASA to the north, Disney World to the west, the ocean at your feet—and you can imagine what rapid growth has wrought: miles of malls, restaurant rows, gas stations and convenience marts, all jockeying to fill whatever square footage is not occupied by all those condos.

So if it's hard to gauge the soul or center of a town that has none, it is at least gratifying to be able to say that Cocoa Beach has some of the best surf on the East Coast. If there is a cult of charisma to be found anywhere outside of the astronauts' ranks (and they are nothing like the paragons of pop culture they once were), it's in the packs of surf bums who haunt the beach in the vicinity of the town's 800-foot Canaveral Pier. California guys ain't got nothing on these peroxide punks, who when they're not in the water are looking at it, usually from the hoods of their cars, with radios blaring.

The beach at Cocoa, unlike those to the north, is composed of loose brown sand of medium coarseness. It slopes steeply down to where the waves break. The waves ride in on long swells that begin a good ways out. Maybe it's not the Pipeline at Malibu, but Cocoa Beach draws surfers from all over the East Coast. Overheard one afternoon, when an already visible full moon was bringing in tall, churning breakers that enveloped the beach in a cloud of mist, was this conversation between a couple of golden boys with boards:

"How's the surf?"

"Killer, and it's still comin' in."

"You goin' back out?"

"Aaah, I dunno. . . ."

"GO FOR IT!"

Now, compare the surfer's slang with the space-age techie talk just up the road and you've got an idea of the intellectual range of Cocoa Beach. In other words, they might be calling it the Space Coast for more than one reason.

Driving is a hazard all over Florida, but it is particularly tricky here. Between the geriatric slowpokes and the hot-rodding space cowboys, you're caught in double jeopardy. And for some reason, there are more indigent automobiles on the road than you can shake a dipstick at. Station wagons with doors staved in. Rambling wrecks spewing blue-gray clouds all over creation. Muffler-less monstrosities, jacked up high and grumbling horribly.

At this point, you're probably wondering how Cocoa Beach got its name. Because the sand's the color of cocoa, right? Wrong. Cocoa Beach is a lately established (1925) adjunct of the town of Cocoa, several miles inland along the Indian River. At the time of its incorporation in 1872, the town founders wished to name their community "Indian River City." The post office protested that this was too long to fit on a postmark, so the wiseacres at the general store took a look at the latest arrival on the shelf—a tin of Baker's Cocoa—and off went a lightbulb. Cocoa! And Cocoa it was. And Cocoa Beach as well.

Another famous name in the area, Cape Canaveral, has been around for a while longer. Apparently one of the oldest place names in America, Cape Canaveral appears on the earliest maps of the region. Renamed Cape Kennedy in the wake of the President's assassination, it has since reverted to its original name. *Kennedy Space Center*, however, continues to commemorate the president whose vision of landing a man on the moon by the end of the sixties vaulted the world into the space age.

Parts of the space center are open to visitors, and a million people a year come here. At the visitors' center, near the intersection of FL 3 and FL 420 on Merritt Island, one can ooh and aah over motion pictures and moon rocks, lectures and exhibits. The Sensaround documentary *Hail, Columbia*, shot onboard the first space shuttle, costs $2 to view. Most everything else within the visitors' center complex is free, including parking.

Bus tours run continuously throughout the day, and they do cost. Four dollars is not a lot to pay for a 2-hour tour, but be advised that NASA security restrictions limit access to all but a few areas. We found that staring at launch pads and vehicle assembly buildings from the streaked windows of a moving bus was not really all that enlightening. And the prerecorded narration, which crackled inaudibly through ceiling-mounted speakers, competing with the roar of the bus engine, was a tad on the tacky side.

Oddly, wildlife abounds on the grounds of the Kennedy Space Center and on Canaveral National Seashore, which adjoins it to the north. *The Merritt Island National Wildlife Refuge* alone accounts for 134,000 acres of protected lands, visited by some 200 species of birds, including many winter wanderers and some endangered ones. It is strange to ponder that our nation's space center, which is taking us into the future, is a haven for many types of animals that might have become part of the biological past were these grounds not a haven for them and other wildlife. In any case, the sight of a rail-thin egret in a lagoon patiently spearing fish in the shadow of a looming rocket-launching pad is one of the more incongruous real-life collages one could hope to see.

Accommodations

Holiday Inn has three locations in the Cocoa Beach area. As we'd begun realizing since we hit Florida, the best nightspots are often found at Holiday Inns, and they certainly offer dependable accommodations. We, however, strongly recommend two nonfranchise resort motels in Cocoa Beach, the *Crossway Inn & Tennis Resort* and the *Polaris Ocean Club International*. The Crossway Inn is a modern motel, lounge and recreation complex just across the street from the beach. Rooms are large and most have at least partial kitchen facilities. On the premises are well-kept tennis courts and a huge Olympic pool. For the recreation-minded, the Crossway would have to get the nod.

The Polaris is directly on the ocean, and its 90 rooms surround an attractively landscaped courtyard with shuffleboard courts and a kidney-shaped pool. We found ourselves up against some fearsome competition on the shuffleboard courts, which are generally the refuge of the over-60 set. This may help explain why our overeager shots would not glide to a graceful stop within the pyramidal scoring area but would sail off the court entirely, like hockey-puck slap shots. We figured that with practice, we'd hone our game by the time we got to Miami Beach and blue-hair country.

Restaurants

No one should pass through Cocoa Beach without experiencing *Bernard's Surf* restaurant. Bernard's Surf, in southern Cocoa Beach, has one of the biggest, oddest and best menus on the whole of the East Coast.

- Biggest: If it takes two hands to handle a Whopper, it takes four to wrangle with Bernard's oversized menu.

- Oddest: Exotic foods are a specialty. They arrive from all over the world—New Zealand, Africa and Japan, to name just a few places. If you have a yen for the unusual, ponder these tasty delicacies: buffalo steak . . . venison . . . zebra . . . chocolate-covered ants . . . chocolate-covered baby bees . . . fried grasshoppers . . . fried caterpillars. We divvied an alligator-meat appetizer, which was not unlike a cross between pork chops and chicken. If you've ever had nightmares about being chomped by an alligator, here's your chance to bite back.

• Best: Beyond the novelty of the exotic dishes, Bernard's Surf is a terrific place for steak and seafood. A few favorite entrées include the sirloin steak and fried quail combination, the cold seafood platter and Snapper à la Surf. The latter consists of a large red snapper fillet, topped with shrimp and crabmeat, smothered in a cream sauce and baked in a metal dish. Prices are moderate, given the outstanding atmosphere and food. Each table has a clear resin top, into which have been embedded sand dollars, starfish and fragile shells. Bernard's is famous on the Space Coast, and you might even spy an astronaut dining here. So daring is Bernard's Surf that if they do ever find life on another planet, it'll probably wind up on the menu.

Nightlife

Ever since the word "astronaut" was coined, those few lucky enough to get the job have been among the most eligible bachelors in the world—married or not. Remember *An Officer and a Gentleman*, when all the local girls would go to any lengths to snare a crew-cut young air force sharpie, hitching her wagon to his star in order to escape a humdrum life on the wrong side of the tracks? So it is in Cocoa Beach, we are told. But obviously, there aren't nearly enough astronauts to go around—a couple dozen, maybe?—and hell, some of them are women these days. So what's a girl to do? Well, the British navy docks up at Port Canaveral several times a year and . . . you take it from there. Many a Cocoa Beach sweetheart has been tossed overboard like unwanted fish bait after a boorish limey with a heart of stone has had his way with her. Or so we're told.

There are all sorts of places for meeting and mating in Cocoa Beach. Be forewarned, though, that there is a hefty redneck presence here. Check the parking lots before entering—a high percentage of choppers and pickups is a good tipoff that you'll want to bend an elbow elsewhere. And whatever you do, don't stare too long at that bad ol' boy with the T-shirt that says, I'D RATHER SEE MY SISTER IN A WHOREHOUSE THAN MY BROTHER ON A HONDA. You may get a tire-track tattoo across your face.

Here are some of the more habitable watering holes: *Spirits*, on the beach near the FL 520 causeway, is a laid-back, friendly place, with large wicker easy chairs and candles burning. Rock 'n' roll lounge bands and mellow vibes predominate. *Brassy's*, on the other hand, draws a young crowd into hard and heavy music; it gets loud and crowded. *The Clique*, on the Merritt Island Causeway about a mile west of the bridge, is a chummy kind of place with a varnished pine decor and empty frames adorning the walls. It's full of friendly regulars. Just down the road, back toward Cocoa Beach, are *C.W. Bandy's* and *The Banyon Tree*, both located at the *Holiday Inn*. You'll find a more upscale disco crowd, wearing proper attire without being told they have to. Both feature a massive bar, video screen, the latest Top Forty hits and a touch of class, if class be what ye are seeking in Cocoa Beach. Turn up that collar, bud.

FOR FURTHER INFORMATION

Cocoa Beach Area Chamber of Commerce
431 Riveredge Boulevard
Cocoa, Florida 32922
(305) 636-4262

Melbourne
Satellite Beach
Indian Harbour Beach
Melbourne Beach
Indialantic

Never feed a Fig Newton to a hungry cat. This is the lesson learned in Indialantic, one of the small beach communities that front the ocean for the big city of Melbourne. A trek through the town of Indialantic is over in a hurry—it's just a half-mile from the Intracoastal Waterway to the beach—but if you feed a hungry cat a Fig Newton, you can stretch it out for, oh, another half-hour or so. A stray cat followed us into a used paperback store, past the Gothic romances, the science fiction and occult literature, all the way back to the back room, where they keep the illustrated classics and the shrink-wrapped *Playboy*s. Nobody was around. The friendly feline looked like a malnourished Morris. We gave him a Fig Newton. All hell broke loose.

Just at the moment the hungry cat greedily grabbed the treat, the bookstore's proprietress, a matronly Aunt Bea lookalike, entered the back room. Surely she was used to the specter of solitary-looking men pawing through the piles of *Penthouse* and *Playboy* back issues. Somehow, though, the sight of two solitary-looking men feeding a Fig Newton to a solitary cat got her goat. She looked at the cat. Looked at the remaining shard of Newton. Looked up at us. And shrieked to beat the band.

After she calmed down, we learned that the cat matched the newspaper description of one that had been lost for days in the community. The classified ad had been signed "Heartbroken," and a reward of $100 had been offered. This is what made her shriek. She was on the phone in two shakes of a cat's tail. She probably would have split the reward with us, but the breakneck pace of life in Indialantic was more than we could handle, so we left without fanfare. And to think we had heard it was such a quiet place.

Indeed, it is a quiet place. The beach towns of Satellite Beach, Indian Harbour Beach, Melbourne Beach and Indialantic are predominantly residential. Many of the residents work for the high-tech firms across the bridge in Melbourne. There is a distinct suburban quality to the subdevelopments—S-shaped back streets with sloped curbs, men with Weed Eaters and hedge trimmers stalking about their yards like big game hunters, station wagons with fake wood-grain siding. Across the Indian River, the city of Melbourne has been growing rapidly, tipping the census scales at 50,000. Most of that growth is due to the electronics and computer firms that have lately been locating here, at arm's reach from the

Kennedy Space Center. A mini microchip revolution is going on in Melbourne, and in the spring the city plays host to the Minnesota Twins during their preseason baseball training, but not much more than that goes on here.

For the record, yes, the city was named by an Australian, presumably the same man who introduced the Australian pine trees that grow along the coast here (and were entirely stripped of their greenery, owing to some strange blight, making late summer in Melbourne look like late fall in New England). As for the beach, it is not one that invites big-time resort development. The sand slopes dramatically down to the water and the waves crash hard and loud 24 hours a day. It was easy to see why this part of Florida's coast is popular with the surfers, less so with family vacationers.

Accommodations

First, let it be said that Melbourne and its beaches are not widely known as a vacation area, nor do they wish to be so known. This is not meant to warn the vacationer away, however. In fact, a very pleasant, albeit quiet, time can be found at Indialantic, the tiny town that meets the beach at the Melbourne Causeway. Lodgings at the *Sharrock Shores Motel* are a rare sort of treat. Not often will you find rooms so close to the ocean, nor will you find them priced so reasonably. (Rates are about half those at the *Holiday Inn* up the road.) The rooms include such extras as a refrigerator, a couch, a balcony, and a picture-window view of the churning ocean. Come prepared to sit out a weekend. Pretend you're in Maine or something—it's not as farfetched as it sounds.

Restaurants

The beach communities that service the Melbourne area, from Satellite Beach to Melbourne Beach, run along a thin strip of barrier island that's traversed longitudinally only by Route A1A. Jimmy Buffett's rhapsodic treatment notwithstanding (he named an album after the highway), A1A can be as irritating as I-95—especially if it's pitch dark and pouring down rain and you're trying to make a tricky left turn across several lanes of traffic. (We, needless to say, met all three conditions.) Be that as it may, you will find a great raw bar in Satellite Beach, if you're willing to look for it. *Bunky's Raw Bar* is housed in one of a number of shopping centers along A1A. This particular one is known as A1A North. Bunky's is divided like a Woolworth's luncheon counter into U-shaped troughs, and it serves boatloads of oysters. A dozen good-sized oysters costs only $3, there are weekly beer specials, and the local clientele puts up a friendly racket. What more can you ask? Well, on top of that, the bar has an Oyster Happy Hour (4:00-5:30 P.M.) when the little buggers are only 15 cents apiece.

The more subdued 'burb of Indialantic boasts Lebanese and Thai restaurants along the main drag, Fifth Avenue. An odd place to find these particular ethnic cuisines, but who's complaining? Melbourne Beach is worth investigating for one restaurant: *Poor Richard's Inn*. Among the top-rated restaurants in Florida, Poor Richard's is located in a restored nineteenth century plantation house. Though the dinner menu and Sunday brunch are much celebrated round these parts, you probably shouldn't come here if, like Richard, you can in any way be described as "poor." *Little* Richard could probably afford it, though.

Nightlife

The center of nightlife on the Melbourne beaches is the *Holiday Inn*. Gone are the days when a night at the Holiday Inn meant a guy who looks like your uncle plinking out "Love Is Blue" on an upright piano. At this particular Holiday Inn, located on the ocean near Indian Harbour Beach, the lounge is called *Jubilation*, and there seemed to be a fair amount of it in the air the night we dropped in. The club looked to be patterned after "Solid Gold": a multitiered dance floor, a museum's worth of mirrors that allow the dancers and watchers to exercise their narcissistic tendencies, a hidden emcee who periodically urges everyone to "celebrate" and, of course, all the latest hits, hitting you from all sides.

Jubilation is immensely popular and draws not only from the inn's guest register but from as far away as Cocoa and Canaveral. The folks that come to Jubilation are as attractive and stylish as the club itself—rugby-shirted surfer boys, and girls clad in everything from leotards to gowns. All seem to salute the party line of *Glamour*, *Cosmopolitan* and Spa Lady.

As if this weren't enough, Jubilation held a fashion show on the night we visited. The male models paraded a "rugged" wardrobe of jeans and flannel shirts, and the gals flashed scanty lingerie. It was almost more than the jubilant throng could handle. At one point, a group of gleeful pranksters drunkenly joined the onstage procession with beer bottles in hand, strategically gyrating their hips and pelvises at the audience. The show ended, the music slammed on and—what's this?—out strutted a group of white break-dancers in tuxedos. No, they don't miss a beat at Jubilation.

FOR FURTHER INFORMATION

Melbourne Area Chamber of Commerce
1005 E. Strawbridge Avenue
Melbourne, Florida 32901
(305) 724-5400

Vero Beach

Vero is Latin for *truth*. In truth, they should have picked the Latin word for "old" when they went to name Vero Beach back in 1889. Vero Beach is for the oldies but goodies. Senior citizens are drawn to the warm climate and gentrified, lazy ways of this residential community, most of which sprawls out across the mainland west of the Indian River. The "beach" part of Vero Beach is on a barrier island that is bounded by Sebastian Inlet at the north end and Fort Pierce Inlet to the south (a distance of some 30 miles). At the point where the bridge deposits traffic at the oceanfront, there is some light commercial congestion, but this quickly thins out as you head north or south along A1A. And Vero Beach is so well-to-do that what development there is at the beach—a smattering of hotels and restaurants, a few small shopping centers—is restrained and surrounded by private homes and neighborhoods. These suburban neighborhoods are quiet and full of single-story, ranch-style homes built in the Spanish style of vanilla-colored stucco walls and brown- ish-red pipe roofs. On the beach itself, there are a lot of condos kissing the sky.

Like the beaches of Melbourne, Vero Beach offers a bit more quiet than you're likely to find elsewhere on the east coast of Florida—hence, its popularity with retirees. Vero Beach is Miami without high crime and big-city anxiety. The city grows only slightly, perhaps 3 percent a year. Today, the population is a modest 16,000. Age and mortality probably have a lot to do with keeping the population bomb from detonating here.

Age and mortality notwithstanding, Vero Beach does have a fair amount going for it. It's at the center of what is popularly known as the Treasure Coast. The Treasure Coast extends from Sebastian Island, down through Vero Beach and Fort Pierce, to the end of Hutchinson Island, at St. Lucia Inlet. In effect, it encompasses the shoreline of two counties—Indian River and St. Lucie Counties—affording their respective visitors' bureaus a han- dle with which to promote tourism. Vero Beach and Fort Pierce, in particular, have successfully exploited "the Treasure Coast" term ever since it was first used in the early sixties by a local newspaper to describe the loot that was being salvaged from the ocean floor just offshore.

There is, in fact, buried treasure off this stretch of the coast. Back in 1715, a Spanish treasure fleet of eleven ships was headed back to Spain. Its cargo included gold, silver and jewels worth 14 million preinflation pesos, which was desperately needed to pay off war debts back home. The ill-timed excursion ran smack into a hurricane, which wrecked the boats against jagged reefs. All eleven ships sank, 700 sailors died and 14 million in Spanish riches drifted to the sea's oozy bottom, becoming mired in muck and mollusks.

With typical colonial ruthlessness, the Spaniards enslaved the local Indians, who were made to dive for the Europeans' sunken treasure. Nearly 6 million pesos' worth was recovered, but more than half remained unclaimed for over two centuries. Occasionally, an odd doubloon or silver coin would wash ashore, but until the late fifties, no organized attempts at a large-scale treasure hunt were undertaken. Off-coastal dredging met with some scattered success. Then, in May 1964, a team of salvage companies struck gold—by the millions. Since then, everyone has been cleaning up—the salvage companies, chambers of commerce, local merchants and the state of Florida, which claims 25 percent of all treasure recovered from the sea.

The Treasure Coast it is, then. A museum of artifacts and history, the *McLarty State Museum*, documents this period in Florida's early history. It's located on A1A, 1 mile south of *Sebastian Inlet State Park*, which is itself a worthy recreation area, with swimming, surfing, diving, boating, fishing camping . . . all the beach-related "ings" you can think of. Evidence of shipwrecks is everywhere. It's in the eclectic baubles and the very wood that was used to build the Driftwood Inn (see Accommodations). Just offshore from the Driftwood, the boiler of a steamship sunk in 1894, the *Breconshire*, protrudes above water.

Moving from wrecks to recreation, Vero Beach is the springtime home of the Los Angeles Dodgers, who play a short preseason here in late February and March. The ballpark is called *Dodgertown*, and it doubles as the summer training site for football's New Orleans Saints. The Dodgers have been calling Vero Beach their home away from home since 1948, which is when the team—then the Brooklyn Dodgers—was invited to use an abandoned naval air station as their spring-training headquarters. Even after their move to the West Coast, the Dodgers continued to return to Dodgertown. Exhibition games are open to the public.

Vero Beach is the heart of Florida's lucrative citrus industry. Hereabouts, in Indian River County, it is claimed they grow the largest and sweetest oranges and grapefruit in the state. There are lots of roadside stands, many operated by the growers and grove owners. In 1984, however, a virulent citrus canker threatened Florida's groves, many of which were burned to eradicate the blight. Fruit could not be shipped out of state; only juice and juice concentrate could leave. So depleted was the citrus crop that many of the stands we visited were actually selling fruit from California and the Dominican Republic. The state's slash-and-burn program has proven effective, though, and the citrus industry has now returned to a shaky semblance of normalcy.

Down at Vero Beach's oceanfront, out of range of the scent of orange blossoms, visitors will discover no fewer than four city-owned parks and numerous beach-access walkways. Vero Beach occupies the northernmost edge of Florida's tropical zone. It is here the ocean begins to take on a deep emerald tint, which intensifies as you head south. Offshore, there are coral reefs. The warm waters encourage the growth of seaweed, which washes up onshore and stains the beach.

With the tropical extremes of heat and humidity comes a parade of exotic life forms. Inland, one finds mangrove-dominated estuaries, much like a scaled-down Everglades. On the beach, the rare Atlantic loggerhead turtle makes an annual pilgrimage from the sea to the shore, usually on evenings of the full moon in May and June. A more common shore creature is the easily spotted *Touristus obesus*. We sighted a large herd of noisy sea cows (and we don't mean manatees) frolicking in the surf and getting knocked over by waves. So relentless is the surging surf at Vero that beach erosion is a serious problem. Incessant "renourishing" and fortification with jetties and seawalls still can't seem to halt the ocean's steady march inland.

A walk on the beach yielded such disturbing sights as trees whose root systems had been slowly exposed by wave action. With no more sand or soil to grab on to, they finally fell forward. Huge chunks from toppled seawalls lay on the beach. A bulldozer was pushing a pile of dirt toward the ocean, ostensibly to create a barrier between it and the condominium under construction. It seemed a futile gesture. At the time of our stay, a hurricane named Isadore, though hundreds of miles offshore, was causing high tides and heavy surf. The waves that were breaking were taller than we were. The moral of the story might be that Vero Beach—as quiet and well-mannered an oceanside community as you'll find in Florida—is still subject to the punishment of the Atlantic Ocean.

Accommodations

America loves an eccentric, and Vero Beach had a dandy. His name was Waldo Sexton, and he was an entrepreneur, builder, collector, exaggerater and all-around nut case. He built three restaurants and one hotel in Vero Beach. Their outlandishness is quite remarkable in a town this foursquare. His pièce de résistance is the *Driftwood Inn*. Sexton was not an architect by training, but he designed the Driftwood according to a verbal blueprint that he improvised day by day. No building supply company was contracted for this project. Rather, the Driftwood, as its name suggests, was built entirely from wood that washed ashore and was decorated with whatever bric-a-brac—ships' bells, lanterns, cannons, parts of boats—the sea spat up. After it was erected and in business, Sexton continued to festoon the interior with junk and oddments obtained at estate auctions, flea markets and his own ramblings about the world. Paintings, treasure chests, ever more bells, mastadon bones . . . the Driftwood is a museum of the eclectic, unified only by the general nautical theme and Sexton's inspired lunacy.

The original Driftwood Inn and one of his other creations are intact, though Sexton's original "hotel" is now flanked by the towers of a high-rise motel condominium. In a sense, you've got the best of both worlds at the latter-day Driftwood Inn: spacious, modern accommodations with balconies that face the ocean, and access to Sexton's wacked-out wonder from yesteryear. Given the luxurious rooms, well-tended grounds, two heated pools and a generous private beach, the Driftwood is an excellent place to drop anchor.

There is also a *Holiday Inn* and several smaller motels at the oceanfront, and that's about it for commercial lodgings. Here and elsewhere along Florida's Treasure Coast, the condos seem to be gobbling up the beachfront real estate.

Restaurants

This was going to be a rave about our favorite restaurant in Florida, but as it turns out it will also have to be an obituary of sorts. The *Ocean Grill*, one of Waldo Sexton's creations, was unquestionably one of the finest restaurants in the state. By this time, we no longer thought we could be surprised by seafood, but we were wrong. The Ocean Grill served us grouper, broiled in lemon and butter, and swordfish steak, grilled and served with a dill sauce. For an appetizer, we had Indian River Crab Fingers, one of the house specialties, prepared from native Indian River blue crabs, caught right up the road in Sebastian Inlet.

We'd recorded our praise in notebooks, and then learned that the Ocean Grill had been washed into the sea by a vicious winter nor'easter. We dined at the Ocean Grill on October 12, 1984; the restaurant was battered and dashed to bits just six weeks later. The storm, which began lashing Florida's east coast on Thanksgiving Day, did damage elsewhere as well. In Palm Beach, a 230-foot Venezuelan freighter was tossed around by the storm, driven through a seawall and brought to rest at poolside on a rich grande dame's estate. A 235-foot barge loaded with food broke loose from its tugboats and drifted ashore at Neptune Beach, near Jacksonville. Severe erosion of the roadway closed a 15-mile stretch of A1A in Indian River County. St. Augustine lost 900 feet of its brand-new, 1,100-foot pier, which had been rebuilt after having been leveled by a hurricane. In Cocoa Beach, the tempest washed away foundations, and workers did what they could to keep one two-story motel from "flooding into the ocean." Cars were buried in the sand on Daytona Beach. Inland rivers rose to flood levels, and communities from Jacksonville to the Palm Beaches experienced severe beach erosion. The air force lost a big radar balloon known as Fat Albert to the storm.

But the saddest loss had to be that of the Ocean Grill. According to wire accounts, "Its old driftwood and European artifacts that decorated the popular bar were lost when the building collapsed into the sea." While we were eating, we could feel the waves rocking the building, but it seemed invulnerable. The Grill had been built in the thirties by Waldo Sexton as a hamburger and chocolate-cake stand. It was filled with Tiffany lamps, antiques, ship artifacts and bric-a-brac from all over the world. In advance of our arrival, we had written the manager, Charley Replogle, who sent us an informative reply. His words now have an ironic ring:

"[The Ocean Grill] stands on many pilings which are washed by the Atlantic at every high tide. So far, we have survived the annual high winds and tide that come from the northeast every autumn. There has been an occasional collapse, but nothing irreparable. When you see the Grill, you wonder that it stands at all, but its fragility is a fooler. It swings and sways safely."

The good news is that the restaurant has been rebuilt on the same spot—sans antiques, of course, though the food is as good as ever.

Nightlife

Turning on the TV one night in Vero Beach, it did not seem inappropriate that we should be greeted by the sight of a duo known as Guy and Ralna doing a cane-and-top-hat shuffle on "The Lawrence Welk Show." Nor did it seem out of place that their old-fangled *pas de deux* was followed by an ad for undergarments for those who suffer incontinence. We were, after all, in the land of senior citizens.

Skeptical and indifferent, we went out looking for a nightlife that, we were convinced, had to be a mirage. To our great surprise, we stumbled upon a lively club in the wilds of West Vero Beach, called *The Outer Marker*. A lot of people looking for something to do apparently find it here. The cars filled two parking lots and lined both sides of the street for some distance. Inside, we found a relaxed crowd, a decent band and bearable beer prices. Several other Vero-area clubs were brought to our attention: *The Other Place* (country) and *Austin's* (jazz). Something for everyone.

FOR FURTHER INFORMATION

Vero Beach/Indian River County Chamber of Commerce
1216 Twenty-first Street
P.O. Box 2947
Vero Beach, Florida 32961
(305) 567-3491

Fort Pierce

As in Vero Beach, the main portion of Fort Pierce is built on the west side of the Indian River. But Fort Pierce crosses the river over to Hutchinson Island. The area seems to be a boater's mecca, with more vessels docked at its marinas than you'd find cars parked at a suburban K mart during a Founder's Day sale. The central focus for all this activity is the Fort Pierce Inlet, which allows boaters access to the inner harbor. Docks line the inlet's mouth as well as the internal channel, and several motels service the boat people.

Right at the mouth, directly on the ocean, is *Jetty Park*, a city-run stretch of rocks and concrete that stretches out into the Atlantic. It's designed with fishing in mind. Immensely popular with locals, the jetty is lined at all hours with pole-wielding hordes whose patience is apparently rewarded often enough to render them irrepressible. Beyond Jetty Park and Ocean Village (see Accommodations), there is precious little else to lure anyone to Fort Pierce. A lounge, a package store and a restaurant are within walking distance of the jetty. There are two public beaches—prosaically named North Beach and South Beach—with lifeguards and dressing rooms. Of the 22-mile length of Hutchinson Island, 4 ½ are public, and there are 10 beach-access paths to get to them. And that's all, folks.

As stated, the largest part of this town of 40,000 is on the mainland. Unless you have close relatives living here with whom you are on good terms, there is no reason beyond the necessities of hunger or hygiene to linger in Fort Pierce. Along with its nearby

neighbor, Port St. Lucie, Fort Pierce has in recent years been
attracting growing numbers of retirees who either can't afford the
luxury of aging down along the Gold Coast of Palm Beach, Fort
Lauderdale and Miami, or simply are not desirous of the overcrowding. In any case, the rush is on. Port St. Lucie did not exist
until 1961. Today, its population is 24,000, and the increase between the 1970 and 1980 censuses was 4,351.5 percent—higher
than the Argentinian inflation rate!

Between the oldsters and the anglers, there is not much of a
middle ground. To witness how fond the fishermen are of the
beaches of Fort Pierce and St. Lucie County, one only has to
wander the seashell-strewn sands south of town. In addition to
shells, one will encounter countless remnants of the sportsmen's
visitations. Several dumpsters could be filled with the litter,
the rusted hooks, the jagged glass, the plastic jugs, the Styrofoam
cups and the beer cans that have been carelessly tossed into the
sand.

As if the occasional rough surf is not enough to dissuade the
swimmer, the ebb and flow of sharp-edged litter is all the reason
one needs to steer clear of those waters in areas where the sportsmen go. Worse yet, however, is the sad look of some of the dunes
in the wake of joyriding Jeepsters. Tire tracks can be followed into
the dunes where, heedless of the signs that threaten fines, these
"pleasure vehicles" have flattened out dunes and crushed precious
sea oats. At one time, Florida's east coast consisted of 1,200 un-
interrupted miles of dense sea oats. Now, they have all but vanished, and even where they have been reseeded, vehicular vandals
continue to run them over. Perhaps it is a sign of poor law enforcement. Perhaps it is the revenge of the boatless. Who knows.
Who cares?

Accommodations

This is a town with lots of beach but precious few accessible
accommodations upon it. Most of the motels are located on A1A
before it does a right-angle turn down the coastline. These motels
service the fishing and boating crowd. The names give away the

game. One is called the *Dockside Inn*; another—its name written in hot pink neon—is the *Angler Motel*. And so on.

The only oceanfront lodging worth extolling is *Ocean Village*, a condominium resort complex that hugs the ocean for a mile. It is a small world set apart from the world of St. Lucie County or, for that matter, from the real world in general. Ocean Village has been carefully planned to offer a secure setting for quality living with an accent on recreation. It covers 120 acres and might be described as a miniature Amelia Plantation. On the grounds are a beach club, a beautiful pool, a 9-hole par-3 golf course, tennis and racketball courts, four high-rise residential towers and rows of two-story villas lining the fairways. Like many such semiprivate places, Ocean Village is in most respects open to the public. The individual condo units are rented out when the owners are not using them. Most of the rentals are by the week or month, and the accommodations are, needless to say, top-notch.

Restaurants

In a town where there is little competition on the dining scene, restaurants have an irritating tendency not to post their menus outside. Thus, the following scenario can often unfold. It has happened to us on numerous occasions; no doubt, it has happened to you as well. It happened to us a lot in Fort Pierce.

Okay. You park your car in the lot. As you walk toward the restaurant, you note how unassumingly nice it looks. The windows are intact, and it seems to have been painted some time in the last five years. The cars in the parking lot are late-model sedans, not pickup trucks or Volkswagen bugs. You get closer and note that there are a couple of flower boxes to counterpoint the obligatory nautical knickknacks (a rusty anchor, an awning made of fishermen's nets, a wood-carved salty dog). You walk up a ramp and stare at the outside bulletin board. Instead of a menu, you see snapshots of children's birthday parties and fat red-faced men holding dead fish up on a string. You think . . . hmmm, if children eat here, then maybe it's reasonable.

You open the front door. It is made of wood and is thicker than a bank vault. You enter, out of breath. The door shuts behind you with an authoritative thud. A pretty woman walks up and says, "G-o-o-o-o-d evening. Will there be two for dinner?" At this point, you should ask to see a menu, but for some reason, perhaps the residual image of children blowing out candles, you do not. You follow the pretty woman to a table, passing through more rooms than the largest whaling vessel of yore. On the way, you happen to notice the measly portions that are sitting upon the plates of the other diners. Before returning to her post in the lobby, the girl leaves you with this chirpy roll call: "My name is Suzanne. Kristy will be your cocktail waitress, and Sally will be your waitress."

You are relieved. You now have more staff members looking after your well-being than you would in an emergency room. You open up the menu, which is the size of a mainsail. You can't believe it. You look at each other. Neither can speak. The prices are higher than the emergency room. You must make a break for it, before Kristy or Suzanne or Sally arrive. A busboy brings you water. He can read the distress in your eyes. Perhaps he is a former customer who could not pay his bill.

Oh God. When he leaves, you both stand up and fan out, retracing your steps through unfamiliar rooms full of curious customers. Just like in Sartre, there seems to be no exit. You cling to the curtains at the edge of one banquet room and peer out like James Bond. When the hostess walks by with the next group of suckers, you hightail it to the front of the place. You've made it to the foyer. A confused-looking couple stands in the way of the front door. You shove them aside. The door is so heavy it seems locked. Finally, it is heaved open. You stumble down the ramp and spring toward the car. Like criminals, you peel away, leaving a gravel wake.

This is not too farfetched. Not in Fort Pierce, anyway. Of the six restaurants we sought out, both on the riverfront and along U.S. 1, none posted menus or prices outside. All of them were overpriced. And they were not gourmet palaces, either. Is this part of a conspiracy to milk the social security set, who are powerless to rebel and unlikely or unable to ferret out affordable alternatives? Oh well . . . since you are going to pay gourmet prices wherever you go (except for the likes of *Western Sizzlin' Steak House*, where we actually wound up one drizzly night), you might as well dine on real gourmet food at the *Ocean Village Inn*. They run monthly specials (e.g., in October, a full-course German meal) and offer an early diner's discount to complement the regular steak and seafood menu. The wine list is bound in leather and is as thick as a Gutenberg Bible. You can also order mixed drinks with names such as Ocho Rios Goombay and Retreat From Miami. We're telling you this so that you know what you're getting into and won't have to break for the door.

FOR FURTHER INFORMATION

St. Lucie County Chamber of Commerce
2200 Virginia Avenue
Fort Pierce, Florida 33450
(305) 461-2700

Riviera Beach

As you draw closer to the Mink Belt of Palm Beach and points south, the towns begin to show signs of being within this gilded sphere of influence. It happens about the time you cross over the Palm Beach County line. The first towns you pass through—Tequestra, Jupiter and Juno Beach—are largely residential and private. Their beachfronts do not cater to average-Joe-from-Hannibal-Mo vacationers. To be fair, Tequestra does have the indispensable Poodle Puff salons for all the yipping, manic purebreds, Jupiter is the home of the Burt Reynolds Dinner Theatre, and Juno has the beach. That we cannot deny. However, of all the 'burbs north of Palm Beach, the best place for a vacation is the one closest in—the town of Riviera Beach.

Although much of Riviera Beach is inland of the Waterway, the beach hound will find plenty to sniff out on Singer Island—a fragile, toothbrush-shaped island that falls within Riviera Beach's city limits. If you can believe what you read, the warm waters of the Gulf Stream come nearer to land at Singer Island than at any other spot in North America. As a result, the temperatures vary relatively little. Night and day, winter and summer, Tuesdays and Saturdays, the mercury hovers around an average of 76 degrees. In the hot summer months, it generally tops off at a not altogether unpleasant 86 degrees, and cooling ocean breezes make even the most scorching sun bearable.

Singer Island allegedly also has the widest public beach on the Gold Coast. This is not quite the boast that it appears to be, as the beaches south of here aren't exactly sandy pastures of plenty. But it is, we admit, a substantial beach, by Gold Coast standards. At the northern end of Singer Island, the *John D. McArthur State Park* has been established along the wild oceanfront, ensuring that the high-rise mania that currently grips the rest of the teeny island will have to stop somewhere.

A local motel manager described Singer Island as a miniature Fort Lauderdale—the Spring Break kids come here when the latter gets overcrowded. Despite the overwhelming, dominolike presence of too many high-rise condos and luxury motels all over Singer Island, a few smaller motels and a modest town center at the southern end are like a final reprieve before you cross the Blue Heron Bridge into Palm Beach country.

Accommodations

Buried among the luxury towers like villages in a valley are a few relatively small motels that beckon to the passing stranger. Among these, *Tahiti on the Ocean* has the most enticing name, but *The Rutledge* is closer to the bridge and the town. Both are adequate and reasonably priced, by Gold Coast standards, and are smack-dab on the beach.

Restaurants

Although most of the action is on the mainland, you don't absolutely have to leave Singer Island to get fed. There are restaurants with gourmet pretensions at some of the luxury hotels, but the real reason you'll want to come to the *Top O'Spray Restaurant and Lounge* of the *Best Western Sea Spray Inn* is the ocean view, as the restaurant is on the top floor. Over at the newly built *Ocean Mall*, crowded in among all the hair-styling salons and exotic plant shops, are a handful of restaurants. The emphasis at *Portofino* is Italian; at *Joey's*, continental; at *The Greenhouse*, seafood and tropical drinks. The freshest seafood can be had at *The Galley*, which adjoins the *Sailfish Marina*. The restaurant looks out on all the bobbing yachts, and the seafood is brought in fresh off the docks.

Nightlife

The best bar on the island, for anything livelier than arguing the relative merits of the Miami Dolphins' defensive backfield, is *Bristol's*. It is adjacent to the *Sheraton*, and is popular with the locals. For a big night out, the Palm Beaches are just a bridge and a heartbeat away, if you wish to run with that pack.

And now, about this *Burt Reynolds Dinner Theatre*. . . . Burt is a god down this way. He was quarterback at Florida State or something before he grew his mustache and made it all the way into the end zone of Hollywood. Contrary to our expectations, his dinner theater is not large enough to stage a car-chase scene. But then again, the plays that run here do not feature Burt. They do, however, attract such distinguished thespians as Cameron Mitchell, Alan Sherman and Charles Nelson Reilly—all of whom were involved in current productions when we zipped through town. The plays are familiar—*Whose Life Is It Anyway?*, *Educating Rita*, *The Best Little Whorehouse in Texas*—and these productions give locals as well as young, aspiring out-of-towners a chance to work with show-biz veterans without the intense scrutiny of anal northern critics. Maybe some season Burt can wed one of his big flicks to a classic of the stage and come up with a smash . . . you know, something like *Smokey and the Hamlet*.

Singer Island Businessmen's Association
P.O. Box 9509
Riviera Beach, Florida 33404
(305) 844-3311

Northern Palm Beach County Chamber of Commerce
1983 PGA Boulevard
Palm Beach Gardens, Florida 33408
(305) 694-2300

Jupiter-Tequestra Chamber of Commerce
800 U.S. 1
Jupiter, Florida 33458
(305) 746-7111

Palm Beach
West Palm Beach

The first thing to observe about Palm Beach, before we get into the mythology of its fur-lined streets and gold-plated lawn mowers, is that there is none here. Beach, that is. Or there is not much of one. During our visit, giant swells rolled in and crashed against the seawall with a mighty bang, sending geysers of water high into the air and rumbling the very asphalt beneath our feet. This was within spitting distance (though we'd never be so crass) of fabled Worth Avenue, land of furriers and fussy Italian chefs, of stylish wardrobes bearing the cursively scripted initials of top designers. As far as the American Express card goes, if you're a soft touch, then *do* leave home without it.

But back to the erosion problem. A good 10-mile stretch of A1A, that venerable coast highway that had carried us from beach to beach for so long, was closed between Palm Beach and South Palm

Beach. The ocean had surged over the highway, washing away the sand under it, and portions of the shoulder and roadway had buckled and crumbled. A front-page picture in the local paper the next morning, captioned "Another Round of Damage for A1A," told a story that has been repeated all along the Florida coast: "High waves yesterday and over the weekend caused part of State Route A1A to fall toward the sea, the fourth time this year the road has been damaged by erosion. The two-lane highway was closed to through traffic . . . after waves chewed into the northbound lanes."

This stretch of A1A, we learned, had been closed to all but local traffic for two weeks, and we were turned back by a law-enforcement official with a walkie-talkie who threatened us with a ticket. The highway, apparently, has been fighting a losing battle with the ocean for years. Chances are you're not coming to Palm Beach for the traditional family sun 'n' surf vacation anyway. Palm Beach is primarily a winter wonderland for the wealthy, who jet down from their northern playgrounds—Nantucket, Newport, the Vineyard et al.—when the cold weather gets to be a bother. This high-society imprimatur is a drawing card used to pump up Palm Beach County tourism. People like to be around money. The Palm Beach County Tourist Development Council knows this. Its "Mythomaniac's Guide to Palm Beach County" tourist-info package includes, among other things, a brochure that could be subtitled "1001 Ways to Put On Airs." It playfully suggests that you tell little white lies to make it appear as if you were the toast of Palm Beach. That is, you're urged to go back home telling fictionalized accounts of riding high in the saddle down in Palm Beach, when in fact you'll get no closer to the estates of Royal Palm Way than the sidewalk. "When friends ask about the polo matches, don't let on that you missed them. Tell them you were late for a marvelous party in Boca and had to leave in the middle of the second chukker." Got that? What the guidebooks don't tell you is that you stand less chance of penetrating the social whirl than the domestic help. And outside of the winter months, Palm Beach is honest-to-God not happening.

Palm Beach is actually a rather small place, when you get right down to it, with a year-round population of under 10,000. West

Palm Beach, on the other side of the Intracoastal Waterway, is six times as large (and six times less glamorous). The area is expanding rapidly, attracting new industry and elderly people in growing numbers. There are other Palm Beaches as well—North Palm Beach, South Palm Beach, Palm Beach Shores. The name Palm Beach has the ring of class to it, and it is fanning out in all directions these days, with each adjacent community denoting another point on the Palm Beach compass.

Palm Beach County is at the northern end of a regal spread of beaches collectively known as the Gold Coast of Florida that runs down to and includes Miami Beach. The Gold Coast handle refers to the precious metals lost to the sea centuries ago when Spanish treasure ships ran aground. Today's treasure ships bear a cargo of an altogether different, though no less lucrative variety. Hence, at least down around Miami, another appellation might better describe the area. The Cocaine Coast, anyone? In any case, the Gold Coast constitutes an unbroken line of commerce and congestion that does not abate until you get a good distance south of Miami Beach. If you desire to get away from it all, do not come here or anywhere near here. The closest you will come to isolation in this high-density zone would be to lock yourself in a darkened broom closet on the top floor of one of those nosebleed condominiums that line A1A.

West Palm Beach, being an inland city that depends more on industry than tourism, really only bears on this book to the extent that it offers restaurants and nightlife. Palm Beach itself is really a private and cloistered community, and most dining and entertaining goes on behind walled estates. Chances are that if you're reading this book, you're not a Jay Gatsby type, so West Palm Beach it will have to be if you get the itch to go out.

That doesn't mean that it is impossible to *stay* on the beach. The beaches north and south of Palm Beach are generally more relaxed—moderately priced and paced, and oriented toward short-term vacationers. However, they too seem to be moving in the direction of time-sharing and permanent residences. Although the local tourism boards gamely tout the Palm Beaches as a vacationer's paradise, this claim becomes increasingly harder to swallow. The smaller motels that have always been ubiquitous on the South

Florida seascape—those flaking one- or two-story affairs, painted in devil-may-care turquoise, pink or yellow and fronted by a sign with a throbbing neon palm tree—are becoming a thing of the past. In their place stand dormitory-style condos, whose cell-like interiors are priced in the high hundreds of thousands. Where will all the people come from to fill them? we wondered, as we passed one empty parking lot after another.

One wonders what the man who founded Palm Beach would make of it all. Palm Beach was developed by Henry Flagler—yes, him again—and he liked the location so much, he made it his home. (Or one of them.) Flagler was given to building the biggest and best of everything. His Ponce de León Hotel in St. Augustine and Royal Poinciana Hotel in Palm Beach are ample proof of this. They fairly explode with architectural egotism—monuments to a life lived grandly and ostentatiously. It's doubtful that Flagler would approve of today's pricy condos, which are impressive only in their verticality and are otherwise drearily uniform.

He'd probably still be pleased with the look of Palm Beach, which remains lined with private mansions, hidden from view by huge, boxlike, well-trimmed hedges. Flagler's own Palm Beach mansion, Whitehall, can best be described as the San Simeon of the East. Built in 1901 for a staggering $4 million (one shudders to compute that in today's dollars), Whitehall was his gift to his third wife, Mary Lily Kenan. Just a little wedding present, you see. Flagler, who made his fortune as the business partner of John D. Rockefeller in Standard Oil, quite literally had more money than he knew what to do with. In the 1890s, looking for new fields to plunder, he began to pour money into Florida, which was at that time little more than a swampy tropical morass. He saw the boundless possibilities in developing the state as a resort for wealthy northerners like himself. And thus he built hotels in festering mosquito dens like Palm Beach and St. Augustine, and ran a railroad down the east coast. Eventually, it connected Fernandina Beach and Key West.

Whitehall can be toured by the public for $3. Often described as the most magnificent private residence in the nation, it is well worth a visit. Each of the many rooms is designed and furnished after a different period: Italian Renaissance, French Renaissance,

Louis XIV, Louis XV, Louis XVI. We imagined a room decorated in Early Punk Rock: Louie, Louie.

After taking in the splendor of Whitehall, and after dining and shopping in style on Worth Avenue, your options grow rather limited, unless your tastes run to greyhound races and jai alai. Both are betting sports. The hounds run from late October to late April at the *Palm Beach Kennel Club*. The jai alai'ers sling away from late October to late March at *Palm Beach Jai Alai*.

Inland, in West Palm Beach, there are even more opportunities for shopping. It is a city of malls, girdled by freeways. It seems to be a point of pride with south Floridians that there is more shopping-mall footage per capita than anywhere else in the world. There is a store and a line of goods for practically any concept you can conjure, from pet psychiatry to wicker headgear.

Gradually, it starts to sink in that the Palm Beaches are an extension of the Los Angeles principle. If Palm Beach is Beverly Hills, then West Palm Beach is downtown LA. One travels great distances over a freeway (I-95) to get from point to point. There are any number of discrete population centers—Lantana, Lake Worth, the various Palm Beaches. It all adds up to a bulging, spread-out mass of civilization that is utterly dependent on the automobile. So, too, in the emphasis on wealth and living well, and in the ceaseless circularity of a city in perpetual motion, the Palm Beaches bring to mind all of those mythologies that are told about the City of Angels.

Accommodations

Plopped in the middle of a lot of high-rise development is a humble, homey motel called the *Palm Beach Hawaiian Ocean Inn*. It's a modest, two-story structure that rambles from the road down to the beach. The rooms are clean, the color TV works. You can go to the office and get a free newspaper in the morning, which you can then lug up to the motel's restaurant, the *Aloha Room*, to read over breakfast. The Hawaiian Ocean Inn is located between the Lantana and Lake Worth Bridges on A1A in South Palm Beach. Palm Beach proper is about 10 miles north of it, and West Palm Beach is a bit farther, via the bridges and I-95. The beach here is narrow, but there is one, at low tide, anyway.

Typically, you pay more the closer you get to Palm Beach. If you're going to shell out the long green, might as well stay at *The Breakers*, "a very Palm Beach tradition" that's been in business for over a century. Except in the lower-priced summer season, you will pay anywhere from $150 to $300 a night to stay at this distinguished oceanfront fortress.

In toward West Palm Beach, you'll find lots of tall chain hotels and motels near interstate off-ramps. They cater more to travelers than tourists. Of the roadside high-rises, you might save a few bucks by staying at the *Days Inn*, which offers comforts comparable to the bigger names for a few dollars less. From your upper-floor room, you can look down upon West Palm Beach: a city of flatness and concrete. Oh boy.

Restaurants

Rich people eat rich food, and Palm Beach bears out this truism. Not surprisingly, the best of everything is found on Worth Avenue. Italian: *Worth Avenue Café*. Continental: *Café L'Europe*. French: *Petite Marmite*. Expensive: all of them. Jacket and tie are requested.

We ran across a restaurant called *Testa's*, whose sister establishment in Bar Harbor, Maine, we'd eaten at some months before. Testa's offers an Italian-American menu at more moderate prices than the Palm Beach standard. It also operates an inexpensive motel right in the heart of Palm Beach. The season is brief, however, running from mid-December through May.

The other Palm Beaches—West, North and South—offer cheaper alternatives. For seafood, we visited the *New England Oyster House* (with locations in West and South Palm Beach) and the *Fisherman's Café* (in North Palm Beach). At the New England Oyster House, an all-you-can-eat fish fry is featured that even a hitchhiker could afford. You can also choose three from an extensive list of fish available that day and have them fried or broiled and served on a platter. We sampled both the fish fry and a platter with broiled red snapper, grouper and dolphin. The Fisherman's Café is designed to look like an Old Key home—all pastels and sunset colors inside, with ceiling fans stirring overhead. It also traffics in fresh local seafood, reasonably priced.

Just up the road from the Fisherman's Café is *TGIFriday's*, a huge bar and restaurant with a gargantuan menu. If everyone in your party is hungry for something different, come to Fridays. The menu reads like the King James Bible—in a word, endless. They've "begat" many types of salads, burgers, Mexican food and 10 tons of entrées. And everything comes out well prepared, despite the great variety of food served. How do they do it? Volume.

Nightlife

The Palm Beaches put on the ritz when it comes to after-dark entertainment. In Palm Beach, we saw all sorts of studs and man-eaters dressed to the nines, and all for a midweek trip to the disco. At several chichi nightspots, the door was attended by young men in top hats and tuxes, who also offered "complimentary valet parking." For the ultimate Palm Beach disco experience, try *Cyd's* or *Cheers*. To our cynical eyes, all the guys looked like Joe Namath during his reign as clown prince of the *Playboy* philosophy, and the women resembled acid-eyed vixens on those prime-time Texas soap operas.

Looking for a relaxed place to put a few away, our ears throbbing and our eyes flashing test patterns after heavy disco exposure, we proceeded to a place called *The Bowery*. It turned out to be the largest and loudest rock 'n' roll club in the area. It features live bands, including nationally known acts. Good sounds and a frisky young clientele make this the place to go for those weaned on rock 'n' roll in the video age. But this too was no ordinary rock 'n' roll hangout; the interior is plush, the chairs upholstered, the lighting a hot neon red. There is a regular bar *and* a champagne bar.

Scruples, up in North Palm Beach, is a club with a similar slant: casual, with class. Either place is as good as the band that's playing that night, and that can be very good or execrable. But be aware that one must uphold the upscale Palm Beach image, even here.

The dress code, for instance, forbids collarless shirts on men. And be prepared to pay $2.50 for a domestic beer, more for imports and more still for mixed drinks. Drinking in Palm Beach can be more hazardous to your wallet than to your health.

Another popular place in West Palm Beach, somewhere between disco and rock, with several pool tables to bring things down to earth, is *Bogie's Lounge*. Now, many native Floridians prefer a calmer club scene, with wind-blown troubadours in Hawaiian shirts telling tales of wasting time in Margaritaville. For that, you'll have to go to *The Ark* or *The Speakeasy on the Lake*. At the latter, you can contemplate the philosophical pros and cons of time-wasting while watching the lights twinkle on Lake Worth and enjoying an off-shore breeze. We, however, found our Nirvana for aimless living at the *Aloha Bar*, behind the Hawaiian Ocean Inn in South Palm Beach (see Accommodations). It's not much—just a modest open-air tiki bar surrounded by stools, with tables on a patio above it and around the pool next to it, and the ocean making sweet music a few feet away.

FOR FURTHER INFORMATION

Chamber of Commerce of the Palm Beaches
501 North Flagler Drive
West Palm Beach, Florida 33401
(305) 833-3711

Palm Beach County Tourist Development Council
324 Datura Street
West Palm Beach, Florida 33401
(305) 837-3890

Palm Beach Chamber of Commerce
45 Coconut Row
Palm Beach, Florida 33480
(305) 655-3282

Boynton Beach

Boynton Beach is a city of 35,000 spread out along the three main north-south routes: I-95, U.S. 1 and FL A1A. Recreationally, it's of primary interest to fishermen. Its inlet connects the Intracoastal Waterway and Lake Worth with the Atlantic, and the Gulf Stream passes close to shore here. Two of the best fishing holes on America's East Coast are right offshore, and have been christened with names—Kingfish Circle and Sailfish Alley—that suggest the big-game fish that lurk there.

FOR FURTHER INFORMATION

Greater Boynton Beach Chamber of Commerce
639 East Ocean Avenue, Suite 618
Boynton Beach, Florida 33435
(305) 732-9501

Delray Beach

Delray Beach is a cooler, calmer and more collected beach community than some of its noisy cousins to the north and south. Some vacationers prefer to base themselves here rather than in the hubbub of West Palm Beach, as Delray is still quite accessible to the Palm Beach area. But like everything else in Palm Beach County, Delray is growing—and mainly up. Still, it offers more in the way of overnight accommodations than any place between the Palm Beaches and Fort Lauderdale.

FOR FURTHER INFORMATION

Greater Delray Chamber of Commerce
64 S.E. Fifth Avenue
Delray Beach, Florida, 33444
(305) 278-0424

Boca Raton

The last city in Palm Beach County, before you cross over into Broward County and Fort Lauderdale's sphere of influence, is Boca Raton. It's a final gasp of Palm Beach chic. Only the climate is warm here—in all other aspects, Boca Raton is pretty chilly.

Boca Raton is a riches-to-rags story. Established by renowned Florida architect Addison Minzer—the man responsible for the Mediterranean style with which the state is identified—Boca Raton went from glamourville to ghost town in the time it took the stock market to collapse. A classic failed city, Boca Raton in the early fifties had a population of less than 1,000. Now it is forty times that, having profited from the fallout of the real estate boom of the seventies, the tremors of which continue to be felt all over Palm Beach County.

Thus, despite the rolling tide of nouveau riche folk who've washed up on these shores, Boca Raton is not very interesting. It is, in a sense, a city without history, having virtually been rebuilt and repopulated since the seventies. The inland thoroughfares are jammed with cars and lined with restaurants, malls and gas stations. Along A1A, the ocean is all but hidden by all the condos going up. Addison, where are you when we need you?

Accommodations

As a place of repose for the wealthy, Boca Raton has several top-rated resorts: the *Boca Raton Hotel & Club* and *Boca West Resort & Club*. They come equipped with golf courses, putting greens, tennis courts, swimming pools, private yacht slips and the obligatory on-premises pros and "social directors." The Hotel & Club is more expensive than the Resort & Club. The latter sinks to a quite unbelievable $60 in the low season. Both are more oriented toward and built around lakes and the Intracoastal Waterway than the Atlantic Ocean. Down at the beach, small motels are an endangered species. There are lots of them out on the Federal Highway (U.S. 1), but not many by the sea.

Restaurants

Most everything in Boca Raton, from fast food on up, is on U.S. 1. We found a real pearl in the midst of it all, the *Seafood Connection*. In Palm Beach County, where everyone's got their hand out and you're lucky to survive a trip to the 7-Eleven without tipping three people, the good souls who run this place have proudly priced their fine fare in preinflation dollars. Perhaps this explains the massive volume of business done here—or maybe the massive volume explains the low prices. In any case, everyone wins. The menu is full of seafood prepared in all sorts of clever ways. There's a platter called the Alaskan Connection, which includes heaping helpings of snow crab legs, baby lobster meat and salmon steak. Closer to home, there's fresh snapper, as well as barbecued chicken and ribs—a combo that's known as the Hungry Farmer. A hungry farmer might afford it, too. You will have difficulty spending more than $20 for two on *everything*—soup to dessert.

Nightlife

The automobile rules the Gold Coast. Come prepared to do battle, and wear your crash helmet. After a harried drive up and down U.S. 1, we finally settled on *Abbey Road*, where a lot of people seem to come together. Abbey Road is a restaurant/lounge that draws a sophisticated crowd. The walls are lined with dark-stained bookcases filled with books. A closer look revealed works by such literary titans as Sidney Sheldon and Heloise. A closer look at the crowd confirmed the opinion of a talkative confidant—i.e., that men come here looking to get picked up by rich heiress types. With studied nonchalance, one told us, "I work in advertising, only handle accounts over 1.5" (million, that is). The club had a ladies' night promotion the evening we chanced by that allowed the gals to drink *for free*. We, on the other hand, paid $3 per Budweiser. Sex discrimination!

FOR FURTHER INFORMATION

Greater Boca Raton Chamber of Commerce
1800 N. Dixie Highway
Boca Raton, Florida 33432
(305) 395-4433

Deerfield Beach

As you exit Palm Beach County and head south, A1A makes a hard right turn and then a hard left before resuming its straight and steady course. Positioned around this series of turns is Deerfield Beach, perhaps the most palatable of Florida's smaller Gold Coast communities. What makes it special is the ease and informality—it's a hidden pocket of pleasure that calls to mind some of the unprepossessing summer haunts along the coast of the Carolinas.

Most of Deerfield Beach (pop. 40,000) is located over the Intracoastal, along Route 810 and U.S. 1, the nation's ugliest highway. But along A1A, Deerfield Beach is a compact, personable vacation community that lends itself both to quiet seaside reveries and to frolicsome commingling. A sidewalk runs along the beach, as do many joggers. The beach itself is a tropical delight: golden sands, green seas, large breakers, and a 710-foot fishing pier. The beaches and walkways are lined with benches, cabanas and so forth. A small shopping area, a few restaurants and some cozy bars hug the curves of A1A, and a strip of motels commences at the intersection of A1A and 810, and continues south toward Fort Lauderdale. All in all, Deerfield Beach is inspirational in its tempered normalcy. Its blessed-by-nature beach is the focus, which is how it always ought to be.

Accommodations

Motels are plentiful, and range from a multistoried *Howard Johnson's* and a *Best Western* to numerous small motels that have their tropicolored charms. Oddly, some of the newer, more luxurious chain motels, e.g., Ho-Jo's, were undercutting the plainer competition, price-wise. Especially in the May–December off-season, coupons and vouchers good for cut-rate deals can be picked up at the chamber of commerce. We were especially partial to Mr. Johnson's lodge, with its roomy rooms and panoramic balcony views. It was from one of these very balconies that we witnessed one of the strangest sights of the trip. There was a convention of clergymen at the hotel. We returned home late one night, companionless, and looked down on the street, where we saw several men of the cloth escorting hot-looking women into a place called *Big Daddy's Lounge*. From the protection of our darkened room, we cheered them on: "Go for it, Father!"

Restaurants

The *Whale's Rib*, a raw bar/restaurant just a stone's throw from the beach, quickly became our favorite enclave. It's mostly light fare— sandwiches, salads, seafood baskets—served in an atmosphere of unself-conscious banter. A step up, but not out, is *Pals Captain's Table*, which glitters alongside the Intracoastal Waterway. Fish is featured, the desserts are lauded, and Pals has been around for twenty-five years, which is saying something in South Florida. If you start squealing for barbecue, get thee to the *Pig on the Pit*. No restaurant so named will ever be acclaimed by *Gourmet* magazine, but there are those of us who believe barbecue is served at least twice a week in heaven, and Pig on the Pit makes it the North Carolina way—rare in this land of Texas-style barbecue.

Nightlife

Located in its own little vest-pocket corner of the Gold Coast, Deerfield Beach offers enough diversions to keep you close to the motel without having to deal with the madness of U.S. 1. There are patio and indoor bars at *Howard Johnson's*, and *Whale's Rib* is a good place to stop in for a brew. There are also a couple of pizza and beer joints and *Big Daddy's Lounge*, where everyone had on cowboys hats and made lots of noise. If you've got Saturday Night Fever, there's a bottomless supply of nightlife at arm's reach, however. Pompano Beach and Fort Lauderdale are but a 20-minute spin away, and north of Deerfield are the upscale restaurant-lounges of Boca Raton and Palm Beach County. The best of both worlds—trashy and trendy—at your fingertips, and the option to ignore it all, too.

FOR FURTHER INFORMATION

Deerfield Beach Chamber of Commerce
1601 East Hillsboro Boulevard
Deerfield Beach, Florida 33441
(305) 427-1050

Fort Lauderdale
Pompano Beach

Fort Lauderdale is the Daytona Beach of the Gold Coast. Like Daytona, Lauderdale is a lively town that is not so distracted by wealth, industry or centuries of tragic history that the beach winds up playing second fiddle. To the contrary, there is more action down on the Lauderdale strand than on any other beach in Florida. To hundreds of thousands of college kids, the words "Spring Break" evoke an exodus to Lauderdale. And if not Lauderdale, then Daytona. It's one or the other. They are *the* Florida fun spots.

Now, there are crucial differences between the two places. Unlike Daytona, there is money in Fort Lauderdale. Nothing is allowed to decay here. There are no boarded-up storefronts, abandoned cars or horse-stable-like strip clubs. If something goes bust, it is torn down before the ink is dry on the bankruptcy papers, and cranes are busy erecting a new addition to the skyline in its place by morning. Kept afloat by a huge boat population and an inflated drug economy—even the tour guides admit this—Fort Lauderdale is a city of perpetual movement. The appearance of transience extends even to the "permanent" population—i.e., those who've built houses here. Were the real estate and tax laws not written in such a way that second homes provide a windfall in shelters and write-offs, Fort Lauderdale might not be the economically thriving city it is today. More than 70 percent of the listed residents in Broward County are not natives, and many of those spend only a fraction of the year here.

But if Uncle Sam is going to make it worth your while to build an expendable domicile, you could not choose a nicer place than Fort Lauderdale to build it. Lauderdale is frequently referred to as "the Venice of America." There are 165 miles of canals within the city limits. Somehow, so much water in a city makes decay seem impossible—the real Venice notwithstanding. In Fort Lauderdale, the water functions like fresh blood that is constantly being pumped into not only the major organs but the remotest back-street tissues as well. To extend the medical metaphor, this translates into a city whose vital signs are chic boutiques and specialty shops; more per capita gourmet restaurants than anywhere else in the nation; yachts lashed to docks in front of huge homes, and impeccably manicured yards over which droop all manner of tropical flora. The New York Yankees make Fort Lauderdale their spring home. Now, would the Yanks train in just any old Ocala, Kissimmee or Tuna Town? Of course not.

In some corners, Fort Lauderdale can appear to be a ghost town of palatial residences. But there's another side to Fort Lauderdale that makes for interesting contrasts. Lauderdale is accommodating in the most profound sense: 3 million tourists visit every year. They come in boats (30,000 of them are docked here year-round). They come here on planes (there is a large international airport, as well as a smaller executive airstrip in North Lauderdale). They whiz by on buses, bikes and skateboards. They get around in regular taxis and water-borne motorized gondolas. They rent cars, hitchhike or drive their own. They quickly learn the U-turn, which is the unofficial state maneuver of Florida. Some of the younger ones run away from home. Others flee college campuses for a bit of Sodom by the sea. Thirty or forty people a year wind up as floating corpses in the canal, after unsuccessfully trying to outrun the drawbridges. (Some call it cocaine courage.)

A lot of the big kids who come here (i.e., adults and senior citizens) are drawn to the tracks of Lauderdale and Hollywood to bet on the pari-mutuel sports—the greyhounds, the thoroughbred and harness races, jai alai. One of us had a grandmother who would stuff herself into an early-morning Trailways coach for an hour-long ride to the dog track. She'd handicap the races en route, and spend a full day gambling her social security income (and usually winning). She did this well into her eighties. It was also she who would disparagingly refer to Fort Lauderdale as "Fort Liquordale."

For the college-age kids, Fort Lauderdale is not just a tourist town, it's part of a rite of passage. A better setting for hijinks could scarcely be found. The beach has been spared. Stringent zoning laws prohibit any building on the oceanfront. It is thus unobstructed—a claim that few other coastal cities in Florida can make. If the annual influx of sun worshippers weren't so astronomical, one would be inclined to say that there is ample free parking along Lauderdale's 6 miles of beachfront. If you get down to the beach early in the morning, you'll still be able to nab a spot. After a late night of rabblement, this may be the furthest concern from your mind, however.

At the very heart of this desirable beach, whose only blemish has been the unfortunate death by blight of many of its palm trees, sits another feather in Fort Lauderdale's cap: the *Hugh Taylor Birch State Park*. Birch is a 180-acre wooded recreation area between the Intracoastal Waterway and the ocean (with a pedestrian underpass that leads to the beach). The grounds include a freshwater lagoon, coastal hammock, mangroves and dense subtropical thickets. Birch State Park looks the way Florida used to, before Europeans came along. As it turns out, Fort Lauderdale was not heavily settled until the 1890s. Named after Major William Lauderdale, it was first a fortification against the Seminoles, built in 1837; second, an area settled by fishermen and farmers in the 1890s; third, a full-fledged township, incorporated in 1911, and last, a thriving resort city to whom marked growth came in the post–World War II years.

There is no mystery to Fort Lauderdale's appeal as a resort. It's summed up in one word: climate. Fort Lauderdale is more temperate than one would think. The average year-round temperature is a near-perfect 75.4 degrees (the mercury has allegedly never topped the 100-degree mark). Contrary to popular belief, it is not a stew pot in the summer. And here's a statistic to ponder on a gray day: Fort Lauderdale boasts nearly 3,000 hours of sunshine per year.

A sight-seeing boat is a good, inexpensive way to see the city. For $4.50 you get to sail the canals of Fort Lauderdale on a mock-paddlewheel boat with the unforgettable name of *Jungle Queen*. It's here that you come to understand where the money goes in Fort Lauderdale, and how it was made. (There is continuous narration, chockful of anecdotes about the wealthy and the wanted.) One millionaire made it picking up garbage. Another blows up buildings for a living. One has antique cars in his living room. Another is the heir to a catsup fortune. One is a real estate mogul . . . oh, there he is now. Hello, Mr. Johnson! (You're supposed to wave at them in their backyards.) Nobody seems to work very hard on anything other than their boats and gardens.

The tour proceeds to a brief layover on a small island full of monkeys and baboons and birds in cages. A weary-looking Seminole wrestles with bad-tempered alligators in what looks like a giant toilet bowl. He raps them on the head with a pole to wake them up. He holds their mouths open. People snap pictures. Afterwards, he walks around with a cup, and folks drop in coins. You learn that he had two fingers bitten off by an alligator. This is his first gig back in the alligator bowl since their surgical reattachment. You would like to grant him a reprieve from this life, but instead drop four bits into the cup and walk away.

The *Jungle Queen* retraces its steps and makes a final foray into the mouth of the booming, man-made Port Everglades, Florida's deepest harbor. Like most sight-seeing tours, there is a heavy emphasis on celebrities. The name dropped most often belongs to . . . the envelope, please . . . Burt Reynolds! He owns that restaurant off to your right . . . here's the yacht that such-and-such movie of his was shot on . . . and so forth.

When all is said and done, there really is no point in trying to cover up or play down the overdevelopment of the Gold Coast. Nor is there any wonder that this is so, given the weather and the Gulf Stream, the palm trees and the evening breezes. But somehow, out of the sun-kissed metropolis that stretches from Palm

Beach to Miami, Fort Lauderdale has managed to carve the most distinctive and appealing personality. Blending divergent elements and lifestyles—casual and elegant, relaxed and intense—Fort Lauderdale may be part of the tropics, but it comes out smelling like a rose.

Accommodations

The 3 million visitors who come to Lauderdale annually are never at a loss for places to stay. *Holiday Inn* has six locations in the area. *Howard Johnson's* has five. *Sheraton*, *Days Inn* and *Best Western* each have two. From Pompano Beach south to the border of Hollywood is one unbroken motel room, but you should pick your location carefully. Depending on what you have in mind, a room in one area of town, even at bargain prices, might not turn out to be such a bargain. Getting around Fort Lauderdale can be a challenge, what with drawbridges, cement medians, concrete junctions, U-turns, left turns and Bat Turns, not to mention competition with other determined drivers.

The best place to stay to experience the maximum amount of Lauderdale madness with the minimum amount of movement is on the Strip—the section of Atlantic Boulevard (a.k.a. A1A) between Sunrise Boulevard and Las Olas Boulevard. The Strip is where all the Spring Break mayhem happens. The Strip is where all hell breaks loose on weekends (see Nightlife). The Strip is where the action is, where the beach is, where the girls and the guys are. Here the contrasts are the greatest, and at least one night on the Strip is an essential part of the Lauderdale experience. (Families, beware! Quarantine your daughters from this chaos! Stay elsewhere—perhaps the airport Holiday Inn.) More important, if you stay at a motel on the Strip, you are guaranteed a parking place at the beach.

Book well ahead of time, particularly for February, March and April, when Spring Break is going full-tilt. The two Holiday Inns along Atlantic—one at the corner of Las Olas, one at the corner of Sunrise—act as bookends to the pandemonium. The one at Las Olas, designated *Holiday Inn Oceanside* (though both are), is the real party palace. The fact is, it accepts *only* students in March and

April. Of course, every motel along Atlantic Boulevard becomes an instant animal house come Spring Break. Most of them are fine places to stay all year round, when you get down to it. In the summer and fall, one can just about name his or her price down here (and, indeed, all over Florida).

The *Jolly Roger* and the *Tropic Cay* are a couple of smaller motels that offer the same amenities as the big boys, plus a touch of personality and less of a bite on price. Neither will win any best-dressed awards when stacked up against such opulent pleasure domes as *Pier 66* (which comes complete with a revolving rooftop lounge), but they are personable places with their own pools and lounges and what seems like a faithful clientele. The Jolly Roger is especially nice. Its lounge curves out and above the street, offering a vantage point from which to view the nighttime parade.

Restaurants

According to a local and probably partial estimate, there are more restaurants in the Fort Lauderdale area than in any town its size (approximate pop. 160,000) in the United States. There are almost 2,500 of them. Because of the intense trading that goes on in this bull market, restaurants come and go with every season, and the prospect of choosing a reliable one (i.e., one that will still be around when this book is published) is a bit intimidating. We learned that the average life span of a restaurant in Fort Lauderdale is six months.

The gourmet will direct you to the French and Cajun restaurants along Las Olas Boulevard or *The Mai-Kai*, a popular Polynesian restaurant. Again using a biased estimate, there are more than 200 gourmet restaurants in Lauderdale. The tour guides will tell you to go to *Pier 66* or to Burt Reynolds' new place, both overlooking lovely, industrial Port Everglades. The trend sniffers will direct you to waterfront locales like *Yesterday's*. The saloon keepers will hold up their trash-can-lid–sized burgers, which come with funny names and a chalkboard list of optional toppings, and tell you not to leave your stool. The motel owners will assure you that you can't beat their steaks and chops. The septuagenarians will steer you to *Morrison's*—cafeteria food goes easy on the digestive system and the pocketbook. The kids will hunt out slabs of pizza, no matter where they lie—even upside down in the middle of the sidewalk. Obviously, you will not, you can not, go hungry in this town: 2,500 restaurants is 2,500 restaurants.

Nightlife

As it is in Daytona, so shall it be in Fort Lauderdale. Both towns cover a lot of ground. Both attract scads of young people (and we don't mean Cub Scouts and Brownies). And both defer to the needs of their young guests, particularly their need to party. In the case of Fort Lauderdale, it might be best to divide the nightlife into sections, to avoid confusing the issue, because the town obviously has more to offer than wet T-shirt contests and drawbridge leaping. After all, this is "where the fun never sets," as they say. There is literally something for everyone.

(1) Pompano Beach—This northern 'burb of Fort Lauderdale is actually a separate city of 57,000, with its own government, FM rock station, spring baseball team and beach. Just south of Deerfield Beach, Pompano is characterized by an endless wall of hotels, motels and condominiums that makes your entrance into Lauderdale's cement acreage a little easier to take. Pompano is all mall sprawl, with big complexes stretching to the west like high-rises overturned on their sides. And in these malls they have some bars, eee-aye eee-aye oh. And in these bars they have a nightlife, eee-aye eee-aye oh. With a sip-sip here and a strip-strip there. . .

Yes, the Pompano side of Fort Lauderdale boasts an inordinate number of "adult-oriented" bistros, places with names like the *Love Boat*, *Cheetah III* and the *Doll House*. The latter is a "complete adult complex" that lists its featured forms of erotic entertainment as if it were advertising sale prices on radial tires. From the outside, the place resembles a stack of psychedelic poker chips, and the entranceway looks, from the perspective of Federal Highway at any rate, like a certain feminine orifice. The anatomical entity in question is, shall we say, celebrated more fully therein.

But that's not all for Pompano. There are clubs for sophisticated younger adults who prefer to talk and disco-dance before the fact. Again on Federal Highway (U.S. 1), you will find *Pickles Pub*—again in a shopping mall. This is a glorified disco saloon with live Top Forty music, guys who wear enough gold around their necks to make Mr. T envious, and waitresses who wear cleft-clinging outfits that would shock Charo. Nearby Pickles Pub is a place with the tragic name of *G. Willikers*. Surprise and whoopee! It too is located in a shopping mall and serves up live Top Forty along with overpriced drinks. It additionally encourages you to use its valet parking by charging you $2 to "self-park" your car in front of the steak house next door. There is something fishy going on in Pompano.

Of all these sorts of places, we found *Bennigan's*, the franchise bar, to be the most sane and least bothersome. The music, though lightweight, was at a volume that permitted conversation, and the decor, if stiffly preplanned, was at least comfortably arranged. Americana rules. As for rock 'n' roll in Pompano Beach, you will want to drag yourself over to the *House of Rock*. Whether or not you make it through an entire night here, all we can say is they do indeed rock, and don't say we didn't warn you.

(2) On the Strip in Fort Lauderdale—The real Lauderdale experience, down on the Strip, combines rock 'n' roll with street theater and throws it at you almost as a visceral assault. The real show, in fact, takes place outside the clubs, on the sidewalks and streets. This scene is part *American Graffiti* and part Dante's *Inferno*. But it is so much more like the latter on a majority of nights that the city is attempting to curb it, so to speak. The cause of the alarm—and the lure—can be witnessed any Friday or Saturday night, when the Strip is packed with a noisome parade of revelers, rebels, rednecks and runaways. Nothing we'd ever seen—not Daytona Beach, not even *Apocalypse Now*—could compare with it. Add to this simmering stew the periodic influx of thousands of college students, cut loose from any sort of parental or institutional su-

pervision, and you begin to get the picture.

The single most impressive thing about the Strip is the volume of traffic. It is backed up for miles, and indeed pedestrians make quicker progress. It is in this reckless convoy of cars, coupes, vans and jacked-up Jeeps that the real heart of the beast can be heard to pound. Around and around they go, making desultory trips up and down the Strip. The point is, simply, to be there. Something is happening. What it is almost defies description. Here is one lingering image, among many we saw, that perhaps sums up the scene better than a lengthy and sober assessment:

A car pulls up to a traffic light. Inside it are five well-dressed suburban girls. They are old enough to drive, but not to drink in the nearby clubs. Thus, they have been drinking in their car. At the light, the driver announces, during a lull in the giggling, that she is too drunk to continue driving. A Chinese fire drill ensues, with all five girls trading places, either by climbing over the seats or staggering out of the flapping doors to assume new positions. Somehow, a new driver emerges from this ritual. More miraculously, she is at the wheel and ready to assume her duties before the light has changed back to green.

The light finally does change, but the new driver has a sudden, acute and untimely case of the giggles. There is no known cure for this. Contagiously, it spreads around the car until all of the girls are giggling like an insane choir—so hard that the car shakes and the driver can't move it forward, lest she drive it into a motel swimming pool or the circle of oblivious pedestrians barking Spanish at one another above the din of a Twisted Sister tape. Horns begin honking. What begins as a gentle note of impatience crescendos to a mile-long symphony of car horns. A shirtless drifter sporting a baseball cap leans into the car window and suggests that he join them, wherever they're going. "Grossed out," they sober up and pull hurriedly away. The drifter shoots the finger at them.

Just another moment on the Strip.

For the record, we found three rock 'n' roll clubs on the Strip—*Summers*, *The Candy Store*, and *The Button*. For some reason, the latter was repeatedly referred to as "the World Famous" Button, but our visit there turned up a smallish rectangular room with a stage, two bars and some burping video games—definitely a no-frills atmosphere. One supposes that the club's noble reputation depends on the magic of the moment. If the music is bad, the Button is inclined to look like a dive. If it's good, the place is a palace. On the night we were there, the music was egregious.

One block off the Strip, near Atlantic and Sunrise, is the *Parrot Lounge*—a great nest if you need a rest from the goings-on in Gomorrah. The Parrot is a booze and raw bar that serves as a bunker for the locals, much like the Oyster Pub in Daytona Beach. No cover, decent jukebox, humanized decor. Just like everything back home always seems to be, in hindsight.

(3) Elsewhere in Fort Lauderdale—If the Strip were the only source of nightlife, Lauderdale could become wearisome after a few days. There are, however, other music outlets and watering holes, of which *Shooters* and *City Limits* are among the most popular. Shooters, on the Intracoastal Waterway, is representative of the other side of young Lauderdale—the upwardly mobile, well-dressed, imported-beer set who don't seem too particular about their music. City Limits sits out at the southern edge of the city, off U.S. 1 beyond Port Everglades. Inside this musical complex, there are three bars—a disco, a less noisome saloon and a rock 'n' roll club with live music seven nights a week. Come early. Parking is at a premium.

FOR FURTHER INFORMATION

Fort Lauderdale/Broward County Chamber of Commerce
208 Southeast Third Avenue
P.O. Box 14516
Fort Lauderdale, Florida 33302
(305) 462-6000

Greater Pompano Beach Chamber of Commerce
2000 East Atlantic Avenue
Pompano Beach, Florida 33062
(305) 941-2940

Hollywood

The name evokes long avenues of fantasy and wealth, swimming pools, movie stars, divine decadence . . . a place you go to make it big or to get a job in a restaurant and wait for your lucky break. Well, of course, that is sunny California's version of Hollywood. Florida's Hollywood is a lot less cinematic, more like a bad made-for-TV movie. Although it was the Roaring Twenties baby of a California land speculator named John W. Young, this East Coast Hollywood is, in effect, a buffer zone between Fort Lauderdale and Miami, and our nominee for worst supporting actor in an American beach real estate drama.

Much of the town is a residential sprawl of splendid homes and moneyed back streets that extend even farther west than Fort Lauderdale. Hollywood is whispered to receive an inordinately large financial boost from the folks who make their money through illegal importation. Over 120,000 people live within this rectangular slab of solid development. It is as quiet a six-figure city as you are likely to find anywhere.

The most scenic axis in Hollywood is, not surprisingly, Hollywood Boulevard, a palm-lined chariot track that runs east to west. It is studded with impressive but not overly ostentatious homes (with curtains drawn), grassy traffic circles and private country clubs. Hollywood has a palm-lined 4½-mile public beach. Additionally, there are 20 golf courses and a major dog-racing track. Beyond this, Hollywood has less character or distinction than both Fort Lauderdale and Miami. Who do you know who has ever vacationed in Hollywood?

Judging from the look of its oceanfront development, Hollywood enjoys a different sort of role—that of a tightly secured haven for the elderly and the chronically nervous. The condos and hotels are like armed fortresses. Many have mandatory valet parking, Checkpoint Charlies in Pinkerton-like uniforms and steep price tags. To get in the door of some of these places without an invitation or reservation would take more negotiating than goes on at the United Nations. Actually, some of these buildings *look* like the United Nations.

Whether this bug for security is related to the high crime rate or is merely a carryover in habit from all those New York City *emigrés*, Hollywood is too imposing for the sensitive vacationer to withstand. When you are surrounded by something far more nerve-racking than what you sought to escape, you are not on vacation.

No, you may wish to make only a cameo appearance in this particular Hollywood. Be that as it may, there are a lot of buildings where you can put up for a night or a lifetime. As you peruse the oceanfront, you practically need a special device to figure out which high-rise is a condo and which a hotel, and, after you arrive at the latter, which employees to dodge and which to approach. There's a price tag on everything, including parking at the hotel you've paid to stay at.

With that in mind, you may wish to stay off the beach, across the Intracoastal Waterway in the main part of the city of Hollywood, if indeed you need to stay here at all. The price structure suggests that this is a fiscally wise move. The in-season rates for the oceanfront *Holiday Inn* top $80, while a comparable room at the in-town Holiday Inn goes for $50. The beach is not that far away.

Of all the large resort hotels on the beach, the most visible is the *Hollywood Beach Hotel*, a huge white whale that rises above the causeway's entrance ramp. The most prestigious, however, is the aptly named *Diplomat Hotel*. This leviathan ought to have its own zip code. There are 1,160 rooms, three swimming pools, a tropical-motif playland in the sand and a number of on-premises eating and drinking establishments.

FOR FURTHER INFORMATION

Hollywood Chamber of Commerce
330 North Federal Highway
Hollywood, Florida 33022
(305) 920-3330

Miami
Miami Beach

"Without adequate planning and zoning, Florida's highways will be lined with roadside stands and clogged with traffic; slum areas in the cities will grow; and public beaches will become unavailable or uninviting. Florida's future should not be open to such possibilities."

These words were written in 1960 in a report to the Florida Economic Development Commission. The author proved to be an astute fortune teller, at least as far as South Florida, and the greater Miami area in particular, are concerned. Miami is indeed a vast urban wasteland, beset by all the worst ills of the modern city: violent crime, much of it emanating from the drug trade; a flood tide of jobless immigrants, some of them hardened felons from Cuba's criminal underclass; accelerated, sudden growth in all directions, including up, that gives the city a look of perpetual chaos, unable to absorb all the changes. Miami Beach, the 7-mile-long island that stands between Miami and the ocean, has slid with its parent into a combination of decay and modern solutions to decay, which often compound the ills they are meant to redress.

Such "solutions," for instance, include efforts to raze many of the glorious, if now moldering, art deco hotels from Miami Beach's storied past. On their sites would go up more of the generic high-rise monstrosities that already run down the Gold Coast like an unbroken line of dominos. Progress? Those tattered hotels and restaurants at Miami Beach's south end, painted in pink and blue and yellow hues, the paint now cracking, are the legacy of Miami Beach in the thirties—when it was every American's "dream vacation."

Today, Miami Beach is, in certain aspects, more like something out of Dirty Harry's worst nightmares. Drugs, guns and violent crime are an accepted fact of life in South Florida. A top-rated prime-time TV show romanticizes this side of the city, and a certain camp curiosity has made Miami fashionable once again. But think of what you see when you switch on "Miami Vice": two alleged vice cops who swagger around the city in smart-looking

leisure ensembles, blowing away enough Latin American drug
smugglers in the course of an hour to keep every mortician in Dade
County working overtime. "Miami Vice" is all about style and
speed. And cocaine and, sometimes, heroin.

We were warned, over breakfast on the outskirts of Miami Beach,
what we were in for. The source of the warning was a bizarre old
battle-axe of a waitress who seemed given to pathological exaggeration. We doubted her sanity. Any lingering doubts vanished
when she confided to us that she used a Jewish surname half the
year and an Irish one the remainder. "Going to the beach?" she
inquired. "Don't take your wallet, and keep just a few dollars in
your shoe. Don't drive after dark. Lock your car and swallow the
keys." She spoke of Miami Beach in the past tense, as something
that *used* to exist. We were made to feel as if we were entering a
war zone.

Such paranoia is largely humbug, as our rambles throughout
the beaches, keys and inner-city neighborhoods of Miami proved.
But it cannot be dismissed entirely. A certain amount of caution
is advisable. The evening news is full of motiveless murders and
drug-related slayings. The randomness of the crime takes some of
the security out of the Golden Rule of traveling in dangerous
places: "Mind your own business and no one will bother you." In
Miami, you never know who may come up and bother you, or
why. You're not even safe in your car—recall the nationally pub-
licized rash of roadside robberies by gangs who'd wait for cars to
slow down or stop on freeway off-ramps.

Retirement in Miami Beach, so much a Promised Land in better
days, is now tantamount to banishment. At night, you rarely see
an elderly face on Collins Avenue, the main Miami Beach thoroughfare. They stay close by their high-rises, most of them self-
contained cities right down to on-premises grocery stores and beauty
parlors. This gives an illusion of emptiness to Miami Beach. In
fact, people are cloistered behind locked doors, looking out at life
from cells of glass and steel.

So why in the Sam Hill would anyone wish to trek to Miami
Beach for a vacation or a convention, when any other city on the
Gold Coast would seem a more sensible choice and the lovely Keys
lie a mere few hours south of this urban disaster?

Well, at least Miami appears to be trying. There is new money everywhere. Miami is becoming a center for multinational business dealings, and the convention trade is growing. Miami's pancultural community also seems to be applying itself with vigor to addressing its ethnic and inner-city ills. With Miami's rapid ascent as a center of international trade and commerce, its newfound cultural vibrancy and self-esteem, and the stylish public-relations facelift afforded it by "Miami Vice," the city is going places. Some claim that it is America's "city of the future."

In the present, good things are happening. The saga of the art deco district wars may turn out to have a happy ending. A strong citizen's group, the Miami Design Preservation League, has been undertaking restorations and lobbying for the district's protection from the wrecking ball. Chalk one up for the good guys. The art deco district runs from Fifth to Fourteenth Streets, between and along Ocean Drive and Collins Avenue. Come on down—parking is easy, and the area makes for entertaining strolling. On the porch of one hotel we passed were stacked toilets of every imaginable pastel hue. We took a picture.

Currently, Miami Beach's art deco neighborhood is the only National Historic District in the country whose buildings were built in the present century. Powerful business interests have been battling the Preservation Society, but the city at last seems to recognize the importance of saving a piece of its past, even as it hurtles into the future. There is also new blood arriving down here. The art deco district is becoming a haven for artists and free spirits, collecting some of those tossed out in the wake of Coconut Grove's gentrification. The Grove, generally perceived as Miami's answer to Greenwich Village, has been losing its bohemian image as it moves upscale, and those who've been priced out are resettling in the more "marginal" areas of south Miami Beach. As a result, they are marginal no longer.

Across the street from the art deco palaces of Miami Beach is Miami's beach. The word on the beach is a good one, too. The U.S. Army Corps of Engineers has pumped $64 million—and uncountable tons of sand—into a program of beach renourishment. It was man who destroyed the beach in the first place, with some ill-advised dredging and development back in the thirties, and man again who put it back like it was. Fortification of the beach has centered upon the creation of three lines of defense against erosion by storm and tide. As a result, Miami Beach now enjoys 10 long miles of wide white sand beach.

Sandwiched in between all of the Fontainebleaus, the Dorals, the Eden Rocs and the other luxury internment facilities are a generous number of public beaches. The 21st Street Beach, at the north end of the art deco district, tends to attract a younger crowd. The 46th Street Beach, in the vicinity of the aforementioned resort hotels, draws families and older couples. There are also beaches at 35th, 53rd, 64th and 72nd Streets, not to mention the *North Shore Open Space Park*, which runs along Collins Avenue from 79th to 87th Streets. In the middle of a concrete and steel jungle, would you believe a 54-acre park full of grass and sand and nothing else?

There are also fine beaches on nearby Virginia Key and on Key Biscayne. *The Bill Baggs Cape Florida State Recreation Area*, on the southern tip of Key Biscayne, is a wild and undeveloped slab of natural habitat, with one of the nicer beaches South Florida has to offer. As on Miami Beach, there's little surf, just gentle ripples, but there's plenty of white sand to spread out on and swaying palms and Australian pines overhead. Botany buffs will appreciate the nature trail, which winds its way through the various plant zones that thrive just a breath away from the ocean. This is all unretouched, pre-European Florida, and it's all the more amazing that it's so near the city.

Speaking of which, if you get a taste for culture, Miami can answer with a veritable lottery of entertainment options—high, low and cretinous. The highs are getting higher, however, and combining culture and relaxation may be one incentive (beyond the expense-account "business trip") for coming to Miami Beach. The beachfront itself is pretty barren of cultural activity. What there is tends to occur in hotel lounges and favors noisy discothèques and Las Vegas–style floor shows.

But Miami proper, accessible from the beach via the causeway of your choice, teems with life. The foremost attraction is the *Metro Dade Cultural Center*, a $25 million complex that occupies an entire city block and was designed in the Mediterranean style by

Philip Johnson ("Florida regional," he calls it). Besides being an architectural wonder—a four-story beauty in the shadow of the towering skyscrapers of Flagler Street, Miami's main drag—the center houses the *Historical Museum of Southern Florida*, Miami's *Center for the Fine Arts* (symphony, ballet, theater) and a library.

No less fascinating are Miami's ethnic neighborhoods, particularly its Cuban district, known as *Calle Ocho*. It runs along SW 8th Street, and is a good place to sample such Cuban foodstuffs as a *medianoche* (a type of sandwich) or amphetamine-powered Cuban coffee. You won't stop talking about it. You won't stop talking, period.

One could go on and on about Miami, unraveling its secrets layer by layer, and never come to the end of it. But today's judgment may not hold true tomorrow—the city changes that quickly. In Miami, life whirls on all around you, on overhead freeways and Metrorails, inside fast cars and secured buildings, metamorphosing by the moment into "the city of the future." Will the future be horrible, tolerable or utopian? It's anybody's guess. At the moment, the city is a little frightening, at least statistically and especially when you turn on the six o'clock news.

Miami *Beach* is a little easier to get a handle on. We can report that there is a boom in hotel building and renovation, that the beach looks fine these days and that the landscaped beach promenade, between 21st and 46th Streets, has made the glittering blue waters even more enticing. But do you really want to come here for a vacation? In the good old days, Miami Beach was, in the words of T. D. Allman, "the Catskills with palm trees." Today, it's more like Riker's Island with palm trees. But with all the new movement afoot—there is currently a *$3 billion* building boom happening across the greater Miami area, and Miami Beach is a principal beneficiary—the place is definitely moving up, building up, looking up. What it is now, during this period of rather furious growth and transition, defies description. But somewhere, in the air, with cranes and building blocks and money from all over the world, they are writing the script for tomorrow. Stay tuned.

Accommodations

Beyond the eternal razing and erecting going on, there are a few
solid observations to be made. After a long period of decline,
during which Miami Beach came to resemble an aged bag person
who couldn't get up and walk away, the old gal is getting her
second wind. With South Florida becoming a new center for international banking and global agribusiness, a new chassis is being
grafted onto the weather-beaten oceanfront. The first new hotel
in fifteen years, *The Alexander*, opened in December 1983, and
others are springing up. And some old favorites, like *The Fontainebleau*, have been made over to the tune of millions. Meantime,
most of the art deco hotels are still out of commission, awaiting
funds and legal stays before the necessary repairs can make them
habitable again.

By way of orientation, Miami Beach stretches for more than 10
miles. Its northern boundary is an area known as Sunny Isles; up
here, Collins Avenue, the main beach drag, boasts five-digit addresses and places with names like the *Marco Polo Resort Hotel*. If
you enjoy one-stop resorts, where every conceivable human need
is met under one roof, then the Marco Polo stands tall.

Restaurants

Two of our favorite restaurants on the whole East Coast are in
Miami Beach. Both specialize in a native delicacy, the stone crab,
which swims in the warm waters off of Florida's Gulf Coast.
They're like nothing you've ever eaten. First of all, you eat only
the claw. The population of stone crabs is a little more stable than
that of most edible crustaceans, because the claw is all that you
are allowed to eat. They are protected under a law that prevents
anything more than the stone crab's temporary capture during a
relatively brief season. The nets scoop them up, a crab is grabbed,
its crusher claw is yanked off, and the crab is tossed overboard.
The claws regenerate, like starfish arms.

Generally, the claws are boiled and served cold. The lucky diner

who faces a platter of chilled stone crab claws will probably dip
them either in a spicy mustard sauce or drawn butter. Before he
(or she) peels off the cracked shell surrounding the claw, he will
surely also note its beauty. It has the texture of fine china, and is
colored ivory and rose, with a border of black along the edges.
The taste is more delicate than that of the familiar blue crab. And
there is a lot to eat, too: no wrestling with a hard-shelled whole
crab, sustaining small cuts aggravated by salts and spices, just to
pick out ant-sized bits of crabmeat. You can fill yourself on four
stone crab claws—and we did, on several occasions.

For the world's best stone crab, and for all manner of excellent
seafood, we strongly recommend both *The Crab House* and *Joe's
Stone Crab*. The Crab House is located on a small key between
Miami and Miami Beach, and is reached via the NE 79th Street
Causeway. The atmosphere is informal and the dining experience
is wonderfully messy. The tables are covered with newspaper, in
the manner of a Baltimore crab house, and standard operating gear
includes a wooden mallet, a nutcracker, plastic baskets for discards
and lots of foil-wrapped wet towelettes for periodic cleanups. The
stone crabs are extraordinary, as are the other house specialties,
particularly the garlic crabs. The latter are conventional blue crabs,
seasoned with loads of garlic and steamed. The Crab House also
serves a superb seafood bisque (for starters) and a sublime Key
Lime Pie, if you have room for dessert.

One of the most memorable things about the Crab House is
the friendly clamor of the place. Miamians drop their crime-
conditioned guard in here and get rollickingly silly. The mallets
figure prominently in what ranks as one of the strangest restaurant
rituals we've ever witnessed. Whenever a member of the restaurant
staff gongs a particular bell—and the usual occasion is someone's
birthday—customers begin banging their mallets on the table in
what becomes a conversation-halting hail of jungle drumbeats. In
the midst of this communal drum roll, Miami came to seem, for
a brief time, positively down-home.

At Joe's Stone Crab, the mallets are raised only to hammer open
the stone crabs, but the meal is no less pleasurable. The waiters
wear tuxes and indulge the clientele in a most solicitous manner.

Joe's is a local institution that has been around forever, or at least as long as Miami Beach. The back of the menu features a disquisition on the stone crab, written by Damon Runyon for and about Joe's *forty years ago*. Joe's has sat on the same spot on the southern end of Miami Beach since 1913.

This is old-style dining elegance—comfortable, not stuffy, in the manner of some of the worthier eateries in Charleston, South Carolina. Just sit back and enjoy the exceptional food, which ranges from stone crabs to broiled grouper and yellowtail. The side dishes do more than play bit parts. In fact, they would enjoy a starring role anywhere else. All who come here are urged to sample the hash browns and coleslaw, which are presented—and justifiably so—with all the ceremony of the main course. The portions are enormous; a plate of coleslaw, for instance, looked like a soft sculpture of Pikes Peak. In an area that balks at tradition in its pursuit of the new, Joe's stands apart as a tradition that's brightened the face of Miami Beach for most of this century.

Nightlife

Thanks to a good friend of ours who was a journalist in Miami (and has since left the area), we were permitted to blow hot air on the subject of South Florida's nightlife in the Sunday edition of the *Miami Herald* back in 1984. Since we got to rant dyspeptically and at great length there, we have pretty much gotten it out of our systems. We will, however, summarize the salient points here.

In deference to those who adore loud discothèques—a contingent that constitutes a majority, in our experience of these things—we will merely observe that there are lots of them (discos, that is). K.C and the Sunshine band, the disco party band from Miami, epitomizes that boogie-down spirit that thrives in these glittery dance palaces. Add to this the other Miamian entertainment preferences, which run toward Vegas-style cabaret, on the one hand, and Cuban music, on the other, and you have a *paella* that really didn't run to our tastes. Still, to each his own.

We did find a "new music" bar down here—something akin to

finding a toucan in the Arctic Circle—although both it and new music have probably since vacated the Gold Coast. (So transient are the clubs and restaurants of Florida that one prominent Daytona Beach nightclub closed the day after we visited it.) Miami does have a great bar for live blues and R&B called *Tobacco Road*. Its reputation is solid as coral, and it draws a healthy crowd, particularly on weekends. There's also a hot club for oldies acts, *Biscayne Baby*. The cover runs about $10 when a "name" act's in town. Beyond this, however, it's all about as redundant as a spinning disco ball, a land of dress-up and make-believe that's about as real as the firearms on "Miami Vice."

FOR FURTHER INFORMATION

Metro-Dade Department of Tourism
234 West Flagler Street
Miami, Florida 33130
(305) 579-4694

Miami Beach Visitor and Convention Authority
555 Seventeenth Street
Miami Beach, Florida 33139
(305) 673-7080

Greater Miami Chamber of Commerce
1601 Biscayne Boulevard
Miami, Florida 33132
(305) 350-7700

Key Biscayne Chamber of Commerce
95 McIntire Street
Key Biscayne, Florida 33149
(305) 361-5207

The Keys

Florida's Keys run for 108 miles from Key Largo down to the end of the road in Key West. As simply as crossing a bridge, you enter another world. The Keys are very different from the urban swath of South Florida, whose pulse is quickened with the terror of high crime, big money and rapid change. It takes a day or two to shake the city tremors and wind down to the lazy ways of the Keys, where a major crisis is deciding what kind of rum drink to have at the tiki bar. Everything seems to bob along at half-speed, from the coconut palms that sway in gentle gulf breezes to the slow rocking of boats at anchor. A lot of people arrive here freighted with worldly concerns, find solace in the worry-free life of leisure almost mandated by these tropical climes and wind up dropping anchor for good.

Technically, it all begins in Florida City, at the eastern boundary of the Everglades, which is where U.S. 1 becomes alternatively known as the Overseas Highway. Here, you encounter the first mile marker—MM 126—and the numbers decrease as you approach Key West. Mile marker zero is located at the corner of Fleming and Whitehead Streets in Key West. Some would call it a countdown to ecstasy.

Before you arrive in paradise, you pass through country that is inhabitable to no man. The 25-mile stretch from Florida City to Key Largo is desolate, a two-lane road whose shoulders are nothing but swamp. Throughout this cheerless stretch, you'll pray your tires have good tread and the gasoline gauge is well above E, for there are no services, no houses, no place to pull over, no signs of life. Just stumps in the swamp. Every so often, you'll pass a string of signs, arranged in word-by-word "Burma Shave" fashion. The message, when strung together, reads: "Patience Pays—Passing Zone 3 Minutes Ahead." You will be glad when you arrive in Key Largo—either via U.S. 1 or, alternatively, Card Sound Road.

One final word: don't come to the Keys looking for sand beaches. They are few and far between, and the irregular bottom can be prickly and the water too shallow to make total immersion pleasurable or even possible. The snorkeling is unexcelled. But for

swimming, the odds are you'll be doing most of your splashing in
a motel pool.

Key Largo

Key Largo (from the Spanish, meaning "long key") is the largest
key. Like most places we'd seen where an island or peninsula kisses
the mainland, it is full of all sorts of entrepreneurial buildup—
everything from Shell stations to shell shops. Regardless, Key
Largo does have one outstanding attraction, *John Pennekamp Coral
Reef State Park*, which is the only underwater park in the country.

Pennekamp occupies 75 square miles of ocean, including coral
reefs, seagrass beds and mangrove swamps. There is an informative
visitors' center and a sand beach on dry land, but the reefs are the
main attraction, and can be visited and explored in several different
ways, all of them park-administered. Your options include a tour
via glass-bottom boat (2½ hours long, 2 of them spent in transit
to and from the reef; if you're prone to seasickness, forgo this);
scuba diving (you must have a diver's license); snorkeling ($15 for
1½ hours of dive time, including gear rental), or you can rent a
boat and take a self-guided tour. In addition, a few private concerns
offer reef trips.

However you get there, the reefs will make your eyes bug out.
Within the confines of Pennekamp exist 40 types of coral and 600
species of fish, many of them in blazing, iridescent colors as psychedelic as any you'd see on LSD. The coral have been building
up their living reefs for hundreds of thousands of years. The coral
creature—a small, fleshy polyp—cements a home around itself,
attaching it to other coral dwellings. The result is an underwater
apartment complex that would put even the most goggle-eyed
developer to shame (which is where they belong anyway). And to
think that after these many millennia, they *still* haven't gone
co-op!

These reefs, like everything else in the world, are now endangered. Our guide at Pennekamp urged all visitors not to buy coral

from anyone, even the hapless old crone at the shell shop who may not appear to know better. It is illegal to chip it off the reef, makes a virtually useless knickknack in the home (it crumbles to dust as it dries out), and supplies of this natural wonder are being depleted through commercial avarice.

Pennekamp is worth a good half-day of your time. Key Largo also houses some Humphrey Bogart memorabilia. The movie *Key Largo* was filmed here, and on the site where it was shot now sits the *Caribbean Club*. Another Bogey favorite is the *African Queen*, and the boat used in the film is in dry dock in front of the *Holiday Inn* at MM 100. Snap a picture of yourself or your companion posing with the *African Queen*, and then beat it down the Overseas Highway to better keys.

FOR FURTHER INFORMATION

Florida Upper Keys Chamber of Commerce
Route 1, Box 274
Key Largo, Florida 33037
(305) 451-1414

Plantation Key

This is a small key with some population spillover from the town of Tavernier, at the western end of Key Largo. It is notable primarily for the *Museum of Sunken Treasure*, which houses a collection of shipwreck reliquary spanning the centuries from the time of Spanish galleons to the modern day—a testament to the treachery of these shallow shoals. At one time, Plantation Key was cleared and planted with limes, tomatoes and pineapples.

Windley Key

This is a minuscule key on the other side of the Whale Harbor Bridge from Islamorada (on Upper Matecumbe Key). Originally, Windley Key was two keys, known as the Umbrella Keys. The narrow cut between them was filled, and the key was sold to a man named Windley. There are several large resort motels on this side of the bridge, as well as the *Theater of the Sea*, a museum of underwater life with aquariums and live demonstrations. Ride a boat. Pet a shark. Feed a dolphin. Reprimand a barracuda.

Islamorada (Upper Matecumbe Key)

Time for a little vocabulary lesson. If you've made it to Islamorada, you're far enough down the Keys that you'll begin hearing some mildly disparaging slang used to describe off-key strangers. If you hear the word "snowbird" muttered, they might just be talking about you, tourist. Snowbird is the name given to northerners down on vacation. In the Keys, "north" means anything above the Everglades.

Okay, snowbirds, there's more. If a snowbird migrates down to the Keys and stays, in time he becomes a "freshwater conch." The Keys, of course, are known as the Conch Republic, and on at least one occasion have threatened to secede from the United States. The conch is the warm-water sea critter that lives in a large, spiral shell that's fiery pink on the inside. The conch is the official mascot of the Keys, and is a staple of the diet down here. In order to be rendered edible, the conch carcass must be pounded to a nearly transparent sheet with a mallet or chopped into fine pieces. It's not the choicest item in Neptune's bounty, but don't tell that to a native.

Try it for yourself, as it is a recurrent item on Key menus. Typically, it is prepared three different ways: conch chowder, a tomato-based soup much like Manhattan clam chowder; conch fritters, in which diced conch is added to a hushpuppy batter and deep-fried, and cracked conch, which is a pounded-out conch that's breaded and deep-fried. It's not exactly delicious, but it's strangely addictive.

Back to the freshwater conchs. Most of the F.C.s we met had long, sad stories to tell, full of disappointments and tragedy, and had come to the Keys to lick their wounds and build a new life. The Keys are for many a tropical Shangri-La, as isolated from the mainland as one can be without surrendering one's citizenship. But still, the immigrants have got that "freshwater conch" label hung on them like a scarlet letter. The name-callers are those born here—one of the smaller subgroups in the U.S. census—and they're known as saltwater conchs. It gets thicker. A white person born in the Bahamas is called a Conky Joe. (Does this make a white woman who was born in the Bahamas and turned to prostitution a "Conky Tonk Woman"?)

All of this nomenclature serves to point up that the denizens of the Keys regard themselves as a breed apart. Life is very different here. You spend every moment on a coral spine that is between 2 and 6 feet above sea level. Most keys are so narrow you can see the Atlantic Ocean out of one eye and the Gulf of Mexico from the other. There is always water around you. Everyone owns a boat, and the canals, channels and passages through the shallow coral seas are the Main Streets and Fifth Avenues down here. The heat of the sun can be crushing at the height of the day, and exhilarating as it sinks and colors the sky in late afternoon. By nightfall, one's vigor returns in full force. The rhythm of life in the Keys is slower, more deliberate. People become more nocturnal, though they never flinch from the warmth of the sun, the glow of a sunset, the feel of wind and water on the skin. It cleans you out, body and soul.

To us, the communities of Islamorada (on Upper Matecumbe Key, pop. 1,400) and Marathon (on Key Vaca, pop. 7,400) epitomize the Keys lifestyle. They are the heart of the Keys, geographically and otherwise. Key Largo is too near the mainland, and is compromised by the proximity. Key West is a virtual city, and everyone flocks here (not to detract from all that is good about it, however). Marathon and Islamorada offer a different sort of vacation experience, something that's closer to the lives of those who call the Keys their home.

Islamorada is, above all, a sport fisherman. largest charter fishing fleets in the country is both sides of the Whale Harbor Bridge. There nas where charter fishing expeditions and boat ranged. You'd have to be the world's unluckiest an something here, for the seas surrounding the Keys breeding and feeding grounds in the world. Here, ...eys, the Gulf of Mexico meets the Atlantic Ocean, with the C ... Stream acting as an incubator. Snorkeling and scuba diving are also extremely popular on Islamorada, as there are underwater coral gardens just offshore. Several dive shops take expeditions out to the reefs.

The town of Islamorada takes its name from two Spanish words that translate, literally, as "purple island." A small town on a medium-sized key, Islamorada exists to serve visitors, with many restaurants, motels, marinas and service stations to be found here. Whether arriving by boat or car, it's a relaxing place to put on the brakes.

Accommodations

For a small town, Islamorada has more than its share of motels. We dropped anchor at the *Chesapeake Motel*, a modern-looking two-story red-brick motel on the south side of the Whale Harbor Bridge. The Chesapeake comes a little better outfitted than most in the vicinity, with a swimming pool, fishing pier and a shaded courtyard—any one of which is a relaxing vantage point from which to lie around and gawk at the colorful flora and fauna. Next door is the *Whale Harbor Inn*, a much-visited restaurant/marina complex. Farther south, the road is lined on both the ocean and gulf sides with motels. All of them have water access, boat ramps and piers. Our eye was caught by a sprawling place called *The Islander*, where many villas and efficiencies were spread out on spacious grounds. The Islander looked like a small village in itself. Serious fishermen might want to lay in at the *Cheeca Lodge*, a sportsmen's complex that caters to all sorts of recreational activities, including golf. It's expensive than the moderately priced motels nearby, but perfect for a pamper-me vacation where money is no object.

Restaurants

Islamorada is also exceptionally well-stocked with restaurants. *Ziggies Conch* specializes in exotic seafood. The outside is painted art deco blue and would grab your eye even if you weren't looking for the place. Top-notch gourmet dining can be had at *Marker 88*, widely regarded as the best restaurant on the Keys, with the possible exception of the perennially popular *La-Te-Da* in Key West. The *Coral Grill* is plainer, but offers a seafood buffet that's a big draw. Good local seafood can also be had at the *Whale Harbor Inn*. The *Green Turtle Inn* is a restaurant and cannery that specializes in the offbeat: turtle consommé, conch chowder and so on. It even cans its own Key Lime Pie filling.

Nightlife

Once you've accustomed your eyes to the dark, you'll realize there's more going on here after sunset than you might have thought. The *Tiki Room* at the *Holiday Isle Resort* and the *Harbor Bar* at the *Whale Harbor Marina* offer live entertainment. Often, it's an island troubadour singing of smuggling and sailing, smoking and loafing, with a generous helping of inspiration—if not repertoire—from Jimmy Buffett. As many of you will know, Buffett is a singer/songwriter who offered his Key Westerly visions of life and lore to the world. Big-name acts sometimes appear at *J.'s*, a club in Islamorada.

FOR FURTHER INFORMATION

Islamorada Chamber of Commerce
P.O. Box 915
Mile Marker 82
Islamorada, Florida 33036
(305) 664-4503

Lower Matecumbe Key

If there's an Upper Matecumbe Key, there must be a Lower Matecumbe Key, right? There is, it's here, and that's about all.

Indian Key

This tiny key southwest of Islamorada is a state historic site. It is accessible by boat only, and all plant and animal life, not to mention artifacts, are protected by the state. Some of the earliest experiments in tropical agriculture, under the aegis of Dr. Henry Perrine—a pal of John James Audubon, whom he coaxed down to the Keys—were conducted on Indian Key. Some bloody Indian massacres were conducted here as well. Among the victims was Dr. Perrine.

Lignum Vitae Key

This key is a state park, under the protection, preservation and administration of the government. You can't get here by car, but it is accessible by boat and eventually there may be some kind of ferry service. Tours are given by park officials thrice daily. Lignum Vitae is 16½ feet above sea level at its highest point, which is one of the highest elevations in the Keys. One of the last surviving stands of tropical virgin forest is here; hence, the need to preserve its 365 acres from any kind of development, ever. Lignum Vitae ("wood of life") is the Latin name for a type of small tree with dense wood that grows here. It is a hardwood that doesn't float, and this key is the last place in the western hemisphere it is known to grow. Other offbeat flora thrive here as well, including the gumbo-limbo, which is not an obscure fad dance from the fifties but a native tree.

Fiesta Key

A tiny triangular key with camping and boating facilities, this key has been through several name changes. First, it was Jewfish Bush Key. Then it was Greyhound Key, so named because the bus stopped here.

Long Key

Not the longest key at all, but one with a few interesting historical footnotes. The small town of Layton on Long Key was frequented by that beloved author of Westerns, Zane Grey. Henry Flagler built his Long Key Fishing Club here. The fishing club, and Flagler's railroad out here, thrived from 1912 to 1935. Then came the legendary hurricane of '35, which obliterated Flagler's Key West Extension Railroad. The supports he sunk in the waters between keys later served as foundations for the Overseas Highway.

The first bridge on Flagler's cross-keys railway went up here at Long Key. Nowadays, it is the home of several campgrounds and resorts—e.g., the *Lime Tree Bay Resort*—and an extensive state recreation area. Most of the south end of the island is parkland, equipped for picnicking, fishing, camping, hiking and swimming. The natural tropical ecology of the predevelopment keys can still be found on Long Key. The small town of Layton at mid-island has its own chamber of commerce; the zip code is 33001. Tell 'em Goober says hey.

Conch Key

This is a small fishing village, with a boat rental facility and one store. If this were New England, the word "quaint" might apply. Somehow, though, it seems out of place in Florida.

Duck Key

In the middle of the stretch of sparsely populated keys between Islamorada and Marathon sits Duck Key. One of the most elegant spots in the Keys, *Hawks Cay* (advertised as "the great resort of the Florida Keys") squats here, as do the *Duck Key Botels*. At a botel, you can pull up to your room in your yacht just as if you were arriving by car. There's even a disco on the key. Is this where the term "Disco Duck" came from?

Grassy Key

This key is home to a research center, *Flipper's Sea School*, where young porpoises are trained for the show-business life, and where older ones are sent to recover from the jangled nerves that this demanding line of work can instill in even the most steely pro. There are also a few motels and resorts (e.g., *Rainbow Bend Fishing Club*), as well as private trailer parks and a seaplane base. At the latter, you can charter a flight over to the Tortugas, the keys that lie beyond Key West.

Crawl Key
Key Colony Beach
Marathon (Key Vaca, Boot Key)

For those who suffer from a fear of bridges, Marathon might be the place to end a southern sojourn. It is the unofficial midpoint of the Florida Keys, and although the motorist must cross fifteen bridges to get to it, the real test of nerves is the bridge that lies just beyond the southern limits of Marathon. There, looming toward Key West, sits the Seven Mile Bridge. Chances are that if you have come this far, you are fully prepared to go all the way, as they say, to Key West. However, should your resolve not be as tough as a fillet of conch, you might want to pull over for a breather in Marathon.

Though Marathon is hidden from view by the nondescript jumble of huts and stores that line U.S. 1, you will find the full Keys experience here. In the heat of the day, it is true that Marathon does not possess the blue, green and red vistas of a postcard vision. But once the sun starts to fall upon the brow and the boats return to port, the town and the keys it's spread over take on a Caribbean charm that helps explain why people come here to live, while they go to Key West to visit. In Marathon, people find sanctuary from stormy lives on the mainland. One tanned and bearded bartender ditched his businessman's life in Denver ("I got stupid and got respectable . . . don't know what got into me") and now dreams only of living rent-free on a boat anchored off nearby Boot Key. "And in the evening, I can float to every bar on the island," he rhapsodized. Another man left Detroit after eighteen years on the assembly line and a family tragedy; nowadays, he works in a restaurant kitchen, a habitat unfamiliar to him until a few years ago. Already, his face glows with a look of contentment we saw all over the Keys.

If you stick around too long, the keys might begin ensnaring *your* soul as well. Marathon, the heart of the so-called Middle Keys, is the likeliest net to drag you in. With a total population of 8,000, Marathon is the second largest city on the keys. (Key West has a population about four times that.) Marathon stretches from Crawl Key to the foot of the Seven Mile Bridge—from MM 56 to MM 47, in mile-marker parlance—and takes in the "suburbs" of Marathon Shores and Key Colony Beach. In this mid-Keys metropolis, you'll find motels and restaurants, modern shopping centers, an airport with daily flights to Miami and Key West, marinas and boats for charter, fishing opportunities galore and, believe it or not, a beach.

To find the sand, you must cross a causeway over to Key Colony Beach, a pleasant, quiet development. "You're Here Now, So What's the Hurry?" a sign queries before you have driven more than 50 yards into the town. The beach is a small, pearly-white stretch of sand, all of it privately owned, so you'll have to check into a motel to check out the beach. All in all, this dainty beach is a fitting place to close the book on the Marathon area. Who knows, you may never have to cross the Seven Mile Bridge . . . and the next thing you know, you'll be explaining to some Hawaiian-shirted newcomer just why you ditched it all back North to come here just so you could wipe a rag across a bar top.

Accommodations

Howard Johnson's is the first noticeable rooftop in the Marathon area, a familiar Day-Glo orange on the south side of U.S. 1. You can price lodging places all day long on this highway and do no better than HoJo's for cost and cleanliness. Not to mention that you need only to stumble a few steps and you're in the restaurant (with its unbeatable $3 Big Breakfast, though you'll want to scrounge up something more authentic for dinner). There's also a bar on the premises with a Happy Hour, which is about the length of time one can spend listening to the wafting Muzak. And no, they don't have twenty-eight flavors of beer.

Normally in the Keys, you simply cannot veer off the main highway down some perpendicular side street. They simply are not wide enough to allow for much lateral development. The road to Key Colony Beach (first left turn after HoJo's) is an exception—a half-mile stretch of pavement that delivers you to yet another road that runs along the ocean. In Key Colony Beach, you'll encounter a well-mannered, almost secret society of homes, condominiums and beach resorts. The logical motel choices here are the *Continental Inn* and the *Key Colony Beach Motel*, both of which are affordable in the off-season and a minor luxury during the choicer months. (The "on" season runs from mid-December to mid-April.) Both are clean, quiet and claim a slice of the precious beachfront. The Key Colony Beach Motel is a few clams less expensive.

Restaurants

Even though the fast-food joints are present and accounted for in Marathon, you needn't sprint in their direction. To get through

arathon" of three square meals, start at *Perry's* or at
Skillet for breakfast. You will find cheap breakfast
he former and homemade biscuits and more at the
y's is a franchise confined to the Keys, with four of
them scattered thereupon. At night, they are a raw bar (a designation painted in huge letters on their roof) and also serve reasonably priced lunches and dinners.

For lunch, jog on over to one of two places, located side by side
near the foot of the Seven Mile Bridge. One is called, fittingly,
the *7 Mile Grill* and the other is *Porky's*. Both are open-air restaurants. Porky's serves barbecue on picnic tables, and the 7 Mile
Grill dishes out its seafood around a dinerlike counter. Both are
inexpensive, and the Grill, in particular, is a Keys institution.

Your dinnertime finish line should, by all means, be *Herbie's*. If
it were up to us, it would get a gold medal, the national anthem,
the applause of its countrymen and an endorsement contract with
a razor-blade manufacturer. From the outside, Herbie's is not much
to look at, but looks are deceiving. Herbie's is a triple-threat wonder, with an outdoor restaurant, indoor bar and screened-in bar/
restaurant area. We feasted on ice-cold raw oysters, piping-hot
conch chowder, autumn salad (a healthy house specialty), conch
fritters, grouper fingers (not little fish digits, but strips of grouper
that have been coated and fried), butterflied shrimp, fried scallops
and cracked conch. We washed it all down with cold draft beer
and finished up with Herbie's homemade Key Lime Pie. Herbie's
often posts several nightly specials, mostly seafood. Best of all,
Herbie's practically defies you to spend more than six bucks for a
meal.

Nightlife

Marathon will never be able to boast of the unbridled outrageous-
ness of Key West, nor would its inhabitants wish to. *The Side Door*
discothèque is about as far as it goes in that regard. A deejay sits
in a boat cockpit above the dance floor and urges the local crowd
to "get down," occasionally taking pot shots at Key West's tendency to do so ass-backwards, as it were. This *is* the liveliest spot

between Miami and Key West, however, so come prepared to party hardy, if you are so inclined.

For a quieter night out, angle over to the *Angler's Lounge*. Located above *Kelsey's*, a gourmet restaurant near the boat docks on the bay side of Vaca Key, Angler's Lounge has a Happy Hour, a dart board, restrained middle-of-the-road tapes and occasional live jazz or jazz-like music.

The Brass Monkey is the local rock 'n' roll hangout. Though sparsely attended the night we were there (surrounded mostly by guys arguing the relative merits of their boat engines and shouting for Black Sabbath songs), a credible sixties cover band assayed a now-familiar raft of Doors and Hendrix classics. In a darkened environment that Hemingway would have understood—to wit, men without women—tempers began to get edgy. After a few beers, the guys started in on one another, getting more vociferous in their point-making until one large fellow, who was wearing a cowboy hat that looked like it had been chewed by an outboard motor, leaned over toward his alleged buddy and growled, "I *know* about the fucking *ocean*. You don't have to tell *me* about the goddamn *ocean*. . . ." When they began making gestures that portended an imminent squaring off, we slipped out the side door and made for our motel, dropping by the U Tote M Quick Mart for a six-pack.

FOR FURTHER INFORMATION

Greater Marathon Chamber of Commerce
3330 Overseas Highway
Marathon, Florida 33050
(305) 743-5417

Key Colony Beach Chamber of Commerce
Key Colony Beach, Florida 33051
(305) 289-1212

Pigeon Key

The *Institute of Marine Science* is located on this tiny, private key, but alas, no pigeons were sighted.

Sunshine Key

A privately owned "camping resort" is spread out over most of the 75 acres of this small key. Far from roughing it, you'll find yourself surrounded with stores, facilities, game rooms, grills, laundromats, tennis, shuffleboard, a fishing pier and a beach.

Bahia Honda Key

Bahia Honda Key is the site of the southernmost state park in Florida. *Bahia Honda Recreation Area* has a concession stand, boat rentals, a marina and a dive shop, as well as campsites beneath coconut palms and swimming on a long, sugar-white beach. At the far end of the island, a section of one of Flagler's original railroad bridges still stands.

Spanish Harbor Key

Boy and Girl Scouts camps, on separate ends of the island.

Big Pine Key

Big Pine Key is the second largest key in the chain. At 8 miles long by 2 miles wide, it is bested only by Key Largo. You have now officially entered the Lower Keys. There is a chamber of commerce at MM 31. Big Pine Key is rapidly emerging as a new population center on the Keys, and is already under the knife of development. It is a shame to see this happen. For one thing, Big Pine Key is one of the final refuges for Caribbean pines and key deer, both of which are endangered. The key deer is a true zoological oddity: a tiny deer the size of a greyhound. Don't feed them—too much junk food has already reduced their numbers. And for heaven's sake, brake if you see one on the road. Their numbers have dwindled to 300. The *National Key Deer Wildlife Refuge* takes up most of the northern end of Big Pine Key, and a road and nature trail pass through it.

FOR FURTHER INFORMATION

Lower Keys Chamber of Commerce
Big Pine Key, Florida 33043
(305) 872-2411

Looe Key

Reachable by boat only, Looe Key is 7 miles southeast of Big Pine Key. The attraction? A coral reef that offers unsurpassed snorkeling and diving opportunities. It's a designated National Marine Sanctuary, which means the habitat is protected, but you can explore to your heart's content. The reef skirts the edge of the Gulf Stream, and the waters are warm, warm, warm.

The Torch Keys

Like the three little bears, these three little keys are a happy family, with a papa key (Big Torch Key), a mama key (Middle Torch Key) and a baby key (Little Torch Key). A "scenic drive" runs up Middle Torch Key, then crosses over and winds out to the end of Big Torch Key. Look for the turnoff from the Overseas Highway.

Ramrod Key

One has visions of what's to come in Key West by the name alone. In actuality, "Ramrod" is the name of a ship that wrecked against a reef just off this key.

Cudjoe Key

Wherein a new low in real estate mongering has been conceived: the "condominium trailer park."

Summerland Key

A poodle-shaped key that rates an airstrip and a post office.

Sugarloaf Key

You're nearing Key West with every mile. Sugarloaf Key is a large ear-shaped island that's destined for commercial expansion as the backwash from Key West floats in this direction. There's a naval airstrip here, a fashionable resort (*Sugar Loaf Lodge*), a post office (in the *Sugarloaf Country Store*) and a few bare-bones communities that merit dots on the map—Pirates Cove and Perky, which isn't.

The Saddlebunch Keys

A grouping of smaller keys, numbered, not named (numbers 1 through 5).

Big Coppit Key
Rockland Key

Sparsely inhabited by service families from the nearby naval air station.

Boca Chica Key

Boca Chica ("little mouth") has been the site of a U.S. Naval Air Station since 1941.

Stock Island

This little island is the welcome mat for Key West. It gets its name from the fact that livestock were kept in holding pens here, pending their delivery to local markets. It's a lot more built up now, boasting a junior college, a golf course, a dog track and Key West's desalination plant. You've got just one more bridge left. Cross the 159-foot Key West Bridge, and you're home free.

Key West

Key West is the last piece of land in America, the tiny dot at the bottom of our map, the period at the end of our sentence. It occasionally gets mentioned during hurricane season to remind us of its fragility. At the same time, we are reminded of its ability to dodge yet another meteorological bullet. Key West has been dodging bullets and changing faces, languages and costumes for 200 years now. Located closer to Cuba (only 90 miles away) than to Key Largo, it has always been on the cutting edge.

Today, the sorts of questionable activities that were once endemic to tropical isolation—piracy, gambling, whoring, rumrunning, salvaging—have given way to a more conventional activity, tourism (which can be a form of piracy in itself). Drugs and illegal aliens are still smuggled in via Key West—indeed, in sufficient numbers to inspire a near-blockade of the island by federal authorities (which, in turn, inspired a local movement to change the name of the island to the Conch Republic and secede from the union). However much illicit trade remains, it takes a back seat to the tourist industry.

Most tourists who have made the leap of faith (and crossed fortytwo bridges) to get here find Key West to be a worthwhile pot of gold at the end of the asphalt rainbow. Perhaps it is the isolation or the tropical setting (technically, it falls shy of the tropics by a mere 30 miles) that makes Key West so appealing. As in any farflung province, the rules that are in force "up there" are more relaxed "down here." In fact, they almost don't apply at all. People simply do not judge or ask too many questions. The proof of this is in the peaceful coexistence of two disparate groups—the nofrills, beer-chugging, working-class fishermen and the flamboyant homosexuals—on an island that is only 4 miles long and 2 wide. Thirty thousand people live here.

Of course, it is not all coconut milk and mangrove honey in Key West. With the tourists has come a certain loss of intimacy, and some things have passed from legend to caricature. Although Ernest Hemingway was once quoted as saying, "I like Key West because people don't stare at me on the street," it is doubtful that Papa could make it half a block nowadays without being asked to pose for a snapshot or scrawl a signature.

For those visitors who are obsessed with "seeing things," there are overpriced sight-seeing boats and the well-known *Conch Tour Trains*, which wind their caterpillarlike way through the tiny streets, clogging traffic. The latter seem ideally suited to the older, less perambulatory visitor. You are taken to sixty historical sites, among them *Hemingway's house*, Harry Truman's *"Little White House,"* the *Audubon House* and *Mallory Square*. But for those who eat their Wheaties, these places can be discovered more joyously on foot, and all you need is a decent town map. These are readily available, and indeed are given away at most motels.

For its size, Key West has a lot to offer the eyes and ears. On a Conch Train, you might miss the Spanish being spoken and sung, the lizards scurrying underfoot, the six-toed cats that wander the Hemingway estate. You'll also miss the bright blue sky and the way the tropical sun plays on the lush vegetation. And if you are not careful, you might miss the beaches. There are two public ones: Smather's Beach and Monroe County Beach. The former is longer and more isolated, but the sand is of a hard, blindingly white and brittle consistency—more like cement that has crumbled to bits—and the water is difficult to wade in. There are big rocks underfoot near the shore and primordial ooze everywhere, and it never gets deep enough for a proper swim. However, you will rarely find an ocean that *looks* more gorgeous from the dry side of a beach blanket. Monroe County Beach offers poor swimming but fantastic snorkeling. Paddle around off the end of the pier for some excellent fish sight-seeing.

The townspeople and tourists of Key West gather daily to watch the sun set at Mallory Square. The sunsets are legendary, as is the ritual of watching them, which is done with quiet reverence and followed by a round of applause for Old Sol. As the sun goes down, the sky fills up with a glorious red glow. The disc seems to hover afloat on the watery horizon, and then finally and with surprising swiftness, *glop!*, it falls like a blob of honey into the teacup of the gulf.

When we were in town, Mallory Square was temporarily hemmed in by an enormous barbed-wire fence, which had been built at the very lip of its unofficial sunset-viewing amphitheater, around which the crowd was herded like cattle in a stockpen. We found ourselves standing on a small side pier that seemed dangerously unprepared for so many people. A written inquiry into the permanence of this arrangement elicited this response: "Mallory Square is under construction to enable our cruise ship to dock. . . . It will soon be the sacred spot of sunset once again." One wonders what sort of reverse mutiny will ensue should this mysterious cruise ship block the view of the sunset.

In any case, the event is greeted daily in the carnival atmosphere for which Key West is best known. Groups of performers and "characters" gather to entertain, spout off or cadge quarters—a rubbery-limbed Rastafarian who does pretzel impersonations, an Uncle Sam on stilts, several long-haired guitarists and the usual profiteers circulating pamphlets promising remarkable gifts for visits to condo villages. After sunset, the best thing to do—either to get over your shock or to sustain your party mood—is to hit the bars on Duval Street. Actually, a more sensible thing to do would be to eat dinner, but this is, after all, Key West.

As one saltwater conch boasted, "We have more bars than churches," and this sums up the bent in this neck of the ocean. Everything is a little bent here. Even the name Key West derives not from its westerly locale but from a mispronunciation of its original name. In the sixteenth century, Spanish explorers named the island Quay Hueso, which means "bone island." After a couple of Dos Equis or Red Stripe beers, "Quay Hueso" becomes "Key West" to the untrained ear. The town was incorporated in 1828, and Key West it was. Fortunately, it *is* the westernmost key. As a sign on the south side of town points out, "America ends here."

Out at the end of the road, people tend to get a little more surreal and devil-may-care. It can be something as incongruous as a guy walking up to you on the street with a bucket full of lobsters, or the distant sound of Bob Dylan's protest songs being re-sung to people wearing flip-flops and Hawaiian shirts. Everyone is topsy-turvy, everything is at its southernmost. You are reminded of the proximity to the Caribbean in the languages you hear. Some people who live hear speak only Spanish. You can, in fact, walk for blocks in this tiny town and hear nary a word of English. Do they want someday to go home, or are they at home right now? The people who speak English don't necessarily want to go home. That's why many who live here came here. One supposes they could leave any time they want, but there is something in the blueness of the sky, the greenness of the water, the crazy quilt of people, the endless singing, whistling, shouting, parading and drinking that tells you this is it. This is land's end.

Amigos, America ends here.

Accommodations

Here at the end of your road, you'll find many of your preconceptions will have to be loosened up. This includes your ideals about lodging: one must come prepared for the funky. Many motels, guest homes and houses are a bit frayed around the edges. It's the sun, the moisture, the tropics. It's okay.

Fear of decay is no reason to seek out the first respectable-looking chain motel you see and plunk down $80 for a night in a room that looks like every other you've slept in on the road. If you did that, you'd wind up on the wrong end of the island, stranded away from the fun. Most of the franchise motels sit like a group of sentries on guard duty at the entrance to the island. If you *do* crave one of the stalwarts, follow Roosevelt Boulevard around to the ocean side, where you'll pay just a tad more to stay at the *Best Western Key Ambassador Resort Motel* or the *South Beach Oceanfront Motel*. Both have abundant oceanfront acreage, swimming pools and all the other creature comforts.

But even here, you are still a long ways away from the old part of town, where the action is. It's too far to walk and ponderous to imagine driving there, having to face narrow streets and limited parking spaces. Closer to town, you can find adequate and more economical lodging. There are plenty of inns, motels and guesthouses, and they are funky but comfy. An upstairs shutter might need a little paint and the air conditioner might groan like a sea cow with indigestion, but it's nothing to get freaked out about.

On Truman Avenue, you will find, side by side, the *Red Rooster Inn* and the *Key Lime Village*. The former is a large house that has been converted to a motel, with air conditioning, color TV and room refrigerators. Key Lime Village is the real sleeper, though. Painted a sun-faded greenish yellow and hidden among a small forest of midget trees, the "village" is a series of cottages distributed almost randomly around the property. There is a well-shaded pool and lounging area off in a corner. The rooms don't have TVs, but there is a common game room with a color set that's always on. You wind up trading the dubious pleasure of having a television in your room for a real break on price. Plus you get these priceless grounds, and you are a short, dinner-digesting stroll from the heart of town. And, oh yes, don't worry about the lizards that scurry among the trees. They come at no extra cost.

As for the guesthouses closer into town, you might want to be a bit more selective here. Many are for adults only—*sophisticated* adults, no less. You can take that any way you want, but the fact that the phrase "We give good paradise" is included in the blurb for one of these places leads us to suspect that in Key West, "sophisticated" means "homosexual." The *Eden House*, on Fleming Street, is one guesthouse we're sure about. Built in 1924, it is a traditional Key West hotel—clean and simple rooms, ceiling fans and a garden café.

For the record, there are two luxury resorts that are frequently mentioned in the literature about Key West—the *Pier House* and the more historic *Casa Marina*—but they seem to miss the concept of their location. That is, by anywhere from $100 to $200 a night.

Restaurants

In Key West, the night does not have to end with a meal, but this is how many visitors exercise their freedom of choice. Here, dinner becomes not merely a meal but a "dining experience." There are any number of places that will wine and dine you like royalty, for a king's ransom, of course—e.g., the *Pier House*, *Claire* and, at *Marriott's Casa Marina Hotel*, a place called *Henry's*. A restaurant informally known as the *La-Te-Da* is at the top of the gourmet heap; it's openly gay but open to everyone. *Kyushu Restaurant* is that rarity on the ocean—a place where you can get sushi. There is a full listing of other Japanese dishes as well.

One restaurant that might escape your notice is the *A&B Lobster*

House. You take an elevator up to a dining room that overlooks old Key West Harbor. The prices are a lobster's whisker above moderate, but the food is excellent. Try the broiled yellowtail or the Florida lobster, and if you do nothing else down here, order a bowl of its conch chowder. It's the best we had on the Keys.

If you want a setting that captures the joyful looseness of Key West, then you must try *Shorty's Diner* on Duval Street for breakfast or lunch. (It does not serve dinner, or we would have inquired about a Shorty's meal plan.) You sit on stools, which surround a huge U-shaped counter. If you happen to spot an unoccupied stool, better grab it fast because Shorty's is popular and no one stands on ceremony. The prices are low, the food is hearty and filling.

If you can't find a seat at Shorty's you might try the *Rooftop Café*. Here you can either sit on a balcony overlooking the Mallory Square shopping district or inside beneath whirring fans. The food and ceremony are more elaborate, and it's worth it for the privilege of eating outdoors, overlooking the bazaar. For the record, we will at least mention the *Pier House*. Everyone else does. Here are two items from its "brunch menu": Eggs Benedict, which go for $10, and, for those on a tighter budget, something called a Piña Colada Waffle, which can be had for a mere $7.75.

Nightlife

The nightlife of Key West actually begins during the daylight hours. Toward afternoon, when the town is mentally preparing itself for another lovely sunset, the folksingers start to crawl out of the woodwork. Suddenly, Duval Street is transformed into Bleecker Street. A hairy minstrel leads a pack of scraggly dogs through the streets, plucking idly at the strings of his battered acoustic. His blue gypsy kerchief matches those around the throats of his canine flock.

From out of *Sloppy Joe's Bar* a solo strummer is lecturing curious tourists just prior to playing an ancient Dylan tune. "Of course, you remember Mr. Dylan, his words still ring true. . . ." Then he launches into "The Times They Are A-Changing." (This, just one week before Ronald Reagan was reelected by an unprecedented landslide.) Up the street, at a place called *The Bull*, a sculptured bull is forever frozen at the very moment it rams through the wall onto the sidewalk. Onstage, a bull-sized crooner is doing it acoustically to Bob Seger. And everywhere you look, it is Happy Hour.

Later on, the town metamorphoses again, and if after dinner you'd rather move your feet anywhere but back to your motel room, here are some places you might go. First, for history and a great jukebox (not necessarily in that order), you must visit *Capt. Tony's Saloon*, which, the sign out front will tell you, is "the oldest bar in Key West." The place is ugly, cluttered with old calling cards, yellowed newspaper clippings (see Tony posed with Woody Strode!), knickknacks, broken seats and bad bathrooms; huge carved wooden heads stare out from the littered walls, and it is hot as hell in here. In other words, it is a wonderful place to knock back a few cold mugs and peck out some songs on the jukebox. Captain Tony, incidentally, made a well-publicized bid for mayor of Key West in 1985.

Rick's is another fitting place to drink a contemplative beer. It is, as Papa Ernest might say, a clean, well-lighted place compared to Tony's, if lacking his unique rag-bag decor. Located on Duval Street across from *Sloppy Joe's*, Rick's is an ideal vantage point from which to study the sidewalk parade before venturing back out to join it. If you want live music, especially rock 'n' roll, you might give *Dirty Harry's* a try. It's near Rick's in a shopper's cul-de-sac. You can't miss it . . . just follow the bouncing hordes.

Finally, there is Sloppy Joe's. Located front and center on a Duval Street intersection, and open on both sides to the perpendicular sidewalks, Sloppy Joe's is an institution. Tourists come in during the day because the sign out front says, in overlarge lobster-red lettering, "Hemingway's Favorite Bar." (Wouldn't a simple, respectful plaque have done the job?) At night, however, the place is a hotbox of rock 'n' roll, and a great place to drink and enjoy music—one of the best on the East Coast. The music goes on until three or four o'clock in the morning, as did our celebratory drinking on this, the last night of our long, long trek southward. Now . . . lessee, where was it that we parked our motel? . . .

FOR FURTHER INFORMATION

Key West Chamber of Commerce
P.O. Box 1147
402 Wall Street
Key West, Florida 33040
(305) 294-2587

Directory

The following is a complete listing of names, addresses and phone numbers for all restaurants and lodging establishments mentioned in the text. Readers should bear in mind that this is comprehensive only as far as the province of our travels is concerned, and by no means is intended as an exhaustive directory of every worthy place to sleep and eat on the East Coast. We know that there are numerous other gems out there waiting to be discovered on subsequent visits, and any reader with a hot tip about a favorite haunt is invited to share it with us (write the authors in care of McGraw-Hill Book Company, General Books Division, 1221 Avenue of the Americas, New York, NY 10020). We promise to consider any and all suggestions for future editions. Finally, the addresses below are as complete as we could determine. (A) = Accommodations. (R) = Restaurants. (A,R) = both. Happy beaching.

DELAWARE

Dewey Beach
Rusty Rudder, Dickinson St., Dewey Beach, DE 19971; (302) 227-3888. (R)

Lewes
Lighthouse Restaurant, Fisherman's Wharf, Lewes, DE 19958; (302) 645-6271. (R)

Rehoboth

Blue Moon Restaurant, 35 Baltimore Ave., Rehoboth Beach, DE 19971; (302) 227-6515. (R)

Fran O'Brien's, 59 Lake Ave., Rehoboth Beach, DE 19971; (302) 227-6121. (R)

Front Page, 52 Baltimore Ave., Rehoboth Beach, DE 19971; (302) 227-0948. (R)

Henlopen Hotel, Box 16, Lake Ave. at Boardwalk, Rehoboth Beach, DE 19971; (302) 227-2551. (A,R)

FLORIDA

Amelia Island

Amelia Island Plantation, Amelia Island, FL 32034; (904) 261-6161. (A,R)

Boca Raton

Boca Raton Hotel & Club, 501 E. Camino Real, Boca Raton, FL 33432; (305) 395-3000. (A,R)

Boca West Resort & Club, W. Glades Rd., Boca Raton, FL 33432; (305) 483-9200. (A,R)

Seafood Connection, 6998 N. Federal Highway, Boca Raton, FL 33432; (305) 997-5562. (R)

Cocoa Beach

Bernard's Surf, 2 S. Atlantic Ave., Cocoa Beach, FL 32931; (305) 783-2401. (R)

Crossway Inn & Tennis Resort, 3901 N. Atlantic Ave., Cocoa Beach, FL 32931; (305) 783-2221. (A)

Holiday Inn Cocoa Beach, 1300 N. Atlantic Ave., Cocoa Beach, FL 32931; (305) 783-2271. (A,R)

Holiday Inn I-95, 900 Friday Rd., Cooca, FL 32922; (305) 631-1210. (A,R)

Polaris Ocean Club International, 5600 N. Atlantic Ave., Cocoa Beach, FL 32931; (305) 783-7621. (A)

Daytona Beach

Castaway Beach Motel, 2075 S. Atlantic Ave., Daytona Beach, FL 32016; (904) 255-6461. (A)

Chez Bruchez, 304 Seabreeze Blvd., Daytona Beach, FL 32018; (904) 252-6656. (R)

Chez Paul, 927 N. Beach St., Daytona Beach, FL 32018; (904) 252-3588. (R)

Hog Heaven, 37 N. Atlantic Ave., Daytona Beach, FL 32018; (904) 257-1212. (R)

Klaus' Cuisine, 144 N. Ridgewood Ave., Holly Hill, FL 32017; (904) 255-7711. (R)

Oyster Pub, 615 Seabreeze Blvd., Daytona Beach, FL 32018; (904) 252-9235. (R)

T-Bone's Steak and Bar-B-Q, 2075 S. Atlantic Ave., Daytona Beach, FL 32016; (904) 255-6461. (R)

Deerfield Beach

Best Western, A1A and Hillsboro Blvd., Deerfield Beach, FL 33441; (305) 428-0650. (A,R)

Howard Johnson's Ocean Resort Hotel, 2096 N.E. 2nd St., Deerfield Beach, FL 33441; (305) 428-2850. (A,R)

Pals Captain's Table, 1755 S.E. 3rd Ct., Deerfield Beach, FL 33441; (305) 427-4000. (R)

Pig on the Pit Bar-B-Q, Route 441, Deerfield Beach, FL 33441; (305) 427-6209. (R)

Whale's Rib, 2031 N.E. 2nd St., Deerfield Beach, FL 33441; (305) 421-8880. (R)

Duck Key

Hawks Cay, Mile Marker 61, Duck Key, Marathon, FL 33050; (305) 743-7000. (A,R)

Fernandina Beach

Bailey House, Box 805, 28 S. 7th St., Fernandina Beach, FL 32034; (904) 261-5390. (A)

Crap Trap, 31 N. 2nd St., Fernandina Beach, FL 32034; (904) 261-4749. (R)

1735 House, 584 S. Fletcher Ave., Amelia Island, FL 32084; (904) 261-5878. (A)

Snug Harbor Restaurant, N. 2nd St. and Alachua Ave., Fernandina Beach, FL 32084; (904) 261-8031. (R)

Fort Lauderdale and Pompano Beach

Best Western Marina & Yacht Harbor, 2150 S.E. 17th St. Causeway, Fort Lauderdale, FL 33308; (305) 525-3484. (A,R)

Best Western Sea Garden, 615 N. Ocean Blvd, Pompano Beach, FL 33062; (305) 943-6200. (A,R)

Days Inn Lauderdale Surf Hotel, 440 Sea Breeze Ave., Fort Lauderdale, FL 33316; (305) 462-5555. (A)

Holiday Inn Fort Lauderdale Beach, 999 N. Atlantic Blvd., Fort Lauderdale, FL 33304; (305) 563-5961. (A,R)

Holiday Inn North Beach, 4116 N. Ocean Dr., Lauderdale-by-the-Sea, FL 33308; (305) 776-1212. (A,R)

Holiday Inn Oceanside, 3000 E. Las Olas Blvd., Fort Lauderdale, FL 33316; (305) 463-8421. (A,R)

Holiday Inn on the Ocean, 1350 S. Ocean Blvd., Pompano Beach, FL 33062; (305) 941-7300. (A,R)

Howard Johnson's Motor Lodge, 4660 Ocean Dr., Lauderdale-by-the-Sea, FL 33308; (305) 776-5660. (A,R)

Howard Johnson's Ocean's Edge Resort, 700 N. Atlantic Blvd., Fort Lauderdale, FL 33304; (305) 563-2451. (A,R)

Howard Johnson's Pompano Beach Resort Inn, 9 N. Pompano Beach Blvd., Pompano Beach, FL 33062; (305) 781-1300. (A,R)

Jolly Roger Hotel, 619 N. Atlantic Blvd., Fort Lauderdale, FL 33304; (305) 564-3211. (A,R)

Mai-Kai, 3599 N. Federal Highway, Fort Lauderdale, FL 33308; (305) 563-3272. (R)

Morrison's Cafeteria, 1700 N. Federal Highway, Fort Lauderdale, FL 33308; (305) 565-3242. (R)

Morrison's Cafeteria, U.S. 1 and N.E. 23rd St., Pompano Beach, FL 33062; (305) 781-7676. (R)

Pier 66 Hotel and Marina, Drawer 9177, 2301 S.E. 17th St. Causeway, Fort Lauderdale, FL 33310; (305) 524-0566. (A,R)

Sheraton Yankee Clipper, 1140 Seabreeze Blvd., Fort Lauderdale, FL 33316; (305) 524-5551. (A,R)

Sheraton Yankee Trader, 303 N. Atlantic Blvd., Fort Lauderdale, FL 33304; (305) 467-1111. (A,R)

Tropic Cay, 529 N. Atlantic Blvd., Fort Lauderdale, FL 33304; (305) 564-4386. (A,R)

Yesterday's, 3001 E. Oakland Park Blvd., Fort Lauderdale, FL 33306; (305) 561-4400. (R)

Fort Pierce

Angler Motel, 1172 Seaway Dr., Fort Pierce, FL 33450; (305) 466-0131. (A)

Dockside Inn, 1152 Seaway Dr., Fort Pierce, FL 33450; (305) 461-4824. (A)

Ocean Village, 2400 S. Ocean Dr., Hutchinson Island, Fort Pierce, FL 33449; (305) 465-5900. (A,R)

Grassy Key

Rainbow Bend Fishing Club, Box 2447, Mile Marker 58, Grassy Key, Marathon Shores, FL 33052; (305) 289-1505. (A,R)

Hollywood

The Diplomat, 3515 S. Ocean Dr., Hollywood, FL 33019; (305) 457-8111. (A,R)

Hollywood Beach Hotel, 101 N. Ocean Drive, Hollywood, FL 33019; (305) 921-0990. (A,R)

Islamorada

Cheeca Lodge, Mile Marker 82, Islamorada, FL 33036; (305) 664-4651. (A,R)

The Chesapeake, Box 909, Mile Marker 84, Islamorada, FL 33036; (305) 664-4662. (A)

Coral Grill, Box 373, U.S. 1, Islamorada, FL 33036; (305) 664-4803. (R)

Green Turtle Inn, Mile Marker 81 1/2, Islamorada, FL 33036; (305) 664-9031. (R)

The Islander, Box 766, U.S. 1, Islamorada, FL 33306; (305) 664-2031. (A)

Marker 88, Mile Marker 88, Plantation Key, FL 33036; (305) 852-9315. (R)

Whale Harbor Inn, Box 632, Mile Marker 84, Islamorada, FL 33306; (305) 664-4959. (R)

Ziggie's Conch, U.S. 1, Islamorada, FL 33036; (305) 664-3391. (R)

Jacksonville

Cajun Catfish, 1927 Beach Blvd., Jacksonville Beach, FL 32250; (904) 249-7365. (R)

Friendship Inn Gold Coast, 731 N. First St., Jacksonville Beach, FL 32250; (904) 249-5006. (A)

Hilltop Club, 2030 Wells Rd., Orange Park, FL 32073; (904) 272-5959. (R)

Holiday Inn Oceanfront, 1617 N. First St., Jacksonville Beach, FL 32250; (904) 249-9071. (A,R)

Howard Johnson's on the Ocean, 1515 N. First St., Jacksonville Beach, FL 32250; (904) 249-3711. (A,R)

Pier 6 Oyster House and Seafood, 2777-1 University Blvd. W., Promenade Shopping Center, Jacksonville, FL 32211; (904) 731-8258. (R)

Ragtime Tavern, 207 Atlantic Blvd., Atlantic Beach, FL 32233; (904) 241-7877. (R)

Sailmaker Restaurant, 9927 Atlantic Blvd., Jacksonville, FL 32211; (904) 724-1755. (R)

Sea Turtle Inn and Restaurant, One Ocean Blvd., Atlantic Beach, FL 32233; (904) 249-7402. (A,R)

Key West

A & B Lobster House, 700 Front St., Key West, FL 33040; (305) 294-2536. (R)

Best Western Key Ambassador, 1000 S. Roosevelt Blvd., Key West, FL 33040; (305) 296-3500. (A)

Claire's, 900 Duval St., Key West, FL 33040; (305) 296-5558. (R)

Eden House, 1015 Fleming St., Key West, FL 33040; (305) 296-6868. (A)

Key Lime Village, 727 Truman Ave., Key West, FL 33040; (305) 294-6222. (A)

Kyushu Japanese Restaurant, 921 Truman Ave., Key West, FL 33040; (305) 294-2995. (R)

La-Te-Da, 1125 Duval St., Key West, FL 33040; (305) 294-8435. (R)

Marriott's Casa Marina Resort, 1500 Reynolds St., Key West, FL 33040; (305) 296-3535. (A,R)

Pier House, One Duval St., Key West, FL 33040; (305) 294-9541. (A,R)

Red Rooster Inn, 709 Truman Ave., Key West, FL 33040; (305) 296-6558. (A)

Rooftop Café, Front St., Key West, FL 33040; (305) 294-2042. (R)

Shorty's Diner, 215 Duval St., Key West, FL 33040; (305) 294-5725. (R)

South Beach Oceanfront Motel, 508 South St., Key West, FL 33040; (305) 296-5611. (A)

Long Key
Lime Tree Bay Resort, Long Key, FL 33001; (305) 664-4740. (A,R)

Marathon
Continental Inn, Box 209, Key Colony Beach, FL 33051; (305) 289-0101. (A)

Herbie's, Mile Marker 51, Marathon, FL 33050; (305) 743-6373. (R)

Howard Johnson's, U.S. 1, Box T, Marathon, FL 33050; (305) 289-1400. (A,R)

Kelsey's, Mile Marker 48 1/2, Marathon, FL 33050; (305) 743-9018. (R)

Key Colony Beach Motel, 441 E. Ocean Dr., Box 53, Key Colony Beach, FL 33051; (305) 289-0411. (A)

Perry's, Mile Marker 51, Marathon, FL 33050; (305) 743-3108. (R)

Porky's, Mile Marker 48, Marathon, FL 33050; (305) 743-5100. (R)

7 Mile Grill, Mile Marker 48, Marathon, FL 33050; (305) 743-4481. (R)

Vernon's Iron Skillet, Mile Marker 48, Marathon, FL 33050; (305) 743-4100. (R)

Marineland
Quality Inn Marineland, Box 122, U.S. 1, St. Augustine, FL 32084; (904) 471-1222. (A,R)

Melbourne Beach
Bunky's Raw Bar, 218 N. A1A, Satellite Beach, FL 32935; (305) 777-CLAM. (R)

Holiday Inn Oceanfront, 2600 A1A, Indialantic, FL 32903; (305) 777-4100. (A,R)

Poor Richard's Inn, 522 Ocean Ave., Melbourne Beach, FL 32951; (305) 724-0601. (R)

Sharrock Shores Motel, 1441 S. Miramar, Indialantic, FL 32903; (305) 723-3355. (A)

Miami and Miami Beach
Alexander Hotel, 5225 Collins Ave., Miami Beach, FL 33140; (305) 865-6500. (A,R)

The Crab House, 1551 79th St. Causeway, Miami Beach, FL 33141; (305) 868-7085. (R)

Doral Hotel On-the-Ocean, 4833 Collins Ave., Miami Beach, FL 33140; (305) 532-3600. (A,R)

Eden Roc Hotel, 4525 Collins Ave., Miami Beach, FL 33140; (305) 531-0000. (A,R)

Fontainebleau Hilton, 4441 Collins Ave., Miami Beach, FL 33140; (305) 538-2000. (A,R)

Joe's Stone Crab, 227 Biscayne St., Miami Beach, FL 33139; (305) 673-0365. (R)

Marco Polo Resort Hotel, 19201 Collins Ave., Miami Beach, FL 33160; (305) 949-1461. (A,R)

The Palm Beaches

The Breakers, S. County Rd., Palm Beach, FL 33480; (305) 655-6611. (A,R)

Café L'Europe, 150 Worth Ave., Palm Beach, FL 33480; (305) 655-4020. (R)

Fisherman's Cafe, 661 U.S. 1, North Palm Beach, FL 33408; (305) 848-9600. (R)

New England Oyster House, 302 E. Ocean Ave., Lantana, FL 33462; (305) 588-9424. (R)

Palm Beach Hawaiian Ocean Inn, 3550 S. Ocean Blvd., Palm Beach, FL 33480; (305) 582-5631. (A,R)

Petite Marmite, 315 Worth Ave., Palm Beach, FL 33480; (305) 655-0550. (R)

Testa's, 221 Royal Poinciana Way, Palm Beach, FL 33480; (305) 832-0992. (A,R)

TGIFriday's, 1201 U.S. 1, North Palm Beach, FL 33408; (305) 622-7860. (R)

Worth Avenue Café, 237 1/2 Worth Ave., Palm Beach, FL 33480; (305) 655-0950. (R)

Pompano Beach (see Fort Lauderdale)

Riviera Beach (Singer Island)

The Galley, 90 Lake Dr., Sailfish Marina, Riviera Beach, FL 33404; (305) 848-1492. (R)

Greenhouse Restaurant, 2410 N. Ocean Ave., Riviera Beach, FL 33404; (305) 845-1333. (R)

Joey's, Ocean Mall, Riviera Beach, FL 33404; (305) 844-9710. (R)

Portofino, 2447 Ocean Blvd., Ocean Mall, Riviera Beach, FL 33404; (305) 844-8411. (R)

Rutledge Inn, 3730 Ocean Dr., Riviera Beach, FL 33404; (305) 848-6621. (A)

Tahiti on the Ocean, 3920 N. Ocean Dr., Riviera Beach, FL 33404; (305) 848-9764. (A)

Top O'Spray Restaurant and Lounge, Best Western Sea Spray Inn, 123 S. Ocean Ave., Palm Beach Shores, FL 33404; (305) 845-0402. (A,R)

St. Augustine

Aldo's Restaurant, 60 San Marco Ave., St. Augustine, FL 32084; (904) 824-0373. (R)

Cap's Seafood Restaurant, A1A North and Intracoastal Waterway, St. Augustine, FL 32084; (904) 824-8794. (R)

Days Inn, 2800 Ponce de León Blvd., St. Augustine, FL 32084; (904) 829-6581. (A)

Econo Lodge, 3101 Ponce de León Blvd., St. Augustine, FL 32084; (904) 829-3461. (A)

Raintree Restaurant, 102 San Marco Ave., St. Augustine, FL 32084; (904) 824-7211. (R)

Ramada Inn Downtown, 116 San Marco Ave., St. Augustine, FL 32084; (904) 824-4352. (A,R)

Scottish Inn, One Corporate Square, St. Augustine, FL 32084; (904) 829-5643. (R)

Singer Island (see Riviera Beach)

Sugarloaf Key

Sugar Loaf Lodge, Box 148, Sugarloaf Key, FL 33044; (305) 745-3211. (A,R)

Vero Beach

Driftwood Inn, 3150 Ocean Dr., Vero Beach, FL 32963; (305) 231-2800. (A,R)

Holiday Inn Oceanside, 3384 Ocean Dr., Vero Beach, FL 32963; (305) 231-2300. (A,R)

Ocean Grill, 1050 Sexton Plaza, Box 3301, Vero Beach, FL 32964; (305) 231-5409. (R)

GEORGIA

Jekyll Island

Buccaneer Motor Lodge, 85 S. Beachview Dr., Jekyll Island, GA 31520; (912) 635-2261. (A,R)

Hilton Inn, 975 N. Beachview Dr., Jekyll Island, GA 31520; (912) 635-2531. (A,R)

Holiday Inn, 200 S. Beachview Dr., Jekyll Island, GA 31520; (912) 635-3311. (A,R)

Ramada Inn, 150 S. Beachview Dr., Jekyll Island, GA 31520; (912) 635-2111. (A,R)

The Wanderer, 711 N. Beachview Dr., Jekyll Island, GA 31520; (912) 635-2211. (A,R)

St. Simons Island

Blanche's Courtyard, 440 Kings Way, St. Simons Island, GA 31522; (912) 638-3030. (R)

Brogens, Mallery St. and the Pier, St. Simons Island, GA 31522; (912) 638-1660. (R)

Emmeline & Hessie Seafood Restaurant, Golden Isles Marina, St. Simons Island, GA 31522; (912) 638-9084. (R)

King and Prince, Box 798, 201 Arnold Rd., St. Simons Island, GA 31522; (912) 638-3631. (A,R)

Queens Restaurant, 407 Mallery St., St. Simons Island, GA 31522; (912) 638-2493. (R)

Rib Cage, 313 Mallery St., St. Simons Island, GA 31522; (912) 638-2768. (R)

Savannah

Chart House, 202 W. Bay St., Savannah, GA 31401; (912) 234-6686. (R)

Crystal Beer Parlor, Jones and Jefferson Sts., Savannah, GA 31499; (912) 232-1153. (R)

East Bay Inn, 225 E. Bay St., Savannah, GA 31401; (912) 238-1225. (A)

Hyatt Regency Savannah, 2 W. Bay St., Savannah, GA 31401; (912) 238-1234. (A,R)

Johnny Harris Restaurant, 1651 E. Victory Dr., Savannah, GA 31404; (912) 354-7810. (R)

Palmer's Seafood House, 80 Wilmington Island Rd., Savannah, GA 31410; (912) 897-2611. (R)

River House Seafood, 125 W. River St., Savannah, GA 31401; (912) 234-1900. (R)

17 Hundred 90 Inn, 307 E. President St., Savannah, GA 31401; (912) 236-7122. (A,R)

Shrimp Factory, 313 E. River St., Savannah, GA 31401; (912) 236-4229. (R)

Spanky's Pizza Galley and Saloon, 317 E. River St., Savannah, GA 30401; (912) 236-3009. (R)

Williams Seafood Restaurant, 8010 Tybee Rd., Savannah, GA 31410; (912) 897-2219. (R)

Sea Island

The Cloister, Sea Island, GA 31561; (912) 638-3611. (A,R)

MAINE

Bar Harbor

Atlantic Oakes By-the-Sea, Route 3, Bar Harbor, ME 04609; (207) 288-5801. (A)

Bar Harbor Motor Inn and Restaurant, Newport Drive, Bar Harbor, ME 04609; (207) 288-3351. (A,R)

Cadillac Motor Inn, 336 Main St., Bar Harbor, ME 04609; (207) 288-3831. (A)

Jordan's Variety, 80 Cottage St., Bar Harbor, ME 04609; (207) 288-3586. (R)

Mary Jane Restaurant, 119 Main St., Bar Harbor, ME 04609; (207) 288-3410. (A)

National Park Motel, Route 3, Bar Harbor, ME 04609; (207) 288-5403. (A)

Testa's, 53 Main St., Bar Harbor, ME 04609; (207) 288-3327. (R)

Belfast

Belfast Cafe, 90 Main St., Belfast, ME 04915; (207) 338-2949. (R)

City Boat Landing Restaurant, Main St., Belfast, ME 04915; (207) 338-5253. (R)

Jed's Restaurant & Lounge, Route 1, Belfast, ME 04915; (207) 338-3241. (R)

Penobscot Meadows Country Inn and Restaurant, U.S. 1, Belfast, ME 04915; (207) 338-5320. (A,R)

Yankee Clipper Motel, Route 1, Belfast, ME 04915; (207) 338-2220. (A)

Boothbay Harbor

Boothbay Harbor Inn, Waterfront, Boothbay Harbor, ME 04538; (207) 633-6302. (A)

Fisherman's Wharf, Pier 6, Boothbay Harbor, ME 04538; (207) 633-5090. (A)

The Harborage, Townshend Ave., Boothbay Harbor, ME 04538; (207) 633-4640. (A)

Hilltop House, McKown Hill, Boothbay Harbor, ME 04538; (207) 633-2941. (A)

Lobster Loft, Commercial St., Boothbay Harbor, ME 04538; (207) 633-4449. (R)

Lobstermen's Co-op, Atlantic Ave., Boothbay Harbor, ME 04538; (207) 633-4900. (R)

Welch House, 36 McKown St., Boothbay Harbor, ME 04538; (207) 633-3431. (A)

Camden

Fox Island Inn, Box 60, Carver St., Vinalhaven, ME 04863; (207) 863-2122. (A)

High Tide Inn, U.S. 1, Camden, ME 04843; (207) 236-3724. (A)

Peter Ott's Tavern and Steak House, Bayview St., Camden, ME 04843; (207) 236-4032. (R)

Swan's Way, 51 Bayview St., Camden, ME 04843; (207) 236-2171. (R)

Waterfront Restaurant, Harborside Square, Camden, ME 04843; (207) 236-3747. (R)

Whitehall Inn, 52 High St., Camden, ME 04843; (207) 236-3391. (A)

Castine

Castine Inn, Main St., Castine, ME 04421; (207) 326-4365. (A,R)

Pentagoet Inn, Box 4, Main St., Castine, ME 04421; (207) 326-8616. (A)

Deer Isle (see Stonington)

Eastport (see Lubec)

Higgins Beach

Higgins Beach Inn, Scarborough, ME 04074; (207) 883-6684. (A,R)

Kennebunkport

Arundel Wharf Restaurant & Inn, Ocean Ave., Kennebunkport, ME 04046; (207) 967-3444. (A,R)

Beachwood Motel, Route 9, Kennebunkport, ME 04046; (207) 967-2483. (A)

Breakwater Restaurant and Inn, Ocean Ave., Kennebunkport, ME 04046; (207) 967-3118. (A,R)

Captain Fairfield House, Plesant and Green Sts., Kennebunkport, ME 04046; (207) 967-4454. (A)

Lubec and Eastport

Cannery Wharf, N. Water St., Eastport, ME 04631; (207) 853-4800. (R)

Cobscook Bay State Park, U.S. 1, Dennysville, ME 04628; (207) 726-4412. (A)

Hillside Takeout, Route 189, Lubec, ME 04652; (207) 733-4323. (R)

Home Port Inn and Restaurant, 45 Main St., Lubec, ME 04652; (207) 733-2077. (A,R)

Ogunquit

Barbara Dean's, Shore Rd., Ogunquit, ME 03097; (207) 646-5562. (R)

Barnacle Billy's, Perkins Cove, Ogunquit, ME 03907; (207) 646-5575. (R)

Blue Water Inn, Beach St., Ogunquit, ME 03907; (207) 646-5559. (R)

Captain Lorenz Perkins Inn, Box 1249, N. Main St., Ogunquit, ME 03907; (207) 646-7825. (A)

Einsteins' Restaurant, 2 Shore Rd., Ogunquit, ME 03907; (207) 646-5262. (R)

Grenadier Motor Inn, 64 Main St., Ogunquit, ME 03907; (207) 646-3432. (A)

Hayes Guest House, 133 Shore Rd., Ogunquit, ME 03907; (207) 646-2277. (A)

Neptune Inn, Beach St., Ogunquit, ME 03907; (207) 646-2632. (A)

Old Village Inn, 30 Main St., Ogunquit, ME 03907; (207) 646-7088. (R)

Old Orchard Beach

Biarritz Motel, 78 East Grand Ave., Old Orchard Beach, ME 04064; (207) 934-2983. (A)

Chez Marie Antoinette Restaurant, 9 East Grand Ave., Old Orchard Beach, ME 04064. (R)

Waves Motor Inn, 87 West Grand Ave., Old Orchard Beach, ME 04064; (207) 934-4949. (A)

South Portland
Lobster Shack Restaurant, Two Lights Rd., Cape Elizabeth, ME 04107; (207) 799-1677. (R)

Stonington and Deer Isle
Bayview Restaurant, Stonington, ME 04681; (207) 367-2274. (R)
Captain's Quarters, Box 83, Main St., Stonington, ME 04681; (207) 367-2420. (A)
The Clamdigger, Route 15, Deer Isle, ME 04627; (207) 348-6187. (R)
1872 Inn, Box 83, Main St., Stonington, ME 04681; (207) 367-2420. (A)
Fisherman's Friend Restaurant, School St., Stonington, ME 04681; (207) 367-2442. (R)

Wells Beach
The Greygull Inn, 321 Webhannet Dr., Wells, ME 04090; (207) 646-7501. (A)
The Webhannet Motor Court, Wells Beach, ME 04090; (207) 646-9400. (A)

The Yorks
Bill Foster's Downeast Lobster and Clambake, Route 1A, York Harbor, ME 03911; (207) 363-3255. (R)
Wooden Goose Inn, U.S. 1, Cape Neddick, ME 03902; (207) 363-5673. (A)

MARYLAND

Ocean City
Paul Revere's Smorgasbord, 2nd St. and Boardwalk, Ocean City, MD 21842; (301) 289-6181. (R)
Roy Rogers Family Restaurant, 7601 Coastal Highway, Ocean City, MD 21842; (301) 524-7117. (R)

MASSACHUSETTS

Gloucester

Bass Rocks Motor Inn, 119 Atlantic Rd., Gloucester, MA 01930;
   (617) 283-7600. (A)

Captain Courageous, 25 Rogers St., Gloucester, MA 01930; (617)
   283-0007. (R)

Down East Oyster House, 116-118 Main St., Gloucester, MA 01930;
   (617) 283-2037. (R)

Gloucester House, Seven Seas Wharf, Gloucester, MA 01930; (617)
   283-1812. (R)

Lynn

Cap'n Jack's Waterfront Inn, 253 Humphrey St., Swampscott, MA
   01907; (617) 595-9734. (A)

Martha's Vineyard

Beach Plum Inn, Basin Rd., Menemsha, Martha's Vineyard, MA
   02552; (617) 645-9454. (R)

Black Dog Tavern, Beach St., Vineyard Haven, Martha's Vineyard,
   MA 02568; (617) 693-9223. (R)

Chez Pierre, S. Summer St., Edgartown, MA 02539; (617) 627-
   8947. (R)

David's Island House, Circuit Ave., Oak Bluffs, MA 02557; (617)
   693-4516. (R)

Edgartown Delicatessen, Main St., Edgartown, Martha's Vineyard,
   MA 02539; (617) 627-4789. (R)

La Grange, Box 312, Chilmark, Martha's Vineyard, MA 02535; (617)
   645-9098. (R)

Lambert's Cove Country Inn, Lambert's Cove Rd., West Tisbury,
   Martha's Vineyard, MA 02575; (617) 693-2298. (R)

Ocean Club, 5 Corners, Vineyard Haven, MA 02568; (617) 693-
   4763. (R)

Ocean View Restaurant, Chapman Ave., Oak Bluffs, Martha's Vineyard, MA 02557; (617) 693-2207. (R)

Point Way Inn, Upper Main St., Edgartown, Martha's Vineyard,
   MA 02539; (617) 627-8633. (A)

Wesley House, Box 1207, Lake Ave., Oak Bluffs, Martha's Vineyard,
   MA 02557; (617) 693-0135. (A)

Nantucket Island

Atlantic Café, S. Water St., Nantucket Island, MA 02554; (617) 228-0570. (R)

The Brotherhood, 23 Broad St., Nantucket Island, MA 02554. (R)

Chanticleer Inn, 40 New St., Siasconset, Nantucket Island, MA 02564; (617) 257-6231. (R)

Downy Flake Restaurant, S. Water St., Nantucket Island, MA 02554; (617) 228-4533. (R)

Jared Coffin House, 29 Broad St., Nantucket Island, MA 02554; (617) 228-2400. (A,R)

Obadiah's, 2 India St., Nantucket Island, MA 02554; (617) 228-4430. (R)

Opera House, 4 S. Water St., Nantucket Island, MA 02554; (617) 228-9755. (R)

The Second Story, 1 S. Beach St., Nantucket Island, MA 02554; (617) 228-3471. (R)

The Upper Crust, 7 West Creek Rd., Nantucket Island, MA 02554; (617) 228-2519. (R)

Wauwinet House, Box 628, Wauwinet, Nantucket Island, MA 02554; (617) 228-0145. (A,R)

Plymouth

Bert's On the Beach, Route 3A, Plymouth, MA 02360; (617) 746-3422. (R)

Governor Bradford Motor Inn, Brewster and Water Sts., Plymouth, MA 02360; (617) 746-6200. (A)

Governor Carver Motor Inn, 25 Summer St., Plymouth, MA 02360; (617) 746-7100. (A,R)

McGrath's, Town Wharf, Plymouth, MA 02360; (617) 746-9751.(R)

Provincetown

Café at the Mews, 359 Commercial St., Provincetown, MA 02657; (617) 487-1500. (R)

Ciro & Sal's, 4 Kiley Ct., Provincetown, MA 02657; (617) 487-9803. (R)

Everbreeze, 429 Commercial St., Provincetown, MA 02657; (617) 487-0465. (R)

Hargood House, 493 Commercial St., Provincetown, MA 02657; (617) 487-1324. (A)

Landmark Inn Restaurant, 404 Commercial St., Provincetown, MA
    02657; (617) 487-9139. (R)
Lobster Pot, 321 Commercial St., Provincetown, MA 02657; (617)
    487-0842. (R)
Mayflower Café, 300 Commercial St., Provincetown, MA 02657; (617)
    487-0121. (R)
The Moors, Bradford St. at Beach Hwy., Provincetown, MA 02657;
    (617) 487-1342. (A,R)
Pilgrim House, 336 Commercial St., Provincetown, MA 02657; (617)
    487-0319. (R)
Poor Richard's Buttery, 432 Commercial St., Provincetown, MA 02657;
    (617) 487-3825. (R)
Ship's Bell, 586 Commercial St., Provincetown, MA 02657; (617)
    487-1674. (A)
Surfside Inn, 543 Commercial St., Provincetown, MA 02657; (617)
    487-1726. (A)
White Winds Inn, Commercial and Winthrop Sts., Provincetown,
    MA 02657; (617) 487-1526. (A)

Salem
As You Like It, Essex Street Mall, Salem, MA 01970. (R)
Beef and Oyster House, 143 Washington St., Salem, MA 01970; (617)
    744-4328. (R)
Café L'Espresso, 106 Essex St., Salem, MA 01970; (617) 744-
    1741. (R)
Chase House, Pickering Wharf, Salem, MA 01970; (617) 744-
    0000. (R)
Folsom's Chowder House, 7 Dodge St., Salem, MA 01970; (617) 745-
    1230. (R)
Hawthorne Inn, 18 Washington Square W., Salem, MA 01970; (617)
    744-4080. (A,R)
In a Pig's Eye, 146 Derby St., Salem, MA 01970; (617) 744-
    9577. (R)

Wellfleet
Wellfleet Oyster House, E. Main St., Wellfleet, MA 02667; (617) 349-
    2134. (R)

NEW HAMPSHIRE

Rye

Hector's Country Kitchen, Lafayette Rd., Rye, NH 03870; (603) 964-6900. (A,R)

NEW JERSEY

Asbury Park

Howard Johnson's, 1213 Boardwalk, Asbury Park, NJ 07712; (201) 988-3434. (R)

Oceanic Inn, 201 Sixth Ave., Asbury Park, NJ 07712; (201) 988-0300. (A)

Pier Six Hotel, 307 Sixth Ave., Asbury Park, NJ 07712; (201) 988-5577. (A)

Atlantic City

Atlantis, Florida Ave. at Boardwalk, Atlantic City, NJ 08401; (609) 344-4000. (A,R)

Bally's Park Place, Park Place at Boardwalk, Atlantic City, NJ 08401; (609) 340-2000. (A,R)

Caesar's Boardwalk Regency, Arkansas Ave. at Boardwalk, Atlantic City, NJ 08401; (609) 348-4411. (A,R)

Claridge, Indiana Ave. at Boardwalk, Atlantic City, NJ 08401; (609) 340-3400. (A,R)

Golden Nugget, Boston Ave. at Boardwalk, Atlantic City, NJ 08404; (609) 347-7111. (A,R)

Harrah's Marina, 1725 Brigantine Blvd., Atlantic City, NJ 08401; (609) 441-5000. (A,R)

Harrah's on the Boardwalk, Mississippi Ave. at Boardwalk, Atlantic City, NJ 08401; (609) 441-5000. (A,R)

Resorts International, North Carolina Ave. at Boardwalk, Atlantic City, NJ 08404; (609) 344-6000. (A,R)

Sands, Indiana Ave. and Brighton Park, Atlantic City, NJ 08404; (609) 441-4000. (A,R)

Tropicana, Iowa Ave. at Boardwalk, Atlantic City, NJ 08404; (609) 340-4000. (A,R)

White House Subs, 2301 Arctic Ave., Atlantic City, NJ 08404; (609) 345-1564. (R)

Avalon

The Beachcomber, 7900 Dune Dr., Avalon, NJ 08202; (609) 368-5121. (A)

Golden Inn, 78th St., Avalon, NJ 08202; (609) 368-5155. (A,R)

Cape May

Carney's, 401 Beach Ave., Cape May, NJ 08204; (609) 884-4424. (R)

Carroll Villa, 19 Jackson St., Cape May, NJ 08204; (609) 884-9619. (A)

Congress Hall, Congress St., Cape May, NJ 08204; (609) 884-8421. (A)

Harvey's, 408 Washington Mall, Cape May, NJ 08204; (609) 884-5648. (R)

Mad Batter, 19 Jackson St., Cape May, NJ 08204; (609) 884-5970. (R)

Sea Crest Inn, Broadway, Cape May, NJ 08204; (609) 884-4561. (A)

Washington Inn, 801 Washington St., Cape May, NJ 08204; (609) 884-5697. (R)

Watson's Merion Inn, 106 Decatur St., Cape May, NJ 08204; (609) 884-8363. (R)

Long Beach Island

Amber House, 118 Amber St., Beach Haven, NJ 08008; (609) 492-2017. (A)

Bill's Seafood, Division St., Surf City, NJ 08008; (609) 494-5928. (R)

The Ketch Restaurant & Bar, 529 Dock Rd., Beach Haven, NJ 08008; (609) 492-3000. (R)

Morrison's Seafood Inc., 2nd St., Beach Haven, NJ 08008; (609) 492-5111. (R)

Owl Tree, 80th St., Harvey Cedars, NJ 08008; (609) 494-8191. (R)

Pier 18 Mall, 3rd and Bay Aves., Beach Haven, NJ 08008; (609) 492-0107 (R)

Show Place Ice Cream Parlor, Centre St., Beach Haven, NJ 08008; (609) 492-0018 (R)

Victoria Guest House, 122 Amber St., Beach Haven, NJ 08008; (609) 492-4154. (A)

Ocean City and Somers Point

The Chatterbox, 9th St. and Central Ave., Ocean City, NJ 08226; (609) 399-0113. (R)

Culinary Garden, 841 Central Ave., Ocean City, NJ 08226; (609) 399-3713. (R)

Gregory's, Shore Rd., Somers Point, NJ 08244; (609) 927-6665. (R)

Mac's, 908 Shore Rd., Somers Point, NJ 08244; (609) 927-4360. (R)

Port-O-Call, 1510 Boardwalk, Ocean City, NJ 08226; (609) 399-8812. (A)

Sting Ray Motor Inn, 1280 Boardwalk, Ocean City, NJ 08226; (609) 399-8555. (A,R)

T.R. Fenwicks, 1200 Boardwalk, Ocean City, NJ 08226; (609) 398-0324. (R)

Sea Isle City

Garrity's, East Landis Ave., Townshend's Inlet, NJ 08249; (609) 263-3164. (R)

Somers Point (see Ocean City)

Spring Lake Heights

Old Mill Inn, Old Mill Rd., Spring Lake Heights, NJ 07762; (201) 449-5370. (R)

Stone Harbor

Shelter Haven, 96th St. and Ocean Dr., Stone Harbor, NJ 08247; (609) 368-2163. (A)

Touché, 96th and Third Sts., Stone Harbor, NJ 08247; (609) 368-3012. (R)

Villa Maria by the Sea, 1101 1st Ave., Stone Harbor, NJ 08247; (609) 368-4761. (A)

Strathmere

Deauville Inn, Box 406, Willard Rd., Strathmere, NJ 08248; (609) 263-2080. (R)

The Wildwoods

Zaberer's, 400 Spruce Ave., North Wildwood 08260; (609) 522-1423. (R)

Maple Leaf Motel, 320 E. Maple Ave., Wildwood, NJ 08260; (609) 522-1689. (A)

Neil's Steak and Oyster House, 222 E. Schellenger Ave., Wildwood, NJ 08260; (609) 522-6060. (R)

Pink Orchid Motel, Orchid Rd., Wildwood Crest, NJ 08260; (609)
    729-3770. (A)
Swan Motel, 510 E. Stockton Rd., Wildwood Crest, NJ 08260; (609)
    522-3459. (A)

NEW YORK

Fire Island

Flynn's Hotel, Ocean Bay Park (c/o Ocean Beach Post Office, Box
    334, Fire Island, NY 11770); (516) 583-5000. (A,R)
Morning Call, Ocean Beach, Fire Island, NY 11770. (R)
Peppermint Stick Restaurant, Cherry Grove, Fire Island, NY 11782;
    (516) 597-9816. (R)
Skimmers, Ocean Bay Park (c/o Ocean Beach Post Office, Box 334,
    Fire Island, NY 11770); (516) 583-8438. (R)

The Hamptons

Barefoot Contessa, 46 Newtown Lane, East Hampton, L.I., NY 11937;
    (516) 324-0240. (R)
Barefoot Contessa, 103 Main St., Westhampton, L.I., NY 11977;
    (516) 288-1243. (R)
Carol's "The Great Hampton Chicken & Rib Co.," 419 North High-
    way, Southampton, L.I., NY 11986; (516) 283-5001. (R)
Casa Albona, Montauk Highway, Amagansett, L.I., NY 11930; (516)
    267-6433. (R)
Club Burgundy, Suffolk County Airport, Westhampton Beach, L.I.,
    NY 11978; (516) 288-6900. (R)
House on Toilsome, 15 Toilsome Lane, East Hampton, L.I., NY
    11937; (516) 324-3003. (R)
Old Stove Pub, Montauk Highway, Sagaponack, L.I., NY 11932;
    (516) 537-3300. (R)
PB's Tequila Flats, Dune Rd., East Quogue, L.I., NY 11942; (516)
    653-5144.(R)

Montauk

Beach House Ocean Resort, S. Embassy and S. Elmwood, Montauk,
    L.I., NY 11954; (516) 668-2700. (A,R)
Clam Bar at Napeague, Montauk Highway, Montauk, L.I., NY 11954;
    (516) 267-6348. (R)

Gosman's, West Lake Dr., Montauk, L.I., NY 11954; (516) 668-5330. (R)

Gurney's Inn, Old Montauk Highway, Montauk, L.I., NY 11954; (516) 668-2345. (A,R)

Hither Hills State Park, Montauk Highway, Montauk, L.I., NY 11954; (516) 668-2554. (A)

Lobster Roll, Montauk Highway, Montauk, L.I., NY 11954; (516) 267-3740. (R)

Royal Atlantic Motel, S. Edgemere St., Montauk, L.I., NY 11954; (516) 668-5103. (A)

Salivar's Restaurant and Marine Bar, West Lake Dr., Montauk, L.I., NY 11954; (516) 668-2555. (R)

Shagwong Restaurant and Tavern, Montauk Highway, Montauk, L.I., NY 11954; (516) 668-9881. (R)

Stingray Motor Lodge, S. Emerson St., Montauk, L.I., NY 11954; (516) 668-3344. (A)

NORTH CAROLINA

Atlantic Beach, Morehead City and Beaufort

Atlantis Lodge, Box 310, Salter Path Rd., Atlantic Beach, NC 28512; (919) 726-5168. (A)

Beaufort House, 520 Front St., Beaufort, NC 28516; (919) 728-7541. (R)

Channel Marker Restaurant, Box 427, Atlantic Beach Causeway, Atlantic Beach, NC 28512; (919) 247-2344. (R)

John Yancey Motor Hotel, Box 790, Salter Path Rd., Atlantic Beach, NC 28512; (919) 726-5188. (A)

Mrs. Willis' Restaurant, Box 1646, Bridges St. Ext., Morehead City, NC 28557; (919) 726-3741. (R)

Sanitary Fish Market and Restaurant, 501 Evans St., Morehead City, NC 28557; (919) 247-3111. (R)

Smithfield's Chicken 'n' Bar-B-Q, Box 349, Salter Path Rd., Indian Beach, NC 28575; (919) 247-2749. (R)

Bald Head Island

Bald Head Island Inn, Box 11058, Southport, NC 28461; (919) 457-6763. (A,R)

Beaufort (see Atlantic Beach)

Calabash
Original Calabash Restaurant, Waterfront, Calabash, NC 28459; (919)
    579-6875. (R)

Carolina Beach and Kure Beach
Big Daddy's, K Avenue, Kure Beach, NC 28449; (919) 458-8622. (R)
Harbor Master, 315 Canal Drive, Carolina Beach, NC 28428; (919)
    458-8270. (R)
Sea Ranch Motel, Box 176, U.S. 421, Carolina Beach, NC 28428;
    (919) 458-8681. (A)

Hatteras Island
Cape Hatteras Court, Box 339, Route 12, Buxton, NC 27920; (919)
    995-5611. (A)
Channel Bass, Route 12, Hatteras, NC 27943; (919) 986-2250. (R)
Diamond Shoals Restaurant, Route 12, Buxton, NC 27920. (R)
Lighthouse View Motel, Box 39, Route 12, Buxton, NC 27920; (919)
    995-5680. (A)
Outer Banks Motel, Box 428, Route 12, Buxton, NC 27920; (919)
    995-5601. (A)
Soundside Restaurant, Route 12, Waves, NC 27982; (919) 987-
    2383. (R)

Kill Devil Hills (see Nags Head)

Kure Beach (see Carolina Beach)

Long Beach
Jones' Seafood House, 6404 Oak Island Dr., Long Beach, NC 28461;
    (919) 278-5231. (R)
Ocean Crest Motel, 1411 E. Beach Dr., Long Beach, NC 28461; (919)
    278-6674. (A)

Morehead City (see Atlantic Beach)

Nags Head and Kill Devil Hills
A Restaurant by George, Milepost 11, Beach Rd., Nags Head, NC
    27959; (919) 441-4821. (R)

Carolinian Hotel, Box 370, Milepost 10 1/2, Beach Rd., Nags Head, NC 27959; (919) 441-7171. (A,R)

Midgett's Barbeque Shop, U.S. 158 Bus., Kill Devil Hills, NC 27948; (919) 441-5636. (R)

Papagayo (at the Croatan Inn), Milepost 7 1/2, Beach Rd., Kill Devil Hills, NC 27948; (919) 441-7232. (A,R)

Quality Inn John Yancey, Box 422, Milepost 10, U.S. 158 Bus., Kill Devil Hills, NC 27948; (919) 441-7727. (A,R)

Quality Inn Sea Oatel, Box 489, Milepost 16 1/2, Beach Rd., Nags Head, NC 27959; (919) 441-7191. (A,R)

Spencer's Seafood Safari, Nags Head Causeway, Nags Head, NC 27959; (919) 441-5633. (R)

Tanglewood Motel, Box 386, Beach Rd., Milepost 8, Kill Devil Hills, NC 27948; (919) 441-7208. (A)

Ocracoke Island

Anchorage Inn, Box 130, Ocracoke, NC 27960; (919) 928-1101. (A)

Back Porch Restaurant and Bake Shop, Ocracoke, NC 27960; (919) 928-6401. (R)

Berkeley Center Country Inn, Box 220, Ocracoke, NC 27960; (919) 928-5911. (A)

Island Inn, Box 9, Ocracoke, NC 27960; (919) 928-4351. (A,R)

Maria's, Ocracoke, NC 27960; (919) 928-6891. (R)

On Their Banks, Ocracoke, NC 27960. (R)

Pelican Restaurant, Ocracoke, NC 27960. (R)

Topsail Beach

Breezeway Motel and Restaurant, Box 11, Topsail Beach, NC 28445; (919) 328-7751. (A,R)

Jolly Roger Motel, Box 8, Topsail Beach, NC 28445; (919) 328-4616. (A)

Wilmington (see Wrightsville Beach)

Wrightsville Beach and Wilmington

Blockade Runner Hotel, Box 555, 275 Waynick Blvd., Wrightsville Beach, NC 28480; (919) 256-2251. (A)

Bridge Tender, Airlie Rd., Wrightsville Beach, NC 28480; (919) 256-4519. (R)

Crystal Pier and Restaurant, 703 S. Lumina Ave., Wrightsville Beach, NC 28480; (919) 256-9093. (R)

Days Inn, 5040 Market St., Wilmington, NC 28405; (919) 799-6300. (A)

Econo Lodge, 4118 N. Market St., Wilmington, NC 28403; (919) 762-4426. (A)

Edgewater Inn, 10 W. Columia St., Wrightsville Beach, NC 28480; (919) 256-2914. (A)

Holiday Inn, Box 599, 1706 N. Lumina Ave., Wrightsville Beach, NC 28480; (919) 256-2231. (A,R)

Sheraton Wrightsville Beach Hotel, 1706 N. Lumina Ave., Wrightsville Beach, NC 28480; (919) 256-2231. (A,R)

RHODE ISLAND

Block Island

Harborside Inn, Water St., Block Island, RI 02807; (401) 466-5504. (A,R)

Highview Hotel, Box 580, Block Island, RI 02807; (401) 466-5912. (A,R)

National Hotel, Box 64, Water and Dodge Sts., Block Island, RI 02807; (401) 466-5577. (A,R)

Spring House, Box 206, Spring St., Block Island, RI 02807; (401) 466-2633. (A,R)

Surf Hotel, Water and Dodge Sts., Block Island, RI 02807; (401) 466-2241. (A)

Misquamicut

Pleasant View House, 65 Atlantic Ave., Misquamicut, RI 02891; (401) 348-8200. (A,R)

Sandpiper Motel, 53 Winnapaug Rd., Misquamicut, RI 02891; (401) 348-8748. (A)

Narragansett

Café at the End of the Wall, Ocean Rd., Narragansett, RI 02882. (R)

Phoenix Inn, 29 Gibson Ave., Narragansett, RI 02882; (401) 783-1918. (A)

Newport

Salas' Raw Bar, 343 Thames St., Newport, RI 02840; (401) 846-3781. (R)

S.S. Newport, Waites Wharf, Newport, RI 02840; (401) 846-1200. (R)

Sea View Motel, Route 138A, Box 392, Newport, RI 02840; (401) 847-0110. (A)

Watch Hill
Inn at Watch Hill, Bay St., Watch Hill, RI 02891; (401) 596-0665. (A)

SOUTH CAROLINA

Charleston
Colony House, 35 Prioloeau St., Charleston, SC 29401; (803) 723-3424. (R)
Cotton Exchange Restaurant, 36 Market St., Charleston, SC 29401; (803) 577-5000. (R)
Heart of Charleston Motor Inn, 200 Meeting St., Charleston, SC 29401; (803) 723-3451. (A)
Henry's, 54 Market St., Charleston, SC 29401; (803) 723-4363. (R)
Indigo Inn, One Maiden Lane, Charleston, SC 29401; (803) 577-5900. (A)
Kings Courtyard Inn, 198 King St., Charleston, SC 29401; (803) 723-7000. (A)
Mills House Hotel, Box 1013, Meeting and Queen Sts., Charleston, SC 29402; (803) 577-2400. (A,R)
Philippe Million Restaurant, 2 Unity Alley, Charleston, SC 29401; (803) 577-7472. (R)
Planter's Inn, 112 N. Market St., Charleston, SC 29401; (803) 722-2345. (A)
Silks, 110 N. Market St., Charleston, SC 29401; (803) 722-2234. (R)
Vendue Inn, 19 Vendue Range, Charleston, SC 29401; (803) 577-7970. (A)

Edisto Island
Oristo, Box 27, Edisto Beach, SC 29438; (803) 869-2561. (A,R)

Folly Beach
Atlantic House, 304 W. Atlantic Ave., Folly Beach, SC 29439; (803) 588-9563. (R)
Holiday Inn, 1 Center St., Folly Beach, SC 29439; (803) 588-6464. (A,R)

Fripp Island

Fripp Island Resort, Fripp Island, SC 29920; (803) 838-2411. (A,R)

Hilton Head Island

Adventure Inn, Box 5646, S. Forest Beach Dr., Hilton Head Island,
    SC 29938; (803) 785-5151. (A,R)

Fisherman's Lagoon, Hilton Head Plaza, Greenwood Drive, Hilton
    Head Island, SC 29925; (803) 785-8878. (R)

Holiday Inn Oceanfront Resort, S. Forest Beach Dr., Hilton Head
    Island, SC 29928; (803) 785-5126. (A,R)

Hudson's Landing, Box 1056, Hudson Rd., Hilton Head Island, SC
    29925; (803) 681-2772. (R)

Hudson's, the Original Seafood House on the Docks, Box 1056, Hud-
    son Rd., Hilton Head Island, SC 29925; (803) 681-2772. (R)

Hyatt on Hilton Head, Box 6167, Palmetto Dunes Plantation, Hilton
    Head Island, SC 29938; (803) 785-1234. (A,R)

Mariner's Inn, Box 6165, Hilton Head Island, SC 29938; (803) 842-
    8000. (A,R)

Marriott's Hilton Head Resort, 130 Shipyard Dr., Shipyard Plan-
    tation, Hilton Head Island, SC 29928; (803) 842-2400. (A,R)

Palmetto Dunes Plantation, Box 5606, Hilton Head Island, SC 29938;
    (803) 785-1161. (A)

Porky's Southern Style Barbeque, 200 Triangle Square, Hilton Head
    Island, SC 29925; (803) 681-4004. (R)

Port Royal Plantation, Box 1786, Hilton Head Island, SC 29925;
    (803) 785-4256. (A)

Sea Crest Motel, N. Forest Beach Dr., Hilton Head Island, SC 29928;
    (803) 785-2121. (A,R)

Sea Pines Plantation, Sea Pines Circle, Hilton Head Island, SC 29928;
    (803) 785-3333. (A)

Shipyard Plantation, Box 1786, Hilton Head Island, SC 29925; (803)
    785-4256 (A)

Isle of Palms

Wild Dunes Beach and Racquet Club, Box Y, Isle of Palms, SC 29451;
    (803) 886-6000. (A,R)

Kiawah Island

Kiawah Island Resort, Box 12910, Charleston, SC 29412; (803) 768-
    2121. (A,R)

Litchfield Beach
Litchfield Inn, Litchfield Beach, SC 29585; (803) 237-4211. (A,R)

Murrells Inlet
Planter's Back Porch, U.S. 17 and Wachesaw Rd., Murrells Inlet, SC 29576; (803) 651-5263. (R)
Sea Captain's House, U.S. 17, Murrells Inlet, SC 29576; (803) 651-2416. (R)

Myrtle Beach and North Myrtle Beach
Cabana Terrace Motor Inn, Box 745, 1908 N. Ocean Blvd., North Myrtle Beach, SC 29582; (803) 249-1421. (A)
Cagney's Old Place, Kings Highway, Myrtle Beach, SC 29577; (803) 449-3824. (R)
Christy's, Box 2218, Kings Highway, North Myrtle Beach, SC 29582; (803) 272-5107. (R)
Gabby's Rib, Kings Highway, North Myrtle Beach, SC 29582; (803) 272-5922. (R)
Morrison's Cafeteria, Myrtle Square Mall, Kings Highway, Myrtle Beach, SC 29577; (803) 448-4302. (R)
Outrigger Seafood, Kings Highway, North Myrtle Beach, SC 29582; (803) 272-8032. (R)
Rice Planters, 6707 Kings Highway N., North Myrtle Beach, SC 29582; (803) 449-3456. (R)
Sea Banks Motel, 2200 S. Ocean Blvd., Myrtle Beach, SC 29577; (803) 448-2434. (A)
Sea Captain's House, Box 218, 3002 N. Ocean Blvd., Myrtle Beach, SC 29577; (803) 448-8082. (R)
Sea Crest Motor Inn, 803 S. Ocean Blvd.,Myrtle Beach, SC 29577; (803) 626-3515. (A)
Sea Oats Motel, 702A S. Ocean Blvd., Myrtle Beach, SC 29577; (803) 448-8494. (A)
Sheraton Myrtle Beach Inn, Box 391, 71st Ave. N. and Oceanfront, Myrtle Beach, SC 29578; (803) 449-4441. (A,R)
Slug's Choice, Kings Highway, North Myrtle Beach, SC 29582; (803) 272-7781. (R)
Slug's Rib, Kings Highway, North Myrtle Beach, SC 29582; (803) 449-6419. (R)
Steere's Calabash Seafood #2, Kings Highway, North Myrtle Beach, SC 29582; (803) 449-0421. (R)

North Myrtle Beach (see Myrtle Beach)

Seabrook Island
Seabrook Island, Box 32099, Charleston, SC 29147; (803) 768-1000.
  (A,R)

Surfside Beach
Holiday Inn Surfside Beach, 1601 N. Ocean Blvd., Surfside Beach,
  SC 29577; (803) 238-5601. (A,R)

VIRGINIA

Chincoteague Island
Chincoteague Inn, S. Main St., Chincoteague Island, VA 23336; (804)
  336-3314. (R)
Driftwood Motor Lodge, Box 575, Beach Rd., Chincoteague Island,
  VA 23336; (804) 336-6557. (A)
Island Motor Inn, Box 236, N. Main St., Chincoteague Island, VA
  23336; (804) 336-3141. (A)
Landmark Crab House, N. Main St., Chincoteague Island, VA 23336;
  (804) 336-5552. (R)
Sea Hawk Motel, Maddox Blvd., Chincoteague Island, VA 23336;
  (804) 336-6527. (A)

Virginia Beach
Blue Pete's Seafood Restaurant, 1400 N. Muddy Creek Rd., Virginia
  Beach, VA 23451; (804) 426-2005. (R)
Capt. George's Seafood Restaurant, 1956 Laskin Rd., Virginia Beach,
  VA 23451; (804) 428-3494. (R)
Captain Kidd's, 706 Atlantic Ave., Virginia Beach, VA 23451; (804)
  428-2073. (R)
Captain's Table, Third St. and Atlantic Ave., Virginia Beach, VA
  23451; (804) 422-4308. (R)
Carriage Inn, 1500 Atlantic Ave., Virginia Beach, VA 23451; (804)
  428-8105. (A)
Econo Lodge, 1284 Laskin Rd., Virginia Beach, VA 23451; (804) 425-
  0803. (A)

The Lighthouse, Rudee Inlet, Virginia Beach, VA 23451; (804) 428-7974 (R)

MacThrift Motor Inn, Atlantic Ave. at Third St., Virginia Beach, VA 23451; (804) 428-0220. (A)

Steinhilber's Thalia Acres Inn, 653 Thalia Rd., Virginia Beach, VA 23451; (804) 340-1156. (R)

Appendix:
Beach Facts and Opinions

State Boards of Tourism

Connecticut
Southeastern Connecticut Tourism District, Olde Towne Mill, Mill
  St., New London, CT 06320.
State Department of Economic Development, 210 Washington St.,
  Hartford, CT 06106.

Delaware
State Travel Service, P.O. Box 1401, Dover, DE 19903.

Florida
State Division of Tourism, 126 Van Buren St., Tallahassee, FL 32301.

Georgia
State Department of Industry and Trade, Tourist Division, Box 1776,
  Atlanta, GA 30301.

Maine
Maine Publicity Bureau, 97 Winthrop St., Hallowell, ME 04347.
State Bureau of Parks and Recreation, State Office Bldg., Augusta,
  ME 04333.

Maryland
State Department of Economic and Community Development, 54
    Calvert St., Annapolis, MD 21401.

Massachusetts
State Division of Tourism, State Office Bldg., 100 Cambridge St.,
    Boston, MA 02202.

New Hampshire
Seacoast Council on Tourism, Box 4669, Portsmouth, NH 03801.
State Office of Vacation Travel, Box 856, Loudon Rd., Concord, NH
    03301.

New Jersey
Shore Regional Council, c/o Public Information Officer, Monmouth
    County Parks System, Newman Springs Rd., Lincroft, NJ 07738.
Southern Shore Regional Council, Schellenger Ave. and 16 Board-
    walk, Wildwood, NJ 08260.
State Division of Travel and Tourism, Box CN 826, Trenton, NJ
    08625.

New York
Long Island Tourism and Convention Commission, 213 Carleton Ave.,
    Central Islip, L.I., NY 11722.
State Department of Commerce, 99 Washington Ave., Albany, NY
    12245.

North Carolina
State Travel and Tourism Division, Department of Commerce, 430
    N. Salisbury St., Raleigh, NC 27611.

Rhode Island
State Department of Economic Development, Tourism and Promo-
    tion Division, 7 Jackson Walkway, Providence, RI 02903.

South Carolina
State Department of Parks, Recreation and Tourism, Suite 110, Edgar
    A. Brown Bldg., 1205 Pendleton St., Columbia, SC 29201.

Virginia
State Chamber of Commerce, Travel Development Department, 611
    E. Franklin St., Richmond, VA 23219.
State Division of Tourism, 202 N. 9th St., Suite 500, Richmond,
    VA 23219.

Mean Monthly Temperatures
(Daily Highs/Daily Lows)

City	May	June	July	Aug.	Sept.	Jan.
Portland, Maine	64/42	73/51	79/57	78/55	70/47	31/12
Nantucket, Mass.	60/45	68/54	74/61	74/61	69/55	39/26
Block Island, R.I.	60/47	70/57	75/63	75/63	70/58	37/25
Atlantic City, N.J.	72/51	81/60	85/65	83/64	77/57	41/24
Virginia Beach, Va.	76/57	84/66	87/70	85/69	80/64	49/32
Cape Hatteras, N.C.	75/61	82/69	84/72	84/72	80/68	52/40
Charleston, S.C.	83/61	88/68	89/71	89/71	84/66	60/37
Savannah, Ga.	85/62	89/69	91/71	90/71	85/67	61/39
Jacksonville, Fla.	85/64	88/70	90/72	90/73	87/72	69/48
West Palm Beach, Fla.	86/69	88/72	90/74	90/74	88/75	75/56
Miami, Fla.	85/71	88/74	89/76	90/76	88/75	76/59
Key West, Fla.	85/76	88/79	89/80	89/80	88/79	76/66

Source: U.S. Weather Bureau

Toll-Free Hotel and
Motel-Chain Numbers

Best Western, (800) 528-1234
Days Inn, (800) 325-2525
Econo Lodge, (800) 446-6900
Friendship Inn, (800) 453-4511
Hilton, (800) 445-8667
Holiday Inn, (800) 465-4329
Howard Johnson's, (800) 654-2000
Hyatt, (800) 228-9000
Marriott, (800) 228-9290
Quality Inn, (800) 228-5151
Ramada Inn, (800) 228-2828
Red Carpet Inn, (800) 251-1962
Rodeway Inn, (800) 874-7719
Scottish Inn, (800) 251-1962
Sheraton, (800) 325-3535
Suisse Chalet, (800) 258-1980
Travel Lodge, (800) 255-3050

Ten Favorite Beaches
(in alphabetical order)

Block Island, Rhode Island
Daytona Beach, Florida
Key West, Florida
Kiawah Island, South Carolina
Montauk, Long Island, New York
Ocracoke Island, North Carolina
Ogunquit, Maine
Provincetown, Massachusetts
Reheboth Beach, Delaware
St. Simons Island, Georgia

Honorable Mention
Assateague Island, Maryland (and Virginia)
Cape Ann, Massachusetts
Deerfield Beach, Florida
Hatteras Island, North Carolina
Hilton Head Island, South Carolina
Jones Beach, Long Island, New York
Long Beach Island, New Jersey
Marathon Key, Florida
Martha's Vineyard, Massachusetts
Old Orchard Beach, Maine

Ten Least Favorite Beaches
(in alphabetical order)

Asbury Park, New Jersey
Atlantic City, New Jersey
Hampton Beach, New Hampshire
Jekyll Island, Georgia
Kennebunkport, Maine
Miami, Florida
Myrtle Beach, South Carolina
Seaside Heights, New Jersey
Virginia Beach, Virginia
West Palm Beach, Florida

Ten Favorite Places to Stay— Hotels, Motels and Inns (in alphabetical order)

Driftwood Inn (Chincoteague, Virginia)
Henlopen Hotel (Rehoboth Beach, Delaware)
Holiday Inn Oceanfront (Fort Lauderdale, Florida)
Island Inn (Ocracoke, North Carolina)
Key Lime Village (Key West, Florida)
King and Prince (St. Simons Island, Georgia)
Litchfield Inn (Litchfield Beach, South Carolina)
Wauwinet House (Nantucket, Massachusetts)
Wesley House (Martha's Vineyard, Massachusetts)
White Horse Inn (Provincetown, Massachusetts)

Ten Favorite Restaurants (in alphabetical order)

Cannery Wharf (Eastport, Maine)
The Crab House (Miami, Florida)
Henry's (Charleston, South Carolina)
Herbie's (Marathon, Florida)
Joe's Stone Crab (Miami, Florida)
Ocean Grill (Vero Beach, Florida)
Old Mill Inn (Spring Lake Heights, New Jersey)
Original Calabash Seafood Restaurant (Calabash, North Carolina)
Raintree (St. Augustine, Florida)
River House (Savannah, Georgia)

Things We Like About the Beach...

water
sand
sea oats
sea breezes
sea shells
good surf
high dunes
blue cloudless skies
the briny smell of the ocean

surfcasting by dawn's early light
breakfast specials
a smiling waitress with a fresh pot of coffee
driftwood
beach music
cutoff jeans
string bikinis
wearing as little as you can get away with
wearing the same clothes every day
fifty-nine-cent flip-flops
peroxide blond hair
tan lines
surfers
lifeguards
southern accents
sandcastles
sunset at Race Point Beach and Key West
lighthouses
salt marshes
Spanish moss
palm trees
spreading live oaks and towering evergreens
alligators and gator wrestlers
a cold brew on a hot day
heaps of fried seafood on a tray shaped like a fish
bluefish, pompano and swordfish steak
crabcakes and steamed shrimp
clams and oysters on the half-shell
pitchers of presweetened ice tea
southern-style pork barbecue
ferryboats
federally protected seashore
the state of Florida
a room with a view
heated motel pools
hassle-free parking
in-room cable TV
returning to a motel room to watch "Gomer Pyle," "Andy of Mayberry"
        and "The Beverly Hillbillies" during the hottest part of the after-
        noon
bicycles

boardwalks
beach blankets
blue highways
goofy postcards
Skee-ball and Skee-ball prizes
shuffleboard, putt-putt and Jungle Golf
not knowing what day of the week it is and not remembering what
    it was ever like to have a job
speculating about what erstwhile co-workers are doing at that very
    moment
free Happy Hour hors d'oeuvres
the sound of quarters being chucked into a well-stocked jukebox
watching televised baseball games from atop a barstool
bars within parking distance of motels
Brew-Throughs
booze

. . . And Some Things We Dislike

mopeds
beach buttons, badges and permits
broken shells underfoot
rotting horseshoe crab carcasses
crying babies at breakfast
dads who drag their reluctant children into the water
white teenagers bearing ghetto blasters
motorboats and Jet Skis tearing around the water
pounding sun at high noon
sand in hidden places
the ache and throb of a sunburn
forgetting your vows, from summer to summer, to take measures to
    prevent sunburn
being sweaty, salty, hot and bothered, and having no place to shower
horseflies, jellyfish and crabs that nab your toes
oil slicks and other boat spew
discarded pop bottles and potato-chip bags
tank-top T-shirts
traffic jams
traffic circles

poor public transportation on islands where you're discouraged from
     bringing a car (e.g., Nantucket)
car upholstery under the glare of a hot sun
seagull droppings on vinyl car roofs
drivers who flout the speed limit (i.e., everyone with a license)
hurricanes
two weeks of steady downpour that clears up while you're packing
     to leave
motel rooms with no cross-ventilation or a malfunctioning air-con-
     ditioner
motels and hotels with drastically jacked-up in-season rates
rooms that face dumpsters and/or traffic
trailer parks and high-rise condominiums
transient summer workers who bitch about tourists
cashiers who snarl at traveler's checks or bills of large denominations
restaurants that charge for ice-tea refills
fast-food fish fillets that taste like tire tread
fried oysters and clam strips
saltwater taffy
fry dough, fried dough, fry doe—however you choose to spell it, it's
     horrible
ice-cream cones the size of floral bouquets
Christmas shops, old-time photos and T-shirt stores
seeing the same lengthy, vapid paperback best-sellers on every beach
     towel and poolside lounge chair
bogus historicity
the words "Ye Olde. . . " on the front of any business
"Parking By Permit Only" signs
valet parking
cover charges and "proper attire"
video-game parlors
road warriors in bars
unforgivably large beerguts
heavy-metal cover bands
South Carolina blue laws
last call

Index